DMITRY ROGOZIN

THE HAWKS OF PEACE
NOTES OF THE RUSSIAN AMBASSADOR

Glagoslav Publications

HAWKS OF PEACE
NOTES OF THE RUSSIAN AMBASSADOR
By Dmitry Rogozin

Translated by Nadezhda Serebryakova and Camilla Stein
Edited by Camilla Stein and Scott T. Moss

© 2013, Dmitry Rogozin
© 2013, Glagoslav Publications, United Kingdom

Glagoslav Publications Ltd
88-90 Hatton Garden
EC1N 8PN London
United Kingdom

www.glagoslav.com

ISBN: 9781782670063

Glagoslav Publications neither shares nor assumes responsibility for author's political and other views and opinions as expressed in or interpreted from this book. This book is in copyright. No part of this publication may be reproduced, stored in a retrieval system or transmitted in any form or by any means without the prior permission in writing of the publisher, nor be otherwise circulated in any form of binding or cover other than that in which it is published without a similar condition, including this condition, being imposed on the subsequent purchaser than that in which it is published without a similar condition, including this condition, being imposed on the subsequent purchaser.

CONTENTS

By Way of an Introduction 5
Tales of Bygone Years,
  or Russian Primary Chronicle (1985—2009) 7
On the Eve 17
Viy 21
A Nest of Nobles 27
My Universities 30
Dead Souls 39
Crime and Punishment 50
The Possessed 65
The Vampire 80
Humiliated and Insulted 86
The Tales of Sevastopol 97
The Deceitful Newsmaker and the Trusting Reader 102
Medames and Messieurs de Pompadour 109
The Tale of How One Peasant Fed Two Generals 116
Resurrection 121
The Tale of How Ivan Ivanovich
Quarreled With Ivan Nikiforovich 126
Bear on Voyevodstvo 140
Hadji-Murat 143
Prisoner of Caucasus 158
Enemies 175
Poor Folk 188
The Stone Guest 203
Notes From the Dead House 216

Taras Bulba … 220
My Tender and Affectionate Beast … 223
The Gambler … 236
A Hero of Our Time … 247
War and Peace … 258
The Bronze Horseman … 265
Motherland … 280
Fathers And Sons … 292
Idiot … 311
The Duel … 316
A Feast in the Time of Plague … 326
The Inspector … 331
Upon The Hills Of Georgia… … 336
A Misfortune of Being Too Clever … 344
Epilogue … 349

BY WAY OF AN INTRODUCTION

Two and a half years after assuming the post of Permanent Representative of Russia to NATO, I finally succumbed to requests of my new Russian and European friends to share my impressions of the job with them. That's how this book came to be. In it I describe many events and personalities that have shaped the history of post-Communist Russia from the dramatic fall of the USSR to the recent war in South Ossetia. I've covered what I know about the events I consider important and without which it would be impossible to understand the past and envisage the future of the great continental power that Russia is. I wanted to give my readers a rare opportunity to see Russian history through the eyes of a Russian. The outcome is a truthful, if not somewhat wicked, book.

For someone directly involved in the majority of the episodes described in this edition, I have expressed my subjective opinions on some political figures of both Russia and Europe. Some might find these opinions either excessively emotional or politically incorrect altogether. For that I apologise in advance. It is our bizarre Russian way to call heroes and villains for what they are.

I chose the title *Hawks of Peace* for this book. For some reason, doves traditionally have the reputation of so-called "birds of peace". Sweet-natured as they are, political "doves" are at times irredeemable cynics, pretending to be on a peacekeeping mission. Of those feathery items I've observed plenty in politics and came to a conclusion that it is in fact "doves" and not "hawks" that deliver suffering to nations and the whole world.

It is the hawks — high-flyers, governed by firm principles and active citizenship, strong willpower and unflagging energy — that must be in charge of peace enforcement in our harsh and dangerous time. Only then our children will be able to sleep well at night, for a hawk will not pick out the eye of another hawk.

I sincerely hope that this book will make the reader empathise with the Russian post-modern drama, will allow the reader to discover the secrets of the Russian constitutional crisis of 1993 when tanks shelled the Parliament and reflect on the terrible two Chechen wars, on the armed conflicts in Transniestria, Bosnia, and South Ossetia, as well as on the terrorist act against the children and their parents in Beslan, North Ossetia.

For chapters of this book I've borrowed several titles of some of the remarkable pieces of Russian classical literature, and this is not coincidental. The readers who know and love Russian literature will not fail to detect a resemblance between people and events with characters and plots of the Russian classics.

This book is about man-made good and evil; about ordinary people, their sacrifice and heroism; about the complex fate of Russia that tries to follow her path amidst global political intrigues. This is also a book about Russia's big mistakes and her first small victories. It is also the story of my life that is so dramatically connected with my country's history and my people. Every word here is true. I wanted to make everybody aware of what I know.

I would like to present to you my Russia — the only one that I love.

TALES OF BYGONE YEARS[1], OR RUSSIAN PRIMARY CHRONICLE (1985–2009)

1985

March — Mikhail Gorbachev becomes the new Soviet leader on the death of Leonid Brezhnev, General Secretary of the CPSU[2] Central Committee followed by the passing of two of his old-aged successors. Gorbachev announces the start of Perestroika, an effort to restructure the Soviet system. At a later stage it turns out that, while having initiated the reforms, Gorbachev does not fathom their ultimate objectives or consequences. The scale of his personality is no match to the scale of the changes he started. The result is the country's spontaneous collapse.

1990

June — the Russian Parliament[3] adopts the Declaration on State Sovereignty of the Russian Soviet Federative Socialist Republic that provides the legal platform for the collapse of the USSR.

1991

March — Mikhail Gorbachev holds a national public referendum on the preservation of the "renewed USSR". However, the Kremlin cannot control the already undergoing process of disintegration of the Soviet Union. Country wide local clashes break out between the Army and the Militia[4] on one side and activists of separatist movements on the other.

---

[1] *Tales of Bygone Years* or *The Primary Chronicle* is the first comprehensive history of Kievan Rus from 850 to 1100 AD, compiled by the monk Nestor in Kiev. It is also a prime example of the Old East Slavonic literature.

[2] *CPSU* — abbreviation for the Communist Party of the Soviet Union.

[3] In 1990 it was the First Congress of People's Deputies of the Russian Soviet Socialist Federative Republic.

[4] *Militia* — Police force in the USSR and Russia before the reform of 2011.

June — for the first time in history, citizens of the Russian Soviet Federative Socialist Republic within the USSR elect their President. Boris Yeltsin, a career-minded Communist 'apparatchik'[1], takes up the Presidency.

August — a group of top members of the Soviet government announces the formation of GKChP[2] and seizes power temporarily, overthrowing Gorbachev and blocking him in the governmental dacha in Foros in the Crimea. Heavy artillery enters Moscow. Protestors against the junta gather outside the Russian Parliament building. Members of GKChP surrender and publicly declare defeat after the three days of confrontation. Gorbachev, who has shown himself as a weak and impotent leader, is discredited. Boris Yeltsin is at the peak of his popularity.

September — a coup in the Southern part of Russia, in Chechnya. Islamists seize power. In the same month begins an armed confrontation between Armenians and Azerbaijani over the status of Nagorno-Karabakh, a landlocked region in the South Caucasus predominantly inhabited by Armenians.

December — the leaders of the Russian, Belarusian and Ukrainian Republics declare the dissolution of the USSR; they denounce the Treaty on the Creation of the USSR adopted in 1922 and replace the Union of the Soviet Socialist Republics with the Commonwealth of Independent States (CIS).

1992

April — the ultra-nationalist leadership of the Republic of Moldova demands 'Anschluss' with Romania. In protest, a part of Moldovan territory on the left bank of River Dniester proclaims the establishment of an independent Transniestrian Republic. Aided by Romanian volunteers, the Army and the Special Forces of the Chisinau authorities assault the towns of Transniestria. The conflict turns into a civil war that lasts for three months and results in the defeat of Moldovan-Romanian troops and police forces. The 14th Army of the Russian Armed Forces under the command of General Alexander Lebed strikes a final blow to the separatists' plans. Transniestria declares national independence.

---

[1] *Apparatchik (Russian)* is a full-time professional functionary for the Communist Party or government.

[2] GKChP is the Russian abbreviation for the State Committee on the State of Emergency (1991).

July-August — led by Zviad Gamsakhurdia, the Neo-Nazi government of Georgia throws troops, formed mainly from released prisoners, into South Ossetia and Abkhazia — the regions that refused to be parts of the new sovereign Republic of Georgia. The well-armed Georgian troops are defeated despite the advantage in numbers. The Georgian war caused a flow of refugees, the first of many to follow.

1993

March — an initiative to bring together the independent organisations that represent Russian communities in the former Soviet Republics, as well as Russian refugees, results in the formation of the Congress of Russian Communities (KRO).

April — dramatic aggravation of the power race between the Russian Parliament and President Yeltsin.

September-October — Boris Yeltsin announces the dissolution of the Russian Parliament. In turn, the Constitutional Court of Russia declares the Yeltsin's decree to be unlawful, and the Parliament votes in favour of Yeltsin's resignation from the presidential post. This confrontation gradually translates into street protests and clashes, and a shoot-out of the pro-parliament rally near the Ostankino TV centre on October 3d. Military units enter Moscow. Under Yeltsin's order tanks shell the Parliament building to suppress any resistance. Moscow is flooded with hundreds of the killed and the injured on its streets.

1994

November — the First Chechen War begins.

December — on New Year's Eve the city of Grozny is under attack. Maikop Motorised Rifle Brigade of the Russian Armed Forces is killed in the battle.

1995

July — led by the warlord Shamil Basayev, bandits raid the town of Budyonnovsk of Stavropol region in the South of Russia and take hostages in the maternity clinic and the city hospital.

September — KRO nominee, Alexander Lebed runs in the parliamentary elections.

1996

June — having come third in the presidential elections, General Lebed accepts Yeltsin's offer to head the Security Council of the Russian Federation.

August–September — the First Chechen War comes to an end. Federal forces withdraw from Chechnya. A criminal Islamist regime is established in Grozny.

1998

June — The State Duma[1] forms the Committee on the Impeachment of the President. Yeltsin is faced with allegations on five counts, treason and criminal negligence that led to a war in Chechnya. As a result of the Presidential Administration's activity, the State Duma comes short of a few votes required to start the procedure on Yeltsin's impeachment.

August — Russia experiences financial collapse. The Government officially announces default. Yevgeny Primakov, a figure of authority in Russia and worldwide, is appointed Chairman of the Government of the Russian Federation.

1999

April-May — NATO's aggression against Yugoslavia. In protest, Russia severs relations with the North Atlantic Treaty Organisation for a period of three years. Half way across the Atlantic, Russian Prime Minister Primakov cancels his official visit to the United States and orders the crew to fly the plane back to Moscow.

June — 200 Russian paratroopers move from Bosnia to Kosovo in accelerated march and occupy Pristina Airport ahead of the NATO advance forces.

August — thousands of Islamist fighters including mercenaries from Arab countries assault the Republic of Dagestan in the North Caucasus. Director of the FSB[2] Vladimir Putin, a figure unknown to many, is appointed Prime Minister of Russia. Terrorists blow up residential buildings in Moscow and in some other Russian cities, causing hundreds

---

[1] *The State Duma* — the lower chamber of the Parliament of the Russian Federation.

[2] *FSB* is the abbreviation for the Federal Security Service of the Russian Federation. The FSB is the main domestic security agency of the Russian Federation. It is involved in counter-intelligence, internal and border security, counter-terrorism, and surveillance. Its headquarters are on Lubyanka Square in Moscow.

of civilian casualties. The Second Chechen War starts, in which the Islamists are eventually defeated. Many of the warlords, including the former Chief Mufti[1] of Chechnya Akhmad Kadyrov, side with the Federation. Shortly after the war ends, Akhmad Kadyrov is elected the President of the Chechen Republic.

December — Yeltsin submits his voluntary resignation.

2000

March — Vladimir Putin is elected the President of the Russian Federation.

April — the Russian delegation to the Parliamentary Assembly of the Council of Europe refutes the accusations of the radically minded European deputies — the political supporters of Islamists in the Caucasus. As a sign of protest against violation of its own rights, Russian delegation leaves the Assembly in the middle of the session.

August — sinks the Russian nuclear cruise missile submarine *Kursk*. According to some versions, the accidental was caused by the collision with a foreign submarine. 118 crewmen do not survive.

2002

May — reconciliation between Russia and NATO is achieved after both parties realise the need for cooperation. The two parties sign the Rome Declaration that establishes the NATO-Russia Council.

October — the Nord-Ost Siege in Moscow. Chechen terrorists take hundreds of hostages among spectators who came to the theatre that evening to see the *Nord-Ost* musical. Spetsnaz[2] carries out the rescue operation. Toxic sleeping gas used by the Spetsnaz to subdue the terrorists also kills many hostages.

November — Russia and the European Union reach an agreement over the visa-free transit for Russian citizens traveling to and from the Kaliningrad region through Lithuania. The Schengen Law is amended accordingly.

---

[1] *Mufti* — Islamic legal authority knowledgeable on the Qur'an, Sunna and the Shariah Law, and charged with issuing an opinion in answer to an enquiry by a judge or a private individual.

[2] *'Spetsnaz'* is the Russian name for the highly trained Special Task Force in interior forces structures.

2003

December — the unforeseen success of a new political force The Rodina Bloc creates a sensation in the parliamentary elections in Russia.

2004

March — Russian President Vladimir Putin wins a second term in the elections.

August — Chechen female suicide terrorists simultaneously blow up two passenger aircrafts in the air, killing all ninety people on board.

September — a group of terrorists seize a school in the town of Beslan in Ossetia taking hostage over a thousand children along with some of their parents and teachers. Over 350 hostages die.

December — the Orange Revolution in Kiev, Ukraine. Ultra-nationalist Victor Yushchenko, whose opposition to Russia is actively backed by the West, becomes the President of Ukraine. De facto the event signifies a split between the Ukrainian political elite and the general public. Moscow-Kiev relations heat up over energy resources. The West plays the 'Euro-Atlantic future' card for Ukraine and Georgia.

2005

August — President Putin sets forth four National Priority Projects designed to develop social welfare in Russia. Dmitry Medvedev, first as the Head of the Presidential Administration and then as the First Deputy Prime Minister, is delegated with responsibility for the projects' implementation. Soon after Medvedev is officially declared a successor to the current President and becomes the candidate from the ruling party in the forthcoming presidential elections.

December — the Moscow City Duma[1] election favourite, The Rodina Bloc, is scandalously taken off the ballots.

2006

April — Despite the crackdown on The Rodina Bloc, the Russian President supports the ideas expressed in the party's programme "National Preservation". The programme is aimed at the resolution of

---

[1] *The Moscow City Duma* — the Moscow City elected parliament.

the ongoing demographic crisis in Russia. Vladimir Putin refers to the programme as the "crucial national project".

2008

February — the Kremlin expresses a categorical disagreement with the decision to declare Kosovo's independence made by the group of countries under the leadership of the United States despite protests from Serbia.

March — Dmitry Medvedev is elected the next Russian President.

May — the new Head of State introduces Vladimir Putin as the candidate for the Chairman of the Government of the Russian Federation to the State Duma. A bipolar political system is formed.

August — Georgian President Mikhail Saakashvili issues a secret order to his troops to assault Russian peacekeeping posts in South Ossetia. On the night from 7th to 8th August he subjects the sleeping capital of Ossetia to an artillery and missile attack. Two hours into the warfare, the Kremlin decides to render military assistance to inhabitants of South Ossetia, the majority of them citizens of Russia, and to rescue the surviving peacekeepers. The North Atlantic Treaty Organisation prefers not to interfere in the armed conflict directly, however, accusing Russia of the "disproportionate use of force". Russia reacts by suspending all political and military cooperation with NATO and acknowledges the independent status of both Abkhazia and South Ossetia.

2009

April — at the 60th Jubilee NATO Summit in Strasbourg the decision is made to reinstate contacts with Russia unconditionally.

August — NATO assists Russia in the search for the *Arctic Sea* bulk carrier hijacked by pirates with a Russian crew on board. The information provided by NATO's Supreme Headquarters Allied Powers in Europe helps the Russian coastguard vessel *Ladny* to locate the carrier and free the crew a few hundred miles off the West Coast of Africa.

September — the new NATO Secretary General Anders Fogh Rasmussen publicly speaks in favour of building a strategic partnership with Russia.

October — an independent EU expert Commission publishes a report on the causes of the Georgian-Russian war of August 2008. The report holds Georgia responsible; Georgia is named an aggressor and a violator of international law. NATO chooses 'not to notice' the conclusions of the EU Commission.

2010

February — NATO takes on a secret plan to defend Poland and the Baltic States, providing for the transfer of nine divisions to reflect the "aggression from the East." In late 2010, the site "Wikileaks" released information to the media about the decision taken by the Alliance. The act caused additional tension in relations with Russia.

April — NATO gathers in Strasbourg / Kehl for the anniversary congress and decides to create a cyber defense of the alliance.

May — widespread unrest in Kyrgyzstan. CSTO offers support to the Republican law enforcement officers and refrains from direct interference in the internal affairs of the allied countries.

September — Kremlin voices the 'loss of confidence' in Luzhkov and removes him from the city mayor seat for his irresponsible conduct during the heat wave and wildfires and his indifference to the fate of Muscovites. Fearful, the mayor runs for safety to the neighboring Latvia where he pleas for the residence permit for him and his family. Thus, the "chief persecutor" of KRO and the party "Rodina" faces a complete political and moral fiasco.

November — Leaders of Russia and NATO meet during the summit in Lisbon, where they summarize the work of the NRC's review of common security threats in the 21st century. Parties declare the purpose of strategic partnership in the summary Declaration. President Dmitry Medvedev officially puts forward the idea of a "segmental approach" to building the European missile defense system.

December — a chain of 'Arab street revolutions' unfolds in the Middle East and North Africa. The USA tests for the first time the methodology of control over mass protests by ways of social networks such as Twitter and Facebook.

2011

January — terrorists from Caucasus carry out a large-scale attack in the Moscow airport Domodedovo.

February — President Dmitry Medvedev instructs his Special Representative for cooperation with NATO on missile defense to protect

Russia's national interests in connection with the deployment of the United States' global missile defense.

March — NATO, using vague wording of the UN Security Council Resolution #1973, commences an intensive air strike on Libya and joins Libyan Civil War, siding with the opposition against Gaddafi. Russian political leadership seriously questions the UN vote and the alliance's subsequent actions.

May — Prime Minister Vladimir Putin initiates the creation of The Popular Front that spins off into the State Duma election campaign and the presidential elections. International Congress of Russian Communities recovers its legal status.

July — President Dmitry Medvedev meets Sochi with the Secretary General and the Council of NATO and calls "unacceptable" statements of the Romanian President Traian Basescu where he publicly supports his government's decision to attack the Soviet Union in June 1941. De facto, unbalanced Basescu becomes unwelcome in Russia.

September — The United Russia party, after a serious internal debate, accepts the terms of the Congress of Russian Communities in the beginning of the joint struggle for the rights of the ethnic Russians and other indigenous peoples of Russia. All-Russia People's Front takes on a real political definition.

September — The Rodina Bloc and KRO organises a recovery congress and announces its unequivocal and full support of Vladimir Putin. Several representatives of the Rodina Bloc and KRO are placed on the electoral list of The United Russia Party according to the United Russian Front quote, but the alliance was not formalized due to the inability of the "party in charge" to agree to KRO's strict electoral requirements concerning especially the issue of the national identity.

November — President Medvedev initiates the "Open Government" that elects Dmitry Rogozin the leader of the Commission of Defense and the defense industry.

December — United Russia experiences tangible electoral losses in the Duma elections. Mass oppositions rally in Moscow demanding a re-vote. I report on the reform of the military-industrial complex of Russia and receives approval of Prime Minister Vladimir Putin and President Dmitry Medvedev. Prime Minister Putin calls me away from Brussels. Upon President Medvedev's agreement, Putin invites me to join the government as the Defense Deputy Prime Minister. I accept the invitation and go to work. My first test in the new role is the New

Year's Eve fire at a nuclear strategic boat *Yekaterinburg*. The accident is eliminated.

2012

March — Vladimir Putin and his campaign managers take over the initiative and turn the tide in their favor. Putin's victory is ascertained. During the elections, the creation of the Volunteer Movement in Support of the Army, Navy and the military-industrial complex is announced and included into Putin's campaign, playing a major role in his victory. The vast number of national and patriotic organisations leave the liberal opposition camp and start forming new political fractions at their base. The country braces for new political power contests.

ON THE EVE[1]

I developed an interest in politics at an early age. My father, Lieutenant General Oleg Konstantinovich Rogozin, Professor and Doctor of Engineering Science, had held prominent positions in the Defense Ministry of the USSR. In the 1980s, in the capacity of Deputy Chief of Armament, he was practically in charge of the entire state military arena and fostered an interest for it in me.

Our house was always filled up with the most fascinating people — leading technical designers of major engineering firms, prominent scientists and military commanders. My mother used to set the table for the guests in the dining room or in the kitchen, and each time I happened to be an unwitting listener to their engaging conversations.

They talked a lot about military affairs such as the armament programmes or some latest technical developments in weapons systems (here father would always send me out of the room to run little errands for him), but every so often the discussion would turn to the situation in the country, which was a growing concern for all. If only my father could know that now, two years after his passing, fate would have me continuing his path in the similar capacity, taking care of the country's defenses.

My father and his colleagues adamantly disliked the party demagogues and the top leadership of the USSR's Communist Party, who, one by one, in the 1970s started to display worrying signs of senile imbecility. I sensed that there was an underlying conflict between the scientists and the Army on one side, and the Communist leadership of the Armed Forces on the other, and that conflict was based on their opposing views on issues of the national security.

The Politburo's[2] aging reptiles maintained that the so-called "strategic parity" between the USSR and the USA had to be achieved,

---

[1] *On the Eve* is a novel by Ivan Turgenev, first published in 1859. A love story that is unfolding on the eve of the Crimean War with observations of Russia's 19th century society

[2] *The Politburo* was the central and governing body of the Communist party of the USSR.

by which they understood a simple arithmetic equality in the volume of 'muscles' — tanks, cannons and, most importantly, strategic nuclear weapons that the two superpowers were pointing at each other.

My father and his friends held a different opinion. From their point of view, national security did not necessitate equal quantities of deadly metal for the invention and production of which the best forces of science and industry had been mobilised. The arms race, this senseless ongoing manufacture of mountains of weapons that were, on top of everything, morally outdated and suitable probably only for grand tank battles of World War II, was the reason behind the shortage of consumer goods and had ultimately led to the demoralisation of the Soviet society, fatal for the Soviet state and its political structures.

In all probability, the Kremlin elders along with the mature Armed Forces leaders, many of whom had been through the fiery years of World War II, were unable to shake off the so-called Stalin Syndrome. The Armed Forces and the Soviet defense industry were not properly equipped to protect the country in the first months of Hitler's aggression in 1941 due to the strategic errors made by the Government. To withhold assaults by the Wehrmacht, the Government placed high stakes on light tanks and even on horse cavalry, and not on heavy weapons and motor brigades. This is not unheard of — aged military leaders often find themselves in the mental grip of the past war. Once burned, now twice shy, the Politburo demanded that the Soviet industries and the economy in general must be militarised further.

My father and his friends thought otherwise and defended their point of view firmly. Their position was that the strategic parity doctrine, which was bankrupting the state and the citizens, had to be replaced with the arms restraint strategy.

Such a strategy means that a state is capable of responding to a military attack in such a way that would cause an aggressor damage that would by far exceed any expected gain to him. Once my father offered me, then a schoolboy, a plain explanation of the meaning of this strategy:

"Imagine two fighters. One is bigger and stronger than the other and is armed with a machine gun. The other guy is only armed with a pistol. The trick is that both of their weapons are aimed at the each other' chests, and, the opponents are mechanically linked together by force of their respective triggers. The moment one of them decides to pull the trigger, the other will do the same, so they both end up shot. So it really does not make any difference whether they are killed by a single bullet or by machine-gun fire. Both would be dead all the same."

My father cited the Caribbean crisis of October 1962 as an example. At the time the USSR had about seventeen times fewer nuclear missiles and A-bombs than the USA did; however, that proportion had been sufficient to restrain Washington from starting a nuclear war that would have had disastrous consequences for the whole world.

The "Hawks" of Washington realised: yes, the United States had the means to erase the Soviet Union from the face of the earth many times over, or to burn down the whole of Eurasia. However, their enemy, too, was capable of "rising from the dead" and striking back, which could destroy twenty or so American cities. Knowing that, the United States was not prepared to take the risk of having to pay such a price.

Essentially, the underlying principle of the arms restraint strategy is the concept of defensive sufficiency. This means that a non-aggressive state does not need to acquire or produce excessive quantities of weapons, but, at the same time, the weapons' quality and quantity must be just enough to be able to cause an unacceptable level of damage to a foreign aggressor in the event of an armed assault. If a potential aggressor has this information beforehand, it would never risk launching an attack. Therefore, "strategic parity" no longer serves the purpose of ensuring national security. It is enough to have brass knuckles in one's pocket to temper the enemy.

Nowadays the validity of this concept is apparent. Had these ideas been accepted and implemented at the time, then, I am sure, our large state would not have collapsed, and the Soviet civil science and industry would have successfully converted to producing various competitive and up-to-date consumer goods and services using high-end military technologies and finds. In a sense, what my colleagues in the State Military Committee and I are building today, could have been done back in the early 80s, if only such people like my father would have been heard.

Maybe those of my readers who were brought up with the mentality of the West would respond to my ramblings with irony. The majority of the Western world received the news of the breakup of the USSR with profound relief. It is true that our societies got used to existing in a state of mutual confrontation for many years. We piled up a bunch of myths about each other and eventually grew to believe in these myths. People in the West were afraid of the Soviet threat; they believed in the possibility of an intervention by the Red Army and followed the fearless struggles of Soviet dissidents against the KGB with interest, but... to me, the Soviet Union is a country where I was born, raised and educated. There had always existed an alternative for us, young Soviet men and women like myself. We could have chosen to get rid of the Communist idiocies and free ourselves from the total suspicion and isolation from the outer world whilst preserving our large multinational state.

My generation and I, personally, have taken the disintegration of the USSR as a tragedy for which the high Kremlin demagogues carry full responsibility. It was their narrow circle and not the masses of people who benefited from the destruction of the great country. It was they who found the ways to abuse their positions of power in order to pocket all the former state assets and privatise natural resources. It was they and their children and grandchildren who formed the class of oligarchs; and now with their conspicuous consumer habits and lack of social graces they embarrass my country to the astonishment of Europe and America. Money that comes easy, goes easy.

My great country could have been spared its tragic fate, but it was not meant to be. Material factors and economic difficulties were not the principal cause of the decline and death of the superpower. The USSR was killed not by empty shops and 007 agents' tomfoolery, not by the senseless charades of the dissidents seeking truth only on the surface, so eager to become famous political immigrants in the West, not even by the false deceitful tunes of the Soviet propaganda. Despite all the problems within the Soviet defense structures, the Armed Forces were perfectly capable of resisting any external aggressor to target the Soviet State's sovereignty.

This war in fact was lost not by army commanders, but by political crooks and demagogues. The nation was betrayed by the CPSU governors, those Communist bosses who had erected Communism for their private party, outwardly despising their own people for their naive faith in "the bright happy future". In the pursuit of power, many of those governors personally led chauvinistic separatist movements and precipitated turbulent calamities of the late 1980s — early 1990s, leading to the inevitable disintegration of the state.

VIY[1]

The moral disintegration of CPSU leadership created the environment for the rise of Mikhail Gorbachev, along with other "architects of Perestroika", whose main advantage over the party leaders of the preceding generation was their ability to walk unaided. The senseless twittering of the new Secretary General, who was incapable of running such a complex country in critical times, was a macabre omen of impending calamities.

Watching Gorbachev, I realised just how important the role of a personality in history truly is. There is little doubt that a strong, decisive and responsible national leader would have staved off the threat of the collapse of the USSR in spite of all the acute political and economic problems that he had to face. This is what distinguishes a true leader from a hell-raiser placed on top of the political Olympus by chance: a true leader can see a purpose and knows how to take consistent measures and use all suitable means in order to achieve his objectives.

Remarkably, critics of the recently elected US President often compare Barack Obama with Mikhail Gorbachev. They point out that the Soviet Union collapsed in 1991 following the liberal reforms policy initiated by Gorbachev, and fear that Obama's policy of transformation might lead to a similar disintegration of the United States. So Gorby is popular in the West for the very same reasons that he is criticised, or hated even, by many in his homeland.

An interesting comment from an anonymous source was distributed by the White House as a counter argument to the statement "America is in need of its own Perestroika". The comment went as follows: "If we mean an update of some aspects of the US policy, then "Perestroika" is acceptable. However, if President Obama commences a reforms policy without envisaging where it could lead and its potential consequences, the comparison with Gorbachev is not appropriate." So, if you ever

---

[1] *Viy* (1835) is a horror story by the Ukrainian-born Russian writer Nikolai Gogol. The name refers to a demonic entity that is central to the plot.

wondered what his Western admirers who throw grand parties in Gorbachev's honour really think of him, here is your answer.

I vividly remember the series of grand and pompous funeral processions when Brezhnev, Andropov, Suslov, and Pelshe all passed away. I remember, I think it was in 1984, once watching on TV the newly appointed General Secretary of the CPSU Central Committee Konstantin Chernenko's speech. He was gasping for breath, holding a sheet of paper in his trembling hands and struggled to read out loud the script of some unremarkable speech. At that moment I was overcome with sadness and despair, thinking: will these nonentities carry on replacing one another forever, and will the succession of their funerals become the most interesting feature of my country?

And then there was a fresh face. The new man smiled and attempted to joke. He was breathing steadily. When Gorbachev was raised to power in 1985, he had all the necessary tools to transform and consolidate relied on those forces if he had resolved to get rid of the government that was made up of thieves and traitors.

He had modern industry experts, world class scientists and academic schools under his control. All of them would have been receptive to a call for a reasonable conversion of the defense system and military science, and they would have supported Gorbachev. The modernisation of the civil industries on the basis of latest scientific achievements and defense technologies would have eased the socioeconomic tension in the country and become a remedy to the subdued social discontent brought about by empty shops.

A call to join the dominant party and the governmental institutions, addressed to talented and patriotically-minded young people, would have secured loyalty to the proclaimed national development goals among the young generation. Had the nomenclature rebelled against reforms at the time, a true leader could have addressed the nation directly, asking for support which would have been rendered, fully and immediately.

Above all, the outdated slogans of Communism, which by then had exhausted their potential and increasingly seemed hollow to all but very few, must have been replaced by a new doctrine based on national interests and democratic freedoms. It would have been essential to decisively denounce the so-called Leninist national policy that allowed for a nation's right to self-determination including its secession from an existing state, and, at last, to build a nation that would be sustainable in the sociopolitical sense.

In the USSR the Russian nation alone did not have the right to self-determination. Chunks of the Soviet Russian territory were habitually allotted to yet more "brotherly nations", whose interests were secured by the chauvinistically-minded Communist bureaucracy.

In the sad year of 1954, Nikita Khrushchev, a political clown and a petty tyrant, bestowed a very generous gift — the Crimean Peninsula — on his "historical homeland", the Ukrainian Soviet Socialist Republic. Rivers of Russian blood were spilled on the soil of the Crimea in the past. However, it goes without saying that when the Communist leaders decided to present that gift to Ukraine, they did not bother consulting the population of the Crimea or, indeed, the whole of Russia.

Minor forms of extortion of indigenous Russian land also took place within the Russian Soviet Federative Socialist Republic. For example, there were a few occasions when the administrative territory of the Stavropol region in the North Caucasus had been cut down and given over to the people of the Caucasus without any approval whatsoever from the Russian and the Cossack inhabitants of the land. The Kizlyar region has become a part of Dagestan; the Mozdok region has been integrated into North Ossetia, and the Naur and the Shelckov regions were "presented" to the Chechen-Inghush Autonomous Republic.

Extreme nationalists were commonplace in Republican and local Communist governments, particularly on the higher levels thereof. The cynics, anti-Communists and hypocrites were using the party membership for the purpose of advancing their own personal careers.

As for ordinary Russian people, they, on the contrary, hoped that the ruling party would act as a protector of their rights in the struggle with nationalistic separatists. However, the party leadership consisted either of the weak "Mikhail Sergeyevich" types and of downright traitors and chameleons, or of nationalistic separatists who resolved to deploy the ruling party structures in order to destroy statehood and grab power locally. That said, the power structure itself was rotten to the core and did not show the slightest hint of an inner ability to reform.

Had a national leader of a different scale been in Gorbachev's shoes at the time, he would have detected the disturbing symptoms of gangrene that had affected the inner party circles. A surgical intervention, cutting off the contaminated tissue, would have been the best method to prevent the imminent bloody collapse of the country followed by the formation of primitive feudal khanates on its ruins. Dirty commercial secrets of the party bosses were no secrets to the State Security department. Probably those secrets do not withstand a comparison with the scale of today's corruption, but even so, the party degenerates and the embezzlers of state property were guilty of enough wrong-doings to have them prosecuted to the fullest extent of the law.

The example of rapidly developing nationalist China clearly demonstrates that an uncompromising stance on crime in party ranks and among top officials, adopted by the ruling party with society's support, benefits discipline in the political party and integrity of the state; it also helps to achieve increased rates of economic growth.

None of the above was done then. Weak and ambivalent, Gorbachev's personal character only added to the acceleration of the centrifugal force. Then began the calamities in Nagorno-Karabakh, followed by violent outbursts in Georgia, in the Baltic Republics, in Uzbekistan, and then — everywhere. Remarkable was the fact that peaceful Russian civilians were always the first to fall victims of those deranged separatists. Some time in mid February 1990, in Dushanbe of Tajikistan, 1.500 Russians were literally torn to pieces by the Islamists. At the central railway station, women were forced to strip naked and skip around in circles, accompanied by the gunfire thunder and their rapists' cackle.

Today, similar chilling stories are told by those Russian refugees who miraculously survived and who have been seeking housing, citizenship, compassion and support from Russian bureaucrats — in vain for over twenty years now. At the time when this took place, stories like these were obstinately excluded from news reports on Russian TV so as "not to incite ethnic hatred"...

In reality, though, ethnic conflicts that manifested themselves so clearly upon the first signs of the Soviet regime going down, had been stewing for decades, if not longer. Tensions between Armenians and Azerbajani over Nagorno-Karabakh; mutual hatred between Georgians and Abkhazians; the issue of the reunion of the Ossetian people — the history of all these problems is much older than that of the Soviet Union.

Previously, conflicts of this nature were often obscured. Any attempts to rock the boat were instantly cut short along the vertical party structure with the help of the repressive apparatus of the KGB. When these two pivots — the KGB and the CPSU — were pulled out of the fabric that held multinational relations together, the whole structure fell down on the long-glowing coals of mutual hostility.

The Russian people themselves were the only force that had the strength and the authority to act in protest against the disintegration of their once-united country.

True, the Russian elite either perished in Civil War of 1918–1920, or emigrated and became scattered around the globe.

True, the succeeding young generation of brave and strong Russian men and women fell on the battlefields of World War II. Only 3% of the young people born in 1923 emerged out of that war alive!

True, contemporary Russians were often denied the right to be proud of their nation. I still remember a teacher at school instructing us prior to a meeting with our French peers that we were not allowed to call ourselves Russians but, if prompted, were supposed to reply instead that we were Soviets (*'nous sommes Sovietiques'*).

However, it was only the Russian nation that had the potential to organise themselves for the protection of the state unity. This was why the facts of assaults on ethnic Russians in the Baltic Republics, in the Central Asia and the Caucasus were thouroghly silenced by the Kremlin (in the same way that Lenin in an effort to promote revolutionary fervour in Russia during World War I was demanding of the German press to veto all revelations pertaining German atrocities against Russian prisoners of war). Gorbachev, and later his successor Yeltsin, correctly assumed that the truth about the scale of the catastrophe, about thousands of murdered Russian families would have produced excessive anger in the nation, and a call to action in response would have followed.

A true leader would have managed to rely on the active moral support of the nation. In the late 1980s ethnic Russians were spread more or less evenly across the Soviet empire, and, therefore, could have acted collectively in protection of the integrity of that empire.

Decisive measures, introduced by a strong national leader, would have also been supported by the masses of non-Russian ethnic groups and peoples who wanted to preserve the good features of the Soviet structure. The results of All-National Referendum on preserving the Union state held in March 1991 confirmed that. Despite the uncanny Gorbachev formula of the referendum, the vast majority of the population voted in favour of maintaining the USSR.

However, such a national leader — a head of the state who would have displayed an ability to assume the full extent of power during that most critical time of the nation's history — never appeared. God had left us one on one with the marasmic Politburo and the bubbly General Secretary. "Decembrists awakened Gertsen"[1] in the 19th century, but the times that we faced were more dramatic: the disintegration of the Soviet

---

[1] A famous quote from Vladimir Lenin which is a reference to the Decembrist uprising of the army officers that took place in the Senate Square in Saint Petersburg in 1825. Alexander Gertsen is a revolutionary of the late 19th century who had been greatly influenced by Decembrists.

power awakened Viy — the anti-national and the anti-state evil. If I were writing a horror movie script, I would describe the political situation of the 1990s as follows: *"The bloody political dawn of Boris Yeltsin arose from the east. A little more time, it seems, and the massive door of the Supreme Soviet will open widely and the Prince of Darkness will enter the hall. 'Open my eyes!' the Prince of Vampires croaks, and the vampires jump onto the terrorised Russia pushing one another aside"*.

The Soviet party recruitment system was fit to produce and bring to the highest levels of power only such grey mediocre characters like Mikhail Gorbachev. Undoubtedly, Gorbachev is respected in the West for triggering the collapse of the Soviet Union, and exactly for that he is despised and even hated at home. However, in the spirit of fairness to Gorbachev, I have to admit that he is not a bad person. His weakness was his main weakness (pardon me for this play on words).

The scale of his personality simply did not match the scale of the changes that he had initiated. That is why the Revolution swallowed its father. Yeltsin, on the contrary, was quite a different fish. This stubborn and charismatic despot knew what he was doing. He betrayed and sold Russia.

A NEST OF NOBLES[1]

In 1981 I was facing a dilemma: I could either apply to the Moscow State Aviation Institute (MAI), where they had a great handball team, and pursue a professional sporting career (I had already been playing handball professionally then) or to take entry exams at the Lomonosov Moscow State University (MGU). My father was inclined towards MAI and advised me accordingly. His reasoning was that I would acquire a solid engineering profession at the Moscow Aviation Institute, where my grandfather Konstantin Pavlovich Rogozin used to be a lecturer in his time, and a starting platform for a brilliant military career would be built.

My father devoted his whole life to aviation. Upon graduating with honours from the First Chkalov Air Force academy in Orenbourg (named after a celebrated Russian pilot Valery Chkalov), he met my future mother, Tamara Vasilyevna Prokofieva, who was a graduate of the local medical college. My sister Tatiana was born there, in the South Urals, in 1953, and the family moved to Moscow. They lived in the old Moscow quarter of Tishinka. Later the state allocated them a flat at the outskirts of the capital in the newly built district of Tushino.

Once upon a time my grandparents lived in the vicinity of Smolenskaya Square, where the well-known building of the Russian Foreign Ministry now towers. In 1941 a German bomb destroyed the house where they used to live.

At the age of 13, my father ran away from home to the front. He served as a ship boy on secondary ships of the 9th Division of 'EPRON' (Special Expedition for Underwater Operations) assigned under the Dnieper Fleet. Participated in the operation to free Smolensk. He was sent back when seriously ill with a form of poisoning, but the Moscow flat was no longer there and the family was evacuated to Altai in Siberia. My grandfather Konstantin (my other grandfather, Vassily, died under tragic circumstances in 1935, leaving my mother an orphan at the tender age of five) served as a chief engineer on the battleship *Marat* from the

---

[1] *A Nest of Nobles* (1873) is a novel by Ivan Turgenev about the Russian aristocracy in the 19th century.

onset of the war until 1944. The battleship was eventually taken down by the Germans in shallow waters near Krondshtadt, but not before it became famous for turning into a living marine barricade when it did not give up under ongoing enemy air strikes and hindered the advance of the German Army on the besieged city of Leningrad.

Many generations of my family served in the military. One of my ancestors, the grandfather of my paternal grandmother, Nikolai Antonovich Mitkevich-Zholtok graduated from the 3rd Military Alexander Academy and from the Alexander Military Law Academy in Saint Petersburg. He was a Cavalier of the Orders of St.Vladimir, St.Stanislav, St.Anna, as well as the Order of the White Eagle. He took part in the Russo-Japanese war of 1904–1905 and in World War I. In 1908 he was appointed Chief of Moscow Police and was promoted to General Major in 1912. He returned to military service and took an active part in planning the famous Brusilov Offensive in 1916.

My great-great-grandfather did not accept the Bolshevik Revolution of 1917. He continued to serve in the Headquarters of Lieutenant General Denikin, the Commander-in-Chief in the South of Russia, having thus become an active participant of the White Movement.[1] Unfortunately I haven't yet found any information on what happened to him after his evacuation from Sevastopol with parts of the Volunteer Army in 1920.

His cousin, a hero of the Russo-Turkish War of 1877–1878 Vyacheslav Kupriyanovich Mitkevich-Zholtok, also served there in the Caucasus. He, too, was a General Major and up to 1903 was the Chief of Staff in the Terek Cossack Army.

A son of Nikolai Antonovich was my great-grandfather Boris Nikolayevich, who graduated from Gatchina[2] military aviation school shortly before the outbreak of World War I. He was awarded the Crosses of St.George for bravery. After Civil War my great-grandfather resolved not to emigrate. The Red Army had been in need of professionals and Boris Nikolayevich was invited to serve there as a "military specialist". As they say, he had a God-given talent as a pilot and was at once duly appreciated in the Army. It is known that in the late 1930s he was under scrutiny by the NKVD[3] in connection with the alleged "espionage

---

[1] *The White Movement* — political and military forces that fought the Red Army in Civil War after the 1917 Bolshevic Revolution. The White Movement Army is known as the White Army, or the White Guards.

[2] *Gatchina* — A picturesque town situated 46 km southwest of Saint Petersburg.

[3] *The NKVD* — People's Commissariat for Internal Affairs, the Secret Police organisation in the Soviet Union from 1934 to 1946.

activity" but the persecutors laid their hands off him at the outbreak of World War II. My research of family and state archives brought to light the following information about the Mitkevich-Zholtok dynasty. The family roots go back to three Prussian princes who took to Lithuania in an attempt to organize resistance against German knightly invasion, first swordsmen, then Teutons. By the way, one of my ancestors actually struck a Master of the Order of the Teutonic Knights in the Battle of Grunwald. More about the story in my new book *Baron Zholtok*.

As concerns the Rogozin dynasty, whose name I am carrying, they come from an area near the city of Rostov. Now their patrimonial village Gari is in the Ilyin district of the Ivanovo region.

Entire generations of the Rogozins were bogatyr[1] blacksmiths and quite prosperous. When the Bolsheviks came to power, my grandfather Konstantin Pavlovich together with his father and uncles took a wise decision — they left their homes behind and moved to Moscow, where it was easier for them to keep out of the commissars' sight.

There were some famous people among my ancestors, such as Boyard[2] Vassily Rogozin. He left his imprint in Russian history by being a loyal companion-in-arm to the celebrated Russian Prince Dmitry Pozharsky. Together with citizen Minin, Prince Pozharsky led the patriotic uprising to liberate Moscow from Polish invaders in the early 17th century.

Historians also mention Boyard Gherasim Rogozin and his son Fyodor, both of whom participated in the liberation of Eastern Ukraine from Lithuanian occupation in the second part of the 17th century.

That is to say there have been some rather decent people in my family tree.

---

[1] *'Bogatyr'* is an epic character, hero of Russian folk tales and legends, Russian heroic warrior of exceptional physical strength and powers.

[2] *Boyard* — a member of the privileged aristocracy in czarist Russia, ranking just below the ruling princes; the rank was abolished by Peter I.

MY UNIVERSITIES[1]

Strangely enough, before I was even born I had radically influenced my father's choice of career. He dreamed of the skies and wanted to become a test pilot, but my expectant mother categorically objected to that. Father had to obey. He graduated with distinction from the Zhukovsky Aviation Engineering Academy and immersed himself into military science and the development of advanced armament systems.

Nobody in my family had any doubts that I would continue the military engineering dynasty, but in senior school I developed an interest in another field — politics and international affairs. In high school I volunteered to carry out mandatory political readings to my peers and teachers. In compiling the reports for each reading, I was digging through diplomatic literature and memoirs of army and government figures in search of interesting material. I went as far as to regularly use news broadcasts on *Radio Freedom* and *Voice of America*, received with the aid of our huge domestic radio-gramophone.

By making presentations in front of other students and teachers, I was developing public speaking skills, invented debate techniques to convince a large audience, and was generally improving my speech and learning the great art of the Word.

Only now I can imagine what the old Communist governors of our school — the principal Yuly Mikhailovich Tseitlin and his deputy Joseph Yefimovich Reizis — thought of it all. Finally, when the principal had had enough of my political readings, he gave me an overall mark of 'four'[2] in social sciences, even though my marks in the subject throughout the year had been excellent. I don't know exactly what liberties in my interpretation of the material moved our old Tseitlin to reduce the mark by one grade. At the graduation prom the principal saw me off with an even stranger comment, "You are not much of a Marxist, Rogozin, are you?"

---

[1] *My Universities* is a part of the autobiographic trilogy by Maxim Gorky, a Russian/Soviet author, founder of social realism in literature and a political figure.

[2] In the Soviet school system Mark 'four' was an equivalent of B grade.

I did not know the dangers that phrase might have implied, but it was after that conversation that I decided to enroll into Moscow State University, the Faculty of Journalism, International Department, no less. In those days the Faculty of Journalism was a proper nursery of dissidents.

My father, who had always been my main authority, went into a great length — but to no effect — to convince me to change my mind. He was never fond of party nomenclature and of Soviet propaganda specialists, whose children constituted the student core of the elitist international department of the Faculty of Journalism.

The international department admitted young men only. International reporting was considered to be an unsuitable profession for a woman. The reason for this was that in the Soviet missions abroad it had been always easy to place a wife of a diplomat, a journalist, or of one of the KGB staff into a job of a schoolteacher, or a librarian, or a nurse. But what was there to do with a husband of a Soviet woman who was sent abroad to work as a journalist? How were you supposed to deal with him? Typically, the husband remained back in the home country, and as to his more fortunate spouse, the KGB used to watch over her in order to "guard the morality". In general, only girls with connections at the highest levels had the chance to study in our department of the faculty.

As I came from a family of a military officer, they did not admit me easily either. I was "cut short" after the exam essay, which had received the examiners' verdict that "the theme was not duly developed". What that was supposed to mean was a mystery except to those who had the monopoly over admitting an offspring of "blue blood". Needless to say, a son of a military officer did not belong to the elite. All the other exams were orals and I passed them with excellence. Still, I was short of a coveted half a mark, as the average mark of my school diploma had been four and a half.

The Physical Education Department came to my rescue. Unfortunately, I cannot remember who had advised me to go there and show them my certificate of Master of Sports of the USSR. They liked to take sportsmen in the Faculty of Journalism. Firstly, someone had to defend the Faculty's sporting honours, and, secondly, one could always become a sports commentator upon graduation. That prospect did not inspire me much, but, still, it was a way in. So I was admitted to the evening department of the Faculty of Journalism of the Moscow State University "with the right to attend daytime lectures" as some "dumb muscle bag", incapable of passing entry exams like normal people.

Seeing my sufferings, my father helped me to get a part-time job in the publishing department of the Kurchatov Institute of Atomic Energy, where I obtained a letter from my employers confirming that I "was working somewhere", as was required by the Dean's Office. Reduced in rights, I nevertheless began my daytime education along with the Hispanic group of the international department.

I had studied in a specialised French school, and knew how to explain myself in French rather well, and even won the city poetry translation competition once (at the time I was fascinated by poems of Paul Verlaine). That is why I firmly resolved to study Spanish. I knew that there was nobody who could help me to advance in the world of international journalism, a world that was alien to my family. As the saying goes, help the gifted and trust the talentless to push through on their own. So I realised that I had to push through on my own, and that is why I needed to have a command of foreign languages and gain the kind of knowledge that would give me more room for manoeuvre and a competitive advantage over the privileged sons of the elite. In retrospect, this turned out to be a well calculated move.

I studied Italian in my third year. On top of that, it was compulsory to learn a language of one of the socialist countries.. I picked Czech, although Serbian would have been a better choice. Ten years later, traveling as a reporter through Bosnia and Serbian Krajina at war and later Macedonia and Kosovo, I deeply regretted not being able to speak the language of my Balkan brothers. Still, in the extreme circumstances of war a language is picked up faster than usual, and soon I had no difficulties in communicating with locals. I will tell more about it later.

After the third year, students were given internship assignments in various locations all over the country. That was how I got to know my vast country for the first time. I asked to be sent to Novosibirsk, the capital of West Siberia and a major scientific and industrial centre located over the Ural Mountains. I never regretted my choice.

In that summer of 1983, the builders of the Metro service in Novosibirsk were spanning the wide and beautiful Ob River with a rail bridge. The bridge was being built from one riverbank; it had been extended gradually, literally by a couple of centimetres per hour. Probably only the unhurried and carefree fishermen sitting by the riverbank could watch the space over the river being built up day by day.

During my internship in Novosibirsk a funny incident occurred, although we did not see the funny side of it at the time. Every day I was on the outlook for worthwhile events to put on the morning news programme. On one occasion, I decided to stay up all night with a fire brigade on duty. To my joy and to others' misery, the fire brigade was called that night — a men's dormitory of an aviation plant was on fire. Never in my life had I seen a sight more scary and mesmerising at the same time — the burnt carcasses of the ruined building towered against the background of crimson dawn. The hot air filled with ash made up a heat haze. In short, it was like a scene from a Hollywood thriller about the end of life on Earth.

In those days, the TV studio of Novosibirsk used French-produced cinematic cameras; video cameras (television reporting sets) were heard of, but no one had had as much as a glimpse of the modern equipment so far. In our news making we had to economise on film as 30 metres film rolls were strictly rationed. The technology did not allow for remaking any faulty material, but I had not thought of it then.

A sweaty moustached Major firefighter was standing in front of me. He was in a state of extreme agitation due to the scale of the disaster, but pulled himself together in order to make his comments for the TV camera. I did not even notice when the Major had sworn using the word 'mother' in the course of his brief interview. The rude and improper swearing had been very appropriate under the circumstances; it seemed natural and did not even register with me.

And so the piece was filmed. We dashed across Novosibirsk back to the studio in our minibus together with the cameraman and the sound engineer. There the film was taken out of the camera and passed for urgent processing. The audiotape that contained all the sound including the Major's voice was cut and synchronised with the film. Nobody, neither the film cutter, nor the editor noticed anything wrong. At nine in the morning, still in agitation over the nightly events, I was sitting in a comfortable chair in the office of my internship supervisor. Transfixed, I was looking at the screen and couldn't wait to see my first "proper grown-up" material.

...When my moustached firefighter had finished his emotional comments I felt like sinking through the floor. The chief editor was looking at me the way a partisan squad commander would look at a just-discovered traitor. The phone rang in less than 30 seconds. The chief editor picked up the receiver with a trembling hand. I realised that the call was from the first secretary of Novosibirsk Regional Party Committee — the number one boss in the whole of West Siberia. Apparently, he had watched the news and was now heading for the studio in order to inflict punishment on us.

I immediately figured that I would be expelled from university, at best, and that my assignment supervisor would get a punitive admonition by the Party. Pulling myself together, I risked suggesting to the chief editor to try to find a solution to this, so to say, delicate situation together. The editor was not listening and kept saying: "It's all over! We are finished!"

But, the solution was found soon. My plan was to find a man in the studio with a voice similar to the Major's and to record him saying any suitable phrase, no matter which, containing the word "mother"; then to strip it in the audio tape and synchronise with the firefighter's speech. In addition we needed an overlay of some background noises, which were readily available in any studio, to make the transition in the Major's words unnoticeable. So we did just that.

The entire studio immediately turned into a swarming anthill; people started rushing around, and in twenty minutes time we were inserting the phrase "someone's mother suffered" into our unfortunate piece. How was it relevant to the news of the burnt-down men's dormitory, did not matter. The crucial thing was to complete the cut in time before the grandee arrived, and we managed to do that.

Soon we heard from the outside the sounds of a car breaking and a car door being shut. The fearsome party boss entered the studio, himself swearing at reporters whom he bumped into on his way. Upon noticing me he looked at me with his Lucifer's eyes and promised to "grill me without oil." Prior to his arrival we all had agreed to act innocent and surprised as if we did not understand the reasons for the big boss's anger. The chief editor, looking annoyed, offered the party boss to see the piece once again to point out what it was that the boss had not liked about it. The first secretary sank into his chair and stared at the monitor grimly.

"Someone's mother suffered!" the Major spoke in not his voice. "I don't get it. Rewind it again now!" the old Communist exclaimed. We obeyed and played the fake tape that we had just pieced together once more. The boss got up from his seat, muttered something under his nose, and left the premises quickly. "Thank God!" exhaled the chief editor, plunging into the same chair in which the fearsome party official had been sitting minutes ago. At a moment's notice his office was filled with staff. People winked surreptitiously, sniggered, and rubbed their hands together.

Truly, we were an inch away from a grand scandal, which was all my fault, but the scandal was avoided due to my bold idea. Soon the reporters came back to their senses all together and were roaring with laughter. Some of them only recovered from their bouts of laughter by the evening. As for myself, I was endlessly happy to know that I could continue to study at MGU. Wishing to thank my senior colleagues who had saved my student skin, I brought some food and drink into the studio and invited everyone to join in the celebration. All my scarse savings that were supposed to pay off my living expenses during internship, had been thus spent. Yet, here my wits saved me again.

My university friend Igor Vasilkov (currently a radio host on City-FM) and I had to somehow last for three nights and two days on the train from Novosibirsk to Moscow with no financial means of getting any food. Hunger could not wait, and so we resorted to a trick. We went to the restaurant car and pretended to the cooks and waitresses there to be employees at central television. We explained that we were producing a TV feature about railroad workers. Strangely enough, the naïve women believed that the massive Soviet-made photo camera in my hands was nothing other than a digital video camera of the latest technology. All the way to Moscow the kind unsuspecting women were competing with one another to give us interviews as well as some tasty food left untouched by restaurant car customers. Of course, I am ashamed of having deceived the trusting waitresses, but God knows — if it was not for our bluff the country would have lost two of its young know-alls.

In my fourth year I came very close to be recruited by the KGB. They called my home number, promised me an interesting job, and arranged a meeting the next day by the Park Cultury[1] Metro station. I agreed to meet. To be honest, I had been dreaming of working for the Intelligence and could hardly restrain my excitement. I was picturing my future life, full of exciting adventures and heroic deeds. I was even ready to agree to do undercover work, especially because due to my southern-Russian appearance — dark eyes, broad nose and cheek bones, dark chestnut hair — I could have easily passed for a Spaniard, a Serb, an Arab, a man from the Caucasus, or even, as my wife sometimes joked, for a giant Japanese. In short, my facial features reflected all the Russian Imperial Army wars of conquests, like a mirror.

Shortly afterwards, Tatiana, my young wife and the mother of our baby son, herself a third year student of the Faculty of Philology of MGU, and I were requested to undergo some tests, including various psychometrical ones, in some medical establishment of the KGB. I informed my recruiter that I was due to go to Cuba for a six months deployment after my fourth year at the university. I was eager to be entrusted by the USSR Foreign Intelligence service with a task. I wanted to become "our man in Havana" and at last do something useful for the Motherland.

But things turned out differently. While I was in Havana, they forgot

---

[1] *Park Cultury*, or *Park of Culture* is known as Gorky Park, made famous in the West by the eponymous Martin Cruz Smith spy novel and the film adaptation.

about me altogether. Having found myself on the Freedom Island I was keen not to waste any time. I was studying the work practices of the US Special Services that managed to establish active radio broadcasting to Cuba. I gathered the most interesting material that became the basis for my diploma thesis *Psychological War of the USA against Cuba*. There, in Havana, I wrote another thesis on the subject of France's defense policy — *The Paradoxes of President Mitterrand*.

At the university I became seriously interested in military and defense issues. I obtained access to the Special Repository of the Foreign Literature Library, where I could read extracts from the French newspapers. Despite my imminent deployment in Havana, I stuck to my original choice of studying the global history of wars and armed conflicts.

I returned to Moscow in 1986, boasting a great dark beard and two completed theses and with an impatient desire to find out when I could start working in the organs of State Security.

The "organs", however, were not returning my calls for a long while. At last, I got through to my old acquaintance in the KGB staff department who matter-of-factly passed on the most unpleasant news to me. It happened that, shortly before his death, General Secretary Yury Andropov had issued an instruction not to employ in the 1st Chief Directorate (foreign intelligence and espionage) of the KGB of the USSR the offspring and sons-in-law of employees of the same directorate, and signed a relevant order on "fighting nepotism". That was a bombshell. My father-in-law, Gennady Nikolaevich Serebryakov, was a colonel in the 1st KGB Chief Directorate and he had been working in the USA directorate. That was the reason why I was denied access to "the office". My dream was shattered right then and there.

I defended both of my papers with distinction, passed the state exams, got my certificate of graduation from the prestigious Moscow State University and... found myself on the street with no fixed employment or job prospects.

Vremya ("Time") programme, the newscast on Channel 1 of the Central State Television of the USSR, for the international section of which I had worked a lot in my student days and even had done simultaneous translations for them a few times, as well as for the political programme *In the World Today*, so popular at the time, declined the offer of my services and employed a boy from a proper nomenclature Soviet family instead.

I rushed to the Western Europe desk of the Novosti Press Agency[1]. As a tip, I had been given the name of the chief editor — Igor Mikhailovich Rappoport. His surname sounded so unusual that I was terrified of getting it wrong or forgetting it, which was exactly what happened. Nervous, I knocked at the door of his office and upon hearing his "Who's there?" opened the door ajar and said: "Howdy, I am looking for Igor Mikhailovich *Ribbentrop!*"

Rappoport yelled: "Get lost!" and threw a book in my direction. To make a long story short, the Novosti Press Agency did not employ me either.

In pursuit of happiness, work, and a chance to be able to feed my family I tried to land a job with the then popular youth newspaper *Komsomolskaya Pravda*. I knew quite a few of the people there. Some of them remembered me from the spring and the summer of 1983 when I had taken an active part in editing the *Komsomolka* supplement *Alyi Parus (The Scarlet Sail)*. That was the time when tempers were running high between the USA and the USSR. In the Far East, the Soviet fighter-interceptor plane made a tragic error and shot down a South Korean civilian airliner, sending it, as the Soviet mass media provocatively put it, "in an unknown direction". The Americans raised hell; the spiral of the Cold War was about to make another turn.

The Soviet newspapers were damning "American Imperialism" as best as they could. The popular *Komsomolskaya Pravda* wasn't slacking either. Sacks of angry readers' letters, addressed to the US President, were delivered to the editorial office. The editors were sending the letters over to Washington without sparing any expense. I made several copies of one such letter and pinned them on the walls of the office. It was so silly and hilarious at the same time, this message from an unknown Soviet Komsomol member to the world-known master of the White House. Here is it's approximate rendition:

> *Don't threaten, Reagan, with your missiles*
> *Don't scare the people with your war*
> *Know, that we have enough capacity*
> *To deal with you forever more*
> *The furies of fire — fire of the damned,*
> *And deadly rays will bring you to your end.*

---

[1] *APN* — Novosti ("News") Press Agency — the leading information and press body in the USSR. It is now a leading multimedia agency under the name RIA "Novosti".

Now, isn't it just a masterpiece? However, for some reason my irony was not to the taste of the newspapers' bosses; I earned myself an admonition but they remembered who I was. And so, came the time when I decided to remind them of my existence and made a phone call to the editorial office. On the phone, someone told me to wait while he switched to another line to talk to his friend from the Committee of Youth Organisations of the USSR (*KMO*). He then informed me that I was supposed to go to KMO for an interview, and only then would *Komsomolka* consider my chances of employment.

At the time I did not have the slightest idea what this organisation represented. Little did I know that the beginning of my life in politics was to be linked to that strange abbreviation and the even stranger institution that stood behind it.

DEAD SOULS[1]

Formally, the Committee of Youth Organisations, set up during the Great Patriotic War under the name of "Anti-Fascist Committee of Soviet Youth" had been autonomous from the apparatus of the Central Committee of VLKSM[2]. The two organisations were under the same administrative body and shared the same building on Bogdan Khmelnitsky Street, which has since reverted to its original name of Maroseika. The first and the second floors of the building were occupied by about a hundred employees or, as they were being referred to, "workers of a responsible position".

In reality, it was a true nest of spies. A good half of all the KMO staff were at the same time employed either by Foreign Intelligence or by Counter Intelligence. Because of that they were nicknamed "multi-tasking operators". The two-timers often used to leave the office during working hours with an excuse that they needed to "contact the Centre". The rest of us, however, suspected that instead they just went for a beer or shopping in a hardware store. Perestroika was at its height, and the elements of decline were evident even in trivial matters like those.

After going through a number of interviews I was accepted and immediately appointed a junior desk officer in the South Europe, the USA and Canada sector, assigned to work with European countries of my language group — Spain, Italy, and Portugal. The desk officer's circle of responsibilities included the following: establishing personal contacts with potential "agents of Soviet influence" among young and promising politicians in the assigned countries; organising and maintaining regular communication with the youth leagues of leading political parties; specific tasks delegated to us once in a while by our "curators" from the International Department of the CPSU Central Committee.

---

[1] *Dead Souls* (1842) by Nikolai Gogol is one of the most prominent works of the Russian 19th century literature. It is a satire set in Russia before the liberation of serfs in 1861. The title refers to the dead serfs that are still accounted for in registers.

[2] *VLKSM* — This acronym stands for All-Union Leninist Union of Young People, usually called Komsomol — a youth wing of the Communist party of the USSR.

I loved my new job right from the start. The level of political responsibility of a young professional in the Committee of Youth Organisations was not inferior to that of a diplomat of a counselor rank, and the creative aspects of the job were far superior. In a few years, the skills of self-reliance would save members of the KMO from extinction along with the USSR; despite their critical attitude toward "the wonders of Russian democracy and of the wild market" all of them would move on to find a place in the new environment. The majority turned into successful entrepreneurs.

I was the youngest on board. The corporate spirit of the KMO and the special culture shared by the people who worked there suited me very well. All of my colleagues were older than me by just a few years, but they already had solid experience of working in the international field. Never was I refused advice on how to handle a task better.

There, in the KMO, I had an opportunity to weigh the pros and cons of the Western model of democracy. I learned the codes of the Cold War and understood why we were losing. My experience led me to believe that there could be no place for idle talk and excessive sentimentality in relations between different countries and political systems, something that the hypocritical "fathers of Perestroika" were trying to implant in us. The skilful psychologists of the West invented tales of "new thinking" and "universal human values" in order to break through the weak and demagogical defenses of our political commissars.

The Western policy towards Russia has traditionally been the one of attempting to control and weaken. The extent and direction of this policy have never depended on the state structure of Russia at any given historical stage of her development. European connections of Russian reigning dynasties (very few Russians by blood among them); military and political alliances between the Russian Empire and the leading Western European powers; the crucial contribution of the USSR to the victory of the Anti-Hitler Coalition; peaceful and touchingly naïve statements of the young Russian democratic post-Perestroika government — all of the above failed to melt the heart of the Ice Queen of the West.

Fyodor Dostoevsky in his *A Writer's Diary* analysed a publication in the *Petersburg Gazette*. Reading bulletins from the Balkans (it was the time of another war in which Russia fought against Turkey and succeeded in freeing the Slavic peoples from the Ottoman oppression), Dostoevsky came across a description of a "strange" behaviour by a British Member of Parliament who decided to spend his otherwise boring leave in the headquarters of the Russian Imperial Army:

Near the retinue appeared some Englishman in a pith helmet and a pea-green civilian overcoat. Some reports claim that he is a member of Parliament who is taking advantage of the Parliamentary recess to write dispatches 'from the front' for one of the London large newspapers (The Times); others maintain that he is simply an amateur, and yet others that he is a friend of Russia. Whatever the case may be, one can't help but notice that this 'friend of Russia' behaves rather eccentrically: for instance, he remains seated in the presence of the Grand Duke while everyone else, including His Highness, stands; at dinner he get up from the table where the Grand Duke is seated whenever he pleases, and today he even asked one officer he knows to help him pull on his pea-green overcoat. The officer measured him from head to foot with a rather surprised glance, smiled slightly shrugged shoulders and without demur helped him put on his overcoat. Of course, there was nothing else to be done. The Englishman acknowledged this by carelessly touching his hand to the pith helmet.

Surprised and hurt by this story, Dostoevsky wrote:

The Petersburg Gazette called this a comical fact. Unfortunately, I see absolutely nothing comical in it; I find it quite infuriating, enough to make one's blood boil. Besides, from childhood we've been inculcated with belief (from novels and French farces, I suppose) the Englishman is a queer fellow and an eccentric. But what is a queer fellow? He is not always a fool or so naïve to be unaware that practices elsewhere in the world are not just the same as they are over there in his own corner of home. Englishmen are, rather, a very intelligent and broad-minded people. As navigators — and besides, enlightened ones — they have observed very many different peoples and customs in all countries of the world. There are very keen and talented observers. They discovered humor among themselves, gave it a special word, and explained it to humanity. Could such a man, and a Member of Parliament besides, not know when to stand and when to sit? Why, there is no country where the etiquette is more rigidly observed than in England. For instance, English court etiquette is the most elaborate and refined in the world.

If that Englishman is a member of Parliament, naturally he might have learnt etiquette from the very manner in which the lower House communicates with the upper one, and precisely who may sit and who is obliged to get up in the other's presence. If, in addition, he belongs to fashionable society; again, nowhere is there such etiquette as at the receptions, dinner, and balls of English aristocracy during their London season.

Nay, judging by the way this anecdote has been related here we have something altogether different. Here is English haughtiness, not simply haughtiness, but an arrogant challenge. This "friend of Russia" cannot be her great friend. He sits there, looks at Russian officers and ponders: "Gentlemen, I know you are lion-hearted; you undertake the impossible and carry it out. You have no fear of an enemy; you are heroes; you are Bayards — each one of you, and the sense of honour is fully familiar to you. Indeed, I cannot deny that which I see with my own eyes. Nevertheless, I am an Englishman, while you are only Russians; I am a European, and to Europe you owe 'politeness'. No matter how lion-hearted you may be, nevertheless I am a man of a superior type. And it pleases me very much, it pleases me particularly, to study your 'politeness' in relation to myself, your innate and irresistible politeness, without which a Russian cannot look at a foreigner, all the more so, at a foreigner such as myself. You think these are but mere trifles. Well, these trifles comfort and amuse me. I went to take a trip. I heard that you were heroes. I came to take a look at you. But nevertheless I shall go home with a conviction that, as a son of Old England (at this point his heart quivers with pride) I am the superior man on earth, while you are a bit of second rank..."

In the above account the last lines are particularly curious:

"The officer measured him from head to foot with a rather surprised glance, smiled slightly, shrugged shoulders and without demur helped him put on his overcoat. Of course, there was nothing else to be done."

Why this "of course"? Why was there nothing else to do? On the contrary, something quite different, reverse, opposite could have been done: it was possible to "measured the Englishman from head to foot with a rather surprised glance, smile slightly, shrug shoulders", — and pass by, without so much as touching the overcoat. Could it not be noticed that the enlightened navigator was playing a trick; that the most refined connoisseur of etiquette was seizing upon the moment for the satisfaction of his petty pride? — Therein is the whole point. Maybe, at that very moment is was impossible to bethink one's self of the situation — our enlightened 'politeness' stood in the way — not toward that member of Parliament wearing some sort of a pith helmet (what's this pith helmet?) but toward Europe, toward the obligation of European enlightenment in which we grew up, in which we have got stuck to the point of losing our independent personality, and from which it will take a long time to extricate ourselves.

One cannot help but agree with these profound thoughts on the inherently Russian attitude towards Europe, expressed by the great Russian writer. It has always been an excessively delicate attitude, and it confirmed false assuredness in foreigners in their own indisputable superiority over Russia.

The contempt with which the West usually treats us is nothing new.

My personal conviction of that was reinforced when I studied the historical archives.

Interesting evidence of this phenomenon is contained in the book *Russia and Europe* by an outstanding Russian thinker and biologist Nikolai Danilevsky, first published in 1871:

> *Over 13 years passed since the Russian government turned its system around and committed an act of such high liberalism, that it even makes it shameful to apply this much discredited word in this instance; the Russian gentry showed unselfishness and generosity of spirit, and broad masses of Russian people showed exemplary moderation and kind nature. From then on, the Government continued to act in the same spirit. A series of liberal reforms followed. The Government no longer applies any pressure in foreign relations. And has Europe altered her attitude to Russia by an inch...? This courtship of foreigners with the view to show them the face of Russia is laughable, as are the attempts to educate the misled public of Europe and make them see the light.*
>
> *The fact remains, Europe never accepts us as one of her own. She sees something generally alien to her in Russia and in Slavs, as well as something that cannot be utilised as simple material from which Europe may draw benefits.*
>
> *However much we try, in this or that aspect of Russian behaviour, we will never find reasons behind this injustice, this distaste that Europe feels for Russia; we will not find an explanation or an answer that would be founded on facts. There is nothing conscious in this attitude, nothing that Europe herself could explain with objectivity. The root of this phenomenon lies deeper. It lies in the unexplored depths of ethnic sympathies and antipathies that form an instinct of a nation.*

Admittedly, Soviet society of the mid 1980s was in a state of political virginity; we expected the West to bestow its grace upon us immediately in reward for our exemplary zeal for a democratic ideal. Overly emotional and open to the whole wide world, the young Russian national character pushed us to swallowing the bait of all things "fresh and fashionable" that the West had to show us.

Concepts that were merely hypothetical in the West were accepted in all faith and undisputed in Russia. Every European theory was turned first into an axiom, then into a dogma, and then into a new political reality. The same had been happening in the Russia of Peter the Great, in the era before him, and in the time of the Decembrist revolt.

"A spectre is haunting Europe," Karl Marx and Friedrich Engels wrote in their *Communist Manifesto* referring to the homeless ideology of communism, which failed to find a shelter in any of the European countries. In Russia, though, this illegal immigrant charmed everyone and became a rightful mistress for long decades to come. Essentially the same thing happened during Perestroika. The USSR gave up its areas of influence in South-Eastern Asia, Latin America, Africa and, most importantly, in Eastern Europe and the Middle East, under the banner of the "campaign for universal human rights". The USSR left behind its assets — to be looted, and its friends — to be harassed. Following that, the USSR itself collapsed under the banner of this "new thinking".

I still do not understand how it happened that the Soviet leadership, having sanctioned the unification of the German nation, not only did not receive any significant political and material dividends (personal ones not included, of course), but instead rendered our country heavily indebted to the West. How could that leadership possibly have trusted the words of the Americans who made promises to Gorbachev that the united Germany would never join NATO and that the Alliance would not expand to the East? In any other country such phony 'negotiators' would have been all but lynched on the nearest birch tree, but not in Russia, where a thief and a traitor may expect not just forgiveness, but glory and respect.

Twice in my work in the KMO I personally encountered circumstances in which Western Special Services almost openly used "youth contacts" in organising activities aimed at undermining the two federative states — the Soviet and the Yugoslav.

I saw this for the first time at the Global Youth Meeting for Freedom and Democracy, hosted in the vast premises of industrial exhibitions in Paris in August 1989. A large delegation of Soviet youth attended. My estimation was that the average age of the participants was 45. In the spirit of the time, under the instruction of the CPSU Central Committee the Soviet delegation included representatives of nationalist movements of the Baltic Republics — People's Fronts of Latvia and Estonia, and

Sayudis.[1] To my utter surprise, these worthy delegates who had come to the French capital at the expense of the USSR, organised a protest against "the Soviet occupation of the Baltic Republics" outside the pavilion of our delegation — in the company of some hippies. A strict order from Moscow not to make any scene notwithstanding, I immediately gave instructions to throw these political gigolos out of the fully paid hotel and, driven by hurt patriotic feelings, had one of them kicked out of the door. However, the British delegation adopted the opportunists and gave them a chance to speak at semi-official events on behalf of Baltic "liberty lovers".

Western Special Services were doing much of the same thing to the Yugoslav delegation, but the format was even more cynical; they were literally tearing the delegation into pieces and encouraging Slovenians, Bosnians and Croatians to set up exhibition pavilions separately from the Yugoslavs. It is common knowledge that civil wars start with trivial quarrelling on street markets and fairs. I doubt that the Global Youth Meeting organizers and their backers were not aware of that.

A couple of months later I witnessed another episode of the Special Services open games against the integrity of the USSR. I was in London on a week-long training programme organised by the Atlantic Association of Young Political Leaders. One evening I stayed late in the library of the Association where I became an involuntary listener of a conversation that was taking place between some people in plain clothes and one of the secretaries of the Komsomol Central Committee of Ukraine. It was not just a conversation but a mix of recruitment, instructions on the subject of where and when Ukrainians were to leave the Soviet "prison of nations", and assurances that the West would stand by Ukraine should things go wrong. It was the autumn of 1989, and nobody in their right mind could fathom a possible forthcoming collapse of the USSR.

The systematic brainwashing of the Party and Komsomol officials of the Baltic and the Caucasian Republics and Ukraine was not done by Special Services with the purpose of recruiting more "agents of influence" or "the fifth column", or, at any rate, that was not the main objective. By that time the CIA had long secured serious positions in the far more influential Soviet circles — among members of Politburo and the CPSU Central Committee secretaries with "noble greyness in their hair".

The Special Services of the Western world were looking for "raw

---

[1] *Sayudis* is a movement for the Lithuanian independence from the USSR, active in the late 1980s. Ceased to exist and disintegrated into numerous ultra-national parties after the Lithuanian Republic acquired state sovereignty.

material" — young people who could potentially be trained to organise anti-Russian pogroms or at least lead proactive street protests, which would shake the USSR from within. That is why, no matter what my European and American colleagues might say to me now, I know for certain that the West had long been making efforts to instigate ethnic conflicts in the USSR.

Such policy is still well and alive today. Here is a recent example. In December 2008, on New Year's Eve in Brussels, I bought a DVD of *Transporter-3*, a film by Luc Besson and Robert Mark Kaman. Typically, the plot was simple, but ordained with plenty face beating of senseless cruelty. One scene drew my attention. The heroine, a Ukrainian girl, wants to demonstrate her irresistible charm and ethnic advantages to her boyfriend, and, pointing at both her head and her generous bosom, says that in these places Ukrainians differ from Russians.

Why this stupid detail? Why was some dumb blockbuster politicized so provocatively? Or could it be that the whole film was made to revolve around that particular scene?

It is very sad and unfortunate that Europe would much rather embrace people from the Arab or African countries than Russians as "their own". And this regardless of the great contribution of the Russian people to the historical development of the European culture! Are the cities of Ankara and Tirana, each a capital of a NATO member country, more European than Moscow or Saint Petersburg?

However, if we look closely at the situation in Europe today, we should not be overly surprised by such an attitude. The colossal influx of illegal immigration, the unrestrained expansion of Euro-Atlantic structures into the South and the East — all this is suicide for the European culture. European politicians, while working on the draft of the European Constitution, misinterpreted the concept of tolerance and crossed out all references to the Christian roots of Europe. That was a straightforward betrayal of Europe's future. With my highest respect for Islam and for civilisations and cultural values of others, I would not like the Notre Dame Cathedral in Paris to repeat the fate of the Church of Sancta Sofia in Constantinople.

Politicians of Europe calmly observe the current social and cultural degradation; they succumb to the cult of blunt cruelty and historical cynicism imposed on them from across the ocean. Another masterpiece by Tarantino is *Inglourious Basterds*, a film about World War II featuring a group of Jewish American gangsters who mercilessly slaughter the battalions of German Nazis. Then they blow up a Parisian cinema with

Hitler, Goebbels, Bormann, and the likes inside. In short, the "inglourious basterds" win the world war.

The fact that the celebrated cynic Tarantino touches upon the subject of World War II instead of his usual gangsters is only part of the disaster. But the fact that people in Brussels, whose grandfathers had not been exactly widely renowned, to put it mildly, for displaying excessive heroism in that war, gave the film a standing ovation, brings out a feeling of grave concern about the moral and aesthetic condition of the Europeans today. And don't even get me started on the issue of their historical memory here...

Unfortunately, contemporary European governance is generally characterised by weak willpower and absence of principles.

There are practically no individuals in their ranks who are capable of envisaging the united Europe as one single civilisation.

They are simply firefighters who barely manage to extinguish a political fire if and when it is lit. They lack a clear vision of the European future, and their memory is not very good either.

In the 70s and the 80s of the last century the political class of the USSR was suffering from the same disease. Disintegrating morally and politically, they stupidly blew off the huge resources that were available to them. Could Komsomol — at that time the only all-Union political youth organisation with 25 million young men and women in its ranks and with immense financial funds and property — had effectively resisted the infighting that eventually tore the Soviet Union into shreds? No, it was too late for that. The Republican Komsomol Central Committees were crammed with young career mongers brought up in the spirit of anti-Russian chauvinism. Those activists who held top positions in the Komsomol central apparatus in Moscow (such as a former Komsomol activist Mikhail Khodorkovsky) were only ever preoccupied with their private business ventures.

When Yeltsin came to power, the apparatchiks quietly privatised the old Moscow mansions that had been expropriated from gentry and industrialists in 1917 and delivered to various governing bodies of the youth Communist organisations. During Perestroika the Komsomol leaders proceeded to use these premises as office spaces for their newly set up private banks and companies. Tour operators' and large-circulation newspapers' profits, monthly "voluntary-obligatory" contributions by millions of ordinary Komsomol members — all those funds were being converted into hard currency. The resulting USD were transferred to Lebanese bank accounts via the Budapest residence of the World Federation of Democratic Youth (Youth Communist International) and the Prague office of the International Union of Students and vanished without a trace. A little later, a newly hatched generation of yesterday's Komsomol leaders turned New Russians would grow fat on this Komsomol cash. They were the ones who appropriated the economy of the great power for mere pennies.

I never took a liking to that rotten crowd who, like a pack of jackals, attacked the inheritance of VLKSM. Cynics, liars and oath breakers — such was the would-be replacement that the dinosaurs of the Politburo had nurtured for themselves. The slogan-chanting group employed by "the fathers of Perestroika" was made up out of the same corrupt crowd. With "faithful sons" like them, the decline of the Motherland was inevitable.

At the end of 1989, I had the first serious problem at work. While in the leading role of the International Organisations Sector in the KMO, I experienced certain pressure to join the CPSU, something that I adamantly did not want to do. Possibly, sometime earlier, I would have become a Party member "like everyone else", but Perestroika and the general atmosphere of lies around me finally discouraged me from any further affiliation with Soviet Communists. That was why I decided to leave the KMO.

By that time I was respected at work and regarded as a sound expert on international affairs. Possibly for that reason the Party Committee of the VLKSM central apparatus did not make a fuss. Besides, they had other matFters to deal with, and soon the incident of my refusal to join the Party was pushed under the carpet. Then, something else happened that completely threw me off balance.

According to an unwritten custom, the KMO senior staff used to conduct all negotiations and meetings with the participation of the big bosses (Secretaries of the CPSU Central Committee) on their own, without resorting to the services of interpreters. This was done not as much due to the extent of sincerity and intimacy of such meetings, but because the bosses wished to stress their exclusive high status. Usually it worked. When I used to personally lead a foreign visitor into a spacious office of a Party Secretary, close the doors and leave the accompanying interpreter behind, typically the visitor would get a little confused and regained his composure only half way into a conversation. Translating from Russian into Spanish or French, regardless of the level of difficulty, had never been a problem for me, since a high degree of proficiency in foreign languages was a requirement in my line of work.

On one occasion, I took a delegation of socialists from Spain to meet the newly appointed Party Secretary who had been promoted from a provincial town to Moscow and who had a reputation of "a great democrat of the Gorbachev kind". The meeting went on as usual and was about to be finished when that Komsomol boss casually quoted the Bible in support of one of the finer points of his speech. Theatrically tossing his head with his eyes half-covered with the palm of his hand, he, as if in a state of deep contemplation, cited a piece from the Gospel of Matthew.

I was amazed. Until that very moment I had never imagined that it would become possible to encounter a truly sophisticated and intelligent person, moreover one adept in the Christian faith at that, in the circle of bureaucrats and hardened cynics. Besides, the ball was in my corner as I did not expect anything of the kind and struggled to translate the quote well.

I figured that the new Secretary of the Party Central Committee might come up with more unexpected surprises in future, and so I read the Bible from cover to cover in every language that I knew.

I eagerly anticipated our next meeting, ready to jump over my head just so that those wise words and ardent arguments of that noble man would reach the blurred minds of his guests from overseas.

I was feeling like a knight called by Richard the Lion Heart for the Crusade in Palestine to deliver the Tomb of Lord from the hands of the infidels. But, I was heading towards a severe disappointment and my romantic episode was soon to be over.

My new idol would still conduct meetings with foreign guests, would still toss his head with his regular theatrics roll his tearful eyes, and quote the same passage from the Bible, over and over again. He never read the Scriptures in his life, and the smart manoeuvre with the quote was incorporated in his personal PR. My hero turned out to be a mediocre Komsomol trickster — one of the "dead souls" of the Soviet nomenclature who rose to the surface in the murky waters of Perestroika. Not wanting to continue with this plankton, I made an irreversible decision to leave KMO.

Only now I am thinking: maybe the artful dodger was sent to me by God Himself to make me read the Bible in three European languages?

CRIME AND PUNISHMENT[1]

Moscow of the late 1990 — early 1991 resembled a city bracing for evacuation. People were stocking up on flour and salt; children and elderly parents were being sent off to the country; many were looking for new jobs — whatever they could find, not always very serious, but just to switch careers. Nobody seemed to be doing any work. All were preoccupied with listening to live radio broadcasts of debates in the two Supreme Soviets[2], one of the USSR and another of the Russian Federation.

In the course of my work in the KMO of the USSR I established friendly contacts with many deputies of the young Russian Parliament. It was there, within the walls of the Supreme Soviet, where a non-Communist patriotic opposition movement known as the "Russian Popular Assembly" was formed. The core of the movement was a coalition of three political groups: Democratic Platform Party of Russia headed by a deputy Nikolai Travkin; Russian Christian-Democratic Movement, led by an energetic deputy and philosopher Victor Aksyuchitz, and the Constitutional Democratic Party (Party of National Freedom) of Michael Astafiev, a deputy who had, as we used to joke, the characteristic "Lenin's squint".

At the time I developed an interest in the political history of pre-Communist Russia and discovered many parallels between the era of the last Russian Emperor Nicholas II and Perestroika, initiated by the first and last Soviet President Mikhail Gorbachev.

I was particularly fascinated by the following questions: had there been a real alternative to Bolshevism, could the outbreak of Civil War and the downfall of the Russian Empire have been prevented, and which

---

[1] *Crime and Punishment* is one of the great novels of Fyodor Dostoevsky, published in 1866. The novel is set in Saint Petersburg. Dostoevsky focuses on the mental anguish and moral dilemmas of Raskolnikov, an impoverished ex-student who carries out a plan to kill an unscrupulous pawnbroker for her money.

[2] *The Supreme Soviet* was the common name for the legislative body of the Soviet Republics. The Supreme Soviet of the USSR was established in 1938, its delegates were elected at the unopposed elections.

political movement could have consolidated and led forward all patriotic forces from 1910 till 1917? I knew that my great grandfather, who had been in charge of the Moscow City Police Force during that time, did everything in his power to restrain Bolshevism, however, it seemed to me that it had not been possible to stop the advancing catastrophe by use of special services alone.

The politicians who appealed to me the most were the leaders of the Party of National Freedom (Constitutional Democrats) — conservatively inclined liberal intelligentsia, represented by such bright figures as Pavel Milyukov and Pyotr Struve. Having studied literally loads of literature, old periodicals, proclamations, and other sources of the history of constitutional democrats, and at my own expense having mounted the memorial plate on the house where Struve was born, in the city of Perm, Urals, I decided to acquaint myself closer with the newly reinstated Constitutional Democratic Party and attended one of their meetings.

The deputy clinic of Mikhail Astafiev was located in the Dzerzhinsky district council of Moscow, by the Prospect Mira Metro station. It occupied a modest space of just about enough room for one and a half dozen people. The Party members greeted me warmly and at once invited to take part in a discussion on the subject of why the cadet[1] leader Milyukov was nicknamed "Dardanellian" on the eve of the Revolution.

The topic of the discussion confused me a little, as it was so obviuolsly irrelevant to problems of the present day. However, the people who were discussing the minor historical fact of little significance with such enthusiasm evoked nothing but sympathy. Of course, it became instantly apparent that what I witnessed was not a serious political party meeting, but a gathering of a local history club. Still, I was under the impression that those very people were the convinced patriots and true guardians of the Russian heritage. My new friends seemed much more proper as compared to hypocritical top figures of Lenin's Komsomol. At their next gathering I announced my desire to join this simple circle. There, on the spot, I was formally admitted to the party and, like the true intellectuals that we were, we all went to a beer tent to wash down this happy occasion.

I resolved to use all my experience of propaganda and management, accumulated during the four years in the Committee of Youth Organisations, for the benefit of my new party. Soon, the first regional party divisions were opened in the cities of Obninsk, Perm, Minsk and

---

[1] *Cadets* — constitutional democrats.

Leningrad (the Northern capital was renamed back to St. Peterburgh in just two years onwards). Due to the effective work of its regional divisions the party grew in numbers. Membership fees were charged, but there were never enough funds to develop party activities on a proper scale, as the impoverished "intellectuals" did not have too many pennies to contribute.

I left the KMO and joined a more than bizarre organisation that called itself the Russian-American University (RAU) and was founded and run by one Alexey Podberezkin. I met this proactive individual, who also used to work in the KMO for some time, on one of our trips abroad. He offered me a job in RAU on a number of occasions and, with the absence of other, more attractive options, I finally accepted his offer. RAU employees made a decent living by the standards of the time. RAU had absolutely nothing to do with America, aside from the fact that among its upper management there were quite a few scientists and ex-intelligence services' employees with the past experience of working against "the primary enemy".

The university had business interests in just about anything. You name it — we did it. Opening new private schools and beauty parlours, reselling of something to somebody and even monitoring UFO. In my position of the first vice-president I tried to carry out my duties with maximum efficiency and be in the office on very few occasions, spending all my spare time in the Supreme Soviet, in my party's headquarters, or on field trips recruiting new membership. I used to donate to the party half of my monthly salary, despite the protests by my wife. Strangely, this money was enough for starters.

In a mere six months, the Constitutional Democratic Party turned into a significant political force. Television, general public, parliamentary deputies and foreign missions in Moscow, all started to pay attention to our public actions and rallies. We were recognised amongst the camp of the "Democratic Russia", which gathered all the dregs of that time under its umbrella. And there were all sorts of these: a jester and "professional anti-fascist" Proshechkin, who had clearly escaped from an insane asylum; Gleb Yakunin, who wore priestly attire and skilfully impersonated a man of spiritual profession; a guy from Sverdlovsk who was a teacher of historical materialism and an anti-Communist at the same time. Boris Yeltsin relied on such adventurers and "prophets of democratic storm." He came to power with them.

Throughout the summer of 1991 Yeltsin and Gorbachev bickered about the Union Treaty, or, to be precise, openly fought for power. In order to get rid of the President of the USSR, Yeltsin was prepared to get rid of the USSR itself. He had no shortage of accomplices in that dirty deal.

The Communist Party leadership longed to divide the superpower; they dreamed of taking full, single handed possession of its massive inheritance. Heads of the Communist Party Central Committees of the Soviet Republics encouraged extreme Russophobia. In the Baltic Republics the Neo-Nazis and veterans of Latvian, Lithuanian, and Estonian Waffen-SS marched across the streets and squares. Gorbachev tossed and turned, losing control over his government and his country. The Army and those divisions of the Force who remained loyal to the oath were acting on their own accord, whereas the cautious KGB was burning its archives. In Georgia, Armenia, and Azerbaijan more and more weapons were seized from warehouses, and gradually more and more rebels' squads were being armed under the open connivance of the Party and government bodies. Weapons were transported to the North Caucasian regions via mountain crossings and tunnels. Everything pointed to a big war in the south of Russia. The government had already matured for the crime but the nation was not quite as ready for the punishment.

Regular, but unproductive idle gatherings of Gorbachev with Yeltsin and other leaders of the Soviet Republics were coming to their logical end. The time had come to sign the Union Treaty — the legal base for maintaining the Soviet Union whilst rejecting its Communist ideology. The document had been rewritten so many times that it was unclear what would constitute the basis of the fragile integrity of the "renewed Soviet Union". Nevertheless, we hoped that it contained something that would give advocates of the state integrity some advantage in time, at the least.

In the evening of 18 August 1991 I was at home finalising the article that explained our position on the issue of the USSR preservation. I remember the opening words very well: "What was discussed for so long by constitutional democrats, has finally happened! The Union Treaty is signed!" But the morning of 19 August turned everything around. All TV channels only broadcast the ballet *Swan Lake*. During breaks hosts would repeatedly read the same declaration of GKChP that had been formed that very night by a group of top Soviet leaders in an attempt to prevent the collapse of the USSR. Tanks rolled into Moscow. Yeltsin's whereabouts were unknown. Some said that Yeltsin was somewhere in the vicinity of the Supreme Congress building, others insisted he had been seen standing on top of a tank reading out some proclamation or other. There were rumours that Yeltsin had cross-dressed and escaped to Finland. All in all, the coup-d'etat seemed to be a farce.

If GKChP happened to have at least one truly brave, consistent individual in its ranks, then it would not have needed to tease the people who were already sick and tired of their weak government by ordering heavy machinery into Moscow. In fact, nobody believed that GKChP were ready to use armed force against civilians. What should have been done first, before sunset, was the arrest of Yeltsin and his more or less capable team, pull them out of their warm beds and send in their pyjamas straight to Lefortovo[1]. And remove immediately scared Gorbachev, who was swallowing Valium in Foros, Crimea. GKChP should have addressed the nation with a clear message, requesting nation's support in overcoming the political and economic crisis.

True, Soviet society could not wait to get rid of the Communist power, naively expecting it to be replaced by democracy, prosperity and order. Still, even the most reckless opportunists would not have jerked and dared to resist a confident and respectful government, if the latter had announced a concise plan of leading the country out of the crisis. But, to quote a famous Russian bard Vladimir Vysotsky, "no real hotheads — no leaders".

Instead of calculating possible and necessary measures to establish order and correct the past mistakes, which had pushed the USSR to the edge, the incapable cowards of the party and government showed that they were afraid of their own shadows.

Under those circumstances, when the threat of elimination of the constitutional power became all too real, no steps, up to internment of the top Soviet and Russian Federation government officials, represented by Gorbachev and Yeltsin, and neutralisation of their most aggressive aides, could have been deemed excessive. Selective use of force against inveterate enemies of the country, even though they had managed to climb up to the very height of institutions of power, would have been absolutely justified. No one would have had a heart to judge the spirited people, if they were to assume responsibility for preservation of both the constitutional democracy and the state of civil peace, and if their actions were consistent, understandable to the public, and tough on particular high profile traitors and defectors.

But as life would have it, real men ceased to be in charge of the Communist Party a long time ago. Idealists and romantics of the past who led soldiers into battles by their own example and who honestly

---

[1] *The Lefortovo* — a prison and a criminal investigation isolation ward.

believed in the Communist utopia and were ready to sacrifice their lives for the Motherland, were not listed among the Party nomenclature of the Yeltsins, Gorbachevs, Shevardnadzes and the like. The latter only wanted to save their skins. They saw their purpose in clinging to power and stealing from their country, bit by bit.

As averse to the Communist ideology as I was, I often asked myself why the Soviet Union became a superpower under no one other than Stalin and why this superpower was losing its position after his death? Brezhnev decided to open up the North Siberian hydrocarbon reserves and began to sell it in large quantities to the West. Exactly at the time the USSR spiralled into a rapid decline. Russia's leading position in global oil and gas trade and short-listed Russian oligarchs among the world's richest will never bring back Russia's former status of a superpower. Even the nuclear weapons that lie idle underground will not add to Russia's glory and respect across the globe. So what was the secret of Stalin's success? Quite simple — under Stalin, nobody from the Communist nomenclature was allowed to steal from the state. That is probably, the main merit of his era. It is also the key reason of his undying popularity, particularly today. Not to sound like a political medicine-man, I do predict Stalin's popularity to reach its peak when last remaining victims of his repressions pass away, along with the last of the generation that remembers his iron grip. As they say, if a man takes one life, he goes to prison, but if a man takes a million lives, he stays in the memory of a nation as a great leader. This will be true for as long as mankind continues to be motivated by fear and greed.

No, I do not belong to the category of men that regard Stalin as "our everything". In what way did the launch of the first space satellite and victory in the most atrocious war necessitate the physical destruction of one third of the opposition and the imprisonment of millions of "seemingly suspicious" people? If it were not for the Bolsheviks' experiments on our nation and Stalin's habit to throw behind bars anyone who would as much as glance at him in a wrong way, Russia could have made a far greater progress.

An international monthly magazine *Sovershenno Secretno ("Top Secret")* in the August 2009 issue published an interesting article, *Russians Do Not Surrender* by Vladimir Voronov, which I quote:

> *For three years, the Russian Imperial Army sustained attacks by the military machine of three other Empires — German, Austro-Prussian, and Ottoman — on the huge front from the Baltic Sea to the Black Sea. Tsarist generals and soldiers never let the enemy to advance deep into*

the Russian land. The generals were forced to retreat but, under their command, the Army was retreating in an organised and disciplined manner, strictly obeying orders. As for civilians, the Army did its best to evacuate them and never abandoned them to be abused by the enemy.

It never occurred to the so-called "oppressive Tsarist regime" to repress families of war prisoners, and the so-called "oppressed nations" did not defect to the enemy in quantities equal to entire armies; prisoners of war did not subscribe to legions that fought against their own country, the way that hundreds of thousands of Red Army soldiers did in twenty-five years time from then. A million Russian volunteers never fought on the Kaiser's side; there was no General Vlasov Army[1]. Back in 1914, no one could fathom, not even in their worst nightmare, that Cossacks would join German troops.

It is hard not to agree with these words. Yes, I understand the reasons behind Stalin's popularity today, but terror and repressions cannot be a driving force of progress or a pledge of a war victory. Our victory in that war was gained at a terrible cost, which was exactly what made that war so atrocious.

A nation cannot be rolled in the asphalt of a personality cult. Communism did not break the Russian nation of great talents and willpower. On the contrary, Russian people altered Communism, assimilated Stalin's regime, adapted to it as much as it was humanly possible, and made great achievements despite the Stalin's order.

No, I am not at all inclined to downplay the gravity of Stalin's atrocities. Neither am I keen on the ways of our modern "elite", which are more noticeable when observed from a distance, or after some time away from Russia.

During a recent leave from Brussels my wife and I went out to a dinner at a fashionable upmarket restaurant in Moscow. The only aftertaste that it left was a feeling of disappointment. There were all sorts of patrons there. A pair of ragged glamour girls with overdone faces were broadly eyeing the customers; a group of mobster-wannabe types were loudly cracking up over something; an old rich paedophile was impatiently waiting for his underage girlfriend to finally finish her Italian dessert; a bohemian gay couple nervously rubbing each other's knees under the table.

---

[1] General Vlasov Army is a name for ROA — the Russian Liberation Army that was formed by a former Red Army general Andrey Vlasov during the WWII. The proclaimed objective was to unite Russians opposed to the Communist regime.

What are we turning into with our notorious Rublevka[1]?

I would suggest renaming Novo-Rizhskoe Chaussee to Nouveau-Riche Chaussee or New Rip Off Chaussee. Decent people, who have been living there before the place became the 'New Russians' habitat, are now embarrassed to mention their addresses — such a cloaca this 'elite district' has turned into. The more our so-called elite and their extravagant pastime habits are being reported in the media, the more of the outraged Stalinists come to surface.

Upon reading this, if you are thinking that Rogozin went into opposition again, don't. What I just wrote is not my exclusive opinion. The true intelligentsia is not alone in painfully observing the country's current cultural degradation. Every decent person in power understands that the elite should behave in a dignified way, abide by law and conscience, and not get above themselves. The time has come to put an end to permissiveness and debauchery without waiting for a relevant directive from the Government. A change must start from within, and this equally applies to all.

But let's go back to the events of August 1991. In those historic days of GKChP's irresponsible demarcation I saw all kinds of people on the streets of Moscow. Unsuspecting of consequences, not knowing much about finesse of politics, people instinctively sensed that the power and the history belonged to Yeltsin now. The masses trusted Yeltsin and were ready to march under his banners. Many sincerely thought that Russian leaders — Yeltsin and Gorbachev — would manage to lead Russia out of the crisis and preserve the Soviet Union. As early as at dawn of 19 August, defenders of the Russian Supreme Soviet started to gather outside the parliamentary building on the Krasnopresnenskaya Embankment. By the evening the crowd had grown, and in the morning of 20 August the square between the House of Congresses and the Pavlik Morozov Park was filled with hundreds of thousands of people.

I saw all sorts there: concerned-looking activists of democratic movements; MPs looking over their shoulders in a conspiratorial manner; excited mob, onlookers.... Yet mainly the crowd consisted of ordinary citizens who were offended by the GKChP provocation and were provoked, in turn, by its apparent cowardice and indecisiveness.

Back then I certainly did not notice either any of the Soviet Communists of the latest branding, or any of Komsomol slickers — my

---

[1] *Rublevka* is an unofficial name of the notorious residential area west of Moscow along Rublevskoe Chaussee. Rublevka is often called "The Beverly Hills" of rich Russians. Real estate prices there are some of the highest in the world.

old acquaintances. They did not have the guts to either join "partisans in the woods", or merely gather together and publicly state their attitude to the ongoing events. The lost people were utterly lost.

Upon learning about the GKChP declaration, I rushed to the Supreme Soviet in search of my Constitutional-Democratic comrades. The Russian Parliament was deserted — the deputies had reasonably decided to stay home. Only the wing where the offices of Aksyuchitz and Astafiev were located, buzzed like a hive. Putting aside our dislike for Yeltsin for a while, we decided to get on with the swift distribution of his latest statement and called for our supporters to gather outside the building of the Supreme Soviet of the RSFSR[1] and hold a rally against GKChP.

That night, together with my wife and son we decided to stay at my parents' place. My father debated with me at length about the whole situation; he acknowledged that the Vice-President of the USSR Yanayev and Co. made a tragic mistake that might cost the country its existence, but he categorically insisted that I stayed well out of these "disputes". I did not hear him and soon locked myself up in his study. By dawn I had finished the draft statement to be made by Mikhail Astafiev on behalf of the party at the rally next day. I chose the words carefully, but still, the final text came out overly emotional. That night I did not manage to get any sleep as if sensing the next day's life changing events.

In the morning, the space around the House of Congresses was swarming. It was hard to tell exactly how many people gathered there, but they were definitely in the hundreds of thousands. Astafiev and I met at an agreed spot. I handed him the text of his statement that I had printed out that night, and we both started elbowing through the crowd towards the parliament's entrance. To my surprise, Astafiev's face was recognised by many (Oh the power of television!); he was greeted warmly and let through the crowd closer and closer to the coveted destination — the entrance to the parliament where a bottleneck of MPs had already formed. I followed Astafiev along the human corridor, trying not to fall behind my celebrity boss.

Militia could hardly keep the human flow into the building under control and gave preferential treatment to the actual deputies and the foreign press. For some reason, "the guardians of order" were not quite as favourable towards national journalists. "Representatives of the ancient profession" encircled the entrance, voicing their indignation.

I couldn't believe my luck — in the pocket of my leather jacket

---

[1] *RSFSR* — the Russian Soviet Federal Socialist Republic.

I found my Moscow International Press-club membership card. The membership had long expired, but I hoped that the militiamen were too busy to pay attention, especially, given that the membership card was worded in English. However, a young lieutenant took his time to study the document, despite the crowd and excitement around him. I felt it was time to take over, held out my hand to shake his, and said, "*Merci!*" That seemed to do the trick, and in a blink of an eye "a French journalist" was running up the stairs to the second floor, which led to the spacious balcony of the White House[1]. On the balcony everything was set up for "revolutionary leaders" to address the crowd. The leaders showed up that very minute — President Yeltsin, Vice-President Rutskoy, and Chairman of Congress Khasbulatov. In a mere two years, these "leaders" would be ripping at each other's throats over the division of power and would flood the streets of Moscow with puddles of blood of their supporters, not sparing random passers-by who'd get caught in the gunfire. But on that day, 20 August 1991, they stood together, and the human sea beneath them moved and hummed.

The balcony was over crowded but I still managed to get closer to the microphone. The brightest episode from the Russian uncertain times unfolded right in front of my eyes, and I was afraid to miss anything important. At last, Astafiev was called out to speak. Mikhail Georgievich pushed through the crowd towards the microphone, fixed his eyes on the text that I had written the night before, and read it out with great expression and diligence. I listened to the reaction of the crowd on the square. People met the speech with approval.

Some other important democrats spoke after my boss' speech when suddenly the balcony went into motion; there were excited exclamations: "Shevardnadze! Shevardnadze!"; people on the balcony were stepping aside to make more space. The Grey Fox approached the microphone slowly, carrying himself with great dignity and conscious of the effect that he produced on others. The human corridor closed behind him, and, pushed from the back, I unexpectedly found myself right behind this man. Perhaps I was mistaken for one of his bodyguards due to my height and build. I cannot remember exactly what the freshly resigned Minister of Foreign Affairs was saying but I do remember what happened after his speech. The spokesman said good bye to "the Great Georgian", turned

---

[1] *The White House* (also known as *"the Russian White House"*) is a name for the government building on Krasnopresnenskaya Embankment in Moscow that used to house the Parliament and now houses the Russian government.

around, spotted me and inquired, barely hiding his annoyance, "So, are you going to speak, or what?"

I do not know whom I was mistaken for at that time, but I reacted instantly and stepped out to the microphone. I started out quietly and without much confidence, but in just a few moments my voice started to sound firmer and firmer.

I felt like I had prepared for, expected, and sought this moment all my life. All my concerns for my huge and miserable country, for its future, hidden behind a thick fog, for its national integrity that we had to protect despite GKChP's provocations and rebellions of national separatists — all the words that were so important to me came out of my mouth and fell into the waves of the human ocean. The crowd echoed my words, and, at that moment, it seemed that hundreds of thousands of people in the square in front of the Supreme Soviet were united into one wholesome nation. That day saw the awakening of a politician in me.

The speeches ended soon but the crowd did not dissipate. The euphoria was gone. What remained, was the uneasy expectation of the imminent climax.

It wasn't until much later that we would learn of what was happening in the Kremlin, in Moscow City Council, in the Military Headquarters, and in the offices of Yeltsin and Khasbulatov. We will never learn what *really* happened there. But at the time it was the last thing on my mind. I swiftly made my way to the office of RAU, which was just five minutes walk from the White House, got on the phone and called all my friends and acquaintances. Soon we formed a volunteer squadron of about sixty people, all set to go to the building of the Supreme Soviet building for the evening and possibly night watch. By seven o'clock in the evening we arrived there in an organised fashion. The square was filling with people, just like in the morning. Like ants, people carried logs and some armature. Something resembling barricades was erected. Skips loaded with construction rubbish arrived under an instruction from the Mayor's office, loyal to Yeltsin.

The loads were immediately taken down by the ant-people. Apparently, someone rather smart commanded hundreds of people, thus setting an example to thousands.

I do not think that the heaps of construction rubbish around the building of the Supreme Soviet could withstand a Special Forces' assault, should an order to storm the building be issued. The ring of desperate obstacles could not have stopped heavy artillery from coming close to the building and descending there. However, the mountains of metal and concrete would have definitely obstructed movements of thousands of people. In case of an offensive, the majority of "defenders of democracy" would have been trapped in the sack of their own making. In panic, masses of people would have crushed one another; such casualties would have been written off as victims of "the bloody regime".

Who knows, that could have been Yeltsin's exact plan, to call tens of thousands of Muscovites for the defense of "freedom and democracy", thus building a human fortress around the building of Congress; then, using human shields, to give GKChP a choice either to storm the building, which would have meant a massacre of civilians right in front of global TV networks, or to give up the political initiative and shamefully surrender, acknowledging total fiasco.

Our group located next to entrance #24 by the Gorbaty (Hunch) Bridge. Trucks omitted that area, and so there was a wide-open space in the improvised defense position. Without asking anyone, we lined up in a thick human chain along the glass windows by both sides of the entrance, and took the zone under our control. I gave my name to the armed militia guards and told them firmly that all security issues on this part of the building's perimeter "in the defense sub-district assigned to me" were to be agreed upon with me. The militia officer nodded indicating that he understood.

In about one hour I exercised the authority that I had usurped so boldly. A rumour was spread that Special Forces intended to use gas. A group of drunken lads climbed up on one of the trucks and tried to tear off a piece of the Russian flag in order to wet the shreds and use them as masks. We could not let that happen and had to use physical force getting the guys out of the barricaded area. With this harsh and immediate restitution of order we demonstrated that random actions without our sanctioning would not be tolerated. Selective use of physical force in situations like these has a great educational effect. If those drunken youths did not exist, it would have been necessary to invent them; the diverse crowd, worn out by the long wait for an attack, needed a manifestation of some kind of order and authority.

I noticed the two processions among the masses of people moving about. One of them was the limousine of Russian Prime Minister Ivan Silayev. For him to pass through, we had to take down some of the barricades built by the "ants." The other procession consisted of military men — senior officers. I noticed the tall, grim man among them — Deputy Commander-in-Chief of the Russian Ground Forces. That was my first sighting of General Lebed who was yet to play a significant part in my life. Much later, recalling the events of that night, Alexander Lebed said to me: "By supporting Yeltsin, we managed to avoid shedding floods of blood". But this was not so. All the blood was yet to be shed. The violent collapse of the USSR claimed hundreds of thousands of human lives. The civilian conflicts in Transniestria, Abkhazia, South Ossetia, and the two Chechen wars were conceived on that warm night, when GKChP grumbled impotently, and both the Army and the KGB refused to carry out its orders.

As the curfew hour ordered by GKChP to be at 23:00 approached, the tension in the square rose. I kept glancing at my watch, as people usually do around festive tables on a New Year's Eve waiting for the clock to strike midnight. When arrows indicated 23:00, we spontaneously hugged one another. Everybody was happy and resolved to fight till the end. For the first time in my life I, the son of a Soviet general, "a golden youth", crudely overstepped the bounds of the old life and broke curfew! That was a point of no return.

Loud speakers were installed from the White House onto the buzzing square. They broadcast the news on an independent radio station *Echo of Moscow*, exhilarant speeches of deputies and visiting "prominent intellectuals", as well as emotional chattering of young journalists from the TV programme *Vzglyad (Glance)*.

My impression was that they all were intoxicated with adrenaline from their own statements that periodically seeded panic in the square. News that "tanks and APCs[1] breached the first echelon of our line of defense on the Kalininsky prospect" and the like, combined with machine-gun fire that we were hearing from the distance in the direction of Sadovoe (Garden) Ring, caused an unhealthy commotion among demonstrators. When the radio of the Supreme Soviet reported that there were casualties as a direct result of a clash between the Army and demonstrators, the tension reached its climax. Any sound would have been taken for a sound of a shotgun, any whisper — for a scream.

If anyone suddenly "detected" silhouettes of soldiers on approach, rumours of that traveled momentarily along the human chains, with "observations and information" added along the way. Suspiciousness towards anyone who could cause suspicion, at least in theory, rose along with the overall tension. As I was head of a squadron, people regularly came up to me, dragging along the captured "discovered KGB agents". The "insurgents" demonstrated miracles of security awareness in those hours of the Great Night Watch, and in some cases the "agents" had been beaten up a little. In order to calm down the night-watchers, each time we "arrested" those passers-by and onlookers, led them out of the

---

[1] *APC* — Armoured Personnel Carrier.

danger zone, and let them walk free. I have no idea why those poor things were brought to me. Maybe, because of the way we had treated the banner thieves earlier, my comrades and I turned into some kind of SMERSH-2[1]. I don't know. It was neither the time, nor the place for jokes.

Every now and again, new incidents occurred in the square. In the parking area a light burst in a lamppost, causing real panic. Everyone assumed the attack had begun. People scattered in all directions, crashing into one another. Thank God, there were no victims.

Recalling the events of August 1991 now, I come to the conclusion that a tragedy is not always repeated as a farce in history. The opposite is also true. The ambiguous and incoherent escapade of GKChP; the farcical false arrest of Gorbachev and his voluntary imprisonment in his Crimean residency in Foros; the "heroic defense" of the White House — all this was a farce. The suicides of Marshall Akhromeyev and Minister of Internal Affairs Boris Pugo (they were practically the only two decent individuals in the Perestroika government and could not bear the shame of their defeat); the arrests of key GKChP members (only one of whom, general Valentin Ivanovich Varennikov, did not make use of the declared amnesty but instead waited for his trial, at which he was acquitted); deaths of three young people in a pointless clash with heavy machinery during the endless night from 20 to 21 August — none of these events could change the operetta reputation of 1991 coupe-d'etat. But for my friends and me, the coup was the first political experience, and a priceless one.

It was August 1991 that had fully revealed Gorbachev's cowardice, Yeltsin's cunning nature, and the readiness of both to sacrifice their country's future and their people's lives for their own power dispute. I think that those days had also divided the huge human ocean by the walls of the Supreme Soviet. People who took the collapse of their massive country with a sense of great loss stayed on one shore; on the other shore settled the foam of party officials, and it was they who managed to get hold of the power and the assets of the agonising USSR.

So what was Perestroika, initiated by Gorbachev and killed off by the GKChP Decree? Was it a revolution in people's minds, a search for a national identity, an awakening of our own national identity in the peoples of the USSR, or was it a manifestation of chaos inside the Party bosses' minds? The answer is neither the first, nor the second, or the third. And it is most definitely not the forth.

---

[1] *SMERSH* is an acronym of *'Smert' Shpionam'* ('Death to Spies'), a number of counter-intelligence departments formed in the Soviet Army during World War II.

Perestroika was the fruit of the nomenclature — the Communist bureaucracy that wished to maintain its power and control over state assets in the environment of chaos and disintegration. The bureaucracy needed a peaceful overturn that would have excused the usurpation of state assets and portrayed the ongoing as an inevitable consequence of social calamities on a larger scale. To destabilise the country, experienced manipulators directed the wave of ethnic chauvinism toward the USSR — gigantic masses of people were consciously set in motion, the process that remained under manipulators' control at all times. Then at the crucial moment, these manipulators promoted themselves as "national leaders", using their unlimited administrative power as well as their control over mass media and state finances. The Old System did not die — it merely changed its facade.

Yeltsin so easily outplayed his opponents in August 1991! Would his triumphant stroll for power have been possible without the nomenclature's support while entrenched in the Moscow Mayor's office? Or without the criminal solidarity with his actions on the part of the Communist bureaucracy that sat around in the Smolny Palace in Leningrad, in the Kazan Kremlin, in Russia's regional and local administrative offices, not to mention the hosts of the Republican presidential residencies in Kiev, Tbilisi, Ashkhabad, Almaty, Tashkent, Dushanbe? And could Yeltsin have acted so confidently without the silent approval of his influential foreign advisers? If the CPSU governing body really wanted to preserve the Great Empire, there would have been no place for Yeltsin and his circle in the Empire's history. They simply would not have existed.

August 1991 had a profound influence on the course of my life. I suddenly realised that I, too, could influence my environment. I felt that I possessed the qualities of a leader. While observing Yeltsin and his retinue, I glanced inside the abyss of political cynicism and averted my eyes in disgust. For the first time ever I came to believe in the power of public speaking, the strength of national vigor, and the importance of initiative in politics. That was when I resolved to have my own destiny always connected with the fate of my nation.

THE POSSESSED[1]

It has been widely believed in the United States and Europe that Russia lost the Cold War. Hence, the Western world, seeing itself as a victor, feels it to be within its right to dictate terms to the Kremlin. This belief is wrong. The West has nothing to do with the victory in the Cold War. The Soviet Union was destroyed not by the West, or NATO, or the Baltic States, and not even by little Green men from Mars. The USSR was destroyed by Russia, and I intend to prove it here.

In my final year at the Committee of Youth Organisations I decided to establish our own version of the Atlantic Association of Young Political Leaders, an organisation that successfully functioned in Western Europe and the USA under the umbrella of NATO. AAYPL casually recruited promising young politicians into its ranks, educated them in the spirit of Atlantis at various forums and training courses, and helped them to move up the ladder without losing already established contacts and informal partnership leads.

I was thinking of setting up something similar. As a result, "Forum-90" was created — the Association of Young Political Leaders of the USSR. I invited such promising leaders as Andrey Kozyrev[2], who was in charge of the Department of International organisations in the Ministry of Foreign Affairs, the MP Nikolai Fedorov,[3] and many other bright young politicians of the new Russia to join the new association. In some instances the members of Forum-90 expressed such drastically diverse political views that it was hard to imagine how they could possibly co-exist in the same association.

After the GKChP defeat, Mr.Kozyrev, who had been appointed Minister of Foreign Affairs of the Russian Federation shortly before that,

---

[1] *The Possessed* is the initial English translation of the title *The Devils* or *The Demons* of this great 1872 novel by Fyodor Dostoevsky. It is a very political work; the revolutionary democrats began to rise in Russia, and Dostoevsky portrays their ideology as demonic.

[2] *A.V.Kozyrev* headed the Ministry of Foreign Affairs of the Russian Federation from 1992 to 1996.

[3] *N.Fedorov* is President of the Chuvash Republic of the Russian Federation.

offered me to take up the position of Deputy Minister. In comparison with the enormous and powerful Foreign Ministry of the USSR, the Ministry of Foreign Affairs of the Russian Federation, located in some premises on Mira Prospect, paled in significance. Naturally, I turned the offer down. In the aftermath of the events of 1991, pushing paper in the office did not tempt me much; I was eager to get into action as if sensing the impending storm. And the storm came indeed.

Under my initiative the 1st Congress of Young Political Leaders of the USSR gathered in the conference hall of Russian Academy of Social Studies on 8 December 1991.

The delegations of young parliamentarians, ministers and public figures from the majority of capitals of the Soviet Republics arrived in Moscow. Gorbachev, Rutskoy, and Kozyrev, who had been due to return from Minsk where he had accompanied Yeltsin at some meeting, confirmed their attendance. None of us knew that on that very day the Presidents of three of the Soviet Republics — Boris Yeltsin (Russia), Leonid Kravchuk (Ukraine) and Stanislav Shushkevich (Belarus) — gathered together in Belovezhskaya Puscha[1] of Belarus to sign the Accords on dissolution of the Union of Soviet Socialist Republics.

Gorbachev did not make it to our congress but sent his press secretary instead, who upon his arrival informed the astonished audience that the country they were born in no longer existed, and that "Mikhail Sergeyevich also found out from TV". "So he must arrest the conspirators immediately!" I shouted out from the presidium, which sparked a burst of applause from the audience. The press secretary grimaced pathetically and retreated. Two of our VIP guests, Rutskoy and Kozyrev, arrived simultaneously in the next hour. About 400 delegates watched the unseemly squabble between the Vice-President, who had also just "found out from TV", and the Foreign Minister, who shared with us the details of his business together with Yeltsin earlier in the day in the government residency in the suburbs of Minsk.

Morbid silence fell. Not many believed the genuine nature of the tragedy, unfolding right in front of their eyes. Only Kozyrev was comfortable and paid little attention to Rutskoy's threats. He was looking forward to exchanging his modest office on Prospect Mira for luxurious premises, formerly occupied by the legendary 'Mister No'[2] in the high-

---

[1] *Belovezhskaya Puscha* — Place of residence of President of Belarus near Minsk.

[2] *Mister No* was a nickname with which Western diplomats referred to Andrey Gromyko, the eternal Foreign Minister of the USSR who was first appointed by Stalin and remained in the post until mid 1980s.

rise on Smolenskaya Square, and was already fantacizing about moving furniture there.

A very short time would pass before the chain of professional diplomats, who didn't wish to continue working under Mr. Kozyrev, would start leaving that high-rise to try their luck on the job market. On average, starting from the early 1990s, about 900 highly qualified diplomatic staff left the Ministry of Foreign Affairs, significantly weakening Russia's position on the global political arena. This wound would never heal. The same would happen in the Defense Ministry and in the KGB, where Yeltsin would throw the last remaining professionals out onto the streets.

The whole country, like a city besieged by the enemy, was left open for looting by the army of demons. The Supreme Soviet of the Russian Federation was the last obstacle in the way of the nomenclature gang that divided the USSR and came to power in the "independent Republics". The Supreme Soviet had less than two years left to live.

Inevitably, the forced breakup of the USSR led to a series of bloody civil conflicts. The Leninist national policy, in contradiction to the Russian national interests, allowed for nations' rights to self-determination to the extent of secession from the Union and formation of independent statehood. A year before the start of World War I, the leader of the world proletariat wrote:

> *As for the rights of the nations, oppressed by Tsarism, to self-determination, i.e. to secession from state and to formation of independent states, the socialist democrats must advocate such a right unconditionally. This is required by the basic principles of international democracy in general, as well as the unprecedented national oppression of the majority of the population of Russia by the Tsarist monarchy; this monarchy is the most reactionary and barbaric state structure compared with the neighbouring countries of Europe and Asia. This is required by the cause of freedom for the Great Russian population, which would not be capable of building a democratic state, if the Black Hundred Great Russian nationalism sustained by the tradition of bloody oppression of national movements, is not eradicated.*

Under the term "nation" the Bolsheviks meant any ethnic group that had been represented in the Russian Empire, and that before becoming a part thereof had not had its own national culture and, in some cases, own writing system, let alone an independent statehood. It is quite obvious why the revolutionary party needed to proclaim such a policy.

Lenin and his comrades were on the outlook for influential allies inside the Empire so that they could channel such allies' feelings of hatred and direct them against the existing regime.

As potential allies, the Slavic peoples that had developed the vast lands of Eurasia and founded the Great Russian civilisation together with various Finno-Ugric peoples were no good to the Bolsheviks. Ethnic Russians always played a silent part in debates over national identity. Russian people were like a piece of clay from which fat chunks were taken for moulding the statehood of "the juniors" (neighboring nations that joined the USSR). "The Big Brother" was labelled a "slave master in the prison of nations" (that was how the Bolsheviks used to refer to Tsarist Russia) and was supposed not only to agree with unprecedented redistribution of its indigenous territory but also pay for all these "reparations and contributions" to benefit other ethnic groups.

The Communist Revolution used the Russian nation merely as a battering ram to demolish resistance of the ruling classes. Russian peasants, soldiers and the working class were pushed into the conflict with Russian gentry, clericals and military. The genius slogans that Lenin had come up with — *Land to peasants! Factories to workers! Peace to nations!* — were none other than a cynical devilish trick. What Russians had been dealt in the end was Civil War instead of promised peace and enslavement instead of freedom. *"It is incorrect to understand under a right to self-determination something other than a right to a separate statehood,"* — this is the quintessence of the Russophobic meaning of the Leninist national policy.

It has to be pointed out that the classics of Marxism and Leninism generally disliked Russia and the Russian people; therefore, the fact that socialism had been established in Russia for the long seventy years is to be regarded as a misunderstanding, a paradox and an irony of history.

The contempt with which Karl Marx refers to the Slavic nations is simply astonishing. According to him Czechs, Bulgarians and Croatians were barbarians and Montenegrins were thieves. Marx writes with irony about Slavic lands, at the time occupied by the Turks: *"This magnificent territory has the misfortune of being inhabited by a conglomerate of various races and nations of whom it is difficult to say which one is the least adapted to progress and civilisation."*

Here is another curious quote from Marx: *"Slavic barbarians are natural counter revolutionaries and the particular enemies of democracy."*

Engels wrote in *Neue Rheinische* in 1849: *"The next world war will erase from the face of the earth not only the reactionary classes and dynasties, but the entire reactionary nations."* Russian nation, naturally, had been the first in line. In 1882 Engels confided in his correspondent Karl Kautsky: *"You could ask me if I do feel any sympathy towards the Slavic nations. I will tell you — damn little."*

There are more of the astonishing revelations by Engels: *"Merciless deadly struggle against counter revolutionary Slavdom is necessary... obliterative war and unrestrained terror."*

No less remarkable were the recommendations offered by Marx during the 19th century Crimean War, when Russia was heroically defending her land in a unfair fight with several European powers: *"... if the plan is implemented insistently and with perseverance, Kronshtadt will fall... if Finland is freed and the enemy is by the gate of the Russian capital, and should all Russian rivers and harbors be besieged, what would Russia be without Odessa, Kronshtadt, Riga and Sevastopol? An armless and eyeless giant..."*

Throughout the Crimean War, Marx and Engels published a series of articles full of spite for Russia in *Neue Oder-Zeitung*. They passionately wished for her defeat, at the same time also expressing a desire that all the European powers would be defeated by a revolution. Frustrated by Russia's success, Karl Marx wrote: *"...the mask of the Western European civilisation has fallen off the Russians and revealed a Tatar beneath"*, and that the Russian Army was *"a sample of guards' parade training"*. Echoing an article by Engels (The *Crimean Campaign, 27 December 1854*) almost word by word, Marx and Engels expressed anger at the British and the French troops for their failure to handle Russians; they excitedly described various scenarios of Russia's defeat in the event of an assault on Kronshtadt or a military involvement by Austria.

As time went by, the hatred that the internationalism theory founders felt for Russia took pathological forms. Engels developed an idea that had also been one of Marx's: Pan Slavism *"puts Europe before the alternative: either to be conquered by Slavs, or to destroy the centre of its offensive force — Russia — for good"*.

Doesn't it sound like a call to action à la Hitler?

In 1866 Engels wrote in the British paper *Commonwealth* of *"the old position of democracy and working class on a right of large European nations to a separate and independent existence"*.

Notably, all references are only ever about rights of the European nations. Russians were constantly left out of the list of nations entitled to self-determination. Engels wrote furthermore: *"...acknowledgement of, and sympathies for the national aspirations have been related only to the large and clearly defined historic nations of Europe; Italy, Poland, Germany, Hungary, France, Spain, England, Scandinavia have not been divided or under a foreign governance, and so have only an indirect interest in the cause; as concerns*

Russia, it can be mentioned merely in her capacity of a proprietor of the great volume of stolen assets, which she will have to return on the day of reckoning".

These texts provide a clue as to why the Soviet political leadership demanded that Soviet students and scholars memorised certain selected quotes from Marx and Engels out of context, and the in-depth academic studies of their written work were not encouraged. Anti-Russian and anti-Slavic revelations were concealed in the works of both classics of communism, the sheer volume of which had been enough to put off anyone with a grain of common sense. In the Soviet Union these texts were available to all; one can imagine the revelations that were contained in the classified historical documents buried in archives.

A Russian historian Anatoly Latyshev was on a temporary parliamentary committee in September-November 1991 where he was allowed access to the Lenin Fund of the Communist Party Central Archives in Marxism-Leninism Institute of the CPSU Central Committee. Latyshev has since published the most fascinating book entitled *Lenin Uncovered,* as well as a series of articles based on his research at the time. He could not discover too much in such a brief period of time, however, what he had found out was enough.

Among the macabre of Lenin's documents, Latyshev discovered the orders to exterminate the Russian people. For example, there were orders *"...to take hostages behind-the-line, to position them in front of the advancing Red Army troops, to shoot them in the backs; to send the Red Army soldiers to the areas where 'the greens' act; pretending to be 'the greens' (we will later blame them), to execute by hanging the officials, the rich, the clergy, the Kulaks*[1]*, the landowners there. To pay the executors 100,000 roubles each..."*

Lenin sent a telegram to the Caucasus: *"We will cut out everyone".* He demanded "the total extermination of Cossacks" from Mikhail Frunze, Chief Commander of the Red Army. By the way, the Cossacks in the Caucasus numbered about one million at the time.

A letter dated 19 December 1919 sent by Lenin to Felix Dzerzhinsky[2] contained more of the same. In reply to Dzerzhinsky's suggestion to execute the captured Cossacks Lenin wrote a brief resolution: *"Shoot down every single one".*

Lenin chose the Russian Orthodox Church as his main target in his terror against Russia. In his letter of 19 March 1922 addressed to

---

[1] *Kulak* — a well-to-do peasant who employed labour force.
[2] *Felix Dzerzinsky* — the Bolshevik revolutionary and the founder of the secret police *Cheka.*

Molotov[1] for the attention of the Politburo, "the Great Leader" insisted on organising a mass starvation in the country in order to put church valuables into requisition citing the need to help the starved as an excuse. The same letter issued instructions to arrest as many as possible of "the reactionary clericals" who would express their discontent.

On 1 May 1919, Lenin gave the following instructions to Dzerzhinsky: *"...it is necessary to finish off with priests and with religion as soon as possible. Everywhere priests must be arrested and shot down mercilessly as counter-revolutionaries and saboteurs, and as many of them as you can find. Churches are to be closed. Church premises are to be sealed and later used as warehouses".*

"It is very probable that someone needs to intimidate Europe with communism that is emerging in Russia, and thus to cause infuriation for Russia in Europe." Dostoevsky made such an ominous remark in his *A Writer's Diary*. Now we know whom the great Russian writer had in mind when he wrote those words. Possibly, no foreign aggressor has ever caused Russia as much damage as the devilish trinity of Marx, Engels and Lenin did.

As soon as the Bolsheviks seized power, they granted "immediate freedom" to Polish and Finnish peoples in accordance with the guidance of the Marxist "classics". The Leninists realised that in their struggle against Tsarism they could and must use the potential of these two large nations adjacent to Europe, whilst understanding that chances of making these nations join the socialist kingdom of Bolshevist Russia were remote. At the same time, the Soviets were not seriously bothered about the short-lived tumults of peoples of the Caucasus and Privolzhie[2]. The Bolsheviks allowed the people in these areas to let off some steam by using Cossacks as scapegoats (Cossacks were subject to real genocide during the Revolution, Civil War, and in the years to follow) and brought them back to the Communist bay, endowing them with the so-called "limited statehood".

Just how false and ludicrous were the claims of Communists that the Russian Empire was "the prison of nations"? Some prison it was, in which not a single ethnic group, however small, and not a single ethnic culture of Eurasia was allowed to perish into oblivion!

The Baltic region that Russians had been developing since primordial times (an Estonian town of Tartu founded under the name of Yuriev by Prince Yaroslav the Wise in the beginning of XII century is one example) changed hands several times in the past, being repeatedly passed over

---

[1] *Vyacheslav Molotov* — a leading figure in the Soviet government since 1920s.

[2] *Privolzhie* — the area around the Volga River.

between Sweden, Prussia and Denmark. The Baltic nations were saved from total assimilation and extinction only under the Russian Crown, when they gained conditions for local education not in Swedish, Danish, or Prussian dialects but in their native languages. This allowed the Baltic people to assume their national identities and form into Latvian and Estonian nations during the Middle Ages.

Stalin's national policy that formed the basis of the 1936 Constitution largely cemented the general line followed by the Bolsheviks on the issue of nationalities. World history does not know any other empire in which the mother country handed out parts of its indigenous territory to former colonies. This was how the Bolsheviks and their successors in power paid to their supporters during the Revolution and Civil War, at the expense of the Russian people.

Of course, Stalin the tyrant could not have imagined in his wildest dreams the sort of crowd that was to run Russia in the end of the 20th century. Stalin did not have enough time to transform the Soviet Union into a single unitary state before he died. Thirty years after "the Great Leader"'s, death the superpower that he had built started to fray along the borders "on paper", drawn out by Stalin himself and formally separating the Soviet Republics.

Boris Yeltsin, blinded by his desire to take revenge on Gorbachev, in signing the Belovezhskaya Accords did not "dare" to raise the question of returning the Crimea to the Russian Federation. Yeltsin "forgot" to negotiate a transit corridor for a million Kaliningrad residents who had to 'thank' him for finding themselves cut off from "the continent" — the Russian mainland. He "overlooked" the fate of 25 million Russians left beyond the border of the Motherland that shrunk drastically after "the Soviet pie" was shared. What a forgetful leader we had, indeed!

Immediately upon coming to power in their regions, the national separatists who were fighting against "Russian imperialistic chauvinism" started to implement chauvinistic policies against ethnic Russians and other ethnic minorities. The "small-scale chauvinism" proved to be much more bloody-minded than the notorious "Russian imperialistic chauvinism".

Having obtained the long-awaited freedom, the Republican nomenclature that yesterday demanded special rights and privileges for title nations of the Soviet Republics, turned the newly formed "sovereign states" into the tiny and mean regimes. These regimes suppressed ethnic Russians as well as other non-title nations. The principle of a nations' right for self-determination was thrown aside overnight. As to the principles of the Leninist national policy, with the deployment of which barbarians managed to destroy the Soviet "Third Rome", they were shoved to collect dust on the top shelves in libraries.

Under the pretence of preventing "further atomisation of post-Soviet area" the new authorities made up of old party nomenclature imposed the unitary statehoods designed to eliminate national autonomies of ethnic minorities.

Starting from December 1991 the almost identical processes took place in Ukraine and in Georgia, in the Baltic States and in Moldova — everywhere with the exception of the Russian Federation, where Yeltsin had proclaimed a notorious formula to "take as much sovereignty as you can swallow" as he was paying off his accomplices out of the lands by right belonging to Russian people.

The disintegration of the USSR by Stalin's artificial borders in combination with chauvinistic rhetoric of the official Tbilisi instantly brought the problem of South Ossetia to the surface. Following suit, people of South Ossetia also decided to exercise their right to self-determination.

The Ossetian self-determination intended to reunite the region that was divided into Georgian (South Ossetia) and Russian (North Ossetia) parts in Stalin's times. For centuries Ossetians lived as a single family with Russians and never insisted on independence in principle. After the reunion Ossetians chose to remain a part of the Russian Federation. As was to be expected, the government in Tbilisi rudely ignored such a decision of the Ossetian people, confirmed in the course of the national referendum. The Georgian government considered that, unlike Georgians, dubbed as "first class citizens", Ossetians were "second class citizens" and thus not entitled to national self-determination. At that, nobody in the Georgian government took the trouble to explain why this should be the case.

More or less of the same happened in Abkhazia. Genetically and linguistically Abkhazian ethnos is a direct relative of Cherkess-Abazin ethnic group that inhabits mainly the North Caucasus in Russia. I would like to point out that independent Abkhazia became a part of Russia only in 1810, whereas by that time both East Georgia (from 1801) and West Georgia (from 1803) had been within the Russian Empire for a good few years, and their people relied on Russia's protection from physical extermination by Turkey and Persia, the two countries that had been constantly attacking Georgia.

Not wishing to remain a part of Georgia, Abkhazia also chose to exercise her right to self-determination and proclaimed independence. Zviad Gamsakhurdia, a psychopath and a biological nationalist, was the first president of independent Georgia. He came up with an interesting method of calming down the Abkhazian population that was inclined towards separatism. Especially for the purpose, Mr. Gamsakhurdia granted amnesty to hundreds of highly dangerous criminals, supplied them with arms and forwarded to Abkhazia to fight. Their leader Jaba Ioseliani, a cruel habitual offender moonlighting as Deputy Prime Minister of Georgia, guaranteed death to Abkhazians if they were to resist: "Democracy is not a feast on lobio!"[1]

The Georgian democracy soon began to thrive not on lobio but on human blood. Armed conflicts in Sukhumi and Tskhinvali stirred centuries-old distaste of Georgians and North Caucasians for each other. Volunteer troops recruited by the radical public movement "Confederation of the Mountain Peoples of the Caucasus" flowed into Abkhazia "to give a helping hand" to brothers. Later these troops would use the same weapons as well as the fighting skills that they developed in clashes with Georgians against the Russian Army in Chechnya.

Russians were the first to suffer from all these conflicts everywhere. On entry to Sukhumi, Georgian gangs put up a banner in the town centre with a slogan characteristic of those tragic times: *"Russian men and women, stay in Sukhumi! We need free labour and prostitutes!"* Cossacks from the South of Russia were outraged by such audacity of the Georgian militants. The Cossacks formed a volunteer squadron and arrived in Abkhazia in order to assist the brave young Republic. Violence led to more violence, and the bloodshed led to more blood.

I had numerous disputes with representatives of the current Georgian government about the origins of the armed conflicts in the Caucasus.

The Georgian government has never missed an opportunity to appeal to global public opinion. They use every international forum to throw dirt at Russia and always try to present events in a way that puts Russia in the most unfavourable light. As if it was Russia that provoked wars in Abkhazia and South Ossetia in the early 1990s, "not wishing to set Georgian people free". Whilst I do not feel the slightest sympathy for Yeltsin and his circle — the people who were defining the Russian domestic and foreign policies at the time — I am adamant that Georgian politicians are not telling the truth.

The roots of both wars, lost by Georgia, lie in classical chauvinism inherent to the Georgian political elite. That elite was brought up in the spirit of their compatriot Josef Stalin and favours methods of physical annihilation of — over a dialogue with — their opponents. The very

---

[1] *Lobio* — a Georgian dish of stewed beans.

idea of negotiating with those who chose freedom over the Georgian ways was unacceptable in principle in the minds of Gamsakhurdia, Shevardnadze, and Saakashvili. The capital of unitary Georgia became the focal point of the decision making process regarding obliteration of independence and self-determination, or even smallest autonomy of the Ossetian and Abkhazian people.

Absurdly accusing the USSR of suppressing the Georgian dissidence, despite the fact that Stalin and many of his close associates were of Georgian descent, the chauvinists from Georgia managed to build such a reinforced radical nationalistic state that even the laziest of nations would have longed to escape from it. As to the hot-tempered residents of Tskhinvali and Sukhumi, they have not taken the new order to heart, to say the least.

Besides, neither Abkhazians nor Ossetians ever made claims on Georgian land or have assaulted cities and villages of Georgia. On the contrary, Georgia was to deploy the criminal elements for assaults on rebellious autonomies of Abkhazia and South Ossetia. It was the Georgian troops that treated civilians with shocking cruelty and savageness. Incidentally these troops were formed not by the Kremlin and not in Moscow, but in Tbilisi, in the governmental residencies in sovereign Georgia.

So what does Russia have to do with all these issues? Maybe our Georgian friends think that Russian men have grown so idle and lost their national and human guise to the extent where they would carry on sipping vodka whilst letting their wives and daughters to be killed and raped?

The Tbilisi's fantasies of the Russian involvement in the armed conflicts in Abkhazia and South Ossetia of the 1990s have one, and one only, underlying reason: the Paper Lions of Georgia are ashamed to have suffered total defeat by Ossetian and Abkhazian volunteers whom they always considered to be worthless. To be seen fighting against a global nuclear power would be, though, quite another matter. Now, that would not be demeaning. Stories like that are worth a lot. For instance, tales of the clinical Russian aggression can be shared with naïve patrons of the European Parliament canteen in exchange for a free bowl of cabbage stew. And if the descriptions of Russian military atrocities are engaging and colourful enough, they might even earn the storytellers some creme-brulee.

Referring to post-Soviet Georgia, I am deliberately putting the words "internal affairs" in quotation marks. Nobody in their right mind would regard the decision of peoples of Ossetia and Abkhazia to remain parts of the Russian Federation after the cessation of the USSR to be an internal Georgian affair. The Russian Federation is a successor of statutory tradition of the USSR. It was Russia of all the Republics that inherited Soviet assets, debts, international agreements, and the status of a nuclear power as well as the permanent membership in the Security Council of the United Nations.

The disintegration of the USSR was the process of the spontaneous detachment of various Russian territories. If Georgia was determined to separate from Russia, it should have done so in strict accordance with the constitutional order of secession of a Soviet Republic from the USSR. This order required a Republican referendum in the course of which people of Georgia were to be given an opportunity to vote for, or against, the secession. If, however, at least one part of Georgia had voted against the separation, the whole Republic was to remain a part of the USSR or of the Russian Federation, the latter being a legal successor of the former.

Simply speaking, if you want to leave, feel free to do so, but leave the others' luggage behind. Citizens of Abkhazia and Ossetia do not wish to leave Russia; by fleeing Georgia they are voting with their feet; they seek any opportunity, legal or not, to obtain Russian citizenship. How can it be regarded a fault of Russia? It is not "a fault" but a direct responsibility of the Russian Federation that arises from its status as the legal successor of the USSR.

It was a duty of Russia to take under her umbrella all ex-Soviet citizens, regardless of their ethnicity and domicile, who refused to adopt citizenships of the newly formed independent states.

I often hear an opinion that Russia deliberately supported separatism in South Ossetia by granting Russian passports to citizens of Abkhazia and Ossetia. This is not the case.

Firstly, in international law there are no restrictions to practical implementation of the dual citizenship principle. When a citizen of the former USSR wishes to apply for a Russian passport, we always review such an application in accordance with domestic procedures. Moreover, it is in our interests to welcome more of the loyal citizens into the country under the circumstances of the current demographic decline. We do not even require an applicant to denounce his or her existing citizenship. It is not Abkhazians or Ossetians exclusively who may become Russian citizens. Representatives of any nation, Georgians included, can do so. About 3.5 million ethnic Georgians live in Russia today. They are our compatriots just the same, our brothers and sisters. So why, if the Georgians are entitled to Russian passports, the same should be denied to people from Abkhazia or Ossetia?

Secondly, we do not impose Russian citizenship on people of the former USSR! Quite the opposite: people queue and wait for Russian passports for months, considering these passports to be a sort of an insurance policy in their complicated lives. I would stress, once again, that granting Russian citizenship to all those former USSR citizens who want it is not a whim but an indisputable duty of the Russian Government, and this duty is determined both by our international obligations and by the Constitution.

Finally, do those who practise issuing national passports to foreigners have a right to criticise us for doing the same? For example, the Government of Poland introduced the "Karta Polaka" ("Pole's Card") in 2007, which is being widely distributed in Lithuania and in Ukraine despite protests from local authorities and the general public. Estonian authorities easily grant citizenship to residents of the Pechorsk area of the Pskov region in Russia, possibly hoping for a future annexation of the area.

The President of Romania, Mr. Besesku, whose idol is the fascist dictator Antonescu, speaking in April 2009 in the town of Pyatra-Nyamts at the forum of local governments of Romania and Republic of Moldova, went as far as to declare: *"Our decisions to expedite the process of granting Romanian citizenship to people from whom it has been taken forcefully, as well as to their family members, is a serious process in which we do not consult anyone and which is gaining momentum with every passing week."*

Doesn't such a statement, coming from a leader of a NATO and EU member country, constitute an instigation to adopt Romanian citizenship?

All this explains why Russia does not need to offer specific justifications for her humanitarian actions in the zones of Georgian-Abkhazian and Georgian-Ossetian conflicts. Such actions are already explicitly justified by the very status of the Russian Federation as the single legal successor and heir of the USSR. This specific position demands that Russian authorities must overcome their hypocritical shyness and the juvenile fear of making a mature decision. Both Republics, Abkhazia and Ossetia, have just as much right to self-determination as Georgia has, and this right was exercised in the course of referendums that were an accurate test of the national will.

Hypocritical sighs of the US-led global community must be taken for what they are — a manifestation of hypocrisy and an inevitable accompaniment to all long-overdue foreign policy actions of self-respected countries. The fuss will die down sooner or later, and the world will realise that Russia is undertaking her duties as a peacekeeper in Eurasia, and that from now on she will not tolerate provocations right at her doorstep.

So far, every effort of Russia to condemn militant impulses of a yet another Georgian "tsar" was met with a barrage of accusations of adopting a policy of double standards: "Just look at those Russians! They are supporting separatists in Sukhumi and Tskhinvali but at the same time they "murder separatists in Grozny in the loo"! (as Putin had once angrily put it).

I can reply to such accusations: the Georgian chauvinists' attempts to draw a comparison between Abkhazia/Ossetia and the situation in Chechnya are as inappropriate as they are provocative. It is blatantly clear what Saakashvili and his entourage were seeking to achieve. What is not clear, however, is why they have been ignoring the reality of the situation with such boldness.

The conflict in Chechnya was a result of an inner confrontation. Chechens fought against Chechens. Russia supported one side, and Russia's enemies supported the other. Moreover, in the aftermath of the two destructive Chechen wars, Russia has assumed responsibility for economic recovery of this long-suffering Republic. Today Grozny is the most improved city in the Caucasus and, arguably, in the whole of Russia. Former militants made peace with Russian people. Former Chechen partisans today are the backbone of Spetsnaz of North-Caucasian Military District.

When Saakashvili's thugs entered Tskhinvali in August 2008 and destroyed this North Ossetian capital in a barbaric nightly bombing, they were resisted by Russian troops together with a Chechen "East" battalion made up of the former militant separatists. Such comradeship-in-arms is the best testimony of the reconciliation between Russians and Chechens.

The war in Chechnya was a hard lesson for us all but we have learnt it well. Today there is no more peaceable country than Russia among those present in the Caucasus.

There is a yet another convincing illustration of the fact that contradictions and hostility between Russians and Chechens, as well as between Georgians and Russians, have never been insurmountable. The argument is as simple as ABC. Where did the Ossetian and Abkhazian refugees flee from war? Did they go to Tbilisi? No, they fled to Russia. And where did Georgians escape from war and starvation? Where a good half of Georgian refugees from Abkhazia are living now, all these natives of flourishing Sukhumi, magnificent Gagra, and spectacular

Pitsunda[1]? They are living in Russia now. Which other country in the world is home to 3.5 million ethnic Georgians, apart from Georgia itself? Russia is. Do people tend to flee to an enemy's territory when they are trying to hide from that enemy? Abkhazians and Ossetians, Georgians and Chechens — in the times of war all of them sought shelter in Russia.

It can only mean that Russia is not an enemy to these people. It also means that the desire of ordinary Georgians to live peacefully side by side with Russians is more powerful than the xenophobic actions of the Tbilisi authorities who desperately want to join NATO. Would NATO provide for Georgian people, would it reestablish peace in this ancient Christian Orthodox nation? Or maybe NATO would install the people of Abkhazia and Ossetia back into Georgia? Of course it would not.

The future of Georgia lies in the mutual friendship with Russia. And Georgian radicals lie when they state the opposite — as they always do.

---

[1] *Gagra and Pitzunda* — picturesque seaside towns in Georgia.

THE VAMPIRE[1]

Unlike armed conflicts in the Caucasus, largely based on a mixture of old grievances, traditions of vendetta and some such dark local specifics, the war in Transniestria was of a purely political nature. Russians, Moldovans, and Ukrainians have lived together on both sides of the River Dniester for centuries. What distinguishes Transniestria from Moldova is not a different ethnic composition of the population, but national instinct and historical mentality. Inhabitants of this land, where the glory of Alexander Suvorov, a favourite of Catherine the Great, is still alive and present, have always been more inclined towards the Russian civilisation.

Until the year 1940 Transniestria was neither a part of Moldova nor a part of the former governing region of Bessarabia. The territorial ambitions of Romania have never been recognised there. Russian language and culture consolidated the multi-national population for centuries, which is a valid proof of the concept that a national instinct is based on culture and spirit to a greater extent than in territory and materialism.

At times the Moldovan nationalists' hatred of everything Russian took schizophrenic forms. In the early 1990s the crowd of hundreds of thousands gathered by the monument to King Stephan. There the slogans of the kind *"Suitcase — Rail Station — Russia!"* were the least extreme ones. One of the women activists from the radical national party "People's Front" in the affect of chauvinistic ecstasy, aided by a local priest, wedded the said monument. Naturally, not without organising a divorce for the King first, as in his lifetime he had disgraced himself by marrying a Russian lady....

In reality, King Stephan (Stephan the Great) ruled Moldova from 1457 to 1504. He managed to suppress the Boyard clans and to build a strong state. Stephan created a strong army and strengthened the defense ability of his kingdom.

---

[1] *Vampire ("Upyr")* is a short story by Alexey Tolstoy, a 19th century Russian poet, novelist, and dramatist. It is the first modern vampire story by a Russian.

Being a ruler of the land surrounded by aggressive neighbours, Stephan looked for allies in the far-reaching countries, primarily in Russia.

In 1463 the King married Eudokia Olelkovich of Kiev, a relative of the Moscow Prince Ivan III. In 1483, Helena, the daughter of Stephan and Eudokia, married Ivan the Young, the son of Ivan III. This connection between Stephan and Ivan III protected Moldova from the Tatar aggression and reduced Poland's ability to put pressure on the Moldovan leader. 529 years later People's Front of Moldova decided to correct the actions of their great king.

The spontaneous division of the USSR and the chauvinisation of society, inspired by the Republican Communist government; inflow of the unitarian emissary from Bucharest to Chisinau; speculations on denouncement of the state with subsequent formation of Great Romania, brought out by extremists of People's Front — all this was met with indignation by the people of Transniestria (it's is worth mentioning that the official Bucharest continues to follow a policy of Anschluss towards Moldova up to this day. For instance, President of Romania Trajan Basesku constantly makes statements to the effect that "he considers it useless to sign such a border treaty with Moldova that would make a Romanian leader on a par with Molotov and Ribbentrop".

On 22 June 2011 on the memorial day of the commencement of the Great Patriotic War when Nazis attacked the USSR in 1941, this Romanian führer declared that had he been in Mashal Antonescu's shoes, he'd surely send Romanian soldiers to cross the river Prut.

Unfortunately, we had never heard a reaction to this challenging speech from Basesku's colleagues in NATO and the EU). The major cause for concern was the resolution on using Romanian military aid against "Transniestrian separatists" adopted by Moldovan chauvinists at the mass rally in the centre of Chisinau on 17 March 1992.

To be fair, I have to admit that it was not Romania but Yeltsin's Russia that mainly rendered military support to Chisinau. Not only the Kremlin ordered General Netkachev, the already intimidated Commander of the 14th Army, to stay out of the conflict, but it had also supplied Moldova with arms and military vehicles belonging to the former USSR.

The borders were opened and hundreds of Romanian volunteers fled into Moldova. They were grandchildren of vampires who had invaded the country together with German Reich troops in 1942–1943, occupied our land and drank our compatriots' blood. My elderly constituents in Voronezh were often telling me stories about the inhumane attitude that Romanian fascists displayed towards civil population. They never showed much courage in fighting against the Red Army and so compensated for their inferiority complexes by atrocities towards defenseless civilians in the occupied territories. At times these atrocities reached such a scale that German commanders had to interfere in order to stop the violence. Now the descendants of those vampires came to Moldova to fight.

As early as in March, 1992, in the place of Bulboki 50 km from Chisinau a formation of a special armed squad began under the guidance of experienced Romanian instructors. Crews of BMP[1]s and BMD[2]s were formed out of the Romanian Army soldiers and officers. In addition, Romania provided thirty-two air fighting pilots and ten interceptor and bombing aircrafts MIG-25, again with Romanian crews, for the operation of air attack on Markuleshty airport in Transniestria (where forty-two of jet fighter aircrafts MIG-29 were stopped and given over to Moldavian Army under a treacherous order of Marshall Shaposhnikov, Commander of the so-called "United Armed Forces of the CIS". The aircrafts had been previously assigned to the Black Sea Fleet.)

Propaganda of Anschluss of former Moldovan Soviet Socialist Republic with subsequent formation of Great Romania was accompanied by threats addressed to the authorities of the Transniestrian capital Tiraspol. Tiraspol reacted soon. People of the autonomy resolved to defend themselves and proclaimed the autonomous Republic of Transniestria.

In Chisinau they hoped that after the Belovezhskaya Accords there was nobody left who could possibly protect the disobedient Transniestria. The USSR no longer existed and Moscow was too busy dividing the inheritance. A possibility of the Russian government negatively reacting to an assault on Tiraspol was not considered seriously. Politicians in Bucharest and Chisinau had noted the ease with which Yeltsin was surrendering Russian interests — land, properties, and capital — to satisfy the ever-growing appetites of governments of the newly independent states. In the spring of 1992 the armed battalions of Romanian and Moldovan unitarians set off to assault Tiraspol; their leaders figured that any actions of theirs would go unpunished.

The operation to destroy Transniestria was named "Trojan Horse". To start with, unitarians planned to stamp out the town of Bendery on the right bank of the River Dniester. The first gunshot sounded in

---

[1] BMP — "fighting vehicle of infantry" — Soviet amphibious tracked infantry fighting vehicle.

[2] BMD stands for Combat Vehicle of the Airborne, a Soviet/Russian airborne amphibious tracked infantry-fighting vehicle.

Moldovan land on 1 April: a police squad shot down a militia patrol and a bus with local workers.

Inhabitants of the autonomy appealed to the commandment of the 14th Army stationed in Tiraspol to protect the lives of peaceful civilians. Local women picketed the headquarters of the 14th Army every day. It was no use. The "not to get involved" order by Moscow was an equivalent of a death sentence for the 150,000 population of Transniestria.

Eventually, the people of Transniestria decided to take initiative into their own hands. All capable men started to form volunteer squadrons. Hundreds of Cossacks and Slavic volunteers from Ukraine and Russia came to Tiraspol, Bendery, and Dubasari in order to help their brothers. However, their numbers were negligible in comparison with the large and heavily endowed army and police of the aggressor. Moldovan side had 14,500 troops and 320 items of artillery and armoured vehicles. This substantial force was supposed to be resisted by the Armed Forces of Transniestria — Cossacks, guards, volunteer units, and the territorial rescue brigade. The Transniestrian side only had small-arms weapons as well as "Alazan" missiles and improvised unaimed mine throwers at their disposal.

It was impossible to stop the aggression while so significantly outnumbered.

The outcome of the conflict was determined by the will of the 14th Army. The country that they had given oath to was no longer there, but there still was a Russian officer's honour to defend. Officers of the 14th Army led their soldiers to the defense line in disseverance with General Netkachev's orders. Betrayed by their political and military governors but infinitely devoted to Russia's national interests, those servicemen wanted to share their people's fate and rose to their defense.

Neither the idle talking of Minister Kozyrev, who in a rush was sent by Yeltsin "to monitor the situation" in Chisinau and Tiraspol, nor the emotional visit by Vice-President Rutskoy, who addressed Transniestrians with many an inspirational word but failed to suggest a viable course of action, could hold back the escalation of the fascistic Romanian-Moldovan aggression.

Headquarters of the 14th Army had never received from the Kremlin an order to separate the conflicting parties and to stop the bloodshed. Fearing a scandal and trying to avoid responsibility for the actions of the 14th Army officers, Moscow procrastinated putting off the decision to place the 14th Army under the Russian jurisdiction. That finally happened on 12 May and, even then, only due to pressure from the Russian Supreme Soviet.

I went to the conflict zone in May 1992 for the first time. I knew the place quite well — back in 1980 our handball team participated in all-Union junior handball championship held in Tiraspol. I still remember the taste of sweet Bulgarian pepper that my teammates and I used to munch on in large quantities.

But this time the city looked entirely different. Tension and anticipation of a fight were hanging in the air. On 19 May we were going to Dubasari in trucks with a small group of Cossacks when we got caught under unitarian fire. One of us, a journalist from Kiev, was lightly injured.

The May clashes near Dubasari were just a nerve-racking exercise before the full-scale attack began exactly one month later. The evening of 19 June saw the outbreak of the real war. Shelling was coming from each and every building. Hundreds of human dead bodies were lying about on the streets under the hot sun. On 22 June, the date of commemoration of Hitler's assault on the USSR, the 'precise' Moldovan aviation attempted a bombing attack on Bendery to cut it off from Transniestrian volunteers — but missed the target.

Moldovan and Romanian militants employed conventional cynical tactics — they were either positioning themselves in residential buildings and kept civilians inside or they stationed their artillery on schools' and hospitals' grounds in order to prevent the 14th Army and Transniestrian troops from firing back. At that the vampires, however, were shooting at everything that moved within their sight.

Tension escalated with each passing day. Moldovan side was drawing more troops and long-range heavy artillery.

The endurance of the defenders of Bendery led to Chisinau's decision to attack Tiraspol with the use of such powerful weapons of destruction as "Hyacinth" cannons and "Hurricane" reactive artillery.

On 23 June our group was on the road between Dubasari and Rybnitsa with a Russian-Ukrainian volunteer squad. We did not find out until later about the arrival of General Lebed along with a Spetsnaz squad into Tiraspol, however the impact of the actions undertaken by the decisive new commander of the 14th Army was felt straightaway. We could see that the real force of the Russian military replaced the previous chaotic actions of segmental militarised units. In the beginning of July, our artillery covered the Kitskan platform and Gerbovetsky forest where the main forces of the opponent were based. It is not known exactly how many Moldovan volunteers lost their lives in the course of that operation. I think there were hundreds.

The "Trojan Horse" stumbled, and this bloody conflict left the most macabre mark in the national memory of Russians, Moldovans, and Ukrainians. That war introduced the name of General Alexander Lebed to the world. As life would soon have it, our paths were to cross one day.

That war strengthened the position of the young Transniestrian Moldovan Republic with her heroic people, who to this day are denied recognition of their right to self-determination in the court of global public opinion, despite having paid gallons of blood for this right.

In March 2012 during one of my field trips pertaining military defense questions, Dmitry Medvedev called to interrupt my conference with the Russian Security Council. The acting president offered me the role of the President's special envoy to Transnistria. I agreed without hesitation, and pledge on pages of this book to do everything in my power so as to stop bloodshed on the shores of Dniester, to protect the people whose only fault is in their decision not to join Romania where Moldovan nationalists are dragging them so persistently.

HUMILIATED AND INSULTED[1]

In October 1992 I filed an application to the Constitutional Court of the Russian Federation questioning the legitimacy of Belovezhskaya Accords that had been signed by the leaders of Russia, Ukraine and Belarus. It turned out that nobody had made a similar application before me. Neither the Russian Supreme Soviet, outraged by Yeltsin's voluntarism, nor leaders of various patriotic movements who had always passionately criticised the Gaidar[2] government, took the time to demand in the Constitutional Court an explanation of the whole Belovezhskaya affair.

After the 14th Army extinguished the fire in Transniestria, it became apparent that the tragic consequences of the illegitimate cessation of the USSR were yet to be seen. I decided to compile a thorough and a clearly defined query supporting it with legal arguments.

I managed to prove in the body of my query that the USSR as a subject of international law could not have been lawfully liquidated by a treaty signed by heads of executive powers of Ukraine, Russia and Belarus. It would be the same, for the argument's sake, as if Texas, North Carolina and California Governors gathered together somewhere in the suburbs of San Diego and declared the dissolution of the United States of America.

I was notified by post that my query was received in the Constitutional Court and was being looked into. A couple of days later I was invited by my friend, a social scientist Leontiy Byzov, to go to Baku in the capacity of the Russian Supreme Soviet expert to accompany an official parliamentary delegation.

On the plane to Baku all members of the delegation discussed nothing else but the latest news: the Supreme Court of Azerbaijan had just ruled

---

[1] A tragic 1871 novel by Fyodor Dostoevsky, also known in English as *The Insulted and Humiliated* or *The Insulted and Injured*. It depicts the harshness of human relations.

[2] *Yegor Gaidar* (1956–2009) was a Chairman of the Council of Ministers of the Russian Federation in 1992. Gaidar is known as an architect of shock-therapy reforms policy in post-Perestroika Russia.

a death penalty for an officer and for several soldiers of the Russian Army. They were found guilty of opening fire on a group of local looters who had trespassed on a military school grounds and tried to seize a warehouse full of weaponry. The Russian servicemen were acting in strict compliance with patrol duty regulations. One other Russian man awaiting his execution was a pilot who had fought on the Armenian side and was taken a prisoner by the Azerbaijani. Typically the Kremlin was keeping the conspicuous silence on the matter. The MPs, though, were very keen to resolve it.

After a short repose in the hotel we were invited to the official residence of the Azerbaijan Parliament for dinner. At dinner all their decisiveness seemed to have deserted the Russian MPs, who were taking turns to toast to "the centuries-long friendship between Russian and Azerbaijani people". An hour or so had passed, and the guests from Moscow, their faces reddened from alcohol, were taken to a palace nearby to meet Abulfaz Elchibey, the first President of Azerbaijan.

He was an old man, bearded, slim, with a piercing pair of eyes on his face. He spoke through an interpreter, slowly and quietly. The Russian MPs seemed to be enjoying his speech a lot.

Then the head of our delegation made a speech in reciprocation, then another deputy, and yet another one....

All of them were praising the mutual friendship of Russians and Azerbaijanis carried through centuries, were offering compliments to the hosts... and not a word about imprisoned Russian soldiers on the death row.

I could not stand it for much longer, so I got up from my seat and said in a loud voice, interrupting one shuffling MP:

> "Mr. President! Your Excellency! Tonight these walls heard a great deal about historic links between our two countries. I am not going to repeat these words, however just and appropriate they were. I would like to take this opportunity to appeal to you to show the strength and wisdom of a national leader as well as your kindness towards the Russian democracy. You are probably aware of the fact that four servicemen and one pilot are near their bitter end in a prison in Azerbaijan. They were sentenced to death merely because they obeyed orders and stayed true to the oath of allegiance that they had taken. They are innocent. Your reputation with people of Azerbaijan is extremely high and your mercy for the Russian soldiers would be yet another evidence to your wisdom. I am asking you to lift the death sentences and to

set the Russian soldiers free. And this would be the best possible confirmation that your Russian guests were right when they said so many words of praise about Your Excellency."

I sat back. Elchibey himself was to break the silence. He looked at me very attentively, nodded, and said in Russian: "Good. I will do that."[1]

I was ecstatic. None of the members of the delegation had scolded me for breaching the state etiquette; on the contrary, everyone cheerfully rushed to congratulate Elchibey on his wise decision.

We left the presidential residence and went on to take part in a scheduled meeting with our Russian compatriots. At the meeting the Russians behaved in an assertive manner, accusing Russia of indulging Armenians in the conflict over Nagorno-Karabakh. A few men in Cossack uniform openly confirmed the fact that Russian volunteers had been involved in the fights for Agdam, Shusha and some other Azerbaijani villages adjacent to Armenian Stepanakert in Nagorno-Karabakh.

At that moment I clearly realised that the tragedy of Russians was not in their artificial division alone but also in the fact that Russians participated directly and proactively in ethnic conflicts of others and fight against one another when they do that.

For our compatriots, who were left without Russian support in their new and unfamiliar role of foreigners in their own countries, this was a way of trying to prove their loyalty to the new chauvinistic regimes.

Russian citizens of Riga and Tallinn applauded 'national fronts' and rallied the streets in demonstrations for the Baltic Republics' independence, thus hoping to earn a right to live in Europe, but they were just voting against themselves. Radical nationalists who had come to power in the Baltic States wanted to get even with the already nonexistent Soviet Union and to do malice for Russia, so they took it out on their unfortunate neighbours — ethnic Russians living in the Baltic Republics. At first, the Russians were denied rights of citizenship, then they were deprived the last remaining political rights and, to finish it off, national schools and culture were taken away from them, too. Now Russian children were not allowed to converse in their native language in schools, not even during recessions.

Why such hostility? Why humiliate and insult the whole nation? It is very shortsighted and not clever. Great numbers of Russians have always lived in Estonia and Latvia, comprising approximately 30–40% of total population. Instead of building the amicable nations of dual cultures

---

[1] Elchibey kept his word — (*Author's comment*).

the Baltic chauvinists are forcing Russians to renounce their roots. What could it lead to? Clearly, it can only bring out feelings of hatred on both conscious and subconscious levels. Russian young people from the Baltic States have a good command of local languages, but they do despise nationalists. Such a discriminative, Nazi-like policy cannot earn respect of any civilised nation. Feelings of hatred lead to estrangement and then more hatred.

In addition, think of the annual military marches and parades of Estonian and Latvian Waffen-SS veterans which are regularly watched by official authorities and representatives of leading political parties, and, my dear reader, you will have a full picture of the historical revenge complex suffered by the Baltic States' politicians and societies in general. In order to justify the anti-democratic suppression of ethnic minorities' civil rights as well as the regular outbursts of recidivism of fascism, the political elite of Baltic States continuously provokes Russia. They are forever at the forefront of all actions that may potentially antagonise Russia and the Western world.

Recently, already in the capacity of the Russian Ambassador to NATO I posed a question to one of my colleagues from the Baltic States as to why his country had taken the unfriendliest stance on relations between NATO and Moscow. Wouldn't it be better for neighbours to live side by side in peace? Besides, if treated with respect, the Russian communities in his country would become more loyal and compliant. My colleague's reply was achingly honest. He revealed that if the political elite of his small country, that is hardly a major player on the political arena, had not used every coming opportunity to provoke Russia, it would have been barely noticed by the rest of the world. However, because they sustain turbulence in their relations with Moscow, politicians and diplomats of his country regularly get invited to Washington and to European capitals where they incidentally settle other issues, including personal ones. I think that such an approach goes beyond cynicism.

But let's go back to the 1990s. After the USSR disintegrated, Russians outside national borders (over 25 million of people) found themselves redundant. In order to earn the right to live in the new ethnocratic state, the Russians were ready to fight on either side in the trenches of Karabakh, shooting at one another. But that was not enough. Soon they had no choice but to pack up and leave for Russia. The new masters of Armenia and Azerbaijan failed to appreciate self-sacrifices of the Russians.

In my view, it was all rather undignified. Self-humiliation, lack of national pride or solidarity — these traits, previously undetected by me, were exhibited in my fellow countrymen; they were the symptoms of denationalisation of the Russians. The ideal of a Russian person, in which I believed my whole life, was being deconstructed right in front of my eyes. I have seen to my shame how my countrymen, prepared to follow any orders, sucked up to various non-entities.

In Russia, too, an icy reception awaited refugees who had fled from beatings and massacre. In the environment of economic and moral crisis hardly anyone in Moscow paid them any attention. Refugees had to settle in miserable conditions, often in dilapidated houses or wagons, in the suburbs of provincial towns. A math professor from Baku could at best count on a job of a village schoolteacher. A director of the exhibition centre in Dushanbe, who had been miraculously saved from being shot during atrocities in Tajikistan, had to make do with a job of an ordinary architect in a small provincial town.

The Soviet Titanic broke down and sank in a huge ocean; people struggled and drowned, dragging others along down to the social bottom.

I couldn't agree with that. In total political darkness I tried to find a new form of self-organisation for Russian people, which was to help us reclaim our entitlement for historical prospects. That visit to Baku gave me an idea of the first step in this direction.

In December 1992 we held a forum entitled *Russian Diplomacy: the Karabakh Syndrome* in the Russian Peace Committee conference hall. Representatives of Russian Diasporas in Armenia and Azerbaijan as well as Armenian and Azerbaijani residents of Moscow were invited. The result went beyond my most pessimistic expectations — the Russians from Baku and Yerevan quarrelled over Karabakh so badly, that they were on the verge of declaring a war against each other right there and then.

Just then a thought came to me — why don't we try to bring together all these amateurish Russian organisations, the groups of our compatriots, the Slavic centres and communities? We could do it not to impose a firm structure but merely to facilitate communication, which would enable them to exchange information and share experiences.

By that time I was actively cooperating with the Union of Russian Revival. It was an informal creative group of young politicians, deputies of the Moscow City Council, business people, and scientists, all of whom held diverse political views but were keen to communicate with one another. In the Union I befriended such people as social scientist Leontiy Byzov, entrepreneur Eldar Kovrighin, Andrey Saveliev, who was a councilor in Moscow City at the time, and Sergey Pykhtin, the head of one of the district councils in Moscow. They began to work together on preparing the Manifesto of Russian Revival — a powerful political proclamation designed to constitute the ideological basis of the Congress of Russian Communities (KRO).

The first edition of the Manifesto was published in March 1993. It stirred a gale of emotions among the patriotically minded. The Manifesto was the first document ever to explain the meaning of a Russian national idea and attribute concise definitions to the political phenomena encountered by Russians:

Following the path of the great Russian thinkers we must say: chauvinism means a bad upbringing of a nation; cosmopolitism means a lack of upbringing whatsoever; internationalism means hard labour of a nation for the benefit of alien interests. This is the platform on which the national patriotic movement has to stand, if it aims to affirm ethical and civilised forms of nationalism without demeaning itself by resorting to aggressive and extreme manifestations of patriotism.

The small-numbered core group of the Union of Russian Revival spent the first quarter of 1993 in preparation for the first assembly of the Congress of Russian Communities. We rented premises in the Parliamentary Centre on Trubnaya Square in Moscow and booked hotel rooms for the delegates.

By that time, the process of spontaneous unification of Russians in the former Soviet Republics was already gaining momentum. After all the misery that people had gone through they have abandoned all hopes for help from the Russian President or the Government and proceeded to set up various Russian communities, societies and centres that would somehow serve to withstand political and cultural aggression of the local chauvinists.

Our job was to identify all those independent organisations, get in touch with them and to ensure their attendance at the founding assembly in Moscow.

The new patriotic organisation has come to life on 29–30 March 1993. It was an international union designed to legally protect the rights of Russians beyond national borders. The delegates did not debate over a name of the new organisation much, and so the Congress of Russian Communities was formed. Some of the patriots whom I know personally later grumbled about the term "congress". Every time I replied that the members chose that name because they were comfortable with it.

The essence of a public organisation is not in its name but in the determination to do useful deeds in the absence of which the chief objective of patriots would be unattainable, that objective being to protect interests of those in whose name the organisation was established in the first place. The Congress of Russian Communities was exactly such an organisation: proactive and fearless, with a clear ideological base set forth in its manifesto, and with an existing wide network of improvised self-organisations of compatriots abroad in place.

The rigid conditions in which KRO had to exist ensured that any career mongers or weak-spirited individuals were thrown overboard. Any provocateurs were easily discoverable in the constant fight for survival of the Russian communities. The very structure of KRO — a network of independently run local Russian communities with the executive representation in Moscow, responsible for coordination and informational work — has freed it from any squabbles for power, which are so characteristic of all political parties.

By May 1993 KRO made a name for itself by winning a few headline cases. In Chisinau four servicemen of Parachute Regiment 300 were arrested in a forged through and through case. That arrest was a form of Moldovan nationalists' revenge for losing the war in Transniestria to the 14th Army. See, Alexey Lebed, a brother of the world-famous 14th Army commander General Alexander Lebed, was in command of the Regiment 300. The regiment was withdrawing from Moldova to Russia, and there was no one left to stand up for the arrested soldiers.

Upon the request of the Russian community in Moldova, KRO executive committee hired a professional attorney to represent the officers in court. We won the case, and the acquitted officers came to Moscow to personally thank my colleagues and me.

In June 1993 a group of Ukrainian extremists attacked the premises of the Russian Cultural Centre in Lviv, beat up the Centre's activists and trashed the place, leaving ripped books and broken windows behind. The Russian communities in Ukraine appealed to the Ukrainian government to introduce security measures that would ensure protection of ethnic Russian population and create a safe environment for Russian organisations.

I requested a meeting with Leonid Kravchuk, the first Ukrainian President, and his Administration, and urgently left for Kiev. The meeting was exceptionally productive. Mr. Kravchuk personally promised me that such attacks would not be repeated in future. He issued relevant instructions to his interior forces ministries. Our meeting was covered by major Russian TV channels, which, as journalists informed me later, nearly gave a heart attack to Foreign Minister Kozyrev. The man in charge of the Ministry of Foreign Affairs of the Russian Federation forgot all about his libertarian attitudes and called TV executives, demanding them to "stop showing Rogozin on TV".

A month later, in July 1993, I went on a visit to Georgia. "My old fellow balcony orator" Edward Shevardnadze was elected the President of Georgia. He agreed to hold a meeting with me at which I intended to discuss the issue of evacuating Russian population from the war zone in Abkhazia.

I stayed at *Iveria Hotel*, formerly a part of a state hotel chain *Intourist*. I happened to stay there a few times back in my younger days, whilst taking part in the Newspaper *"Eastern Dawn"* Cup handball competitions. For years later, when I worked in the Committee of Youth Organisations I often visited Tbilisi with various foreign delegations. Each time we stayed at *Iveria*. But in 1993 the hotel was beyond recognition. Georgian refugees from Abkhazia had set up an improvised camp inside it, and the place gave an impression of ancient Shanghai. The wide-open windows of this front Republican hotel, formerly the best in town, now displayed somebody's rags on dry-lines.

For all that, the electricity in the hotel had not been cut off when we arrived. I switched on the TV and for a while watched the news in Georgian language. Judging by the pictures, the news almost entirely featured events in rebellious autonomies. While flicking between the channels, I suddenly came across something that looked liked an interview of Jaba Ioseliani, a bank robber and the leader of the Georgian paramilitary group Mkhedrioni. It was this heavily armed force made up of criminals on amnesty that had been infamous for the massacres in Sukhumi of Abkhazia.

Jaba Ioseliani was addressing the viewers in Russian, and I still don't understand why he chose to speak Russian and not Georgian on that occasion. I doubted that a single Russian still remained in Tbilisi in the aftermath of the chauvinistic strikes in the heyday of massacres that were the signature style of now oblivious President Gamsakhurdia. Ioseliani couldn't have been speaking Russian exclusively for my benefit!

The notorious criminal was threatening to inflict terrible punishments on ethnic Russians and on Russia as a whole. He was promising to seed death and sufferings for those who would dare to stand in the way of Georgian militants in Abkhazia. In general, he was terrorising. I listened to this remarkable interview till the end, switched off the TV and made my way out along the corridors of *Iveria* that were stuffed with bundles and luggage of the refugees. The city was barely recognisable, too. Sounds of gun machines were distinctly audible in the evening. Someone offered an explanation that these days, firing guns at weddings and jubilees, had become a new Georgian custom. I returned to the hotel and with difficulty managed to get some sleep at last.

In the morning traffic jammed on all Tbilisi roads. As it turned out, trolley wires had been cut off during the night by some starving dwellers with an intention to sell them for scrap metal.

Together with my assistant Dmitry Stupakov and a representative of Shevardnadze's office we had to leave the car behind and walk on foot to the residence of the Republican leader. The Grey Fox wasn't alone. Next, was sitting the very same TV persona from the previous night. "Oh, good, it is you whom I am after!" went through my mind the moment I saw Ioseliani.

It is worth mentioning that by the time of these events Shevardnadze's power in Georgia was purely nominal.

Thieves-in-law[1] were making all major political decisions and it was them who were determining the direction of the Georgian Armed Forces' actions in the zones of conflict. Only they could decide whether to block or to open an exit for Russian refugees from the fire trap that had caught defenseless civilians. In short, not the Grey Fox, but Ioseliani together with his accomplice Kitovani governed Georgia. The twosome played Tsar and God, sealing the fates of thousands of Russians.

Our hosts greeted us rather drily and with some contempt, as if we had interrupted a most important conversation. I think that when Shevardnadze first agreed to talk to me he did not have a clear idea of who exactly was going to take up some of his precious time.

He was informed that President Kravchuk himself had received me in Kiev. That alone was a good enough recommendation. Besides, he also had a phone call about me from Professor Buryak from Kiev, whose opinions the Grey Fox always valued.

I noticed a momentary dismay on the faces of my interlocutors and so decided to take initiative at once. To begin with, I warned Ioseliani that he was being deemed personally liable for all actions of the Georgian militants. I demanded that he must quit insulting Russia and, in a more mellow tone, suggested that he should name a mediator with whom I could discuss the technicalities of the Russian exodus from the conflict zone. Then I addressed Shevardnadze requesting him to oversee the implementation of our agreement.

Strangely enough, that strategy proved to be successful. On one hand, with my tactics I had acknowledged the position of Ioseliani as

---

[1] A *'Thief-in-Law'* is a criminal who obeys "The Thief's Code" — a figure of authority in the Russian and former USSR underground world.

the only person in Tbilisi worth negotiating tangible issues with (which was the case in Georgia at the time). On the other hand, the Grey Fox had been put in his habitual comfortable role of a humanitarian mediator. Our meeting in Shevardnadze's residence was more than effective. In a few days after it had taken place, the process of the Russian exodus started to go smoothly.

The pushy actions of the Congress of Russian Communities — an organisation little known to the general public — started to bear the first fruits in the environment of total helplessness and Yeltsin's irresponsiveness.

KRO acted proactively inside Russia, too.

KRO asserted itself as an efficient organisation capable of protecting citizens' rights even in Moscow of the mid 1990s.

Dealing with a threat of demolition of Neskuchny (*"Not dull"* in Russian) Garden on the bank of the Moskva River was one such scenario. Residents of apartment blocks on Leninsky prospect signed a petition to KRO asking for assistance with the issues surrounding Neskuchny Garden, this fine island of nature in the heart of Moscow. Previously, Neskuchny Garden had been in the Russian Imperial family's possession before it was given over to Count Orlov. The Moscow air is notoriously very polluted as it is, and the greenery and trees are sparse in the city; and then without a prior notice along came demolition workers, fenced a part of the garden, and just about started to uproot the trees and dig up a foundation for "an elite housing project". Local residents worried; they first went to Mayor Luzhkov, but their complaint was met with an all too predictable rejection. Then a delegation of residents, indignant by irresponsiveness of the city authorities, came to KRO.

It did not take us long to organise a street rally in protest. We stopped traffic on Leninsky Prospect for one minute. We were playing at a loud volume the popular song *Don't Cut the Trees Down!* by the rock band *Lube*. Following the rally, KRO addressed the federal Government with a request to interfere and to stop the unlawful demolition of the garden. And... Luzhkov backed off. The builders of the "elite housing" went away, and the campaigners to save Neskuchny Garden have joined the ranks of KRO — the only organisation that had been taking a dynamic interest in all matters of legality and justice in the native city and in the whole country.

The mass meeting in Troparevo in the South-West of Moscow was the next notable action of KRO. The Moscow City Council intended to grant permission for an Islamic Centre to be built there in the place of a children's playground in the park. The finance for the project was supposed to come from Saudi Arabian sources. We found out about the building plans by chance. Olga Uspenskaya, my wife's classmate and friend, lived in the area. One morning she received a leaflet was dropped into her mailbox, distributed by some organisational committee or other. The leaflet cheerfully announced that a madrasah and a large mosque along with an Islamic cultural centre were soon to be erected in the park opposite her house, and that once it is built, the happy residents could feel free to bring their children there. The site had not been chosen randomly — the Troparevo Park is one of the highest spots in Moscow, and the mosque would have towered above all other clerical buildings in the city.

There is another curious detail to complete the picture. Traditionally scientists, teachers and staff of the Moscow State University, predominantly Russians and Jews, inhabited Troparevo. Very few Muslims used to live in that part of the city. The decision to erect a mosque there seemed rather provocative, both essentially and formally.

KRO got involved in that outrageous situation that carried a risk of a social explosion. We acted accurately and politically correctly, so that no one could bring against us an allegation of instigating a national or a religious conflict. I informed the Spiritual Muslims Department of the Central European Russia in advance that we were preparing a demarche, and I visited imam Ravil Gainutdin[1] to discuss the delicate situation with him personally and privately.

The wise imam understood everything at once.

Moreover, he agreed to participate in a joint press conference and to sign a joint statement addressed to the Moscow City authorities. At the same time the KRO executive committee announced the time and date of the mass protest rally. Over 4,000 Muscovites attended.

To his credit, the initiator of the project Abdul-Wahid Niyazov accepted our invitation to appear at the mass meeting, during which he even tried to speak to Muscovites from the tribune. We discussed the matter and in the end this young Muslim activist accepted our arguments. Mr. Niyazov notified the Moscow City authorities that neither he nor his backers from Saudi Arabia insisted on erecting the mosque in that particular location and asked them for assistance in finding a different, more suitable site.

It was an unquestionable victory for KRO — another one in the portfolio of our first successes in the cause of protecting the Russian national dignity and human rights of Russia's citizens.

---

[1] *Ravil Gainutdin* is Chairman of the Council of Muftis of Russia.

THE TALES OF SEVASTOPOL[1]

Reputation of the Congress of Russian Communities grew stronger with each passing year and with every achievement in campaigning for civil rights of the Russian compatriots in the former Soviet Republics. Authorities started to take the Congress seriously. General public awareness of the organisations' name also increased. During the first two years of its existence the Congress won a number of notorious court cases, such as a lawsuit against Pyotr Rozhok, the leader of the Russian community in Estonia; a lawsuit against Raisa Telyatnikova who headed the Russian community in Sevastopol; KRO facilitated the release of journalist Boris Suprunyuk from imprisonment in Kazakhstan and won a number of cases in defense of honour and dignity of dozens of Russian patriots and human rights campaigners.

I would like to elaborate here on one court case against the Russian community in the city of Sevastopol, which we won back in November 1995, as it had been linked to the ongoing debate on the status of the great Russian city of Sevastopol. Boris Yeltsin betrayed Russian interests yet again in May 1997 when he signed on behalf of the Russian Federation a 20-year lease of the Sevastopol military and naval base, as if it is necessary to lease something that belongs to someone by right. The Russian side has indisputable legal reasoning in the debate over the status of Sevastopol. I would like to refer to some documents that legally justify the position of those who back the cause of reinstating the Sevastopol municipality in its Russian status.

The official Kiev's standing position in the matter today is as simple as a concept of hypotenuse. Sevastopol forms an integral part of the Crimean Peninsula, and the territory of the Crimea was taken out of the Russian administration and delivered to the Ukrainian Soviet Socialist Republic by Nikita Khrushchev in 1954.

---

[1] *The Tales of Sevastopol*, or as they are known, *Sebastopol Sketches* is a collection of stories by Leo Tolstoy in which the Count immortalised the defense of Sevastopol during the siege of 1854–1855 by Anglo-French forces in the Crimean War. Leo Tolstoy himself was one of the defenders.

A number of respectable Russian politicians share a different view on the matter, insisting that juristically the municipality of Sevastopol is a part of the sovereign Russian Federation and is being kept under the Ukrainian control unlawfully. Sevastopol has been an important naval and military fortress from its very foundation by Catherine the Great, and by late 19th century it has been firmly established as a major base of the Black Sea Fleet. The general town-planning scheme of 1938 reflected the unique strategic significance of Sevastopol, and all further town planning required an approval of defense authorities and had to be compliant with needs of defense. The new administrative borders of the city have been drawn with consideration of the Black Sea Fleet base objects and quarters' disposition. Accordingly, on 7 March 1939 the Presidium of the Supreme Soviet of the Russian Soviet Socialist Republic had passed a resolution that widened Sevastopol's borders thus expanding the city. Therefore, Sevastopol includes not only residential areas but also the naval base and the living quarters of the Black Sea Fleet. The new borders had clear field marks that were also used as base for the post-war reconstruction plan of the city.

The sheer scale of post-war reconstruction of the city required attention of the highest governing bodies of the USSR. Due to its status of a fortress city, Sevastopol has been taken out of the Crimean region of the USSR by resolution No 403 of the Council of Ministers, dated 25 October 1948, and by the Decree of Presidium of the Supreme Soviet of the Russian Federative Soviet Socialist Republic dated 29 October 1948 and was classified as a municipality excluded from regional governance and as a city under jurisdiction of the Russian Federation. From that time on decisions of the Crimean regional executive council have not applied to Sevastopol, the main base of the Black Sea Fleet. From 19 February 1954 following the proposal by Nikita Khrushchev and "taking into consideration the territorial proximity, economic unification and close economic and cultural links" the Presidium of the USSR Supreme Soviet adopted a resolution to take the Crimean administrative region out of the Russian Federation and to hand it over to the Ukrainian Soviet Socialist Republic. To quote the resolution, it was a gift "to mark the 300th anniversary of the Russian-Ukrainian reunification." I would like to reinforce the point that what was handed over to Ukraine was the Crimea as an administrative unit, and not the Crimean Peninsula in the geographical sense. By the time of that resolution Sevastopol had existed autonomously from the administration of the Crimean region and had been under the custody of Moscow for six years. In the period from 1954 to 1991 there's been no documented revision of the city's status in favour of Ukraine.

As concerns the Belovezhskaya Accords of December 1991 on the cessation of the USSR, when President Yeltsin had placed his signature on the document, possibly under the influence of alcohol, he somehow "forgot" to raise the issue of repatriation of the Crimea as a whole and the city of Sevastopol in particular. Indeed, if Ukraine accepted the Crimea as a gift on the occasion of the 300th Jubilee of Russian-Ukrainian reunification, then, surely, this equivalent of an engagement ring must have been returned after the two parties have split up.

At least, the Supreme Soviet and the Federal Assembly had the nerve to debate the status of Sevastopol at the time. On 9 July 1993 the Russian Supreme Soviet declared the status of Sevastopol as a Russian federal city; the Federation followed with an analogous resolution on 29 November 1996, declaring Ukraine's efforts to separate Sevastopol from Russia unlawful and damaging to Russia as seen by the international jurisprudence.

Such detailed analysis supports the findings that Sevastopol has never been handed over to Ukraine, not in 1948, neither in 1954, nor in 1991. So it seems, it's not the Black Sea Fleet that is based in Sevastopol, but Sevastopol itself is an integral part of Russia's Black Sea Fleet.

Under the Soviet Constitution the matters of national security were in the exclusive competence of the Soviet Union. Being a single legal successor of the USSR, the Russian Federation must be recognised as the only legitimate owner of the main base of the Black Sea Fleet, which is what Sevastopol, a fortress city, is. These are facts, and facts can be a stubborn thing.

Of course, the legal line of reasoning alone is not everything that is required to lodge an official territorial claim with the Ukrainian government. A political decision coming from Russia's government is crucial. Nevertheless, as the expiration date of the Russian lease of Sevastopol is nearing, though recently prolonged by President Yanukovich, and in connection to the clearly unfriendly efforts by Ukrainian politicians to unilaterally revise terms and conditions of the lease, the issue of Sevastopol's status needs to be again included in the agenda of the Ukraine-Russia negotiations. That is, anyhow, my personal point of view.

In case Ukrainian nationalists do something stupid again, there would be nowhere to take the Black Sea Fleet. Sevastopol is home to the Black Sea Fleet, and it would be improper for a fleet to be homeless. If official Kiev starts the procedure of joining NATO, the nature of our relations with Ukraine would undergo dramatic changes. In that case the issue of Sevastopol could not be possibly avoided or ignored. I hope that my smart Ukrainian colleagues realise this.

Of course, in my capacity of an Ambassador I can only research the legal aspects of the debate on the status of Sevastopol. The political will on this matter is to be expressed by the Russian President, not by ambassadors or ministers. However, it is hard to imagine a President of Russia, whoever assumes the office when the time comes, risk ordering the Black Sea Fleet to leave Sevastopol for good.

All participants and witnesses of the notorious litigation proceedings against the Russian community in Sevastopol in 1995 came to a conclusion that the Russian side was right in the debate on Sevastopol. The public prosecution office that was allegedly acting under the instructions of Kiev brought up the case. The claim was that the activities of the Russian community were of "explicitly anti-Ukrainian nature" and that their letters, declarations, addresses, etc., aimed at achieving recognition of the Russian status of Sevastopol, were published "with the aim of initiating the processes of estranging Sevastopol from Ukraine". In addition, the public prosecutor expressed an opinion that the Russian community in Ukraine "engaged in an unlawful activity of facilitating the illegal Russian citizenship for the citizens of Sevastopol and has arranged a visit of Russian consulate group to the city." Another incriminating statement was that the community "was stirring up separatist moods and national hatred and was setting Russians and Ukrainians in Sevastopol and all over the Crimea against each other, thus increasing political and social tension in the area."

The attorney instructed by KRO and the heads of Russian community in Sevastopol not only spectacularly won that case of a great importance to the whole Russian movement, but also managed to include a clause on the territorial dispute between Russia and Ukraine into the final verdict. That was an achievement. In doing so, the human rights campaigners and compatriots managed to gain something that the Russian government and the Foreign Ministry under deposed Kozyrev had failed to do: to protect their honour and dignity and reliably undertake the "third defense" of Sevastopol.

My opinion is that there are only two ways of withdrawing the issue of Sevastopol's status from the agenda of Russian-Ukrainian relations. The first option would be an expression of good will by Ukraine and the acknowledgement that the Russian cause is just. Ultimately, the Black Sea Fleet is safeguarding Russia and Ukraine alike; therefore, there is no reason for it to be perceived as a "foreign military base" in Ukraine. The second, wider option would be the reunification of Russia and Ukraine. In light of tense relations between the political elites of both our countries today this option seems highly unlikely. But who knows, maybe our children would turn out to be wiser than us? Kiev is the mother of Russian cities, is it not? Ergo, Ukraine is the mother of Russia.

The Orange Revolution of 2004 has brought the separators of Slavs and of Orthodox Christians to power. But Russians and Ukrainians managed to overcome far more dramatic times throughout history and always found the heart to come together and live under the same roof peacefully. Let us hope for the best and wait for Mother Ukraine to come back home.[1]

---

[1] When this book was being translated into English, important developments have taken place. The new Ukrainian President Victor Yanukovych agreed to prolong the Sevastopol lease for 25 years in exchange for the discounted prices of Russian gas for Ukraine. The Sevastopol story is to be continued. — *Author's comment.*

THE DECEITFUL NEWSMAKER
AND THE TRUSTING READER[1]

Our numerous campaigns for promoting and protecting the rights of Russian compatriots in the newly independent states, taking initiative and being ahead of the game, regional divisions opening in all former Soviet Republics — all this brought a barrage of hatred and jealousy from Yeltsin and his entourage on the Congress of Russian Communities. Rather than encouraging efforts of Russian compatriots to organise themselves, the Kremlin chose to put obstacles of all kinds in our way. As the Russian media fabricated more escapades against KRO day in and day out, our organisation got the label of "the union of Russian nationalists".

Campaigning for human and civil rights of, say, monkeys in a zoo, seemed more acceptable than standing up for 25 million Russians who had been abandoned by Yeltsin in post-Soviet territories outside Russia to be regularly consumed for breakfast by the local zealots.

Some of my associates used to shiver, feeling the pricks of the so-called free press on their skin. At times they even considered suing the scurrilous authors for libel. However, I've always been more of a sceptic when it comes to taking legal action against libelous rags. What is the point of expecting an apology from a rat? Why bother with all the ritual dancing in various courts and instances of appeal?

At best, one would waste plenty of time, effort and money for justice to finally be served in the form of a microscopic disclaimer printed somewhere on the last but one page of a tabloid next to cheap ads for hair remedies or escort services. Moreover, the yellow press is bound to vengefully publish a disclaimer of their own, repeating the initial odiousness all over again and throwing in a couple of freshly invented insults for good measure.

---

[1] The title is taken from one of the feuilletons by Mikhail Saltykov-Shchedrin, a major Russian 19th century satirist and author. His satiric journalistic works have not lost their appeal with Russian readers to this day.

At one time, back in the mid-1990s, a curious incident happened to a friend and colleague of mine. He took offence when some tabloid in the habitual manner of political yobs named some KRO members xenophobes or extreme chauvinists, I can't remember exactly which.

I tried to persuade my colleague to disregard the insult and bother less about taking legal action. However, he, belonging to the hereditary intelligentsia, would not let it go and kept demanding a 'just' hearing. Well, the hearing took place. Moreover, KRO won, and the monetary value of the received compensation for moral damage was... twenty roubles, equal to about sixty cents at the time. We teased our friend for some time after that, saying that with such a success rate, he became eligible for the honorary title of "the party sponsor".

Of course, there are a great number of decent, highly professional individuals amongst the ranks of journalists. Indeed, I know many of them personally, some since my student days. I encountered quite a few brilliant "golden pens" during my time as Russia's Ambassador to NATO. Being a journalist by training and a publicist by vocation, I have the highest regard for the courage of war correspondents who report from military conflict zones. I do appreciate intelligence and insight displayed by representatives of the diplomatic journalistic pool. I have the greatest respect for the thousands of honest and intelligent reporters who work hard to earn their daily bread. However, my attitude toward the yellow press has always been negative. As a general rule, the irredeemably cynical and superficially-minded reporters end up being employed only by the yellow press. Ever so eager to peep through a keyhole, laugh at the misfortunes and weaknesses of others and ridicule a slightest manifestation of moral standing or principle — people of this kind sneak into all walks of life, but they are particularly dangerous in journalism.

Attempts to court the yellow press are ridiculous. Casting pearls before swine, who habitually go through strangers' dirty laundry, is not worth it.

I first realised that during my freshman year at Moscow State University, after a journalist from the French magazine *Paris Match* had visited us students. Tall and slim, this Queen of Spades was terribly nice to us and very admiring of Russian ballet and Russian culture in general. Madame de la Brosse, this was her name, expressed a wish to attend a students' party, as she needed material for her account of the Soviet students' informal social life. Today I still recall very vividly how one of the students escorted the madam to a birthday party on campus. There, when fellow students cleared the table to set it for tea, the French lady sheepishly placed an issue of *Pravda* on the table and snapped her camera. A week later we were mailed a fresh issue of *Paris Match* with her feature inside. Madam de la Brosse made up her report almost entirely of idiotic clichés from the Cold War era. The report was illustrated with pictures from the birthday party with touching tags such as "Even at a party Russian students are busy reading *Pravda*".

Our own "liberal press" turned out to be even greater spoilers. By the early 1990s the former Soviet media was left with no means of existence. The staff collectives were converting popular newspapers and TV channels into joint-stock companies but still struggled to avoid bankruptcy.

Before long, oligarchs came to the rescue, guided by the urgent need of a tool required to facilitate their blackmailing of the weak government; the Russian media was that tool. Mr. Berezovsky, Mr. Gusinsky and other media tycoons were ready and willing to provide media advocacy services to Yeltsin, particularly when the opposition between the Supreme Soviet and the Kremlin sharply intensified. In return for their favours, oligarchs demanded nothing less than highly profitable chunks of the state assets, with another condition being that the Kremlin would turn a blind eye on their dipsy-doodling. Thus oligarchs not only managed to gain returns on their investments into media, but also retained total control over the Government's actions using that same media as an instrument. What freedom of speech are we talking about here? A gang of oligarchs controlled almost exclusively all access to media channels including television stations and newspapers. They were the ones to decide who and what would be broadcast and for how long, who would be silenced and who would be publicly subjected to lashes.

In the spring of 1993, on the eve of the Parliament's crack down, Yeltsin decided to launch an affair involving a public referendum. The general public was given a clue as to the correct answers to each of the four poll questions regarding the President, the Government, the Parliament, and the new presidential Constitution. "*Yes, Yes, No, Yes!*" — movie stars, television shamans and the rest of venerable masters of Arts and Culture chanted non-stop from the TV screens in that order. "*Yes, Yes, No, Yes!*" — echoed all popular liberal newspapers.

What could those actors, used to playing someone else — with fictitious thoughts, fictitious feelings — all their lives, understand about the ongoing sinister processes in the country? Did yesterday's "Major-boys"[1], this Komsomol of the Gorbachev brand, who despised all things

---

[1] "*Major Boys*" a popular name for offspring of Communist Party officials.

Russian and dreamt of making a quick buck and moving abroad, know anything about the real Russia? Were they ready to assume responsibility for the promotion of Yeltsin's ghastly deeds, for the Constitution defenders' blood, for the Army, destroyed and shamed in Chechnya, and for the people's loss of trust in their country?

Just try to confront the corrupt journalists, try bringing them and their foul trade to justice, and all you'll ever get from them would be righteous indignation and denial of all your 'dirty hints' on the corrupt and lying nature of their publications. Of course, the same journalists would never miss an opportunity to whine tête-à-tête about their bitter fate and enslavement to their owners and, above all, their owners' masters from the Presidential Administration. Such revelations would mean absolutely nothing. Be sure, your former confidante will strike harder next time and then allude to "commissions from above" and complain about his or her "bitter fate" yet again.

In case you succeed in intimidating a corrupt pack of journalists, they will hurriedly come to their "Daddy" who would be bound to think that all this noise is in his favour. It would be yet another opportunity for him to talk about the "independence of democratic press" and "inviolability of democratic values such as freedom of speech". You will discover a vicious circle of cover-up and collective hatred from the entire liberal journalistic community, seasoned with poison coming from "progressive figures". Some anonymous political scientists will commission some compromising material and will try to bring you down again. Be sure, such material will be dug up even if you are not guilty of anything. They will manage to connect unrelated facts and quasi-facts so skilfully that you will be left doubting your own innocence.

If you attempt to appeal to their conscience, or plead to leave your family out of it at the least, or beg the yellow press to keep their dirty hands away from your loved ones, that, too, will only be met with roars of laughter and an excited surge of desire to dig you into a hole, as fast and as deep as possible.

"Truth is a lie multiplied by libel", such is the "freedom of speech" formula adopted by those who use global multimedia as a tool for the distortion of facts. It is one thing when such a distortion concerns you personally. It is quite another, though, when entire nations are subject to abuse and insults, which was exactly what happened on *08.08.08* (8 August 2008), when Mikheil Saakashvili's troops attacked the South Ossetian city of Tskhinvali in the middle of the night.

As that tragic story unfolded, I was far more shocked not by the barbaric actions of the Georgian troops who had zealously bombed civilians in their sleep, but by the subsequent presentation of the events in the US and some of the European multimedia. As a result of that presentation, the actions of the Russian troops who had come to save a small Ossetian nation from destruction were labeled as "disproportionate and aggressive", whilst Saakashvili, the real aggressor, washed the blood off his hands and slipped into a halo of peacemaker.

Major newspapers were displaying expressive photographs "as evidence of the Russian atrocities" on their front pages . A massive anti-Russian campaign started in the West, in which the truth about the events of the night from 7 to 8 August 2008 sank deep in the waves of insults and lies. It became known only later that many of those photos showed not some injured old Georgian women calling for help from the "ruins of buildings in Georgia", but, in fact, the women of Ossetia in the destroyed Tskhinvali; and that these poor women were injured and killed not by "the Russian barbarians" but by the friend of "the civilised world" Mikheil Saakashvili who continued to show off, with the blue EU flag in the background, shamelessly telling lies on each and every TV channel.

I find it hard to believe that none of the Western politicians were offended by such a blunt and audacious violation of one of the fundamental principles of democracy — the freedom of speech. The minds of the millions in the USA, Canada, the European Union and the rest of the world were criminally manipulated against their will by professional newsmakers and con men.

A couple of months after the tragic events in South Ossetia, my son Alexey, who studied NATO communications policy in-depth in the Institute of Foreign Relations in Moscow, interviewed a well-known Belgian PR expert Patrick Worms online. Aspect Consulting, the company for which Mr. Worms worked, communicated from inside Georgia about the events of the dark days of August 2008. Patrick's revelations cannot fail to amaze. This is how he answered Alexey's question about the reasons why *The Times* readers were misinformed about that war:

> **Alexey:** Some of the claims (during the war) veered into outright exaggeration — such as stating that Russian jets were "intensively bombing Tbilisi" or that Russian troops had taken Gori — but the 24-hour news culture meant that many organisations repeated them without independent verification. It's a quote from *The Times*. Can you comment the quote from *The Times* please?

Patrick: Well, Russian troops did take Gori, so that's not a mistake, is it? Re: "intensively bombing TBS", it sure was! I don't know whom *The Times* had on the ground at the time.

Alexey: You say that Russia has bombed Tbilisi?

Patrick: But I was there, and I can tell you we were all panicking that evening :) No, no! I don't say that! I said, "it sure was" a mistake (for *The Times* to say that Russians were "intensively bombing Tbilisi"). But yes, Russian planes did bomb targets in Tbilisi — the radar, the airport, and the aircraft factory. One of the bombs fell not far from where I was, and I can tell you I was s*** scared. But thankfully, there were a few bombs, it was not intensive, it stopped quickly, and they did not hit residential areas.

Alexey: Whose mistake? *The Times* say it was Aspects statement. But if Russia had bombed Tbilisi, there would have been no Tbilisi left.

Patrick: You'll have to send me the original *Times* article for me to comment. Do you have a link?

Alexey: One moment. http://www.timesonline.co.uk/tol/news/world/europe/article4518254.

Patrick: OK, let me read it. Right, I see. And I remember! At the time, things were happening so quickly that it wasn't always possible to check everything before it got out. When I saw that, I went "oh s***". Basically, in a PR war, as I said above, you cannot lie — and if you make a mistake like that, it takes a while to get the media's trust back.

Alexey: So they used lies?

Patrick: Not quite. Remember, none of us had been in a war before. We were all scared.

Alexey: So were thousands of civilians in Tskhinvali....

Patrick: We had no idea then (11 or 12 August, since the piece is dated 13 August) where the tanks would stop, or when the bombs would stop falling. And they didn't bomb civilian targets in Tbilisi: the airport and the radar station. That's all it was, but at the time we had no idea what the Russian air force was planning to do. And man, was it a scary experience.

Alexey: OK. You said in one of the interviews, "That evening, on the 7th, the president gets information that a large Russian convoy is on the move. Later that evening, somebody sees those vehicles emerging from the Roki tunnel [into Georgia from Russia]. Then a little bit later, somebody else sees them. That's three confirmations. It was time to act." But we know now that there were no Russian tanks in South Ossetia on the 7th. Does this mean that somebody misinformed Mr. Saakashvili, and that was the reason for the start of artillery fire on Tskhinvali?

Patrick: The PR team in Tbilisi was a lot of young people, inexperienced in this, who in peacetime were doing things like working for the central election commission or the ministry of education. Mistakes were made, certainly.

So that is that. Like they say, thank you for being honest and open with us. So a professional in his field has as good as put his signature under the statement that Western reporters who went "Oh, s***!" spread lies about the war. It follows from Mr. Worms' concluding words that the same "fearless" reporters, in turn, gave an even greater scare to Saakashvili himself. One way or the other, it becomes clear that the shameless chevaliers of journalism exploit tragic events and design their own virtual war, in which an aggressor becomes a victim, a victim becomes an aggressor, cynics are presented as preachers, and the living are presented as the dead.

To sum it up, the Western media told criminal lies in the course of the war in South Ossetia. With the exception of one honest man, Patrick Worms, not a soul came forward and admitted it. Let us put emotions aside for a while and try to understand what exactly has been happening to the presentation and distribution of information over recent decades, and what the modern methods of informational warfare are. For this purpose, I once again refer to the research conducted by my son Alexey Rogozin.

MEDAMES AND MESSIEURS DE POMPADOUR[1]

Can you guess which media campaign of recent years happened to be the most colourful, bold and successful? Correct! — and I have already described the campaign of lies and disinformation around the tragic events of *08.08.08* in North Ossetia in this book. One must ask how was it possible in this day and age, when Internet users and observant readers and viewers may choose from such a wide selection of media vehicles, to undertake a campaign that was deliberately designed to fool members of civilised societies in their dozens and hundreds of millions? This question is far from being rhetorical. To find an answer, it is necessary to gain an understanding of the extraordinary changes that presentation and consumption of international information have undergone over the last few decades. I am going to use theses and conclusions from a study completed by my son and entitled *"International Information: New Realities"*, which is arguably the most comprehensive and up-to-date research on the subject.

Before I describe today's dramatic events any further, let me provide a historic example that illustrates just how greatly a government may be influenced by the pressure of public opinion into making a political decision.

In 1905 Russia was torn apart by two dramatic events. The first Russian Revolution broke out in Moscow and other large cities. Factory workers together with radical Bolshevist elements clashed with the police. At the same time, the Russian Imperial Army and Fleet suffered continuous defeat from the Japanese in the Far East. Under the circumstances, Tsar Nicholas II appointed Sergey Witte, a prominent public and political figure who previously had been a Russian Ambassador to Japan, as his envoy in the peace negotiations with Tokyo. The United States and the American President Theodore Roosevelt himself, who openly

---
[1] This is a book by Mikhail Saltykov-Shchedrin published in 1873. It is a collection of social satiric stories, many about clerks and bureaucrats.

sympathised with the Japanese, acted as mediators in Russo-Japanese affairs.

In June 1905 Sergey Witte went to Portsmouth, USA, where the negotiations were to take place. Before the voyage Witte had meetings with government leaders and members of financial circles of Berlin, Paris and New York, testing the waters for a chance of a new international loan. He was informed that the world powers expected Japan and Russia to make peace at any price, and that this was conditional for a new loan to Russia. That information had allowed Witte to work out a final strategy which he followed during the peace negotiations. In his *Selected Memoirs* Witte outlined his strategy:

1) Not to demonstrate that we wish to conclude peace; to produce an impression that the Monarch agreed to hold negotiations merely to meet the wish of nearly all world powers to put an end to the war; 2) to carry oneself in a manner appropriate of an ambassador of Russia, i.e. an ambassador of a great power that has few worries; 3) bearing in mind the huge importance of the press in the United States, to be accessible and particularly obliging towards the press; 4) to gain sympathy of the American public, which is very democratic; to conduct oneself simply, democratically, and without a trace of vanity; 5) in view of the considerable Jewish influence, particularly in New York, and that of the American press, to treat them without hostility, which incidentally fully coincides with my personal views on the Jewish issue in general.

Sergey Witte shares his "secrets" further:

I suggested from the start of the talks that the press should enjoy full access to the course of negotiations. I reasoned that I was prepared to repeat anything that I would be saying privately in front of the whole world, and that, as an envoy of the Russian Tsar, I had no hidden agenda or secret thoughts.

Of course, I realised, the representatives of Japan would never agree to that. However, the press learned about my suggestion and the subsequent refusal of the Japanese instantly. Naturally, that could not bring out very nice feelings towards the Japanese.

Witte followed these tactics consistently throughout the talks, and that, in his estimation, helped him to fulfil his mission to the general benefit of Russia. He had numerous meetings with journalists, shook hands with a train conductor that had brought him from New York to Portsmouth, publicly picked up and kissed a child, and the like.

He was genuinely eager to be liked by journalists, even though all this acting did not come easily for him. His position in the negotiations was flexible but firm. As a result of a lengthy and tedious showdown (the conference went from 27 July to 23 August 1905), Witte managed to negotiate rather favourable terms for Russia. At the start of the negotiations, the claims of the Japanese were extremely assertive spreading into the territories of Quantung, Sakhalin, Kamchatka, Primorie[1], as well as three billion of roubles in reparations. Gradually, the appetites became more moderate. The Japanese side demanded concession of Quantung lease and the Port Arthur — Harbin railroad line, the concession of Sakhalin already under the Japanese occupation; the recognition of Korea as a part of the Japanese sphere of influence; the open door policy in Manchuria; the concession in Russian territorial waters, as well as a payment of reparations. Witte agreed to the terms regarding Korea and Manchuria but refused to forego Sakhalin and pay reparations. When negotiations had almost reached a stalemate, the Tsar agreed to cede the Southern part of Sakhalin to Japan upon the insistence of Theodore Roosevelt. The Treaty of Portsmouth was signed. The final settlement for Russia was "almost decent", using Witte's expression. The Russian Emperor personally thanked Witte for his efforts in conducting the negotiations in a firm and capable way.

The Treaty of Portsmouth turned out to be a success for Russia, for her diplomacy, and personally for the head of the Russian delegation.

The Treaty was more like an agreement between two equal partners rather than a post-war settlement. Such are the powers of personal charisma, competent management of the press, and understanding of the nature and the significance of public opinion.

So, what has changed since the last century, when Sergey Witte and some of his contemporaries just started to recognise the media's global political influence? Obviously, the nature of the media has changed with the fantastically fast development of the Internet and the rapid acceleration of informational travel along with it.

That said, the Russian administration pays close attention to the necessity of using modern means of information and the opportunities it opens on state and diplomatic service. In July 2008, at the meeting of the Russian ambassadors in the Ministry of Foreign Affairs, the President, in the first lines of his speech, recommended to the ambassadors to

---

[1] *Primorie* — informal name for the Primorski region of Russia bordered by China, North Korea and warm waters of the Sea of Japan. Primorie is the extreme Southern-Eastern region of Russia, located between 42° and 48° latitude and 130° and 139° east longitude.

start their working days online. Judging by how the new White House resident Barack Obama suggested to the Kremlin "resetting" Russian-American relations, Dmitry Medvedev may find in Mr. Obama a good correspondent, as they both handle modern information technology quite exceptionally. That being said, I'd suggest that Americans don't "reset" but perhaps better run a "system upgrade" in their relations with Russia and clean up their diplomatic bureaucracy from "viruses".

Sadly, many of my colleagues of advanced age hardly know to find the power button on a computer, let alone how to surf the Net. But this recommendation of the Russian President is remarkable, as Mr. Medvedev closely follows all the innovations in the means of global information and leads by example (that I followed, having opened my Facebook and Twitter page in October 2009).

It is well known that the sheer speed of information travel sometimes presents a problem for the audience, because it is impossible to keep up with all the latest news and developments. The flow of information speeds up even more when something extreme happens on a global scale, and the stereotypes that are already deeply rooted in people's conscience — well-established notions and concepts about certain phenomena and events — assume greater meaning.

The Cold War public stereotypes played a crucial and a sinister role in misrepresentation of the information on the war in the South Caucasus in August 2008. So what exactly are these stereotypes?

The first universally accepted concept is that Russia is an heiress to the USSR; therefore, it is an unpredictable country with imperious ambitions.

The second stereotype follows from the first: in the conflict of a "senior" and a "junior" the senior is always to blame. Georgia had a role of a "junior" whilst Russia was a "senior." Incidentally, it never occurred to anyone that Georgia was actually "a senior" in relation to South Ossetia, a country with the population of a mere 60,000, which Georgia attacked. Despite that, the Western media conducted a successful campaign due to the manipulations of stereotypes.

Another change in the global information field is the highest ever growth rate of the information volume. It took 1750 years from the beginning of our era to double the volume of universal knowledge. The second doubling occurred by the year 1900, and the third circa 1950, which took a mere fifty years! This phenomenon is known as the "information boom." By the year 2006, the compounded volume of global digital information amounted to 161 million gigabytes, which has increased by approximately three million times the volume of information contained in all the books ever written. It was estimated that from 2006 to 2010 the volume of that data would further multiply by six.

Why do I quote these figures at all? Mainly, I would like to show the potential scale of data capable of disorientating audiences or individuals. That is why it is crucial to process and classify information.

However, the classification of data may also become a subject of manipulation. Whilst certain data is taken into account, the rest may be ignored. That is why the controversy between the ever-growing need to classify data and the principal and technological limitations for such classification is one of the greatest controversies of the modern day.

Changes in the nature of information affect both the objectivity of information and the methods of its falsification. The more technological the mass media is, the less they can afford to distribute conscious lies. In addition, the role of appraisal has also shifted. Growth in the number of players in the field of handling global data and information has led to the situation when there are, at minimum, two diverse and contradictory opinions on practically any subject at any given moment in time. This provides a space for manipulations, too. For instance, in public opinion polls on any issue, the majority opinion may be represented by a smaller number of responses than an opinion of the minority. Such an unbalanced presentation would not constitute an objective reflection of a situation.

A curious observation of recent times: photographs that once served as illustrations to news nowadays are a medium in their own right. During the military conflict in the South Caucasus, only photographs without comments were often published on the Net or in the newspapers. Pictures replaced written messages of what was happening, or what was allegedly happening. It was enough to publish a photo of the destroyed Tskhinvali in Ossetia with an indication that it had been taken in Tbilisi, and presto, the desired effect of a sense of indignation for Russia's actions was achieved!

Television is a dangerous instrument. An electronic ray cannon (the base of a telescope) is a more powerful and long-reaching weapon of influence and persuasion than a steel cannon. The delusional TV world kills off a sense of reality, placing millions of people in a virtual collective madhouse. And if people are not happy about something they can always complain — to the National Lottery, for instance.

Video materials easily accessible online, such as YouTube, are in direct competition with television. For example, a popular BBC clip in which Saakashvili is chewing his tie has been viewed online 1.5 million times. This number significantly exceeds the number of lucky viewers who have originally watched this display of the unfortunate Georgian führer's schizophrenic behaviour on television.

Online blogs, Live Journal in particular, are playing a greater role, too. Blogs now are a platform for advanced politicians. A vivid example of this are the personal blogs of London Mayor Boris Johnson and of Prime Minister David Cameron, both of whom practically live on the Internet, weaving a web for their potential electorate.

The new media technology is in high demand in NATO. In its public and media relations, the NATO International Secretariat for a while now has relied not just on press-briefings, but on the catalogue of audio and video materials, or documentaries. Undoubtedly, NATO feels the destructive effect of the global mass media that characteristically exaggerate the scale of wars, catastrophes and all other tragic events that claim human lives. In particular, NATO politicians complain about the soul-destroying "unjust" appraisal of the Alliance's mission in Afghanistan. In an attempt to reduce the flow of criticism NATO set up its own TV channel — NATO-TV. But could a channel of an openly propagandistic character be effective? I am not so sure.

It is no longer good enough to be a gifted Public Relations officer; one has to have cross-related expertise, too. For example, NATO called upon Michael Stopford, whose professional background in public relations included a senior executive position in The Coca-Cola Corporation. In the summer of 2008 Michael Stopford occupies the position of NATO's Deputy Assistant Secretary General for Strategic Communications Services that he'd keep for a couple more years. Clearly, Mr. Stopford was not exactly going to promote the Alliance by using a marketing tagline "Enjoy NATO!" but, undoubtedly, his experience in commerce has greatly benefited his new employers, particularly during the Georgian-Ossetian crisis.

Public Diplomacy becomes an area of the utmost significance. The term itself was invented under the presidency of Ronald Reagan. My colleagues in NATO consider cooperation with decision makers and opinion makers alike to be of the extreme importance. Despite the fact that the term "propaganda" is never applied in the official public lexicon of NATO, it is not banned from the internal communication. The word "propaganda" is used widely enough within NATO, and defines more than adequately concrete tasks in the promotion of NATO and USA ideological products with an objective to perform gender reassignment operations on countries that have found themselves under the umbrella of Washington.

Finally, in his findings, Alexey Rogozin points out that governments worldwide have transformed their very approach to multimedia. Some states and even international alliances outsource their needs to professional PR agencies. We know of at least three PR partners that Georgia had in the course of *08.08.08* events. They are Orion Strategies and Squire Sanders Public Advocacy in the US, and Aspect Consulting in Belgium (and I have already referred to the revelations of Patrick Worms about his methods of media warfare against Russia).

The conflict of August 2008 demonstrated that the Georgian PR machine had been of a much higher standard than that of Russia. As the events were spreading, the Russian global information activities clearly lagged behind. At least the good thing is that the government of my country realises this and is addressing the problem. Analysing the information war against the Russian Federation, Foreign Minister Sergey Lavrov said, "As far as the multimedia relations are concerned, we are nothing more than children." I agree with him. So let's grow up.

THE TALE OF HOW ONE PEASANT FED TWO GENERALS[1]

The course of world history, so full of contradictions, proved that the world is dominated by three main political doctrines, namely the Communist, the Liberal, and the National. Society's political life develops within the framework of this ideological triangle. Outstanding political leaders and their parties emerge out of battles between these three ideological forces. What happens in real life is that each one of these forces is subdivided into some very diverse movements. Communism, liberalism, and nationalism alike take a range of forms from moderate to extreme; they have their radicals and their centrists.

The Bolsheviks led by Lenin, the radical Maoists, the Albanian Trozkists of the Kosovo Liberation Army, members of the Italian Red Brigades — they all called themselves Communists. Moderate Communists also exist — various labour parties, opportunists and social democrats — and they do not like to be reminded of their Marxist origin!

No narrower a gap separates radical and moderate liberals. From the bitter experience of the contemporary Russian reformers we have all seen how usurpers, who under the cover of demagogical slogans had gotten hold of the former USSR assets, could bare their teeth. The mastermind of the voucher privatisation in Russia, the "unsinkable" Anatoly Chubais, became a household name for all the wrong reasons. As a result of the privatisation a small group of adventurers, who had formed the nominal group of reformers in Yeltsin's closest circle, grabbed the tastiest chunks of natural resources and entire industries. Now these heroes regularly give the much attended talks in London and Davos, whilst it would be more appropriate to hear them speak inside prosecution offices and to invite them to visit, not snowy Switzerland, but the even snowier Siberia, and for much longer periods of time, as well.

---

[1] An allegoric tale by Mikhail Saltykov-Shchedrin, in which a peasant looks after two self-important but helpless generals who find themselves on a desert island. The generals take the poor man's efforts for granted.)

Of course, not all crooks in Russia call themselves "liberals", and, vice versa, not all liberals are crooks. Personal decency and sincerity of views of the true liberals such as, for instance, the academician Andrey Sakharov, the economist Gregory Yavlinsky and Anna Politkovskaya, who fell prey to the deadly bullet of a hit man, are doubted but a few.

The same differentiated approach must be taken in the analysis of national movements as well as of Communist and Liberal ones. In the 20th century the national energy of peoples of Europe and Asia often took highly dangerous, extremist and even perverse forms. Chauvinistic hysteria, vanity, a sense of superiority of one nation over another — all these are disastrous allies in a political struggle. The horrors of Hitler's fascism must be a warning to all politicians who lean towards the nationalist way. But no matter how hard provocateurs try to portray nationalist ideas as a fascist threat in Russia, there will never be a place for a Nazi ideology in my country which survived the Nazi intervention in the past and paid a terrible price — 27 million human lives! — for freeing the world from the brown plague.

As for the idea of building Communist society, it is a processed and foregone stage in the development of our civil society. The official Marxist-Leninist ideology dominated Russia for seventy years since the Bolsheviks seized power. The slogans "Freedom! Equality! Fraternity!" of the Great French Revolution were interpreted to suit the Marxist ideology, and they led millions of people. The faith in the "bright Communist future" made the entire nation fulfill such grand projects as the GOELRO plan[1], industrialisation, speedy reconstruction of the country after the destructive Nazi aggression, gaining the status of a nuclear power, space research, the virgin lands campaign, and the Baikal-Amur (BAM) Railway.

Sacrificing their comfort and material prosperity, generations of Soviet people lived for a dream of a near, happy Communist future to be enjoyed by their children as was promised by the Politburo. My generation is infinitely grateful to our grandfathers and grandmothers and to our parents' generation for defending the freedom and sovereignty of our country and for bringing it to the status of world power. However, in the 1970s the myth of the forthcoming Communism was shattered and the

---

[1] *GOELRO* is an acronym for the State Commission for Electrification of Russia; GOELRO plan of 1920 was the first ever Soviet plan for economic recovery and development of the country.

Soviet people realised that the Party leadership had regressed and was dying out, soon to be extinct much like dinosaurs, albeit sinking in the web of lies and privileges. The underlying reason for the disillusionment was simple — the social and political class, whose job was to install the Communist ideals in the minds of the masses, lost faith in these same ideals. Communism turned out to be a utopia, a romantic dream of a rise of the renewed and perfect humans. Commissars were throwing millions of men and women into the hearth of history if they appeared to not live up to the perfect ideal.

Though it's not the mistakes and the so-called "excesses" of the Communist Party that were the main problem; the very ideas of Communism were doomed. People were denied one of the most powerful and ancient human instincts — that is propriety. The Communist ideas depersonalised man, estranged him from tools and means of production, and took away a sense of belonging.

The Soviet people were stuffed into communal associations in the countryside, where each family was given a tiny allotment with a rabbit hutch for a house. And that was done regardless of the countless acres of land in Russia! Building of brick houses was officially banned; the detailed building regulations restricted absolutely everything, dictating even an exact angle at which a roof was to be built. Thus, the Soviet leadership exhibited its own stupidity to the whole world.

By the 1970s the country was suffocating. Still, the feeble geriatrics in the Politburo did not open the windows to let some fresh air in, fearing the wind of change that could have blown them away.

Communism as an ideology and socialism as the existing reality were both rapidly losing their appeal. It had not been very clever of the Communists to invent such definitions as "the socialist camp", which only served to intensify a feeling of isolation from the rest of the world and brought about a sensation of premonition that the old order was historically doomed. By and large, it was the apathy of the masses that allowed the party politicos to divide and to privatise the USSR. All wrongdoings of the ruling class were happening in silent connivance of the masses.

Being in opposition later, the Communist Party of Russia tried to rid its ranks of traitors and to correct the mistakes of their predecessors. But, in their criticism of the new Government, the Communists could not help feel a strange sensation that they were spitting at a mirror, i.e. at their own reflection. The opposition of the modern Communist Party to the "party in power" is an internal affair, where former first secretaries of regional Communist Party councils ("United Russia") quarrel with former second secretaries of the same councils (KPRF[1]). There is no place for the diversity of ideas in this dispute of has-beens. This opposition is merely an expression of jealousy and bitterness on the part of those who have fallen overboard from the ship of history.

Today the Communist Party of the Russian Federation has exhausted the inertia of popularity of the Communist Party of the USSR and is going through a deep structural and ideological crisis. As our veterans who preserve faith in the Communist ideals get older and pass away, the Communist Party is becoming a thing of the past. This, too, is an unintended credit to the modern KPRF nomenclature that by its conformism and lack of principles has finished off the nostalgia for "the era of the developed socialism".

Liberalism is another political doctrine that in its perverted form has dominated Russia since 1991. The cult of individualism and personal gain, contempt for law and traditions, total permissiveness and corruption, glamour and perverse abomination — this is all there is to the liberalism in power. Our liberals adopted a very selective approach to the original doctrine, i.e. the American ideology of liberal freedoms. They cynically threw aside the unquestionably great liberal values such as freedom of speech, freedom of meetings and demonstrations, independent justice and parliamentary democracy.

When tested by reality, our liberals proved to be none other than the Bolsheviks, but backwards. They were unlucky to be dealt a bad hand with the Russian people — lazy and ungrateful zilch of a nation, unwilling to submit to new masters. In pursuit of personal success measured by a position in the *Forbes* rating of Russian billionaires, "liberals" were robbing their country on a monstrous scale. At the same time ordinary people were denied any form of ownership of assets, and that happened under the pretense of liberal reforms. To minimise the risk of mass indignation, the "liberals" provoked a war in Chechnya, clashed the peoples of Russia against one another in ethnic conflicts, deconstructed public morale and ethics, and corrupted the Army, that last bastion of the superpower.

With their criminal activities, they discredited the very concept of liberalism, turning it into a concept of national betrayal. These people also discredited the very word "democrat" and lost the moral right to remain in power. They managed to keep the country under financial, information and law enforcement control for quite a while, but the countdown of the timer under their chair had already begun.

---

[1] *KPRF* is an acronym for the Communist Party of the Russian Federation led by Gennady Zyuganov who co-founded the party in 1993.

Lately, our liberals have been rather lively, perhaps under the instruction of the Washington Committee. They quickly mended the old party with a renewed brand, hid away Svanidzes and Gozmanovs, and with a freshly painted gonfalon and "original ideas" came out to the streets to hunt for voters. Well-well.

Indeed, a Russian muzhyk is very patient. He is prepared to forever feed two generals at once — a Bolshevik and a backward-Bolshevik.

RESURRECTION[1]

A national idea is the nation's response at large to Communist or liberal governance. A national idea does not mean that one nation is in contraposition to another. For example, in Russia all the indigenous ethnic groups were building the great nation and great national culture together with ethnic Russians. We all grew accustomed to one another and learned to appreciate and respect the customs and culture of each indigenous resident of our country.

Today, the minority nations within Russia are prepared to embrace the idea of national revival to a greater extent than are the Russians themselves. It is easier for them than for the Russian majority.

The minorities in Russia are not torn apart by political parties. Not being tormented by inner historical guilt, they prefer to forward delegates to represent them directly in the party in power. However, the Russian nation is not integrated either structurally or ideologically. The national self-consciousness is being blurred in Russians, and this is a major disaster. The Russian has been separated from propriety for a long while and lost the sense of responsibility. The Russian aesthetic sense has been eroded; the cult of education and interest in the national and family history were also abandoned. All of the above are the effects of the "national sterilisation" policy that was consistently implemented in turns by the Bolsheviks, by the Soviet nomenclature and by Yeltsin's "liberals".

The National idea reinstates a nation to its natural condition, which is being a master in its own house. No only an individual, but also a collective of people have inherent rights such as the following:
- A right of existence and of national reunion within an indigenous territory;
- A right for self-conservation, development, and growth;

---

[1] *Resurrection* (1899) is the last novel written by Leo Tolstoy. The story is about a nobleman Dmitri Nekhlyudov who seeks redemption for his sins committed earlier in his life. Tolstoy intended the novel to be an exposition of injustice and hypocrisy of man-made laws.

- A right of self-identification and a right to think and communicate in one's native language. Language is power. Protection of our language and its expansion abroad is the basis of reinstating our global political influence;
- A right to sovereignty, self-determination, and self-governance;
- A right to have a Motherland, a right to cultural identity and to involvement in national history and civilisation;
- A right to exercise control over output and distribution of natural riches and resources given to a nation's land by God;
- A right to access the achievements of global civilisations and to use them in national or personal interests.

National idea is the ideology of national revival, which implies eradication of the historical, social, political, and economic injustices. National idea has the power and the virtue of truth, and even those who fiercely hate the national movement acknowledge that.

National idea is an indisputable right of a nation to reunite. The German nation, defeated in World War I

I and artificially divided by winners into three separate states — the German Democratic Republic, the Federal Republic of Germany, and West Berlin — never ceased to hold a sacred belief in its right to reunite. True, the German nation accepted the reality of the segregation, but never agreed with it. Forty years later, the impossible became reality — the Berlin Wall was torn down and Germany was reunited.

So why are the people of my country, the country that carried the heaviest load during the most atrocious World War and sacrificed the prime of the nation when the entire generations were killed or injured, denied their right to reunite? Such a reunion is natural and thus unavoidable; it is additional proof of the inevitable forthcoming triumph of the national movement.

The ideology of national solidarity reconciles different classes of society; it teaches acceptance, tolerance, and mutual support within one political nation. This is what mainly distinguishes national ideology from communism that incites class hatred, and liberalism that claims to protect bourgeoisie from "lumpen proletariat".

The efforts of national capitalists, national elite, and the nationally-minded broad population are of equal importance in reinstating a powerful and independent country. The deep meaning of national solidarity and the social groups' co-operation within a framework of a national state is that it provides the basis for political stability, without which economic modernisation of a country cannot advance.

National political doctrine must creatively embrace and absorb the indisputable socio-democratic values. Patriots must be at the forefront of the campaign for social justice and rehabilitate that principle from the rubbish of left-wing demagogy.

A union of national and social ideas is absolutely natural. A true patriot should care first and foremost about the wellbeing of the whole nation, which depends largely on the material factors — quality of life, life expectancy, effectiveness of social policies, care of the weak and elderly. Swift overcoming of destitution and poverty, bringing a meaning and a purpose back into national life must be an honourable responsibility of a patriot.

As for liberals, we have to adopt their universally significant democratic slogans. Only thieves and traitors are afraid of such democratic achievements as freedom of speech, an independent court system, the people's right to self-expression and to participation in meetings and demonstrations, and a right to put important matters for the public vote in referendums. Promotion of illegal drugs and of alcoholism, degenerative art, prostitution, propaganda of homosexuality and paedophilia, offences against religious and national feelings are those openly anti-national and anti-social manifestations of the perverse liberalism that should be banned unconditionally.

Without the effective use of universal democratic and social values the national idea would be at risk of regressing into the vulgar propaganda of national superiority, brutish self-praise, and bigoted arrogance.

There is a series of problems on the path to the resurrection of the national idea and its affirmation in the state. The enthusiasm for the so-called "national romanticism" in foreign affairs is one of them. Throughout history, Russia too often was prepared to put her national security and sovereignty at stake in the name of "fulfilling Russia's duty to other Slavic nations". Russian governors, politicians and military commanders, not to mention members of the ruling dynasty, were traditionally under the influence of Pan-Slavic ideas.

This was the reason why Russian society remained oblivious to the words of such an exceptional oracle as Prince Meshchersky, the editor of *The Citizen* newspaper.

Less than a year before the outbreak of World War I he insistently called, *"once and for all, get over the routine diplomatic traditions of Slavophil sentimentality that has cost us hundreds of millions in monetary terms as well as rivers of sacred Russian blood, and that, in return, has brought us nothing but the shameful role of our 'brothers'' fool."* Typically, his call was not heard. The result was national disintegration, downfall of the monarchy, and the sufferings endured in Civil War.

Fyodor Dostoevsky treated with scepticism the popular idea to gather all Slavic nations together under the wing of Russia; a Russian poet and Slavophile Fyodor Tyutchev was an outspoken advocate of that idea. Dostoevsky wrote: *"Do them kindness, and pass them by. We cannot be dissolved in Slavism; we are above that. They will bring us discord..."*

Isn't it precious advice to us today? Does anyone in Eastern Europe stand by our side these days?

I would like to quote Dostoevsky some more:

> *Russia must seriously prepare herself to watch all these liberated Slavs rushing rapturously off to Europe to be infected by European forms, both political and social, to the point where their own personalities are lost; and so they will have to undergo a whole long period of Europeanism before comprehending anything of their own significance as Slavs and their particular Slavic mission among humanity. These little countries will be eternally quarrelling, eternally envying one another and plotting against one another. Of course, the moment there is any serious disaster they will certainly turn to Russia for help.*

I think that the Russian Foreign Ministry cannot possibly add anything to the above.

That is why the national ideology prescribes for Russia to exercise national egoism, and not "the Slavophil romanticism" in foreign relations. We should be motivated primarily by our own national interests and only follow the actions that would benefit Russia.

I, personally, never hesitated in answering the question of what comes first — a state or a nation. A nation is certainly above a state. Only God is above a nation. A state is a form of national self-actualisation; it serves to protect a nation's interests; it serves to maintain a nation's territory and its geopolitical influence. A nation should inhabit its indigenous territory. If a part of the inhabited indigenous territory happens to be under foreign control as a result of a war or treachery, then this nation must seek historical revanche.

All of the above fully applies to the Russian people who represent not just a nation, but also an entire civilisation. Our ancestors survived through severe struggles over land and natural resources. The Russian people involved the minority nations into the process of joint development of the great culture and creation of the powerful state. Russians assimilated a small fraction of these minority nations; others, such as Turkic, Finno-Ugric, Mongolian, and Caucasian ethnic groups progressed into developing their own spoken and written languages and national cultures, largely owing to Russians. Separatists of extreme views prefer to be very reticent about the invaluable contribution of Russians into the conservation and development of the minority nations. With their historic heroic achievements and patience, Russians have demonstrated that a right of a nation to self-determination can mean and should mean a right to live alongside Russians within one state.

For the sake of argument, let us classify all nations into three categories. The first category comprises the nations of indigenous cultural and historical types that proved themselves capable of creating significant world's cultures or entire civilisations. Anglo-Saxons, Turks, Germans, Russians, French, Spanish, Chinese, Persians, Arabs, Hindu, Japanese, Italians, Greeks, Dutch, and some other large-numbered ethnic groups all belong to this category.

The second category encompasses the nations that appeared in the world with a single mission of finishing off the agonising redundant civilisations. Having completed the mission, such nations either died out, or were arrested in their collective development.

The third category includes the nations that served purposes of other nations, i.e. they were either assimilated into a larger nation, or played a part in developing civilisations of others. For example, Russians assimilated such Finno-Ugric nations as Ves, Golyad and Muroma, and only geographic names remind us of these ethnic groups today.

Do Russians today represent a great modern civilisation? Are we capable of duly continuing the cause of our ancestors? The answer to both of these questions is no. The Russian nation is segregated — 17% of us live beyond the national borders. No other nation worldwide before us incurred such losses. Today Russian people are disoriented; their historical mission of being the guardians and protectors of the internal and external security in Eurasia is all but forgotten. Russians must be reconsolidated: it is necessary to reunite the fraternal indigenous nations of Russia by means of love and common interests and causes. Only then Russia may join the ranks of confident nations again. However, in order to achieve this, it is necessary to arrive at the realisation of the notion that national progress is based on the sense of national unity, which is something that my compatriots have not experienced for a long time. The most important patriotic task of the present day is to nurture this sense.

THE TALE OF HOW IVAN IVANOVICH QUARRELED WITH IVAN NIKIFOROVICH[1]

On the evening of 21 September 1993 my whole extended family gathered around the dining table at our place to celebrate the birthday of my son Alexey, who turned 10 on that day. The small TV set in the corner of the room was put on mute. I was glancing at the screen every now and again, when I suddenly suspected from the tense expression on the newsreader's face that something dramatic had just happened. The host was reading out the Yeltsin's decree on the dissolution of the Parliament.

Everyone went silent.

"Here it comes," my father remarked.

I excused myself, got up, kissed my boy, and got ready to leave the house. My wife Tatiana accompanied me to the door.

"Just don't be asking for trouble," she told me before going back to the guests.

It took me ten minutes to get there. I parked the car at a fair distance from the building of the Supreme Soviet (it would have been a shame to see it crushed during an attack), rushed towards the White House and into the office of Alexander Rutskoy, Vice-President of the Russian Federation. Andrey Fedorov, an old chap from the Committee of Youth Organisations and Forum-90, welcomed me there. Since resigning from his job at the Foreign Ministry, Andrey held the position of International Relations Advisor to the Vice-President and, naturally, was well informed on the events that were unfolding on that evening and previously.

He told me that the Parliament intended to impeach the President during an extraordinary session to be held in the next hour, and that Rutskoy was to be proclaimed the head of state. Then the new President

---

[1] (In this humorous 1835 Nikolai Gogol story, also known in English as "The Squabble", two landowners — the neighbours and dear friends — fall out over trivial matters. Their pointless dispute escalates and ends in disaster.)

would dismiss all key ministers and appoint the new ones. Only then the new President would present his new plan of further action.

I advised not to distribute ministerial positions at that moment in time under any circumstances, at least not until Rutskoy had firmly secured his position as the President. The logic behind it was simple. Yeltsin by nature was of a very suspicious character. Rutskoy should have done the opposite, namely he should have reappointed all Yeltsin's ministers, consolidating them under his leadership instead of sacking them. Such a decision would have instantly made Yeltsin suspicious of his closest circle and of his generals. In that case, the ministers, too, would have thought twice about whose instructions they'd better follow, given that even the Constitutional Court was backing the Parliament. But if Rutskoy and the demagogic parliamentarians, in front of whom he was to take the oath, would carry on their threats to Yeltsin's circle including death penalties and repressions, which would merely consolidate the current Yeltsin's government further.

However, my voice was no longer being heard. The parliamentary leaders and Rutskoy himself were in a state of euphoria, already dividing Yeltsin's skin and his limitless power in their minds. Their pettiness and hunger for political revenge blurred their vision. In the end, as I predicted, these hasty decisions cost the Parliament the support of top figures in the Army and Militia. Panicked, officers of law enforcement institutions took the Kremlin' side, and this became a deciding factor in the outcome of the clash.

Another silly mistake was made in relation of Moscow's Mayor Yury Luzhkov. Luzhkov's arrogance and self-conceit had always annoyed MPs a lot. Rutskoy was planning to dismiss the Mayor, too, and replace him with Alexander Krasnov, who was the head of the Krasnopresnenskaya borough council at the time. Naturally, Luzhkov threw his support for the Kremlin immediately.

It has to be taken into account that loyalty of the city authorities is of critical importance in times of a civil crisis. The events of August 1991 were proof of that; Yeltsin then easily smashed GKChP with the active help of the first Mayor of Moscow Gabriel Popov who facilitated the erection of barricades around the White House. An attempt to sack Mayor Popov turned out to be very costly, indeed, for the Parliament in the Black October, 1993.

Generally, Luzhkov is not that much of an "eagle". When in 2010 acting president Dmitry Medvedev removed Luzhkov from the mayor's seat for his irresponsible and negligent response to the suffering of Moscovites during extreme heat and forest fires, Luzhkov softened, shrank and applied for a residence permit in Latvia. The mighty mayor turned out to be a schmuck. In 1993 we couldn't be sure whose side he would have chosen should he have traced the slightest hesitation in Yeltsin's standing when confronted with the parliament's determination. Under his hat there's not the head of the city's head, but a shining calvity. However, the ex-pilot Rutskoy had already swooped down on his enemies, not leaving them room for maneuvre. The cornered Mayor of Moscow, who did have a lot to lose, ran into Yeltsin's embrace. He had much to fear indeed.

Here I would like to elaborate a bit more on the phenomenon of our Moscow Mayor. The contribution of this "philanthropist" and "experienced manager" to the development of our capital city, as well as the customary ways of our elite and their entrepreneureal relations, deserve a separate chapter. It is not improbable that Luzhkov's business would attract interest not only of journalists but also of competent authorities in the not too distant future.

All his doings go way back to the day when Yury Mikhailovich had married well. The business of his spouse, Madame Yelena Baturina, flourished due to her unrivalled talents. Even *Forbes* did not fail to admire the speed with which Yelena Baturina had moved from a category of millionaires up to the category of billionaires. One wonders, how the cheerful Luzhkov on his modest City Mayor salary can keep up with his wife; and how does it feel to enjoy a good living at the expense of one's wife's entrepreneurial genius?

Rotten luck, but secrets come out, sooner or later. Thirteen years following the assault on the White House, on 14 July 2009, another Bastille fell, this time in Moscow. The newspaper *Vedomosti* flashed the revelations of Christopher Grierson, a partner in a British law firm Hogan Lovells International and a lawyer of Shalva Chigirinsky, who had been the closest business associate of Ms. Baturina. Mr. Grierson told *The Financial Times* about his witness statement. In particular, he said that Yelena Baturina's influence over the property market in Moscow was so great that "no major projects can proceed in the city without her backing". Furthermore, under the terms of the partnership between Baturina and Chigirinsky "all profits and losses from deals were to be split 50/50", however, Baturina never financed any of Chigirinsky's projects whilst he instead had spent altogether 12 million US dollars "on her behalf", including maintenance of a private jet.

Vedomosti wrote that under the terms of the deal between these two business people, Ms. Baturina was to provide assistance with administrative and political issues and Chigirinsky was to transfer half of his assets to her. It took a single quarrel between the two "lovebirds" for the business secrets of the Luzhkov family to be revealed. I wonder if our Mayor knows at all what corruption is and what the prison sentences for it are.

Another interesting fact of this citizen's life: under the official electorate data of September 2009, the head of Moscow City administration privately owns, apart from four miniscule plots of land in the Kaluga region and a battered vehicle of 1964, one-fourth (!) of a 150-square meter apartment in Moscow.

Thank God, now we know that Luzhkov has a roof over his head and does not have to sleep on the streets. But then again, we are concerned that our dear Mayor does not have a private apartment all to himself and has to resort to communal living. What exactly was Luzhkov thinking when he declared his assets and income as such? Do we really look like complete idiots?

You've got to give it to Yury Mikhailovich — he is a very energetic person. As soon as he had chosen his master in October 1993, Luzhkov did not procrastinate. The building of the Supreme Soviet was barricaded again, just like it had been in August 1991; only this time the barricades were erected not by defenders of Parliament but by those who wished to dismiss it.

Yeltsin and Luzhkov tried to isolate the backers of the constitution from the rest of the world by means of barbed wire and bricks.

With a heavy heart, I left Andrey Fedorov in his office and went one floor down to the office of Astafiev. I needed to see my comrades from the Constitutional Democratic Party, who were heatedly discussing the Yeltsin Decree #1400 on the dismissal of Parliament and weighing chances of an assault on the Parliament. The delegates' fighting spirit prevailed. Someone was going to get grilled. Everybody was eagerly anticipating an announcement for the extraordinary parliamentary session to start and were speculating on how the deputies would react to an attempt of an anti-constitutional coup.

Activists of the Union of Russia's Revival and KRO had quickly gathered opposite Astafiev's office and were working on a statement on setting up Headquarters of Public Movement to Overcome the Constitutional Crisis. Supporters of the legitimate Parliament in its clash with the President queued on the spot to put their signatures under the statement. The Headquarters looked like a ground zero of a revolution, or so I thought.

Whilst patriots were busy preparing addresses and statements, some left-wing radicals managed to get access into the inner radio unit of the

Supreme Soviet. Audible to all, the internal communications speakers were transmitting a radio hysteria of the left-wing Communist leader Victor Anpilov. "These fools are going to spoil the game," my friend Andrey Saveliev said grimly. I nodded.

At last Anpilov calmed down, and the live broadcast from the Assembly Hall of the Supreme Soviet commenced. Ruslan Khasbulatov, Chairman of the Supreme Soviet, was the first to speak, followed by the Chairman of the Constitutional Court Valery Zorkin and finally by Vice-President Rutskoy. Their speeches sounded rather victorious. I had an impression that the speakers were imagining themselves to be queens in a game of chess and were considering Yeltsin to be a cornered king after an shortsighted fatal move.

Yeltsin's yesterday's comrades impeached him for breaching the constitution. Rutskoy took the oath and received a standing ovation. People in the hall started rushing up to the moustached 'Ceasar', asking for his autographs. Sergey Baburin, a Member of the Supreme Soviet and a "devoted patriot", demanded there and then to introduce the death penalty for "the rebels", i.e. for those who were on Yeltsin's side. As they say, all hell broke loose. The adrenalin suppressed a sense of danger in MPs and blocked their ability for making sober decisions.

The thing that is the most unexplicable to me in the whole affair is Rutskoy's behaviour that day. Instead of trying to assume the presidential role and responsibilities, Rutskoy "trenched himself" in the White House. Whom he intended to govern there, apart from the dinner-ladies, remains unclear. The law and public opinion were on his side when he was proclaimed President; as an already lawfully elected Vice-President and with the Constitututional Court ruling in his pocket, Rutskoy became President in accordance with the Constitution. He should have immediately made his way to the Kremlin to assume office. Who could have stopped him? The Chief of the Kremlin security guards?

Chances of Rutskoy being arrested by the officers of Special Forces who were loyal to Yeltsin were slim. At that precise moment in time Alexander Vladimirovich enjoyed a position of a much higher legitimacy than Boris Nikolayevich did. I doubt that with the events of two years ago, still fresh in the collective memory of some officer of a Special Forces division would have dared to take on such a gigantic responsibility. Rutskoy should have shifted the epicentre of people's protests to the Kremlin walls. All public protests should have been made to focus on one major demand: to let Rutskoy take charge as the new President of the Russian Federation.

Nothing of the sort was done. Both Rutskoy and the Supreme Soviet preferred the voluntary isolation in the White House. In contrast to that, the Kremlin did not waste time and did something that GKChP had not had guts for back in 1991. Thanks to the energetic Luzhkov, the water and electric supply, as well as the private communication lines, were cut off in the House of Congresses. Yeltsin ordered to put barbed wire around the building with the defenders of the Constitution inside it, and placed Army units over the entire perimeter. One could still leave the building, but no one could get in.

Rutskoy, a machine gun in his arms, was running backwards and forwards like a caged animal. The deputies called for drastic action. In the absence of electricity they were sitting by candlelight talking about Lenin's plan for an armed uprising — "to seize bridges, telegraph and telephone". All of it, though, was just idle talk. All the steam went into the whistle.

On 27 September I managed to get into this fortress of Soviet power for the last time. At the time my wife was working as an expert in the Constitutional Committee of the Supreme Soviet. In solidarity with the parliamentarians, she, like many other members of staff, refused to leave her station. Despite her protests I insisted that she came home. By then time had slipped away irrevocably. Even the walls there seemed to know that it was doomed, having missed all chances to save itself from an armed assault; the catastrophe was close, and I was not prepared to risk the life of a person dear to me.

The next day, about twenty MPs gathered together with representatives of public and political organisations in opposition to Yelsin in the hall of Krasnopresnensky district council, a five minutes walk from the Parliament. The Headquarters of public support for the Supreme Soviet was located on Shmidtovsky Lane.

As the meeting went on, it became apparent that nobody had thought out or could suggest a concise action plan. However, it was noted unanimously that over the last few days Muscovites had grown noticeably more sympathetic to the 'strikers' sitting in the White House. By then militia squads clashed with civilians, who tried to break through into the White House.

I was scheduled to appear on a popular talk show on one of the independent radio stations in Ostankino TV centre on the morning of the same day. When I arrived in Ostankino, I saw about twenty militants of the Special Forces squadron "Vityaz" ("Knight") on the second and third floors of the TV centre. Fully armed, they were surveying the "catacombs of Ostankino" — a complex chain of corridors interconnecting two buildings of the TV centre — and eyed possible targets for their shells.

Heavily armed vehicles of the Militia Special Squad (OMON)[1] pulled over in the TV center's parking lots. They were barely detectable from the street but clearly visible from the windows of the upper floors of the building. "The vultures are here," grimly commented one of the cameramen.

I gave a detailed description of everything I had seen to Alexander Krasnov, and he promised to pass my message "not to go into the Ostankino trap" to Rutskoy. I know that Krasnov kept his promise. There is no question that the Supreme Soviet was informed about an armed provocation being prepared by Yeltsin; however, despite numerous warnings, the supporters of the Parliament chose to go to Ostankino only to get caught in the mousetrap. On 3 October, hundreds of defenders of the Constitution, fulfilling someone's treacherous order, left the defense line outside the Parliament and went by trucks for the assault of Ostankino TV centre. Why? What for? It remains a mystery to me to this day.

The appearance of a militant squad of Russian National Unity, headed by Alexander Barkashov, and their challenging behaviour by the Parliament building was another unresolved mystery. In great contrast with the inert parliamentary strikers, the young Nazis displayed enviable levels of activity. Raising hands in the Roman salutation, they were posing gladly in front of TV cameras, they were marching across the parking lot.... In brief, their conduct was creating a rather aggressive and intimidating image of the Constitutional defenders. Naturally, such self-promotion of ultra-rights, happening under the noses of Rutskoy and Khasbulatov and all but encouraged by them, did nothing to increase public sympathy or respect towards the Supreme Soviet.

I am certain that Barkashov's theatrics and his army was exclusively advantageous to the Kremlin. Barkashov' squad had not been under Rutskoy's command, nor had it been liable to Rutskoy's MPs or ministers. It was used as a scarecrow. Its provocative charade compromised the true defenders of the Constitution and helped to untie Yeltsin's hands, setting the informational background for the assault on the Parliament.

On 2 October the first major clash occurred between the militia and the demonstrators. Astonishingly, the Moscow City authorities decided not to cancel the annual City Day and went ahead with public celebrations regardless of the incidents between militia and civilians that were already taking place in the area close to the White House. What

---

[1] *OMON* — Special Purpose Police Unit is a generic name for the system of special militia units in the Russian Federation. The system was formed in 1978.

was this decision, an error of judgment or a deliberate provocation? The Moscow Mayor does not come across as a stupid man, and I am sure that he was fully aware of what he was doing when he approved the 'feast in the time of plague'.

On 2 October activists of the ultra-left wing of Victor Anpilov, joined by other Muscovites, undertook a first attempt to break through the cordons of militia to the entrance of the Parliament building. On the same day I was at a rally meeting of non-Communist opposition on Lubyanka square. It was a chilly day; the cold and the tension of the preceding two weeks had got to me and I came down with fever. As I understand now, it had saved me from being involved in some bloody events of the two days that followed.

In the aftermath of the assault, I came close to being incriminated with participation in the resistance to the dismissal of the Parliament, in particular with organising an unsanctioned mass street protest. I was called to the prosecutor's office to give statements once or twice but they soon laid off. KRO received an official warning from the Ministry of Justice but nothing other than that, so we got off lightly.

All our problems were nothing in comparison with the tragedy of families of the defenders who had stayed by the Parliament walls to the end. Hundreds were shot dead or were crushed under the weight of the tanks. There were also casualties among people who just happened to be in the wrong place at the wrong time. It was like a people's hunt in the very heart of Moscow. The tanks of our great country were shooting at the weaponless and defenseless Parliament in front of the whole world! Global media channels munched on the shame of Russia as I stood, in fever, on the balcony of my apartment, ten kilometres away from the shelling spot, and listened to the sounds of cannons and guns that were shooting down the Constitution of my country.

It is hard to describe the turmoil that I felt inside. I wanted to be there, among those few of my friends who fulfilled their duty to the max. I wanted to defend my honour and that of my country with a weapon in hand but I was not sure that I would be able to point it at the Russian soldiers, young guys like myself who were thrown by their officers to storm the Parliament. And the one person who really deserved my bullet was out of reach. He was hiding behind the backs of his cowardly generals, protected by high Kremlin walls. He was watching on TV as the Russian Army followed his order and shot at the Russian Parliament. Helplessness and hopelessness were gnawing at my soul, and this wound will never heal.

There is no doubt that the assault on the Supreme Soviet opened the way for separatists in the North Caucasus. It was not a coincidence that in October 1993 the rebellious general Jokhar Dudaev — the usurper of power in Chechnya, who, in less than a year after the events, would declare a war on Russia, — conspicuously congratulated Yeltsin on a "yet another victory on the way to justice and democracy". Yeltsin did everything he could to prove that under his power there could be no constitution, no law, no honour and no morality in Russia.

Five years later, in 1999, I found myself immersed into the aftermath of the tragic events of Black October. The parliamentary faction "Russia's Regions" delegated me, a young MP, to sit on the Impeachment Committee. The official name of the committee was the Special Committee of the State Duma of the Federal Assembly of the Russian Federation on Investigation and Appraisal of the Procedures and the Factual Basis of the Allegations Against the President of the Russian Federation. The commission was studying and investigating all aspects of the 1993 tragedy in the most thorough manner. Even though the Impeachment Committee status was guaranteed by the constitution, its work could not have possibly made a tangible impact. We did not have a right to enforce attendance of important witnesses, particularly of those who had held senior government positions at the time and whose testimony was required to put the whole picture together.

Even if witnesses agreed to attend the Committee sessions, we could not insist that they testify under oath. However, even those witness statements and materials that we did manage to obtain allowed us to conduct a more accurate appraisal of the events of the autumn of 1993.

The Committee established that Yeltsin had come to the decision of dissolving the legislature as early as in the end of 1992. Possibly, the fact that the MPs appealed to the Constitutional Court questioning the legitimacy of the Belovezhskaya Accords was an immediate ground for such a decision by Yeltsin. Probably the Kremlin took for granted that the Supreme Soviet had always been agreeable, and, albeit sometimes reluctantly, viewed the appeals as a sign of an opposition.

In March 1993, the Presidential Administration issued a Decree on Special Regime of governing the country. The Decree intended to dismiss the Parliament and gave extraordinary executive power to the President. Yury Skokov, then the Secretary of the Security Council, a man much respected among parliamentarians, refused to put his signature on the document initiating the Decree and was sacked instantly.

A month later, Yeltsin staged another show in the form of a public referendum under the slogan *Yes, yes, no, yes!* Using this referendum on public confidence in the President and in the Parliament, the group of 'liberals' in the Chernomyrdin cabinet tried to compromise the Parliament and to push Yeltsin to a brink of an open confrontation with it. The parliamentary leadership expected the bubble to burst in August, as they thought that the President would try to refer to recent historic analogies and parallels with the coup-d'-etat of August 1991. But it came and went uneventfully, and everyone relaxed. Until the evening of 21 September came....

In reality, Yeltsin and his liberal government wanted to get the Parliament out of the way for quite a different reason. Unlike the State Duma later, the Supreme Soviet had real executive powers. It could object to plans of state assets usurpation and their free distribution among the oligarchs. It had the power to dismiss any cabinet minister and to initiate legal proceedings against them.

The work of the first democratic Russian parliament was not without its flaws and drawbacks. The Parliament was led by Ruslan Khasbulatov, a rather brutish man whose doings had largely contributed to the collapse of the Soviet Union and to the ethnic disintegration of the country. True, the members of that Parliament did not always excel either professionally or culturally. However, even bearing all this in mind, the Supreme Soviet had been a truly independent executive body; therefore, the only way for Yeltsin to bring it down was to resort to physical force.

The execution of the Parliament was pre-programmed by Yeltsin's closest circle that kept pushing him towards an anti-constitutional coup. It was they who were dreaming of removing the last obstacle out of their way to unlimited plunder and to riches beyond imagination.

The Impeachment Committee also discovered that the armed conflict between the branches of power, the weakening of the Russian state, and the rise of the modern ruling class had been beneficial to some "third party". That "third party" surreptitiously provoked an escalation of the conflict in both camps. To prove the point, there is a unique piece of evidence provided by Victor Andreyevich Sorokin, one of the key participants in the tragic events of 4 October 1993. At the time General Sorokin was Deputy Commander-in-Chief of Russian Air Forces.

Below is the transcript of the audio recording of his testimony:

> **Gen. Sorokin:** It was around 3am when we were alerted and called to see the Minister. When we arrived, Chernomyrdin, Moscow Mayor Luzhkov, the then Chief of the Presidential

Administration Mr. Filatov, heads of FSK[1], some other civilians, and Interior Forces Minister Yerin waiting for us there. Minister Yerin was the first to speak and he demanded that the Army must assault the White House. His speech was very nervous, his condition was obvious.... At that point Chernomyrdin became agitated, too, and categorically demanded that military units and divisions at our disposal must launch an assault without delay. The Defense Minister said, "I am not going to obey any oral instructions" and told them that he must have an order in writing. Filatov confirmed that such order was being prepared and was about to be issued. They demanded that we start drawing forces to the White House at once, in the middle of the night, and start to unblock the building. I insisted that we must wait until daylight. It would have been unacceptable to insert force in the darkness. They agreed. I advanced at about 7am. I left behind a Special Forces Battalion especially to patrol the Army Headquarters, and along with the convoy of the 119 Regiment we reached Kalininsky Prospect from the side of the Arbat Hotel. By the time we reached our destination, there was some intense chaotic shelling over there already. I ordered the Regiment Commander to advance to the White House as fast as possible and to locate soldiers by the entrances to the building. I ordered to fire in return only and not to open fire first.

At the time of the order the plan was to block the building and to issue an ultimatum to the White House defenders to vacate the building. If the ultimatum were not met, only then to use tanks. The Commander of the Tamanskya Division was in charge of the tanks here. He is my friend from college. I approached him and asked, "Are you going to open fire from tanks?" He said to me, "Victor Andreyevich, I haven't got ammunition". These were his exact words. I replied, "Very well then". We were advancing from the side of the Mir Hotel past the building of COMECON[2]. At around 8am the units advanced to the walls of the White House. I reported 'upstairs' that we had reached the destination and positioned our units at the buildings' entrances, just to warn somehow.... My understanding was that if there were my people beside the walls, that force would not be used.

---

[1] *FSK* — Federal Counterintelligence Service; the State Security Service that was a successor of the KGB from 1991 to 1995, when it was reorganized into the FSB.

[2] COMECON — The Council for Mutual Economic Assistance.

In the course of the advance our losses were five dead and eighteen injured. They had been shot from the back. I'd seen it personally. The shooting was from the roof top of the building of the American Embassy and from the top of Mir Hotel. All the killed and the injured had been shot at from behind. I do not know who was doing the shooting, but I have my guesses.

At around 10am the first ultimatum was put forward. I was scanning the frequencies and heard voices of people who were there, who had radio stations. And, at around 10am, my officers and I started towards the walls of the White House. Having reached that spot, the one that is now occupied by the miners on strike, near the Gorbaty Bridge, I heard the first sound of a tank firing. It had just gone past 10am

I turned around and went back, reached my radio station. After midday, the soldiers of my regiment carried out my order. I categorically ordered not to enter the building and not to take any actions. Their task was to leave and to stand by the entrances. After midday, a division from Tula was drawn. It was getting dark. I cannot confirm which other divisions were there as well, who was there. I gave the Commander the task of gathering up the Regiment and leading them to me; I reported upstairs that I was withdrawing; I had to deal with the killed, the injured, and the weapons. They gave me a go ahead. I gathered my regiment, checked on the people, ascertained the casualty rate, and led them back, to Matrosskaya Tishina, where they settled in the gym for the night.

Rogozin: You were saying now that there was some firing from the rear and that some soldiers were shot at and killed from the back. Did you realise that after the fight, or was it already obvious in the course of the fight? And why, if you had ordered to fire in return only, these fire nests on the roof of the American Embassy were not suppressed by your people? And what are your assumptions as to who was firing?

Gen. Sorokin: I forbade to fire at the American Embassy. My people were advancing in waves: one group ran, another group covered it by firing back. I categorically forbade shooting at the Embassy so as not to raise any unnecessary questions.

Shaklein: After the briefing you met the Commander of the Tamanskaya Division who told you that he did not have any ammunition. In the aftermath of the events, when you were thinking it all over, did you discuss the developments with your colleagues, maybe with Commander of Tamanskaya Division among others? Many things were not clear on that day: why, what, who, what was happening? But did you exchange any information with your fellow commanders? What additional information had you obtained from them? In particular, who was chiefly responsible for the decision to use force?

Gen. Sorokin: The Commander of the Tamanskaya Division did not lie. He told me in all honesty that tanks under his command did not have ammunition. The ammunition was supplied at a later stage. I found out about it later, too. Really, the tanks had not been armed. No one but the President could have pressured the Defense Minister. His deputies were present when the initial decision was being made — not to fire at.... And where — in the capital of our Motherland! I think he was persuaded later. But he couldn't be persuaded just by any lad within two hours. It could only have been the President, no doubt.

Rogozin: Can we make a private definition in preparation of the Committee resume on the issue September-October 1993. It is absurd to think that a fire nest on a roof of a US embassy could be possibly set up without that embassy being aware. If what you are saying is correct, then we are talking about a direct foreign interference in the events of October 1993 on the side of the provocateurs who were shooting at soldiers from the rear in order to produce a desired effect. I consider this information to be very serious as well as very helpful in finding answers to many questions about the Clause 1 today, when we were reviewing the Belovezhskaya Accords. It was done intentionally, and it was a policy of aiding.

Beyond reasonable doubt, a testimony of the kind that we heard would have caused a barrage of emotions and calls for justice followed by a series of further inquiries. Moreover, while working on this book I came across other sources that confirmed the truth of General Sorokin's testimony. There are a few witness statements indicating that the commanders of the tank and airborne units caught under fire were approached by surveillance agents of Interior Ministry with the information that the fire had been opened by "our own" — government snipers and snipers of an unknown origin.

There is no status of limitation on the responsibility for Yeltsin's anti-constitutional actions, such as the forceful dismissal of the Parliament. Unfortunately, these actions have not been fully investigated to the present day, and justice was not done as yet. It remains unknown how the snipers who were shooting at our soldiers as they went forward and had gotten access to roofs of the US Embassy in Moscow. And who were those assassins, if they were there at all? This is a riddle more interesting than the mystery of JFK assassination. The difference is that the American tragedy is still debated and investigated, whereas not many people have any wish at all to think about the tragic events of October 1993 in Moscow.

Back in 1994, commenting on the finding of Impeachment Committee, Alexey Kazannik, former Prosecutor General of Russia, gave a distinguished characteristic to that crime of the century:

> *We have interrogated thousands of servicemen and gathered the following evidence: no peace negotiations took place on 3 or 4 October 1993. The order was issued to assault the building without delay.... During the pause between 3 and 4 October, when the assault began, the people inside the White House received no warning about the shooting or the assault that was about to start. There is no testimony to any attempts to resolve the conflict peacefully. Therefore, the events of 4 October must be classified as a crime, with revenge as a prime motive and by means which had put many people's lives at risk. That crime was triggered by inferior motives.*

Russia is a country with the past that was unpredictable. I think that without learning the truth about that past we have no future.

BEAR ON VOYEVODSTVO[1]

Energy resources in the natural environment of the northern continental land are a factor of politics. Moreover, they are a factor of life as such. Those who have energy resources in their possession are the true masters of the country and, one could argue, of the universe. However, gas and oil resources are exhaustible and will run out sooner or later. There have been talks about alternative sources of energy for decades, however, humankind does not know of any as yet that would be viable safety and cost effective.

Until Russia succeeds in restoring her "parallel economy", high fuel prices as well as the efficient long-term usage of natural oil and gas will continue to be a factor of vital importance. What is the real cost of the Russian energy resources, which we, unlike they do in Arab countries, have to recover from the depths of the earth in the hellish conditions of polar winter and then carry by pipes for several thousands of kilometres to the nearest border for export?

Oil and gas are our strategic resources that represent a guarantee of our sovereignty. These resources are God's award to Russian people for the resilience and hardships in developing cold environments.

However, a buyer and a seller in the regular energy supplies market depend on each other in equal measure. This circumstance requires a clear mutual understanding and an open partnership. The reasons why the European Union countries are keen to diversify channels of energy supply are understandable. Who wants to be in a state of complete dependence, even if such dependence is one of a virtual kind? Likewise, Russia is also interested in diversifying routes of supplying oil and gas to Europe, in particular, in laying gas pipes in the bottom of the Black Sea and the Caspian Sea and building gas liquefaction and deep petroleum refining plants.

We would also prefer not to be affected by turbulence and cataclysms

---

[1] Another satirical tale of the 1880s by Saltykov-Shchedrin about bears who are appointed governors by Lions. The bears install a bloody regime in the land and are killed by rebels.

of the political life in neighbouring states. We do not appreciate, and I am sure nobody would, when our gas is stolen from us. However, the moment we voice our non-appreciation, we are getting blackmailed with shutting down of our gas transit deliveries to Europe.

Ladies and gentlemen, Communism is over! No payment — no gas. We can no longer afford to be excessively charitable in our trade and economic relations as we have our own citizens to look after. If the current pro-Western regime in Ukraine is so dear to the EU and NATO, why don't these organisations offer to cover the cost of gas that was stolen from us by their audacious protégé? Putting pressure or resorting to blackmail does not make sense in this matter. We have been offering the European Union to sign strategic treaties on energy supplies for a while now.

We are prepared to guarantee stability and security of our energy supplies. In turn, we are interested in importing European technology into our economy, particularly in the field of natural resources. In order to secure this partnership, the European bureaucrats should stop politicising the issues that are purely economic and quit scaring ordinary people with "the Russian bear".

There is no such thing as natural energy weapons. However, Brussels has its political preferences and its "pets"; it also has the propensity to blackmail. If all of us wish to act like gentlemen in such a sensitive issue as the provision of our people with heating, we have to stop playing games.

The Russian energy and fuel industry is in need of a profound reform and innovation crucial for the successful rehabilitation of the Russian economy. We have to remind ourselves that the USSR had evolved into a global power due to the industrialisation on a grand scale, not because of the high volume of oil and gas export sales.

The volume of export marginally increased under the leadership of Leonid Brezhnev in the 1970s when signs of economic decline had become all too apparent. We had grown addicted to enjoying large profits from exports and, like all addicts, stopped working hard and looking after ourselves properly.

Our economy's power generation sector must not continue to corrupt our economic mentality; we should not carry on living at the expense of Russia's natural treasures. The power generation sector must become a source and a platform for long-term large-scale investments into other sectors of economy, and serve as a warranty of our sovereignty. It is our golden key to economic revival, and it is utterly important that this key is turned in the correct direction.

In order to do a job well, it is imperative not just to choose the suitable tools, but also to envisage the final product and purpose. As concerns the tools, it is clear that the energy sector is there to pull out the rest of the economy, by setting up investment funds and creating a favourable pricing background. But what is the end purpose of economic programme and what are benchmarks to measure effectiveness and efficiency of the government's efforts in that area of its direct responsibility? I will try to formulate an answer. In my opinion, the purpose of the government's economic policy and the criteria of its implementation should be the following:

1) The growth of the nation's prosperity. In a country where people now are having to pay not just for their food and housing but also for access to education, culture, and medical care, it would mean the growth of absolute income at a rate above inflation.

2) The increase of the birth rate and of life expectancy, as well as prolongation of seniors' working lives.

3) The reinforcement of national security; the reduction of deaths by unnatural causes such as the ones that occur in wars, terrorist attacks, international conflicts, crime, fatalities on the roads, and negligence in the workplace.

The only method of objective appraisal of the government's efficiency is to set tangible, balanced, realistic, and comprehensible goals and measure the results of reforms against them.

HADJI-MURAT[1]

Yeltsin nurtured the revolt in the Caucasus. There is a lot to say, of course, about the history of the militant Chechen people and the Caucasian War that went on for a good half of the 19th century. Studying the archives on the history of wars in the Caucasus, many times I have come across some rather severe epithets used by government figures and army leaders of Russia whenever they mentioned Abreks[2].

General Alexey Yermolov, hero of the Caucasian War offered one such typical description of Chechens in his memoirs:

> *The area down by the Terek River is inhabited by the Chechens, the most dangerous bandits who attack the defense line. Their fairly small numbers have significantly increased in the last few years. This happened because they welcomed the bandits of all nationalities to join them; they accepted those who have left their own native lands for various reasons to do with crimes, committed by them there. Within Chechnya these criminals find accomplices and friends who are ready to take revenge on their behalf or to partake in other crimes; in return, the newcomers are ready to be the Chechen's guides in unfamiliar lands. Chechnya can be rightly called the nest of all criminals.*

The carrot and stick policy of harsh actions by General Yermolov combined with negotiations led by Prince Baryatynsky, who by the end of the long Caucasian War had finally captured the mountaineers' leader Imam Shamil, secured the victory of the Russian Imperial Army in the Caucasus and established peace between the Russians and the peoples of Chechnya, Ingushetia, and Dagestan. The surrendered

---

[1] *Hadji-Murat* is a short novel by Leo Tolstoy. The eponymous main character, an Avar rebel commander, for reasons of personal revenge, forges an uneasy alliance with Russians whom he had been fighting. The novel was published posthumously in 1912.

[2] *Abrek* is "the noble bandit of the North Caucasus," a name for mountaineers who struggled against the Tsarist Army and administration post-Caucasian War.

nations of the North Caucasus went on to serve the Russian Throne faithfully and on a number of occasions were graced by royal gratitude.

During World War I the Chechen and Ingush Regiments of Dikaya ("Wild") division displayed remarkable examples of heroic fighting in the famous Brusilov Offensive of 1916, causing considerable damage to the troops of the German Kaiser. A grateful Tsar Nicholas II admired the courage and skills of Chechen and Ingush fighters and sent the celebratory telegram to his envoy in the Caucasus.

Chechens are proud of their lengthy resistance to the Russian Army, which had been the most powerful in Europe. But the pride that they take in their heroic fighting on the side of that Army is far greater.

This is a proof of the fact that the strong Russian state has always been capable of not merely suppressing rebellions in Caucasia but providing the people there with means and opportunities to benefit both themselves and Russia. By this I mean a state that is both truly strong and Russian, and not a gangster state created by Yeltsin and his werewolves. Immersed in theft and power hunt, Yeltsin's people neither understood, nor cared about the fates of the different nations within the Russian Federation; they disregarded these nations' selective historical memory, their complexes of guilt or bitterness, and their mutual grievances.

Moreover, thieves in power had a vested interest in creating a criminal enclave. They needed a kind of a "black hole" through which it would be possible to transfer unrequited oil, trade arms illegally, and print and distribute fake banknotes and false financial documents. Criminals were also in need of such a black hole where they could bring their disagreeable business partners to be tortured and buried. The criminal greed of the central Government, the indomitable Chechen temper, disintegration of the state, and the overall moral decline — these are the ingredients of a bloody Caucasian cocktail.

In 1991, the Supreme Soviet issued a Decree "On Rehabilitation of Repressed Nations", which was as destructive as it was absurd. The decree provided for the considerable monetary compensation to the Chechen Republic among others few, from where people had been deported to Kazakhstan by Stalin in reprimand "for mass collaboration with enemy during the Great Patriotic War". By adopting this controversial law, the shortsighted people's deputies opened a Pandora box.

In his book entitled *The Chechen Trap*, Andrey Saveliev tells the chronological story of how rebels seized power in Chechnya. The book is the most honest non-fictional account of Civil War and of the genocide of the Russian population in the Republic.

The legal disintegration within Chechnya started with the breakup of the USSR state structure and with spontaneous self-determination of the Soviet and Federative Republics. In 1989, before it was split into two independent Republics, Chechen-Ingushetia had the population of 1,270,000. Russians, Armenians and other ethnic groups accounted for about 40% (around 530,000) of the entire population. Later the proportion of ethnic Chechens grew as a result of the inflow of ethnic Chechens from Kazakhstan and combined with the decline in number of ethnic Russians who were driven out of the Republic due to the aggressive nationalism and the intensifying separatist moods. From 1989 the process of extrusion of those of the non-Chechen ethnicity from the bodies of power was gaining momentum. By 1990 practically all the key positions were occupied by ethnic Chechens.

Islam was rapidly imposed in Chechen-Ingushetia. 211 mosques were erected and two Islamic universities opened in Kurchaloi and Nazran within two years prior to the events of September 1991. That way the political and material platform for the revival of Mouridism — a form of sufi Islam traditionally practiced by Chechens; the ideology preaches the spiritual slavery of apprentices who are to carry out orders and recommendations of their teachers — was secured.

On 27 November 1990, the Supreme Council of the Chechen-Ingush Autonomous Republic adopted the Decree of Sovereignty. The autonomy was proclaimed a sovereign state, which claimed that it would be prepared to sign the Union Treaty on a basis that would be equal to the other former Soviet national Republics only. All-National Congress of the Chechen People expressed support of the decision. This led to the immediate effect of self-organisation of ethnic Chechens and made existing governing structures redundant, establishing a system that totally disregarded interests of the non-Chechen residents.

A Soviet Major-General Dzokhar Dudayev was elected Chairman of the Executive Committee of the All-National Congress of the Chechen People. For this purpose he was invited to come back from Estonia, where he had served as commander of a heavy bombarding division. Soon Dudayev grew dissatisfied with being a puppet. He quickly figured that in that unstable situation he had a real chance of becoming a leader. When a quarrel between democrats and nationalist radicals in the Executive Committee broke out, Dudayev sided with the radicals.

Gorbachev did not see signs of danger in the acceleration of ethnical chauvinism and in Chechnya's spontaneous sovereignty. Then Yeltsin, who notoriously encouraged the national Republics "to take as much sovereignty as they could swallow", put up an appearance in Chechen-Ingushetia.

In May-June, 1991, the Second All-National Congress of the Chechen People declared independence of the Chechen Republic from both the USSR and the Russian Federation. Russian government failed to take any measures against separatists and rebels, not even at that stage.

In September 1991, under the pretence of resisting GKChP, Dudayev and his circle dismissed the Supreme Congress of Chechnya. Head of the Republic, Doku Zagayev, who had been loyal to Russia, was sent into exile. The executive power went to the temporary Supreme Council that had been appointed by the Second All-National Congress of the Chechen People. To a surprise of many, this junta was acknowledged as "the only lawful authority in the Republic" by the Supreme Soviet of the Russian Federation headed by Ruslan Khasbulatov at the time, an ethnic Chechen himself. From the perspective of maintaining the state integrity such a move on the part of federal powers was a climax of insanity.

Soon, Dudayev's armed supporters seized the building of the Republican Council of Ministers and the radio and TV centre. On 27 October 1991 the executive committee of All-Chechen Congress held illegitimate parliamentary and presidential elections. The power went into the hands of criminals completely.

At last, Moscow started to show signs of concern. In November 1991, the Congress of the Russian Parliament overruled the election of Dudayev as the President of the Republic of Chechnya. Initially, Yeltsin was not in a rush to implement this decision made by the Parliament; he signed the Decree on special regime in Chechnya and then... disappeared from Moscow. In his absence, the Supreme Soviet, elected by the Congress of the Russian Parliament, cancelled Yeltsin's Decree upon the initiative of Khasbulatov, thus annulling the decision of the Congress of Parliament.

The public viewed all this as a legal chaos, a downright collusion with the rebels, and a breach of the constitution. A Spetsnaz squad was dispatched to the Chechen capital Grozny only to be blocked on entry by Dudayev's forces. Remarkably, on someone else's order the military cargo planes that carried heavy transporters for the squad, landed in an altogether different airport. This treacherous act gave Dudayev a cause to talk about "his first victory over Russia."

Annihilation of the ethnic Russian population in Chechnya was preceded by dissemination of russophobic literature, direct insults on Russians coming from the government, desecration of Russian cemeteries and compulsory re-registration of 'non-locals' on 10 January 1992. Those Russians who had not managed to re-register on time were labeled "terrorists".

Weapons and ammunition of the Russian Federal Army located in Chechnya were looted or stolen. Dudayev had been greatly assisted by Marshal of Aviation Shaposhnikov, Gorbachev's protégé. While acting as Commander-in-Chief of CIS United Armed Forces, he ordered to transfer to Dudayev 50% of all weapons that were stored in the territory of Chechnya. Russian Defense Minister Pavel Grachev also signed that order. Later Grachev would withdraw federal troops from Chechnya with no heavy artillery that had become Dudayev's military trophy.

In any self-respected state under similar circumstances these two top rank officers would have been sent for tribunal. Alexander Korzhakov, Head of the Presidential Security Service, commented: "I have no idea why Shaposhnikov and Grachev made this decision, although I do have my guesses: it was in fashion then to carry cash in suitcases. Maybe, one of them received such a suitcase. I really don't know".

Treacherous decisions were taken and implemented in the high echelon of the Federal Army amid an ongoing slaughter of that army in the territory of Chechnya. In February 1992 reports of Dudayev's militants taking over yet another military object were streaming in every day. Russian Federal generalship disregarded the fact that their servicemen were being killed in action whilst the guerrilla army was being armed up to their teeth with our own weapons. Exactly during that period were recorded first facts of hostage taking in exchange for army weapons.

Another "know-how" of Dudayev's was to drive a fully fuelled fire engine into federal weapons depots and threaten to set it on fire unless weapons and ammunition were handed over.

On 1 June 1992, Russian generals had the audacity to commit an unprecedented act of treason. They handed over more than 40,000 small arms weapons, about 150,000 grenades, and more than 150 military aircrafts to the unlawfully formed military units. Among these weapons were rocket missiles "Luna-8" and valley fire systems "Grad".

In the autumn of 1994, Dudayev ordered to fit eleven L-39 aircrafts with 100 kg blast bombs and rockets in order to strike civilian objects in the South of Russia. He would have carried out this airborne threat, if it were not for the Russian Aviation that destroyed all Dudayev's planes parked in the airdromes right before the federal troops were brought to Chechnya.

Georgia rendered extra support to Dudayev's regime. Georgian President Zviad Gamsakhurdia paid Dudayev several visits, promising him all kinds of assistance in the struggle against Russians. Weapons to Chechnya streamed from other countries, too — Ukraine and Azerbaijan,

Turkey and Eastern Europe. Chechnya was quickly becoming a striking force that was aimed against Russia and was prepared to use arguments of force, if Moscow weakened further.

According to an unverified version, Chechnya stocked up on weapons with the intention to trade with Islamist countries illegally. In any case, the amount that had been handed over to the guerrilla army in 1991 was sufficient to ensure a combat deployment of seven divisions. In June 1992 Dudayev's army counted 15,000 people, not counting the so-called national guards who were ready for mobilisation.

General Lebed knew what he was saying when he characterised the war in Chechnya as "a commercial and custom-built war". There were 70 million tons of known oil reserves in Chechnya, and it was not the oil of high quality. Chechen oil output never exceeded 1% of the total figure for Russia. The underlying reason for the First Chechen War was not as much the desire of the Russian nomenclature to maintain control over oil reserves per se, but a potential opportunity to smuggle oil from other regions of Russia through Chechnya.

Notwithstanding objections from the Security Council, the government of Gaidar sanctioned supply of around 20 million tons of oil from Bashkiria to Grozny. Illegal oil trading operations brought near a billion of USD to Dudayev and his accomplices. Portions of these moneys were privately invested overseas.

According to Chechnya's State Duma Deputy General Ibrahim Suleimenov, there's evidence of 22 million tons of oil having been exported annually during the four years of Dudayev's ruling. The proceeds were deposited to Dudayev's personal bank accounts and those of his clandestine Moscow protectors.

Profits from oil stolen in the partnership between Chechen gangsters and Russian bureaucrats were also used to acquire weapons in additional quantities. These same weapons were used against the Russian Federal Army in Grozny. Arms of the same origin were also deployed by terrorist groups of Shamil Basayev and Salman Raduyev against peaceful civilians in Budyonnovsk of Russia, Kizlyar of Dagestan, and later Beslan of Ossetia.

However, in 1995, Yegor Gaidar, Prime Minister in Yeltsin's cabinet, during a session of the Parliamentary Committee of Enquiry on Cause and Development of Crisis in the Republic of Chechnya offered a very straightforward explanation of why fuel had been supplied to gangsters. He said that the Republic needed it to make sure that the sowing season in the North Caucasus went smoothly.

Under Dudayev's unrestrained supremacy, the territory of the rebellious Republic became an outpost of organised crime.

Crime rate in Chechnya grew sevenfold since 1990. From 1991 to 1994 a number of reported premeditated murders exceeded 2,000. The majority of murder victims were of Russian ethnicity. Nobody bothered much with murder investigations. After the federal troops were brought in, the airborne and artillery strikes on Grozny finished off the remaining Russian population. The city of Grozny, founded by general Yermolov in the beginning of the 19th century, turned into a mass Russian grave in the North Caucasus. Plenty of Russian bones are buried under the wrecks of Grozny. Before the outbreak of the war, Russians accounted for over half of the city population. The city itself, the largest in the North Caucasus, used to be an important petrochemistry centre of the region.

The Russian civilians were the true hostages in that war. Chechen civilians, sensing a disaster, fled from the city to their relatives in adjacent villages and in the mountains. Those Russians who worked and lived in the city generally had no relatives nearby to seek shelter with. Nor had they any protectors; there was no one in power whom they could turn to and ask for help and protection from their persecutors. Civil Russian population fell easy prey to cruel Chechen warlords.

Even the Cossacks villages of the Naursky and the Shelkovsky regions that were originally part of the Stavropol area before the administrative transfer to the Chechen Republic by Nikita Khrushchev, failed to put up an armed resistance to bandits. It seemed that Cossacks, too, procrastinated and looked up to Moscow; they were exchanging stories about mischievous Abreks only to pack their scarce possessions and leave for "the mainland" in the end.

The breakaway leaders demonstrated excellent propagandistic skills. Dudayev's press office with his ex-Komsomol propaganda expert Movladi Udugov implemented a concise brainwashing strategy. Their message to the ethnic Chechens was that Russians were deserving of contempt, and any criminal actions directed against them would go unpunished. Tales of "the Tsarist atrocities against mountain dwellers" and calls for "pay back" were purposefully widely disseminated. At the same time, Udugov's media machine preferred not to debate origins and causes of the mutual historical grievances and not to elaborate on the reasons behind the mass deportation of Chechens in 1944, namely their collaboration with the Wehrmacht.

The federal mass media were singing in tune with the Chechen propaganda. Television and newspapers largely portrayed the warlords as "freedom fighters." In contrast, the Russian troops were portrayed in papers as a collection of pneumonic hobos and miserable children just weaned off a mummy's breast. As to the Russian civilians who had found themselves hostages to both rebellious bandits and Kremlin cowards, they were hardly mentioned at all.

Disturbing information on the tragic circumstances of the Russians in Chechnya constantly arrived to the Congress of Russian Communities. Badly attired and scared, having miraculously escaped the "Chechen paradise", strangers were forever appearing at our offices on Frunzenskaya Embankment in Moscow. They were telling us what was happening to our compatriots over there. Their stories sounded more like scenes out of Tarantino thrillers — not like something that belonged in real life.

And the bloodshed that they were describing had certainly not been produced in Hollywood. Russians were forcefully evicted from their homes; their property was confiscated all over the Chechen Republic. This totally permitted mistreatment was causing Russians not simply to migrate, but to run away. Dudayev's regime forced around 250–300 thousands of civilians to leave the area, before the federal troops were brought in. According to the data submitted by the head of the Russian community in Chechnya, Oleg Makoveyev, 350,000 were evicted and 45,000 were killed during the three years of Dudayev's rule. Morgues were packed with unidentified bodies. Kidnapping and trafficking women flourished. Rapes and horrid killings of Russian women were a matter of habit. Russians were beaten up right on the streets, children kidnapped. Knives and light arms weapons, kindly donated to the bandits by Minister of Defense Pavel Grachev, were in use all over the place.

The same data was received by the Kremlin as well, but seemed to fail to produce due impression on Yeltsin and his team. Neither Khasbulatov, nor Gaidar, despite KRO public appeals, said a word of reproach to Dudayev in connection with the ongoing Russian genocide.

As early as in May 1994, several hundreds of Russians from the Cossack village of Assinovskaya in the territory of Chechnya signed a collective letter addressed to President Yeltsin, pointing to Dudayev's crimes against them.

Here is an extract from this letter:

> *1 January 1993. Three o'clock in the morning. Unknown people in masks stormed into the house of a villager P.I.Shekhovtsov, opened fire, beat him up and then put him inside a box alive, and nailed the box. His elderly mother was pushed into the kitchen, and the kitchen door was nailed. They have stolen his car, too.*

16 March 1993. Middle of the night. Breaking and entering the house of A.Voystrikov, the armed thugs beat him up as they were saying, "Man, we are on schedule. Each Russian family is on our list." Then they took his car, too.

Under similar circumstances the cars were taken from M.V.Moiseenko, E.I.Popov, V.Labyntsev, A.Fedoseyev, to name but a few. Dozens of motorbikes were stolen from villagers, too. As a result, Russian people of the village were left almost entirely without private transport.

In the same village of Assinovskaya armed warlords took away eleven tractors and several vehicles, once property of the collective farm. The letter to the President also contained the tragic list of Russian women pensioners who were robbed and battered:

A.Fedorova, M.D.Trikovosova, A.Kazartseva, V.Pirozhnikova, M.Vanshina, K.Isaeva, M.Bukhantsova, V.Mtyukhina, A.K.Malysheva, Tilikova, X.I.Mishustina, and many others. Many of these old women are widows of soldiers who perished during the Great Patriotic War.

Some of them could not survive the trauma and the humility, like it happened, for example, with the disabled A.Klimova and with the Hero of the Soviet Union Ivan Fedorovich Sergeyev. They both died from the resulting injuries. On 24 March 1994, Lena Nazarova, a schoolgirl, was kidnapped and savagely raped by a gang of six. In April 1994, the Syedin family — mother, daughter and three small children — were forcefully evicted from their home; the house is now occupied by Chechens and the family has to seek shelter elsewhere. 13 May 1994. Armed gangsters broke into the house of Kaminchenko family, savagely beat up the mother and the grandmother, while 13-year old Oxana was raped and taken in an unknown direction. Altogether over 70 houses were attacked by gangsters. This is why in two years the number of ethnic Russians, whose ancestors lived in the village since 16th century, has fallen from 7,000 to 2,000.

Copies of hundreds of letters of the similar context arrived in the executive committee of KRO. By spring of 1995, KRO set up the Coordinate Centre of Assitance to Russian refugees in Stavropol region. It was based in the town of Georgievsk (once the place where Eastern Georgia signed the Treaty of Georgievsk in 1783 after asking for protection of the Russian Empire). The Centre of Assistance branches were also opened in large villages on the bank of the Terek River, for instance, in the Galyugaevskaya village. When I was helping the volunteers, for the first time in my life I witnessed the quiet stoicism and courage of ordinary Russian people when delivering refugees who sought to escape from massacre to the opposite bank of the river. Those brave people, many Orthodox priests among them, did not expect gratitude or rewards. To me, they are an example of the Russian character that is capable of doing heroic deeds for the salvation of others.

The local authorities were not quite so altruistic. Some of them merely visited the Neftekumsk or the Zelenokumsk regions of the Stavropol area, or came as close as 40 kilometres to the Chechen border, and they already expected awards and recognition from the Government for their "unrivalled courage". If a war serves any purpose at all, it is that it ruthlessly reveals people's true nature and shows who is genuine and who is fake.

Those Russians who managed to flee from the war zone, will never again come back to Chechnya. Nor will they ever receive a compensation for material and moral damages that they suffered. These refugees were met rather coldly in Central Russia too, to say the least.

They could complain to no one and did not expect help from anywhere. The Kremlin had been penetrated by accomplices to the bandits, and society as a whole was depressed and at a loss. The media, however, precept itself occupied with what they loved most, namely thrashing the Federal Army.

"Professional human rights campaigners", their living paid for out of foreign grants, were demeaning their country at an equally "professional" level. I decided to publicly expose one of them — one of the most audacious and notorious haters of our country.

Sergey Kovalev always aspired to become the "next Academician Sakharov", but unlike the world famous "father of a thermonuclear bomb", Sergey had achieved nothing remarkable in his life. Nor had he been particularly prominent in the circle of human rights defenders, perhaps apart from standing out for his utmost hatred of his country and people. That "dove of peace" was also very good at being dirty. It was not beneath him to visit the Dudayev's bunker and watch warlords executing federal soldiers or, at another time, to campaign for the rights of Shamil Basayev, a celebrity bandit in Chechnya, who attacked a maternity hospital in Budyonnovsk in the summer of 1996 and whose gang raped the women there. On another occasion, in one of the tabloids Kovalev published a letter with the following sadistic message addressed to mothers of Russia:

> *Corpses are scattered all over Grozny ruins. These are the corpses of Russian soldiers. Stray dogs are finishing them off. These remains were once somebody's sons — not yours, I sincerely hope.*

The wounded are lying down in a grey and damp bunker. They are the captured Russian soldiers; some of them developed gangrene. They, too, are someone's sons. (...) Some of you will be informed that your son went missing. Don't believe it. He is out there, abandoned on the streets of Grozny, and the dogs are gnawing at his dead body, or else, he died from sepsis in Chechen captivity.

This printed piece had decidedly confirmed my opinion that "the human rights protector" Kovalev was a right beast. Sadly, Kovalev was not alone, as a singnificant part of "democratic" Russian mass media were promoting a similar attitude to Russian officers and soldiers fighting in Chechnya. That is why my public duel with Kovalev that took place in the summer of 1995 on a live talk show, revealed the hypocrisy of those who betrayed their country together with Yeltsin.

I had thoroughly prepared for that talk show. I took an approach of an investigating journalist to cut open my opponent's ideological guts. In the midst of a discussion on air I asked the host to bring into the studio the video recording equipment. As it happened, a couple of months before the show during the terrorist act in Budyonnovsk, where terrorists took hostage thousands of hospital staff and patients and had 150 people killed, Kovalev arrived there to rescue the terrorist leader Shamil Basayev. Terrorists demanded some "voluntary hostages" to cover their withdrawal from the crime scene and drive buses back to the Chechnen territory unhindered. Kovalev was in close communication with terrorists and offered himself as such a hostage to guarantee the extremists their safety and impunity. Later, two hostages testified to me that when the buses with the terrorists and Kovalev on board had reached a safe area in the mountains, the professional human rights campaigner along with his colleagues happily greeted a Chechen crowd that was meeting them as heroes returning from a successful mission. However, no documentary proof of Kovalev's behaviour existed. I decided on a cunning trick.

Kovalev was very afraid of being exposed. He could not know for sure if he had been filmed by anyone from the crowd. My plan was based on a hypothetical possibility that such documentary could have existed and made available to Kovalev's opponents. During the televised debates I produced a blank video tape and, looking my opponent in the eye, claimed that the direct proof of his treachery — a footage of him, Sergey Kovalev, rejoicing with terrorists in the success of a barbaric operation — was in my hands. Predictably, the host, who was not aware that the tape was blank, broke into explanations of why (due to "technical reasons") it was impossible to play the video right there in the studio. Kovalev reacted in the most peculiar way. His face went red. Perhaps this man who had positioned himself as the "conscience of the nation" still had some traces of conscience left in him after all. My tactics hit the target; Kovalev mumbled, betraying the fact that the allegations against him were true. Our victory was close but not final. Kovalev left the studio. Soon, he was on operating sites with the separatists again.

The newspaper *Moskovsky Komsomolets*, this mouthpiece of "progressive liberalism", covered my televised duel with Kovalev. I still remember the title of the article — *A Dialogue between a Drum and a Violin*. I assume that the inkster who wrote it meant under a violin the human rights protector and definitely not me. In any event, the paper affirmed that Kovalev's live performance had been a failure. I took part in many a luscious debate since and appeared on some of the most interesting broadcasts, but that debate, that first brick in the wall, I remember to this day.

Right after the talk show I took a flight to Budyonnovsk.

The ground of the Sacred Cross (the original name of the town) was still hot from a recent fight with the Basayev gang. A newly created cemetery at the bottom of that new Russian Golgotha, where the shot and tortured terror victims had been buried, was covered with flowers. Many people on the streets recognised my face and were coming up to express their gratitude to me for unprecedentedly having voiced on national television the truth about their tragedy.

There, in Budyonnovsk, I made friends with the Militia Colonel Nikolai Lyashenko. As a former head of Budyonnovsk branch of the Interior Ministry he was under prosecution's gun at the time. Things like that happen a lot in our country — a commander of a Militia squad who goes into a non-even fight with a gang of contract fighters is judged by law, whilst high authorities who fail to detect trucks that carry terrorists of Basayev's Abkhaz battalion in the territory of Stavropol, walk free. Fortunately, charges against Lyashenko were dropped soon, and he was reinstated in his position. Appreciative, his fellow citizens elected him head of the city council. This expression of trust, coming from the people who have lived through war, was the best possible answer to the Kremlin; the latter was attempting to shift its own responsibility for failures onto the Army and Militia officers who faithfully carried out their duties.

The First Chechen War brought out into the light all domestic and foreign foes of Russia, like an X-ray. They appeared out of all holes, like rats, in the first signs of Russia's weakening. Milli Mejlis (National

Assembly) of Tatarstan issued the following statement on bringing federal troops to Chechnya: "After Baku, Tbilisi, Vilnius, Riga, and Tashkent, Moscow's bloodstained hand is now stretched out to Chechnya, and it will not stop at that." The Kremlin swallowed the humble pie and wiped the mouth with the bloodied hand. None of the authors of that statement incurred liability for their words. But that was not enough for the Tatar separatists. Not only did they directly support Dudayev, but also started to organise mass meetings in memory of the defenders of Kazan, the city seized by Tsar Ivan the Terrible in 1552. The political objective was obvious — a breakaway from Russia. Now very few people remember how in 1991 the crowds on Kazan's central square carried banners *"Tatarstan — an Independent State!"* and *"Russians, Get out of our Republic!"*

Who exactly was helping the Chechen warlords, is not a great mystery to the Russian government. Influential politicians and business people in Turkey, Pakistan, Azerbaijan, and Ukraine, as well as chiefs of special services of some countries rendered great assistance to the Chechen militants. For example, Turkey accommodated Chechen warlords in her territory. As early as in December 1994, the Turkish Security Council debated the issue of a military aid to Dudayev. Then the Chechen Diaspora in Turkey managed to collect and transfer 4 million USD to Chechnya, and then 10 more million followed. Couriers with fake IDs, disguised as reporters, delivered large amounts of cash across the border between Russia and Azerbaijan. It was not for nothing that Dudayev named the presidents of Turkey and Kazakhstan, along with Shaimiev[1], as his preferred mediators.

The fundamentalist party Jamaat-e-Islami legally acting in Pakistan recruited soldiers of fortune for Dudayev from various Islamic states. The Special Forces of Pakistan facilitated contacts between Dudayev and the masterminds of drug syndicates that had been active in the north-western border province of Pakistan. The drug mafia offered the warlords cooperation in transporting heroin and opium. The proceeds could have been used for the ongoing armament necessary for the continuation of war.

In occupied by Turkey North Cyprus military training camps for Dudayev army and his volunteers were set up. In the spring of 1995, an air corridor between North Cyprus and Chechnya was opened. Warlords, weapons and ammunition were being flown into the parts of Chechnya and Dagestan adjacent to Georgia and Azerbaijan.

---

[1] *Mintimer Shaimiev* is the first President of Tatarstan, a Republic within the Russian Federation.

In Istanbul, a secret agreement to supply about 2,000 fighters, so-called volunteers, to Chechnya was signed between the Afghani and other terrorist groups. From Afghanistan alone up to two hundred was ready to go to Chechnya as a matter of priority. Negotiations on supply of weapons, ammunition, and manpower were held in Istanbul in August 1996 between Dudayev's generals and the inner opposition of Tajikistan. Azerbaijan was the place where warlords went for a vacation and medical treatment. *Baku* and *Apsheron*, the smartest hotels of the Azerbaijani capital were at their disposal. There, in Baku, the militants obtained Azerbaijani passports to travel to Turkey or Russia on criminal business. Those who did not fancy long-distance trips used an opportunity to earn a bit on the side by means of racketing and drug trade.

Azerbaijan became a transit point for weapons delivery from Turkey. In 1995 Russian border guards arrested 53 vehicles and a tractor loaded with weaponry. The guards confiscated a total of seven tons of 240 reactive missiles, 110 units of ammunitions, pistols, machine guns, clothes and medical supplies.

I would like to thank Mr. Ilham Aliyev, President of Azerbaijan, for putting an end to this disgrace.

The Ukrainian authorities almost openly sheltered "the peaceful separatists" who posed as refugees from Chechnya. These people not only spoke out their anti-Russian views without a scruple, but also involved in mobilisation of the Chechen Diaspora with *laissez-faire* of the Ukrainian authorities. In the territory of Ukraine, Chechen militants received an ample opportunity to form public movements and organisations that did not withhold their aggressive attitude towards Russia and her people. The politicians in Kiev condoned the fact that the Ukrainian nationalists participated in military actions against Russia. Militants of the Organisation of Ukrainian Nationalists (OUN) and the Ukrainian Insurgent Army (UPA) went to fight in Chechnya with no objection whatsoever from the official Kiev. Witnesses say that the Ukrainian fascists were particularly cruel towards the captured Russian soldiers. That being said, what could be possibly more atrocious than the way the Chechen warlords treated our servicemen?

The support for the bandits was being expressed explicitly in Western Ukraine: one of the streets in Lviv was named after the rebellious leader Dzokhar Dudayev. The press wrote about the health farms in the Crimea that accommodated injured in Chechnya warlords. A commercial firm in Kiev covered the costs of their stay. At least one group of 200 warlords arrived to the Crimea to recover in the health resorts belonging to the Defense Ministry of Ukraine. Moreover, the Crimean Tatars there were allowed to organise provocative street rallies under Ichkerian banners, where they proclaimed chauvinistic slogans and issued threats against Russians.

The Baltic States also made their contribution to the warfare against Russia. Apart from the unofficial forwarding of militants into Chechnya and the economic aid to the Dudayev regime, the Baltic States organised the political support for an armed squadron of russophobes. The most memorable event of that campaign was the celebrations in Vilnius on the occasion of Madame Dudayev's arrival in the city to present awards for the Lithuanians who had fought against the Russian side. On top of that, the Baltic States were officially turning a blind eye to the fact that the terrorists were using their countries as a location for coordinating their informational resources, primarily the Web-based outlets.

The Polish members of "Russophobe International", too, did not want to be left out. They kept an award for Sergey Kovalev who agreed to accept it only upon the end of the war in Chechnya. The Polish were not ashamed to adorn the Kovalev's neck with an Order of Honour.

The Government of the United Kingdom pretended not to notice the ongoing recruitment of Islamist warlords to fight in Chechnya that took place in London mosques practically openly. The British naively deemed that by cherishing a Wahhabi serpent in their bosom they had insured themselves against a bite. Despite the numerous extradition demands of the Public Prosecutor's Office of the Russian Federation, the British authorities continue to shelter not only the oligarchs in exile who profited from the Chechen tragedy, but also the leaders of the terrorist underground, such as Akhmed Zakayev!

Thereby, Russia's very diverse enemies had their interests "creatively interlinked" during the course of the Chechen war. One can only express regret about the shortsightedness of the "moral sponsors" of the Chechen banditism. Having lost the war in Russia, the bandits moved to the very same countries that encouraged them against Russia, and have built their nests there. Now it is not the FSB and the Russian Army who are facing the task of taming the criminals, but the police and the Special Services of the European Union. Let us wish them the best of luck in this hopeless business!

PRISONER OF CAUCASUS[1]

In December 1995 we missed just by 0.6% the 5% threshold to gain seats in the Parliament. During the three months after the unfortunate for us election campaign we had to reinstate KRO literally from scratch. Some of our key figures left to join the movement "Honour and Motherland" set up by General Lebed to facilitate his campaign in the forthcoming presidential elections. The core figures stayed; they were waiting for my decision on a future course of action. "Older comrades" who had led our election list all went their separate ways. Yury Skokov, who had been #1 on the list and who had been mainly to blame for our failure, took the responsibility for the KRO lack of success on himself. This act partially diminished the criticism of his bungling actions.

Yury Skokov and I first met in April 1993. I telephoned him straight after he had been notoriously sacked from his position as the Secretary of the Security Council of the Russian Federation. In those reckless times practically everyone around me sincerely felt for Skokov. It was he who had received the highest number of votes from the People's deputies in the Supreme Soviet during the election of the Chairman of the Russian Government in December 1992.

However, the President then had a preference for Victor Chernomyrdin, the head of Gazprom, over Mr. Skokov. The former enjoyed great respect in industrial and military circles. Mr. Yeltsin felt uneasy about Skokov's independent standing. In March 1993, six months before the Black October, Skokov was excused from the government service. He attributed his dismissal to his refusal to ratify the draft of the anti-constitutional Decree on Special Order of Governing the State. In fact, with that decree Yeltsin had attempted to dismiss the Supreme Soviet for the first time, but at that stage the internal forces ministers convinced him not to go ahead.

Yury Skokov was older and a lot more experienced than me. He still

---

[1] *The Prisoner of Caucasus* refers to 1872 novella by Leo Tolstoy about a Russian Officer Zhilin captured by Abreks. The story is strikingly relevant to modern times. There is also a famous poem of the same title by Alexander Pushkin.

maintained his contacts in the government structures and in internal forces ministries. He helped me with advice and rendered moral support; I used to keep him updated on the developments and introduced him to my colleagues. Eventually I invited him to be a partner in the KRO governing body. I figured that Skokov's authority would help KRO to strengthen its position not only in the countries of the former Soviet Union, where by that time we had evolved into a major network of Russian compatriots, but also within the Russian Federation. No matter how great a political advisor he was, Skokov turned out to be a poor politician when he was in the public eye, indeed.

That "wise gudgeon" practically wound up KRO pre-election campaign as he had relied on his shadow agreements with Yeltsin's circle to see our election bloc through to a win. Skokov naively deemed that Yelstin's ability to manipulate votes had been unchallenged to such an extent when the public campaign and the transparent competition for people's votes were reduced to a third-rate importance, in his mind. Moreover, Skokov was jealous of Lebed, who was as popular in Russia at that moment as once The Beatles had been. Eventually, Skokov managed to persuade Lebed to take the second place in our pre-election list, and that damaged the course and the outcome of our election campaign colossally.

Following our election fiasco, General Lebed severed his ties with Skokov and moved to KRO offices on the Frunzenskaya Embankment. There he began preparations for his presidential run. A young and prospective economist Sergey Glaziev, the #3 on the KRO election list, announced that from now on he was only interested in science and ... in the Communists. However, Glaziev proceeded to spend most of his time beside Lebed working on an innovative economic programme before the elections.

Interestingly, Lebed had two economic programmes of the mutually exclusive contents. It is still not clear what this maneuvre was supposed to mean. Possibly, the witty commander, who often liked to pass off as a simpleton, thought that it would be rather amusing to have two separate programmes, one that was suitable for liberals, and another for Communists; so to say, to be an "all-weather political bomber". Of course, all this was upsetting and unnerving for Glaziev who just did not understand General's character.

I got to know Alexander Ivanovich quite well. I understood that he was a military officer who had been through the wars of the 1980s and the 1990s, and that deep down he despised all politicians, regardless of their political colours and shades. When he took a decision to become a politician himself, he was still conscious of his own gigantic advantage over the rest of them — in his experience, natural intelligence and wit, his knowledge of matters of life and death. However, instead of relying on own personal decency and dignity, the General tried to outplay politicians at their game. He started to play by the rules that are cynical, and are pre-set so that a political outsider would inevitably end up losing.

I have to admit, having the popular General Lebed on the KRO election list raised the public interest to our organisation and to the elections in general. Back in May 1995, Skokov asked me to go to Transniestria on an urgent mission to facilitate the newly resigned Commander of the 14th Army General Lebed's return to Moscow and to make it as quick and smooth as possible. By that time the relations between the Army Commander and the Government of the new unrecognised Republic had already been seriously spoiled. I was not aware of all the details of the conflict, but I was sure that my good friendship with the President of Transniestria Igor Smirnov and my contacts in the Interior Forces Ministries would be helpful in getting Lebed out of there without a scandal or unnecessary complications. Following Skokov's advice and wishing to come across as more convincing, I invited the former GRU[1] Spetsnaz Commander Vasily Kolesnik along with some other senior officers to come with me.

In Tiraspol the dust was settled rather quickly. At the end of the day, the object that had been causing frustration for the new Government — the roughish and difficult Commander — was leaving with us for Moscow, so the reason for the conflict was removed. Skokov and I had a firm agreement with Lebed that he would publicly declare his intention to enter the political arena on behalf of the Congress of Russian Communities; that declaration was to be made prior to the official announcement of his resignation. It was supposed to sound persuasive and scary to our opponents. As soon as he stepped off the plane, Lebed indeed made such a declaration, which sent political scientists and liberal scribblers into a state of shock. However, our triumphant walk did not last very long.

The internal competition between Skokov and Lebed, combined with the old guard's reluctance to stress the "Russian issue" in the pre-election campaign, played a low-down trick on KRO. Skokov had even

---

[1] *GRU* — Abbreviation for the Main Intelligence Department, the military foreign intelligence directorate of the General Staff of the Armed Forces of the Russian Federation.

thrown to the media a supposedly funny phrase, something like "ethnic Russians do not exist at all". "A Russian is either a Tatar in bad disguise, or a Jew in good disguise" — this expression had been going around in the press, and its origin was attributed to KRO. I think that this poor joke was equally offensive to Russians, Jews, and Tatars.

Skokov and Lebed were so busy trying to outdo each other that they almost forgot about the pre-election campaign, having delegated it to chevaliers of PR. As a result we faced fiasco, disappointment, and the breakup of our political coalition.

But Lebed was not going to surrender at that. He was eager for a revanche, and the presidential elections of 1996 promptly provided him with a chance. To me, the upcoming presidential elections represented an opportunity to reconstruct KRO's integrity and to breathe the air of hope into the people via their involvement in the proactive election campaign with Alexander Lebed as our presidential candidate. President Boris Yeltsin and the Communist leader Gennady Zyuganov were his opponents.

The start of the campaign was slow and shaky. All of January, February, and the first fortnight of March 1996 our candidate was passing the time alone in his office next door to mine, nervously smoking, staring at the silent phone and repeating from time to time: "It's OK. They will call. They'll have no way around it". At first I was slow in understanding what he had in mind, but then it dawned on me. In March, I received a phone call from one of my university mates who then worked in press relations in LogoVAZ[1]. He told me that "Boris Abramovich Berezovsky kindly requests Alexander Ivanovich Lebed and Dmitry Olegovich Rogozin to join him for dinner".

"Are you going?" I asked the General, just to make sure. His facial expression revealed at once that he had been waiting for that very phone call for those three months.

The office of the Grey Cardinal of Russian politics was located minutes away from the Paveletskaya Metro station. Our host did not show up at an agreed time. We were led into a well-lit room where everything had been laid out for tea. Lebed was seemingly nervous. He even looked under the table for some reason, as if Berezovsky would have been hiding from us in such an uncomfortable place.

At last the door opened, and a plain looking, balding, and a very lively man stormed in, talking on two mobile phones at once. He handed over his mobiles to his helpers, sank into a chair opposite us, and, without

---

[1] *LogoVAZ* is the financial empire headed by Boris Berezovsky in the 1990s.

a pause, showered a series of sophisticated political compliments on Lebed. General nodded in my direction and said to Berezovsky that he never kept secrets from me. He then took out his cigarette-holder and asked permission to smoke. It seemed that Boris was ready to turn a tiniest matter into a reason for more compliments. He said that although his was a smoke free office, anything and everything was allowed to such a great man and all. I had an impression that Berezovsky needed Lebed more than Lebed needed him. General did not have to open his mouth to utter a single request. Berezovsky was chattering non-stop.

When he arrived at the subject of the upcoming presidential elections, he stopped talking and, looking pointedly at the Commander, produced a few sheets of paper with some printed text and handed them to Lebed. General assumed an air of importance (he had a habit of doing that when he was being nervous), lit up a cigarette, and only then proceeded to read. Nobody said a word. Lebed took his time to read through the papers, and the pause hanged on for too long.

"So, how is your nationalistic congress doing?" Berezovsky addressed me, apparently in an attempt to break the awkward silence and to taunt me at the same time.

"Preparing pogroms," I answered in the most serious manner.

"Hilarious! Very funny, young man! You'll go far!" Berezovsky would have probably been happy to continue this exchange, but at that point Lebed finished reading and nodded, indicating his agreement. As I understand now, the General was offered to familiarise himself with some plan for the election campaign that provided for considerable financial and informational support in exchange for luring voters away from the favourite of the Presidential rally — the Communist party leader Gennady Zyuganov. The price of the question was about a million votes and a prominent position under Yeltsin with Lebed being Yeltsin's successer. It was the Trojan Horse.

To my surprise, the General swallowed the proffered pill without chewing. What was he counting on? Was he thinking that Yeltsin, who carried on dancing during his field trips despite a recent heart attack, was in poor health? Of course, Lebed did not wish to go under the banner of the existing power for which he felt profound disrespect. Despite the propensity for impulsive and unexpected decisions, the General was a clever man and well-tuned to the moods of the nation. He was prepared to put his reputation at risk for the time being, so as later to appear having outwitted his enemies.

I suppose that those who persuaded Lebed to accept the offer to serve as the Secretary of the Security Council were none other than

General Alexander Korzhakov and Mikhail Barsukov, who were then in charge of the Presidential Security Service and the Federal Security Service (FSB) respectively. Probably, one of them had figured that once their places beside the deteriorating President were secured, they could convince him to hand over the power to the "General Peacemaker", who was much liked by ordinary people.

With the Skokov's case as an example, Lebed was also fully aware how important the position offered to him (Secretary of the Security Council) would be in the hierarchy of Yeltsin's power structure. The only thing he was not aware of was Yeltsin's preference to always play whites and never intend to lose. The position of the National Security Advisor to the President was added to the bargain (to which I commented to Lebed that advisors generally do not become presidents), as well as the firm promise that Pavel Grachev would lose his post as Defense Minister (Lebed could not forgive Grachev the dismissal from the Army). Lebed accepted Boris Yeltsin's offer. The two giants shook hands on it.

After the deal was finalised, the television channels, controlled by Berezovsky and some other oligarchs, began to broadcast Lebed's promotional campaign ads. An appropriate motto was chosen: *"There is such a man, and you know him!"* The General moved out of the KRO offices to a spacious election headquarters and hired hundreds of political consultants of all sorts who ran up and down the hallways all day long. In short, the pre-election campaign was boiling up under the guidance of the demonic Berezovsky.

Our meetings with Lebed were fewer and far in between. The "five minutes to President" Lebed no longer wished to have by his side the people who had previously seen his weaknesses and his less heroic side. His soul underwent a big transformation.

We met again after the first round of the elections. He came to the Frunzenskaya Embankment to see me for no special reason, just to meet up and to catch up on the latest news. I sensed that the General was mixed up; I changed the subject of our conversation and reminded him of June 1992 when he had been in charge of the military troops in Transniestria. The General solemnly remarked that those were the happiest days of his life. Back then he knew where he stood and what he had to do; he could clearly tell friends from foes.

I asked him to do something — to denounce the deal, to quit urging people to give their votes to Yeltsin, and to refuse to take the proffered post out of Yeltsin's hands. I warned Lebed that he would end up covered in dirt and thrown aside. It would be better for him just to quit the malicious game. Six months would pass and the circumstances would change, but he, Lebed, would have stayed true to his honour and dignity; then there will be no other candidate for President but him.

Lebed said good bye and left for the Kremlin. I did not see him again until September 1996 when he returned from Khasavyurt.

My warnings to him proved to be entirely justified. Anatoly Chubais, who was the Head of the Presidential Administration at the time, came running to Yeltsin and requested an immediate dismissal of Korzhakov and Barsukov "on the grounds of a coup-d'-etat attempt". Yeltsin duly did as he was asked and sacked both "conspirators". Out of the threesome, Lebed alone was remaining in a position of authority.

But Chubais did not subside at that. He thought up a clever move of creating a governing body parallel to the Security Council — the Defense Council; a lawyer Yury Baturin was installed as a head thereof. In the fall of 1996, when Lebed was accused of "forming unlawful armed units under the umbrella of the Security Council" and dismissed irrevocably, this Defense Council became redundant; "the universal lawyer" Baturin was sent away initially to join an astronaut squad, and then he was launched into space. This is not an anecdote. When sober, Yeltsin liked practical jokes and sometimes made unexpected decisions.

Such was the end of the inglorious march into power for my old comrades from the Congress of Russian Communities.

In August 1996, the Government appointed General Lebed to be in charge of the Chechen affairs, correctly assuming that he was bound to fail there. Lebed was left with no friends or advisers, and he decided to employ the same tactics in Chechnya as he had done in Moldova. The major difference was that Transniestria had been a part of Moldova, and Chechnya was a part of Russia. One could argue whether the result of Lebed's actions in Transniestria met Russian national interests, but his actions in Chechnya were, beyond doubt, in direct contradiction with these interests.

"I can foresee plenty of criticism from hurrah-patriots and hurrah-democrats alike. I declare that our Internal Force Ministries will find out the residential addresses of such critics; the military will recruit them, and I will form the advance military units out of the critics, giving them an opportunity to fight as much as they like. These squads will be led by the brave generals — deputies of the State Duma. Those who disagree with me or with the peace treaty may appeal to any instances, up to President and God himself. This war will stop. Those to put obstacles to that will be eliminated". I could read insecurity and doubt underneath the intended harshness of Lebed's words. He wished to put an end to the war in Chechnya not because he wanted to stop a waste of human lives: he just wished to liberate himself from the status of "Caucasian prisoner" as quickly as possible.

In a rush, Lebed allowed the wording in a preamble of the Khasavyurt Accords[1] that was unacceptable within the framework of the Constitution: "...in accordance with international law the Parties agree..." Being the Secretary of the Security Council, Lebed should have known that international law regulated relations between sovereign states, not between a subject of a federation and a federal centre. Thus Lebed not only handed the total control over Chechnya to the separatists, but also officially acknowledged their state of independence. Secretary of the Security Council did not have a right to manage Russian sovereignty in such a reckless way, his past achievements in Russia's favour notwithstanding.

On 24 September 1996 KRO issued a statement detailing the measures necessary to formalise the Peace Treaty in order to underline that our standing on the Khasavyurt Accords was different from that of General Lebed:

At that stage of the negotiations the following measures were required to enforce the Peace Treaty:

1) All reconstruction work in Chechnya must be suspended. The funds allocated for the reconstruction must be used for the purpose of paying compensation to citizens who suffered from the war, primarily to the refugees who lost their homes.

2) To relocate federal troops from mountainous and sub-mountainous regions, where they have become a target for warlords, to the Naursky and the Shelkovsky districts on the opposite bank of the Terek River. The troops are to be stationed there until the status of these territories is finally determined.

3) To declare the city of Grozny a disaster zone; to take all governmental institutions out of Grozny and appoint the temporary military commandment to administer the city.

4) To form the temporary coalition government in the city of Urus-Martan or in the town of Shali with the purpose of the preparatory work to hold a people's referendum and elections in which all citizens of the Russian Federation who have lived in the territory of Chechnya until 1991 will participate. Until the referendum and the elections are held, general governance is to be carried out by

---

[1] *Khasavyurt Accords* — the Peace Treaty that marked the end of the First Chechen War signed in Khasavyurt in Dagestan on 30 August 1996 between Alexander Lebed and Aslan Maskhadov.

the Russian side, and the local governance is to be carried out by whichever side controls a particular settlement at the moment.
5) To ensure total evacuation of the non-Chechen population from the areas of crisis and to provide them with a temporary accommodation in the socially stable regions of Russia.
6) To carry out partial mobilisation and to create the territorial army and the Cossack armed units around the areas that are under the separatists' control.
7) To adopt a governmental social rehabilitation programme for Russian refugees and forced migrants (which would include financial compensation, housing, employment, etc.)

In the event of the disruption of the Chechen crisis peaceful regulation, or if military actions against the Russian federal troops continue, the Government must declare the state of military emergency in the territory of Chechnya, as well as the state of emergency in Russia, and on that basis ensure complete breakup of the bandit units. In this case, the separatist leaders are to be prosecuted as war criminals and traitors.

The rebellious Chechen leaders are to be warned in advance that the current negotiations with them are final. They must know that no further negotiations will ever take place. They must know that their accomplices and supporters will be uncovered in any location in Russia and be deported to Chechnya at the least.

General Lebed held a different view and so he broke off with KRO almost entirely. He did not wish to think about the potential consequences of his actions and preferred to enjoy the state of peace instead. Later, the peace achieved on his terms would turn out to be worse than a war for Russia.

The split with Lebed was very difficult for me. Being a son of a Russian general, I have always believed in the officer's honour. I anticipated the coming of the Russian De Gaulle and considered Lebed to be the hope of the Russian patriotic movement. It was unbearably hard to admit to myself that I had been wrong. I wanted to check on things all over again and so decided to see the effect of the Khasavyurt Accords with my own eyes.

In October 1996, I flew over to Budyonnovsk together with my comrades-in-arms. We planned to get to Chechnya from there. A year had passed since the Basayev's terrorist attack, and the life in that town in the Stavropol region still did not come back to normal. Citizens of Budyonnovsk were still grieving for their friends and relatives who had been killed in the hostage taking. We visited the cemetery that was filled with fresh flowers and wreaths.

In the two hours that we spent at our friend, the Militia Colonel Nikolai Lyashenko, we managed to meet members of the Russian refugees community and officers of the helicopter squad. The women refugees knew that we were about to travel to Chechnya. These women carried with them crumpled photographs of their children, mostly girls, who had gone missing, and they wanted us to take those photos to Chechnya. I did not know what to say. I was certain that the absolute majority of these teenage children were no longer alive, that they had been tortured and killed by "freedom fighters" turned beasts, but how could I say such a thing to the mothers! Each one of those poor mothers will believe and hope as long as she lives that her child had miraculously escaped a terrible death and was alive somewhere out there....

We flew over to Grozny by helicopter. It was already dark when we landed in the Severny ("Northern") Airdrome. Federal troops were still based in Khankal, and there were military quarters not far from the airport. The debris of Ichkerian aviation, destroyed by our Army in the first days of the attack on Grozny, were still visible on the take-off runway.

We were taken to see the military commandant. He received us very warmly, offered us tea and accommodation for the night. We declined the offer to stay, reasonably considering that it would be easier to drive in the night out of the city besieged by warlords.

Three Ladas full of Chechens waited for us at the first road checkpoint following the exit from the airport. I was fondly calling them "our tour guides". They were the militants of grim disposition, skilled soldiers and guards, all from the mountainous region of Vedeno. All of them were blood relatives of Borz-Ali, a Chechen friend of mine from the university. Borz-Ali had offered me his help prior to our "inspecting visit" to the rebellious Republic and provided guards and guides for us. I had far greater trust in my friend's reassurances of safety than I did in the declarations of Russian military commanders, who had been busy withdrawing federal troops from Chechnya under the Khasavyurt Accords.

At the commandant's office the "tour guides" passed us a note via the patrol guards. It contained an instruction not to stay there overnight but to leave Grozny and its surrounding areas upon the descent of darkness. Despite the commandant's keep protests and offering us his armed guards and combat equipment, I decided to put ourselves at the trust of Borz-Ali's people and leave quietly without causing unneccesary attention to ourselves. My experience in Transniestria and Bosnia did not go in vain. During a war one should keep a low profile and only wage a calculated risk, thus increasing chances of survival.

On the outskirts of the city a slender boy soldier, who had just been drafted, got out of his concrete hideout at the checkpoint. It was obvious that this guy, left on his own by his commanders in the forest full of blood-thirsty predators, was feeling lonely and scared. He addressed me: "Please, sir, on your way back, flicker your headlights four times. Otherwise I'll shoot." He pronounced those words quietly but firmly, and I knew at once that should something go wrong, this soldier, a mere youngster, would not surrender. Russia fought in Chechnya with youngsters like him. Those yesterday's schoolchildren had fought against seasoned bandits and foreign soldiers of fortune, and won.

We crossed the unpopulated ruins of Grozny within minutes and reached a rural road which led us to the village of Chechen-aul. There we had a bite to eat and went to sleep. I was put on a sofa in the living room. Two of the "guides", fully dressed and with their guns in arms, stretched on the floor carpet in the same room.

In the morning our host, an elderly Chechen man, showed me the spot from which the cannons of Tsarist General Yermolov had fired at the man's ancestors during the Caucasian War in the 19th century. The old Chechen was talking with pride as if he had been firing those cannons personally. "They do respect Yermolov in Chechnya," crossed my mind, "But they despise Yeltsin's today's generals."

The day was spent in conversations with villagers of Shali and Novye Atagi. All the time I was looking out for traces of soldiers in captivity, trying to find out their scores and the places where they were being kept. In the afternoon we were granted a visit by Movladi Udugov himself, the 'local Hebbels', as sneering Borz-Ali had commended him to me. Udugov was accompanied by a certain Isa, who was introduced to us as a "professor and key ideologist" of the Ichkerian regime. The two Chechens were inclined to philosophise immediately upon their arrival. They wanted to explain their views on Islam, war, and the prospects of relations of Caucasians with Russians and Russia. If I had not been aware of the fact that my opponents represented an ideology of the cannibalistic Dudayev regime, then maybe I would have gladly followed a proffered line of discussion. But as things stood, I was talking to the "spiritual leaders" of Ichkeria and tried to understand just one thing, namely, how dangerous their views were? Could the metastases from Dudayev's cancer spread beyond Chechnya and the Caucasus? Were those self-learners really capable of "shifting" the mainstream Islam in

Russia; could they succeed in brainwashing Muslims in Russia, next to whom we, Russians, had lived peacefully for centuries and together with whom we were now building and defending our integral state?

By the end of the conversation Movladi Udugov admitted that Ichkerian leaders themselves were taken aback by the scale of betrayal on the part of the Russian officials. The latter frequently took initiative to pass some valuable information on to the rebels in exchange for a fee; the officials also came out with profitable commercial proposals. In turn, the warlords bought more weapons and more information out of the profits from such joint projects. It did not take much courage to pick on Russia of that kind. Yeltsin still sat in the Kremlin. The metaphorical "Russian bear" was asleep; everyone knew about it and took the liberty to rob and kill.

The meeting ended with a light squabble between Isa and my assistant Yura Maisky. "Professor" made a displeased gesture with his hand and got out of the table. When Udugov was saying good bye, he mentioned matter-of-factly that he was surprised to encounter "a man of such views", meaning me, in the circle of General Lebed who was an esteemed man among the Ichkerian government. I took it as a compliment.

By the evening we were on the road again. We had to cross the mountains to visit the villages of Makhkety and Vedeno — Basayev's sleeping quarters. There in Vedeno I had my random encounter with Khattab, the commander of the Arab soldiers of fortune.

Our companions stopped the convoy in the centre of that big village to pick up some of their people who were to meet the "president" of Ichkeria Zelimkhan Yandarbiyev. I got out of the car for a smoke and saw some odd-looking people in white coming out of a house across the street. At dusk they looked rather like ghosts. Then a man in black appeared at the door. He noticed our convoy and immediately walked in our direction. The man's image was instantly familiar. It was Khattab — the notorious international terrorist, a religious fanatic and an intermediary financier through whom Saudi sheikhs were financing guerilla gangs in Chechnya. He had a face of a Bollywood star, and only his deepest black eyes betrayed his dark soul.

Khattab came up close to me and stared at me inquisitively. His body language spoke "look who is the master here."

It was incredible! The very man who had been chased all over the mountains by the Army Special Forces was standing right in front of me in flesh. He was not sitting in a dug-out or hiding behind bushes; he had not shaved off his beard or moustache not to be easily identified — oh, no! This lowlife who had killed dozens of our soldiers in Afghanistan and

Chechnya was looking at me; he was not afraid of anything or anyone; he walked freely upon our land and felt quite at home there.

Apparently, the people in white whom I had noticed earlier were the listeners of Khattab's "political information course". Likewise, they were not in hiding and felt in control of the situation and of our land, upon which they had shed so much Russian and Chechen blood. Afterwards I felt sorry that I had not had a gun in my hands.

"You, Russian?" Khattab asked me in a heavy accent.

"Yes, I am Russian," I replied.

"Why a Russian here?" the Arab said with a smirk.

At that point my facial expression must have changed because the "tour guides" who had been watching the scene, promptly, as if following a command, stepped in between the two of us. One of the guides opened the door of the car and gestured me in to take a back seat, whilst another said something to Khattab in a low voice in Vainakh[1] language. Then the guides jumped into the car, too, and ordered the driver to take off. Having shut the car doors, they unlocked the bolts of their guns and never took their eyes off the Arab and his militants, who did not move from the spot, until their silhouettes disappeared from our view.

That was how I got to know the Chechen hospitality law. These people were responsible for my life and I could be certain that this was not just a figure of speech. "Khattab is really a merciful man. He took pity on many Russian soldiers," one of the guides said as if in justification. "Sure he did," was all I could say, and nobody spoke anymore through the rest of the journey to Starye Atagi.

Our meeting with "the president of Ichkeria" was furnished with pomposity. In the morning we were taken to a large villa where Yandarbiyev resided. The villa was patrolled by a couple of dozens of young guys in black uniform, armed up to their teeth. The patrol guards searched everyone with the exception of myself and my assistant Yury Maisky, together with whom we had wandered through a good half of Bosnia in our time. Of short height, robust and square-built, this Yura from Simferopol could easily be taken for a Chechen. During our stops for meetings with various Ichkerian "authorities" Yura showcased his martial art in front of the admiring Chechen fighters. Yura elicited instant respect from them. No warlord could withstand his direct stare, and he had no equals when it came to martial fighting. The Ichkerian presidential security, too, did not dare to bother Yura, and so he managed to smuggle one or two guns to our meeting with "the King of the Jungle".

---

[1] *Vainakh people* — Chechens and Ingushs.

Prior to that rendezvous I saw Yandarbiyev only on television. I remember once watching a disgraceful scene, when a Chechen delegation, headed by my vis-à-vis, had somehow made Yeltsin sit not at the head of the table during their meeting, as befits a president of a great power, but opposite them as if they were his equal partners.

I have noted long ago that there are quite a few romantic souls among criminals and Nazis. For example, Adolf Hitler liked to paint pictures, Jaba Ioseliani was a Master of Arts, Zviad Gamsakhurdia fancied himself as a "creative intellectual" and Vytautas Landsbergis is a keen musician. Yandarbiyev was of the same kind — he wrote poetry. It is a shame that we never got around to reciting poems together during our meeting.

The "president" was overtly attentive to me; he was talking sweetly and slowly and tried very hard to make himself understood correctly. The point that he wanted to establish was that Chechens wished to live separately from Russia but, at the same time, did not want to be exiled. I objected that it did not work like that — if Chechens desired to build their own separate state they had to recall all their compatriots back into Chechnya. No matter how hard Yandarbiyev was trying to maintain calm presence, it was obvious that he was annoyed by our conversation.

I was deliberately talking in a low voice; because of that, my opponent was leaning towards me from time to time which was making him remember my words better. The meeting finished with Yandarbiyev solemnly promising to do his best to stop the persecution and bullying of the Russians in the Republic; to get in contact with the leaders of the Russian community in Chechnya (it was actually they who asked me to see the "president"), and to adhere to the demands of the Russians citizens from Grozny who were eager to leave the territory of Chechnya in the shortest terms possible. I knew the true value of his promises but at least they were a proof that Yandarbiyev had heard me.

Somewhere in central Grozny, when we were on our way back to the airport I asked the driver to stop by a semi-destroyed Orthodox church. Three elderly Russian women were quietly sitting inside. At the altar an Orthodox priest was busy cleaning dust and rubble off the tall icons. The icons were shot throughout from machine guns. The priest told us that there were still many Russians in the city, and that the general mood was suppressed because of the ongoing withdrawal of the Russian Army. People were at a loss; they did not know how to leave Chechnya, or where to go. Many of the Russians did not have a choice as they could not move their sick and elderly and could not leave them behind. In short, these were the most tragic circumstances.

As we were talking, suddenly a piece of metal fell down on the ground a metre away from us making a loud noise. What struck me the most was that the women, and even the cats that were asleep at the women's feet, did not move a muscle. People and animals had become so used to the continuous ambient noise of explosions, shooting and bombing that they stopped paying attention to loud sounds altogether.

In the Severny Airdrome our helicopter was ready to take off. Just as we were about to take our seats, a sergeant came up running to tell me that the commandment asked us to delay our departure.

We went to the third floor of the Airdrome office building where the temporary Army Headquarters were located. A few senior officers, two generals and some hot tea awaited us. The officers wanted to know how our trip to the mountainous regions went. I gave them the detailed report of everything that we had seen. One of the generals was very interested; he convinced us to stay for a bit longer, ordered to send our helicopter back to the base in Khankal and prepare another helicopter to take us to Mozdok[1]. At home I learned that the helicopter that we were supposed to take was shot down by the warlords.

Finally, we parted with the commandment and loaded into a "cow", which is a nickname for a huge helicopter MI-26. The helicopter was packed with the Special Forces fighters going back home. The atmosphere was not cheerful; nobody spoke during the whole flight. A truck, parked beside the helicopter, was being loaded with bodies of dead soldiers, wrapped in cellophane.

"Who are they?" I asked a young lieutenant.

"They're our guys".

"But the war is over, isn't it?"

"For your Lebed yes, the war is over," he said through gritted teeth. There was hatred in his voice.

So that was how my first trip to Chechnya ended. Along with it ended my friendship with Alexander Lebed — the ex-Commander of the 14th Army, former Deputy Chairman of the Congress of Russian Communities, and a former candidate for Russian presidency.

An extract from the KRO's Declaration dated 2 March 1997:

> The efforts of traitors and defectors of the Motherland and the endeavours of bureaucrats in power, who had lost their mind, honour and conscience, led to one of the most humiliating defeats in Russia's history — the defeat in the Chechen War.

---

[1] Mozdok — a town in the Republic of North Ossetia.

It was a war in which the Government, the mass media, and at times even the top military officials fought against their national army. They repeatedly undermined all chances of victory by our Armed Forces. Russians failed to make their Government act in that war in the best interests of the nation.

The war now ceased purely because the Russian and the global shadow market entities are profiting from the state of war less than they do from the existing conditions, under which the control over the Chechen Republic is being exercised by the unlawful militant groups. The expansion of instability zones into the North Caucasus is in direct correlation with the interests of oil monopolies that have been spoon-feeding Chechen bandits.

The political clandestine confederacy of bureaucrats and criminals, combined with the fake elections held in Chechnya, resulted in the present situation when not a single issue of the Russian-Chechen relations has been resolved. On the contrary, the conflict is escalating further.

KRO is forced to affirm its position: the guilt of Chechen separatists and rebels who brought great suffering onto the Russian people will not be purged until all those responsible for killings, theft, enslavement and forceful evictions are punished; until the last terrorist is captured and each and every refugee received due compensation for the losses incurred.

KRO does not recognise the legitimacy of the elections of the Chechen president because the Russian citizens were evicted from their land and excluded from participation in these elections. KRO considers Aslan Maskhadov to be not a president or a governor, but a rebel and a thief who must be arrested and subjected to trial without delay. We will officially deem any action directed at securing his status as president of the Chechen Republic to be an act of betrayal of Russian national interests.

KRO deems it necessary to establish a measure of liability for the individuals who allowed Russia's defeat in her fight against rebels. Those who rendered direct or indirect support to the terrorists and the rebels; those who undermined the fighting ability of the Russian Armed Forces; those who carried out propaganda against federal troops in Chechnya must all be called to justice.

Until betrayal and banditism are fully punished, KRO will not agree with the notion that the Chechen War became history.

The Congress of Russian Communities adopted that Declaration at the assembly in January 1997. By that time all the "prominent military figures," "promising economists," and "major statesmen and politicians" had already deserted KRO. But our conscience, dignity and faith in our just cause remained with us even in the most complicated of times.

The Caucasus was on fire. The Balkans were aflame, too. The hearts of Russian patriots were burning with them. The struggle for Russia had only just begun.

ENEMIES[1]

The war in Yugoslavia was instigated by just about anyone who could be bothered. Yesterday's brothers and compatriots were purposefully being turned into the worst enemies. Some supplied matches and others carried diesel canisters in order to set fire to the multinational Balkans. Somehow the fact that the Balkans had cradled two world wars was erased from collective memory. The story of the bloodstained disintegration of the Balkans that ended with NATO bombing of Belgrade is identical to the scenario of the USSR breakup. The only difference was that Russia possessed nuclear weapons. Only this circumstance had saved us from a military intervention of democratic powers that otherwise could have rushed in to assist the Chechen "rebels".

Here's the story behind the war in Yugoslavia.

In February 1991 Croatian Sabor (the Parliament of Croatia) adopted a resolution to cease to be friends with the Yugoslav Federation. The Serbian minority of Croatia reacted with disagreement, and so the National Assembly of Serbian Krajina (the autonomous Serbian region in Croatia) adopted a resolution to "unfriend" Croatia and to maintain the Yugoslav Federation. The emotions were stirred on both sides, and that, along with persecutions of the Serbian Orthodox Church, caused a flow of refugees, the first of many. 40,000 Serbs were forced to leave their homes behind.

Total mobilisation was announced in Croatia in July 1991. By the end of the year the number of Croatian armed groups had reached 110,000 people. Armed divisions of Croatian nationalists carried out ethnic cleansing in West Slavonia. All ethnic Serbs were expelled from ten towns and 183 villages, and partially expelled from another 87 villages.

The Serbian side started to form territorial defense of Krajina. Volunteers from Serbia came in to join. Parts of the regular Yugoslav People's Army had entered the territory of Croatia and by August

---

[1] Set in 1905 in provincial Russia, *The Enemies* is Maxim Gorky's drama about the social ferment that culminated in 1917 Revolution.

1991 pushed the Croatian volunteer troops out of all Serbian districts. However, the People's Army ceased to support Krajina Serbs after the peace treaty was signed in Geneva.

A new Croatian attack forced Serbs to withdraw. For one year starting from the spring of 1991, Krajina was partially taken under the protection of "blue helmets". At that, the demands of the United Nations Security Council to withdraw Croatian troops from areas controlled by the peace enforcement were not met. Croatians continued to launch active military actions with deployment of tanks, heavy artillery, and missile launchers.

The war of 1991–1994 in Croatia claimed 30,000 human lives. Direct financial losses are estimated at over 30 billion USD.

From May to August, 1995, the Croatian Army conducted a well-prepared military operation of returning Krajina back into Croatia. Dozens of thousands were killed in the course of the operation. Another 250,000 Serbs were forced to flee the Republic. In total, more than 350,000 Serbian refugees left Croatia in the period from 1991 to 1995. But the Serbian tragedy was not limited to the loss of Serbian Krajina.

In October 1991, the Skupstina[1] of Bosnia and Herzegovina, in the absence of the Serbian deputies, declared independence. Three months later, the Skupstina of the Serb People proclaimed in retort the formation of the Bosnian Serb Republic as an autonomous entity in the Yugoslav Federation.

In April 1992, the Islamist warlords seized the Militia regional departments and the crucial city objects in Sarajevo. The Serbian Territorial Army resisted that coup. First the Yugoslav Army withdrew from fighting positions, and then its living quarters were blocked by the Islamists. Over 1,300 people were killed. The number of refugees amounted to 350,000 during the forty-four days of the open warfare.

The USA and allies methodically provoked the civil conflict in Yugoslavia and encouraged separatists with words and actions alike. When the advocates of a single integrated country decided to use force against rebels, the West accused the official Belgrade of instigating armed conflicts in Bosnia and Herzegovina. Upon the OSCE[2] ultimatum the Yugoslav troops had no choice but to leave the territory of the Republic. Still, the situation did not stabilise. Then the war started between the Bosnian Croatians and the Bosnian Muslims with the involvement of the

---

[1] *Skupstina* — a Serbian and Croatian word for an assembly, meaning the Parliament.
[2] *OSCE* — Organisation for Security and Cooperation in Europe.

Croatian Army. The leadership of Bosnia and Herzegovina was splitting into independent ethnic groups.

However, the USA still managed to square the circle and harmonise the hostile parties. The Catholics and the Muslims of Croatia reconciled and agreed "to be friends with each other" against Orthodox Serbs. The Muslim-Croat Federation was established in March 1994, and the decision on forming a joint army was made. The Air Force of NATO carried out air strikes on Serbian positions. Americans did not spare funds for the armament and training of the Muslim-Croat Army, which shortly went onto the offensive.

Nobody was helping the Bosnian Serbs. Russia turned away from them. Milosevic did not wish for any complications in relations with the West, and so he also betrayed the Bosnian Serbs. It may well have been the case that the President of Yugoslavia felt something close to envy for their leader, Professor Radovan Karadzic, but the fact remains — the Yugoslav People's Army did not interfere in the conflict.

Thousands of Serbian patriots, many military officers of the Yugoslav Army among them, crossed the semi-transparent Yugoslav-Bosnian border and joined the ranks of the armed resistance.

The Serb militants treated the fighters of the International Orthodox Christian squad with particular respect. Among the soldiers of the squad I met some Bulgarians, some Greeks, and even two United States citizens who had been baptised Russian Orthodox. The Tsarist Wolves — volunteers from Russia — were at the core of the squad. They were reconnaissance scouts; they were at the front lines of the attacks, leading the Serbian units. The Muslim-Croat Army undertook a proper hunt for the Wolves, but the fighting ardour of the "war dogs" subsided following the open fights with the Russian volunteers. I do not know of any incident when a Tsarist Wolf was taken in captivity. I don't think that such a thing ever happened.

In 1994, during the fights near Novo-Sarajevo, I accidentally came across an acquaintance of mine from the times of the war in Transniestria. He was a tall Cossack from the Black Sea area who left his family behind in Ukraine and went to Yugoslavia to fight for the Slavic cause. He fought there for over a year and saw many of his comrades-in-arms dying.

Two years later, when Serbs had to leave Sarajevo for good, they took coffins of their perished friends with them. Not a single Serbian bone was left behind for sacrilege! No Russian burials, too, were left in the territory of the Muslim-Croat Federation. All the Tsarist Wolves killed in battles were buried near the town of Banja Luka, where Serbs had moved their capital city.

Surely, it is easy to find many flaws in the national character of Serbs, just like in any other nationality. But the Serbian attitude to their deceased does not stand a comparison with how we, Russians, treated our own dead and injured, who had often been left behind on the battlefields of Chechnya; or with how our authorities treated the Russian inhabitants of Grozny, the town that was flattened by the Russian Aviation; or with how our bureaucrats dealt with the Russian refugees who were fleeing from the nightmare of the Chechen war covered in rags and carrying starved children in their arms. Serbs are a close-knit and united nation and they remember both the good and the evil for centuries.

Even today, abandoned by Russia and by the rest of the world, having lost half of their territory and great numbers of their people, Serbs are not broken. They remember to this day who their enemies were, and who came to help during the trying days of the struggle for their national honour and independence.

I was often at the front line of the Serbian defense in the capacity of a journalist during the Bosnian war. In January 1995 my friend Mikhail Nuzhdinov, a few Serb soldiers and Russian volunteers, and I were in a vehicle when Islamist militants suddenly ambushed us.

The direct fire killed the driver and the two other people who were sitting to my both sides. The backfire killed two of the attackers. Bullets went through the corpus of the vehicle like a needle in a sewing machine, smashed the front window, and took several people's lives.

I did not have a scratch on me.

In a year after that, I got involved in another incident in Sarajevo. In the corridor of a long crossing between the Muslim and the Serbian parts of town, which looked like a hoarding of a building site, an old woman was held up. She was carrying some bundles and got all messed up in her baggage. For the unchallenged snipers who in those days were running the show in the destroyed Sarajevo, the woman was visible as if she were on a palm of a hand. To avoid becoming a target for snipers who were driven crazy by all the blood, city residents used to stretch ropes or wire across the streets and hang on them some rags, bedding, blankets and anything else that could have obstructed the snipers' view and disguised people's movements. I wanted to help the woman out and ran towards her along the corridor. I managed to literally drag her away from the road for a distance of about fifty metres where the two of us hid behind a French heavy transporter painted in white and blue colours of peacekeepers.

The reaction of the Serbs who accompanied me was rather ambiguous. At first, they admired my courage and expressed an intention to award me for my "heroic deed." Then it turned out that the rescued woman happened to be a Muslim and not Serbian. At that point the chief Serbian officer gave me a proper scolding. He was shouting that I could have caught a bullet of any accurate shooter. He was saying that the total lack of punishment had turned snipers into hunters who would follow any prey. He was right, of course, but for some reason it seemed to me that he would not have been shouting as much if I had helped a Serbian woman. Somehow, the award was never mentioned again.

Truly, a civil war is the cruelest kind of all.

I had a few meetings in Pale with the leader of the Serbian Republic, Professor Karadzic, and with the Chief Commander of Bosnian Serbs, General Radko Mladic. The General was extremely popular among Serbs; he was a symbol of national resistance, a living legend. Once Mladic addressed me with a question whether Russian aircrafts would drop some empty boxes or containers from air above the territory of Serbian Krajina, to make it look as if Russia had resolved to support her brothers in their struggle. "We don't need weapons or ammunition, we got everything we need. If we run out, we acquire more in the course of the fight. But it is important for us to show our Serbian countrymen at war that Mother Russia did not desert them. The Americans assist our enemies all the time. Their aircrafts drop military and food supplies for them. Please, just drop off some empty boxes and we will take care of the rest," requested Mladic.

To say I was deeply ashamed of my country at that moment would be to say nothing at all. Only the Tsarist Wolves with their unprecedented heroism were a living reminder to Serbs that there were some true Russians still present in Russia.

After I became the Ambassador to NATO, my colleagues often asked me whether my opinion on Karadzic and Mladic changed since they had both been declared war criminals and their names were put on the international wanted list, to be located and arrested at a later date. My answer is: I would never heroize a participant of other people's civil war as I think that, by definition, there cannot be any heroes in a civil war. Civil wars are the most horrendous and dirty of all possible kinds, when a brother points a gun at a brother and a father fights against sons; officers who took an oath to serve their country do not know anymore which part of the disintegrated country they must be loyal to. As for the extent of guilt of a certain politician or a military commander, only a fair court in a fair trial can determine it. I do not consider the Hague tribunal to be fair or just. It is a spectacle, and not proper justice. I do not believe in it.

Soon the UN Blue Helmets blockade of Serbs' heavy weapons resulted in the gravest situation for Orthodox Slavs. NATO airborne strikes, that had destroyed military objects, centres of communications and air force defense systems in Serbia, cleared a path for a new advance of the Muslim-Croat Army. By October 1995 the Serbs who were left to deal with NATO single-handedly had no alternative but to sign a cease-fire agreement.

Two weeks into December 1995, the UN Security Council delegated the formation of peacekeeping forces to NATO with the objective of putting an end to the armed conflict in Bosnia and Herzegovina. Russia, the country that in the 19th century trained and armed the professional Serbian Army, the same army that fought alongside Russian troops against the Ottoman and the Austro-Hungarian Empires, against Prussia and even Japan (a Serbian volunteer squad participated in the Russo-Japanese war of 1904–1905), ratified the humiliating terms of the Agreement for Peace in the Balkans at the end of the 20th century. By that Agreement, for the first time in its history NATO secured a right to conduct an overland operation beyond the zone of its immediate responsibility. The United Nations' role in all this was pitiful.

The war in Bosnia and Herzegovina claimed over 200,000 human lives, out of which over 180,000 were civilians. But the main impact of the Bosnian war is that it manifested the unipolarity of the modern world and proved the fact that the USA and NATO are allowed to act with impunity.

Following the Bosnian war, NATO developed a taste for conducting operations beyond its traditional areas of responsibility. In the summer of 1999 the North Atlantic Alliance attacked Yugoslavia by-passing the UN Security Council. As a result of the non-stop bombardment and the blackmail by mediators, the Yugoslav Army had to withdraw from indigenous ancestral Serbian territory — the land of Kosovo and Metohija. Immediately after the withdrawal, the legalised Albanian warlords unleashed terror on the Serbian population that had not had a chance to escape in time. All Orthodox Christian places of worship were violated; Serbian cemeteries were dug up with bulldozers.

The terror and violence continued despite protests voiced by human rights protection organisations and UNESCO (all cultural monuments in the area listed by this international organisation were destroyed). On entering Kosovo, NATO troops did not interfere into the Albanian atrocities, preferring to observe violent actions against ethnic Serbs from a distance. As a result, NATO's reputation suffered colossally.

Nine years passed, and in February 2008 NATO decided to finish the business that had started with the bombings of Belgrade. Energetic protests by the pro-Western government in Belgrade notwithstanding, the majority of members of the Alliance declared acknowledgement of Kosovo's independence. Interestingly, the same countries now disapprove of Russia's acknowledgement of independence of Abkhazia and South Ossetia. I think that at this point I have to elaborate on the Russian stance on the matter so that the reader may not suspect that the Kremlin applies the same cynical double standards in the international affairs as the Western democracies do.

There are two principles in the international law with which not just separatists, but also some respected diplomats and lawyers so often juggle. I mean a nation's right to territorial integrity and a right to self-determination. In fact, there is no contradiction between the two concepts. The right of a state to protect its national borders from external and internal enemies always has priority. However, there is one exception to this rule. A right of a nation to self-determination may happen to be more important than the principle of inviolability of frontiers in the event when such a nation is subjected to systematic violence or a threat of physical extermination. If this is the case, then the global community, or at least one world power, may acknowledge that such a nation has a right for an independent existence and for secession from the country within which it is subjected to torture and violence.

Let's see why it was necessary to acknowledge Kosovo's independence in February 2008. Who represented a threat to Kosovo Albanians? "Evil" Milosevic? But he had been long in the Hague prison where he eventually died under mysterious circumstances.

The new rulers of Serbia? No. President Boris Tadic now occupies the office in Belgrade, and the Western world actively supported him in the elections.

The question is, what was the need to tear Serbia into pieces and assign the powers independent from Belgrade to the former warlords of the Kosovo Liberation Army? Who was responsible for that decision? The "dove of peace" Martti Ahtisaari who put the plan of Serbia's dismemberment down to paper at Washington's dictation? Or maybe those who dictated to him were responsible?

In real life it is the peoples of the Balkans and Europe that will have to pay the price for the mad decision of the war architects. The political map of Europe will unavoidably be redrawn.

As to the acknowledgement of Abkhazia's and South Ossetia's independence by the Kremlin, Russia chose to take this step after all other methods of convincing the Georgian regime not to use armed force against these small Caucasian nations were exhausted. The operation against South Ossetia, launched by Saakashvili, had the code name "Clear Field". It would have been a clear field or, more precisely, scorched earth, left by the Tskhinvali Butcher. If Russians did not interfere in this massacre and did not take the very decision that unfortunate Ossetians were long waiting for, there would be no one left to protect over there. Russia acted in strict compliance with the international law, in particular with a right of a nation to self-determination; Russia's actions saved Ossetians and Abkhazians from total physical extermination. The attempt of Saakashvili to "settle the Ossetian issue for good" aside, the attack on, and despicable killings of the Russian peacekeepers in Ossetia could not have gone unanswered for. For the first time since 1945, an army of a foreign state, following orders of its commanders, massacred our servicemen on their sacred peacekeeping duty. Were we supposed just to forgive the killers? A constitution of any country defines an external assault on an army to be an act of aggression and an immediate cause for war. So it is worthwhile for the people of Georgia, who have so recklessly elected the paranoid Saakashvili as their leader, to think about how they should offer their apologies to Russia. Moreover, the Russian Army resisted a temptation to seize the whole of Tbilisi along with the "Tie Tamer", who was trembling in his bunker, in the heat of revenge. The Army deserves admiration for its self-control.

Sadly, Russia led by Yeltsin displayed an altogether different behaviour. The Government was reluctant to take responsibility or make independent decisions. It was in Bosnia where the Americans waved good bye to the old Russia, to her firm stance in foreign affairs and her capacity to influence peacekeeping processes.

It finally became clear to Washington that the political elite of Yeltsin's power was prepared to betray not only their friends but also own national interests in exchange for promises of financial incentives or titles (such as the Nobel Peace Prize, for example). We let ourselves be stepped over and wiped the spit off our faces.

After the cease-fire agreement was extracted out of Serbs with the silent approval of Russia, the global community established the International Criminal Tribunal for former Yugoslavia (ICTY) in The Hague. I will stress my attitude to it once again: the Hague tribunal became an instrument of direct pressure on Serbia. With its aid, NATO "cleansed" the leadership of former Yugoslavia from Civil War veterans, hiding them behind bars; following the trail, Milosevic and Karadzic, who used to compete for sympathies of millions of Serbs, were arrested and also sent to The Hague. Vojislav Seselj, leader of the Serbian Radical Party, languishes for years there; he was never in the slightest linked to the decisions of official Belgrade during the Balkan wars. Seselj was always in opposition to Milosevic regime. Nevertheless, in the West he, too, is deemed guilty of war crimes. I think that if the desire for it was strong enough, the whole Serbian nation could be sentenced to imprisonment. The only snag is that The Hague is just too tiny for repressions on such a grand scale — its prison and the whole town do not have enough space for every single Serb to be locked up.

The invention of a, so to say, "bird language" is indirect evidence of the fact that the NATO commandment knew that their aggression against a sovereign state and a UN member was in breach of the international law.

By using this coded speech, representatives of the Alliance were shielding from the public the facts of disproportional and indiscriminate use of armed force against civil objects and civilians in Serbia. The propaganda talents of Jamie Shea, who was NATO spokesman and the Deputy Director of Information and Press during the war in Bosnia, are often credited with invention of that "newspeak". (Jamie Shea is now Head for Policy Planning in the Private Office of the Secretary General in NATO; he heads the brainstorming group on a new strategic concept of the Alliance). It is Jamie Shea who was always in the global TV cameras' spotlight for the weeks of incessant daily bombings of Serbia's capital city and her towns, bridges, electric power stations, and factories. Mr. Shea was the man who was the first to introduce the terminology of the concealed war. Unfortunately, this terminology still has not been duly studied and analysed. Below are some samples of the "bird language" — a series of expressions from Jamie Shea's vocabulary. On the left there is a military term; on the right — the camouflaged "translation" in which words are either airbrushed with emotionally neutral daily use expressions, or altogether replaced for the purpose of ideological brainwashing.

The Glossary

Bombardment onto Serbian positions — 1) use of aviation; 2) air campaign; 3) force impact from air.

Combat engagement — a collision or a contact of warring factions.

To eliminate or to destroy — to have an impact on infrastructure.

Blockade — temporary restrictions of external communications.

Search — 1) examination aimed at preventing arms or drugs smuggling; 2) documents verification.

Naval blockade — provision of maritime boundaries security.

Sweep operation — documents inspection.

Combat operation — special actions with the use of military component.

Raid — a terrain study.

To attack or assault — 1) to take preventive measures; 2) to display initiative.

Shell attack — suppression of the enemy fire positions from a remote distance.

Arrest — 1) detention in order to verify identity; 2) to check documents of persons suspected of terrorist activity.

Kill zone — non-secure territories.

Employment of military equipment — use of technical assets.

Airdrop — to reinforce peacemaking component.

Round-up — measures of detection.

To establish a cordon sanitaire — to take a dangerous area under control.

Sanctions enforcement — application of persuasive, or coercive, security measures.

To interrogate — to interview; to obtain current awareness information.

Casualties among Serbian civilian population — 1) incidents; 2) collateral damage; 3) unavoidable casualties.

Aerial reconnaissance — 1) situation assessment from air; 2) monitoring the ground situation.

Serbian refugees — evacuated population.

Radio jamming — radio electronic countermeasures.

A Serb prisoner — a person detained in a conflict zone.

NATO Tank convoy — military equipment moving in an organised manner.

NATO Armed Force — 1) a limited peace enforcement contingent; 2) security presence.

Yugoslav Peoples' Army — a mass consolidation of human force and equipment of the opponent.

NATO Special Operations Forces — divisions with combat experience.

Elimination of Serbian civil objects — liquidation of logistical support of the opponent.

Front line — security zone.

Elimination of civil property of Serbs — 1) Recovery operations; 2) Clearing of dangerous debris.

Curfew — a temporary measure to restrict the movement of population.

Martial law — administrative measures to enhance security of the civilian population.

NATO military instructor — 1) assistant; 2) consultant.

NATO military supplies to Kosovars — assisting the strengthening of the emerging democracy defense capability.

Bringing NATO troops into Kosovo — protection of the young democracy.

Albanian warlord — a freedom fighter.

All is fair in love and war, especially all that helps to conceal genuine intentions and facts. But had this "birdspeak" worked; did it help to hide the facts of massacre in Yugoslavia? And why not a single tribunal in the world takes these facts into account? Were it not the USA fighter jets and missile planes that bombed Belgrade in the spring of 1999, destroying all bridges over the Danube River, killing 2,000 civilians, and rendering another 7,000 disabled? Were they not NATO troops that spread 23 tons of depleted uranium-238 across Serbia, causing radiation sickness in half a million people? Why Serbs, who were protecting their homes from fire and violence, and not NATO, or the Kosovo terrorists from Maoist armed groups were declared real criminals?

The answer is simple: it was done to cover up the true perpetrators of the Yugoslav tragedy — politicos of the West. They sent Serbs to their deaths; the Orthodox Christians died because they merely wanted to defend their homeland.

I vividly remember my final meeting with Milosevic. It took place a month before the elections in Serbia at which he lost infamously.

The two of us talked for over three hours. Many signs betrayed that Milosevic was sensing the approaching finale. He was pulling one cigarette after another out of a Davidoff pack and chain-smoked. His hands were trembling all the time, and he was hiding them under the table.

During the conversation he kept coming back to the same subject: the Kremlin had betrayed him. Milosevic was blaming most of all

Foreign Minister Igor Ivanov as well as Chernomyrdin, who, on behalf of President Yeltsin, negotiated with the Finnish mediator Ahtisaari the terms of the Yugoslav Army withdrawal from Kosovo in exchange for cessation of NATO bombardment.

I don't know if Milosevic realised that he himself had played too many games with the West. Being one of the creators of Dayton Agreement[1], he forced Bosnian Serbs to surrender and sentenced them to a political defeat. Did Milosevic not realise that the same Western politicians, who were condescendingly tapping him on the back, were bound to give him over to The Hague as they had done with other Serbian soldiers and officers?

Even so, the arrests of Milosevic and Karadzic and their deportation to The Hague left the Belgrade liberals with the permanent mark of dishonesty on the uniform and on their conscience. Installed by Americans, they gave their national leaders over upon the very first demand of bloodthirsty prosecutor Carla del Ponte. If, for instance, Milosevic was guilty, then why the liberals of Belgrade decided not to put him on trial in his country? Or did they not believe in the justice and objectivity of their national Court of Tribunal? Or did they have something to be weary of, like national anger or some unwelcome revelations?

Such is the anti-national essence of "liberals" — their own people intimidate them more than death itself. But a national will outlive politicians and time. National memory erases facts and events, but it cannot forget a humiliation. Any attempts to humiliate a nation, to bring it down to its knees, to impose alien ideas and idols are bound to end badly for imposers. In their time, after World War I, the British and French allies treated Germany in much the same way. Germans were not merely defeated; the victors horrendously humiliated them. What were the consequences of that? The spring of the German collective memory straightened and pushed Hitler to the height of power. As a result, German Nazis launched the new world war twenty years after the initial massacre, this time on larger scale. We all know what the price of that war was: 57 millions of human lives. Over a half of them were my people.

Describing a similar situation, the outstanding German military theorist Carl von Clausewitz wrote in his book *Three Principles*:

---

[1] *Dayton Agreement* is the General Framework Agreement for Peace in Bosnia and Herzegovina, also known as Paris Protocol or the Dayton Accords signed on 14 December 1995.

"A shameful mark of cowardly submission can never be erased; a drop of poison will spoil the blood of future generation of a nation. It is quite another matter, if a nation lost its independence after a bloody but a noble struggle. Such a struggle ensures that a nation will be resurrected. The heroic deed of a war will then be the seed that would bring new plentiful fruit."

I can only add that mean tricks, such as arrest and condemnation of a president of an independent country and enforced estrangement of a part of indigenous territory, could never be forgotten. The spring of the great insult in Serbia is tight now. But it will jump. You will see.

POOR FOLK[1]

In 1996 I started to work on my PhD dissertation that was to be defended at the Moscow State University. My paper was entitled *The Russian Question and its Impact on National and International Security*. I conducted an extensive research and set out to transfer all my fresh impressions into a written text. Right from the start, I found myself facing a philosophical dilemma that was virtually insolvable for me at the time: which factor is more important in the process of national revival — is it a spirit or "a body" of a nation?

On the example of the Chechen War, I saw how the disaster, that had affected both Russians and Chechens, had a positive impact on birth rate in one ethnic group and at the same time led to shock, despair, and demographic decline in another. Is it possible to seed and nurture the idea of national revival in a nation that lost all faith? Can a national idea become a banner of national revival when the Russian population is declining by a million a year? If Russians do not perceive themselves as a consolidated nation, would they ever be ready to reproduce? And which factor is of greater significance in improving demographic situation: is it the material component, i.e. financial incentives, or is it the ideology, i.e. national ideas and education in the spirit of respect for large healthy families?

The truth is that there is no such thing as a demographic problem in Russia. There is a demographic disaster instead. The breakup of the country, moral decline and disintegration of the family as an institution, deterioration of the domestic industry and of all aspects of public and social life — all of the above induced the gravest reaction in people. The "poor folk" responded to the uncertain times with an unprecedented fall in birth rate that reflected a lack of desire to continue family lines; with an unheard-of mortality rate exceeding that of a wartime; with the migration of population from the Northern and Eastern to the Medial

---

[1] *Poor Folk* or *Poor People* (1846) is the first novel by Fyodor Dostoevsky. It is written in a form of letters between a man and a woman who lived in impoverished circumstances.

and Western regions of the country, closer to metropolises and the developed economic arteries. This migration process left deserted the same strategic territories that had been developed with great hardship by many generations of Russians throughout centuries.

For this reason, the promotion of a national idea is one of the crucial tasks of the patriotic movement; this task is to form and advance the authentic and the single most important national project "National Preservation, Growth and Development in the Integrated and Consolidated State". The project is based on the profound analytical report prepared by a group of gifted young academics.[1]

It is gratifying that the ideas set forth in our report constituted the base of the new Demographic Programme that was announced by President Vladimir Putin at the Federal Assembly in 2006.

The future success of the Demographic Programme depends upon our willingness to target the three most important national objectives.

The first goal is to solve the current demographic crisis by encouraging fertility in families whilst combating the over-excessive mortality rate. It is necessary to rid the nation of the so-called "Russian cross", which is a name for a graphical intersection of the rapidly declining line indicating birth rate with the sharply rising line indicating mortality. The target population of such a vast and rich country as Russia should be at least 500 million.

Secondly, it is necessary to encourage voluntary repatriation of our compatriots from the Baltic States and the CIS and at the same to start "colonising" and redeveloping the regions of Siberia and the Far East again.

The third imminent task is to sort out the basics of the immigration policy and to drive the unwanted immigration and ethnic mafias out of Russia.

Can there be anything more important than a nation's right to life and limb? According to the forecast of the Commission on Population and Development, a subsidiary body of the Economic and Social Council of the United Nations, the population of the Russian Federation will be reduced by 9–10 million in the period from 2009 to 2020; it will shrink further from 112 to 92 million by 2050. If far-reaching measures are not taken urgently, this exact outcome is inevitable.

---

[1] Authors: Vitaly Averyanov, PhD; Benjamin Bashlachrev, independent system analyst; Andrey Kobyakov, Professor at the Moscow State University; Yuriy Krupnov, author of "Demographic Doctrine"; Andrey Saveliev, Doctor of Political Sciences; Sergey Butin, publicist.

The quality of Russia's evolution as a civilisation must be determined by her ability to double the birth rate coefficient in the next ten years. For this to be achieved, an average healthy couple in Russia should have twice as many offspring as it has today. In other words, it is desirable that people who belong to the middle class and are able to raise their children well, adopt a popular fashion of having three children in a family.

The state is capable of setting such an objective; it can encourage couples to have more children, and it must be willing to do so. In the medium-term perspective this would at least partially compensate for the current drastic shortage of human resources. In Russia today there are about 17 million women of childbearing age. Even if a half of these women come to a decision to have two more children each, 17 million of new lives would be brought into the world.

Another aspect of the sound demographic policy is to resettle people into the strategically important geographic areas and initiate a series of potentially profitable and productive economic projects there.

Our nation must not let others overtake vast riches in our North and Taiga. On the contrary, the avant-garde of the nation must be encouraged to go there, like it was done at the times that were better for the state. National prosperity is based not on the capital city and on ever-expanding metropolises and not on the makeover of the whole country into an endless "Eastern bazaar". The future prosperity depends on building the strong backbone of small towns' network — renewed industrial and economic centres, which are particularly significant in West Siberia, East Siberia and in the Far East.

The future of Russia lies in Siberia and the Pacific Ocean. It is our generation's duty to stop the Russian exodus from this land of the future. This exodus exposes Siberia and our Pacific coastline to an influx of adverse and extraneous immigrants.

The objective of national reproduction must be a priority in the Russian domestic policy today. If this objective fails to be achieved, all other projects and policies aimed at improving people's lives would become void.

Typically, the process of elimination of "unwanted population" by methods of abortions, contraception and vasectomies is more intense in the societies, the weakening of which benefits global oligarchy. Instead of projecting a positive and happy image of parenthood, the mass media are inclined to raise issues of increased cost of child rearing and stress on problems of education and similar aspects of parenthood in a negative way. During the last fifteen years, many obstetricians all over Russia have been trying to convince women in their care not to go through with pregnancies; they recommended abortions, intimidated women with prospects of medical complications in pregnancy that were often grossly exaggerated or altogether non-existent. For all those years an array of foreign-subsidised "non-governmental" organisations specialising in birth control was at work, many of them on a global scale. There are hundreds of such family-planning centres all over the country. They mostly favour in their activities the areas that are already endangered such as Siberia, the Far East, and the non Black-Earth belt.

Generally, these organisations promote a worthy cause: they try to prevent the spread of AIDS and venereal diseases; they raise awareness of methods of contraception and promote maternal health. However, the achieved effect is questionable. In Russia, seven out of ten pregnancies end in a decision to abort the fetus. Cases of syphilis have increased 150–200-fold over the last thirteen years in the Far East; the number of HIV-infected people has grown 4-fold. At the same time, the sales of contraceptives have gone up 5-fold, and the number of live births dropped down by 3.7 million and continues to decrease.

Governmental agencies that specialise in tackling drug abuse can demonstrate a very similar picture. If in 2004 there were about 70,000 drug abuse-related deaths in Russia, in 2005 this figure went up to 100,000 (!), the vast majority of the drug victims being people of young age.

If a mind of a person is being continuously and for a long period of time infixed with a notion that it is unnecessary and even harmful to procreate, and that the resources of the planet are limited and there are not enough of them to accommodate the growing population, then this person would fall under the magical influence of numbers and statistics and would finally accept the idea; an individual cannot test or check it personally. The same individual, though, cannot help noticing the obvious around him or her: the increased proportion of elderly people in the population; fewer children about; the inflow of "foreigners" who take up vital space. All of these are signs that the familiar cultural and social environment is being eroded. By the time these signs become all too apparent, the process is gone too far and it is too late to change anything. That is why the degeneration of the European civilisation and the lack of desire and/or ability to reproduce is not an achievement but a peril.

We as a nation have to denounce this "plague of the white man" and to set upon our own demographic path. If there is a rational seed in the concept of birth control and birth limitation, it does not suit Russia and her indigenous nations. To some extent these ideas might be justified in countries like China, India and Pakistan — geographic regions with high birth rates and the deficit of drinking water, but they could not be reasonable for us!

If the current ominous birth and mortality trend continues, the next decade would see the economically active population of Russia shrink by 10.6 million; thus, the shortage of workforce would present an insurmountable obstacle for Russia in gaining back the equal player status in the global market. Many centrally planned economic and industrial projects in the USSR were accomplished with young generations on call; the workforce was forwarded into certain industries; quotas of places in educational institutions were set; occupational training and professional re-training courses were offered. But no governmental directives or market mechanisms can drive the economy forward if there are not enough young people available.

The question is, can any arguments in favour of the economic growth and national security convince a married couple to have three or four children? Chances are, they cannot. Nobody would start a family for the sake of saving the country, especially if this is an abstract and irrelevant concept advocated by scientists and politicians and mocked by the army of professional scribblers.

The idea of saving the country should be intrinsic to an individual life and to be clear to the vast majority. If the Government adopts and implements concrete measures designed to overcome the population crunch, that in itself would build a framework for resolving economic and security issues. Only at that stage such measures, clear to all citizens, could be supported by ideology and by arguments reverting them from the child free lifestyle. Only then it would be possible to promote the idea of a large family, making it acceptable in people's minds and even trendy.

The record demographic collapse of the early 1990s did not happened overnight. The way for it was paved in the preceding decades. It is very important to understand the roots of the current demographic crunch. Many demographic experts share the view that the reason for the current decline lies in the "mortality shock", which was experienced by our population in 1992–1995 and is still acutely felt today. The uncertain times have put our compatriots in drastically stressful situations and reduced the lives of millions by years. The real cost of the turmoil for the nation is greater beyond comparison, as so many new lives were never conceived at all during that era.

After the year 2000 the birth rate has risen slightly, but the mortality rate is still on the increase. We are still carrying "the Russian cross" that appeared on graphs when the excessive mortality curve crossed the curve that reflected unprecedented decline in live births. According to official data the Russian Federation loses around 800,000 — 900,000 people every year. During the last 13 years Russia's population went down by more than eleven million. Three babies are born and four people die every minute in Russia. In China 38 babies are born and 16 people die every minute, whilst in the USA the figures are eight and four accordingly.

General statistical figures do not reflect the full scale of the demographic losses as they are concealed, to some extent, by the influx of immigrants. If the Government proceeds with the intention to grant amnesty to several million foreigners who are living and working in Russia illegally, the official statistics would be able to report a demographic improvement.

In writing about the demographic crunch I cannot help touching upon the sore subject of mass abortions. Russia's abortion rate ranks second in the world. For instance, the number of abortions per 1,000 of women aged 15–45 is seven in Belgium, eight in Germany and 63 in the Russian Federation. These days abortion falls into the category of free medical services. All attempts of my colleagues in the Rodina ("Motherland") parliamentary faction to put forward a proposal that the state must stop subsidising abortions that terminate millions of unborn lives have been met by officials with fierce resistance.

An introduction of an indirect incentive for a woman to continue with a pregnancy, like a "baby stipend" or a "demographic voucher" valued at 250,000 Russian roubles, clearly is never going to work on its own. The state has to stop the criminal financing of abortions. Imprisonment must be stipulated for such crimes as an abortion performed against will; coercing into an abortion; supply of materials for self-performed abortions. About 2 to 3,5 million of unborn babies are aborted annually; this is comparable to a war on a grand scale. These figures are scary, but even more terrifying are the proportions of the number of abortions to the number of live births — for every newborn in Russia there are two babies killed in their embryonic state. The state makes free abortions available, and this means that every Russian taxpayer is covering the cost of killing an unborn child out of his or her pocket. This is utterly immoral and, I should say, criminal.

Mass abortions must be stopped not merely by the deliberate efforts of the Government, but by collective willpower and a shift in attitude. The Government must initiate a full-scale public campaign to discourage abortions, with the use of media and the inclusion of television, prior to legislative moratorium on artificial terminations of pregnancy. It is no longer sufficient to dispute the subject; official propaganda is required now.

The true meaning of abortion is deeply repulsive, and this must be conveyed to the whole nation. It is necessary to awaken parental instincts in young people. Upon seeing an image of a fetus developing in a womb, many people will resolve never to kill a life that has already been conceived. At the same time, it is necessary to think of the ways to encourage and reward the medics who save an unborn human life from being cut short.

As yet, the negative view on abortions prevails in society, largely due to the efforts of the Russian Orthodox Church. The frequency of abortions has reduced by half in the last fifteen years. I believe that Russia will regain the traditional view on an abortion as a heavy sin; that this act will be amounted to murder and banned at any term of pregnancy with the exception of medical or moral grounds (such as a pregnancy resulting from rape).

Writer Yury Vorobyovsky gives an interesting historical reference against abortions in *The Russian House* magazine:

> *A distinguished French doctor Jerome Lejeune posed a question to a conference of obstetricians and midwives, "Dear colleagues, what would be your advice? You see a family in which the first child is born blind, the other child is deaf from birth, the third child is ill with tuberculosis. The mother has tuberculosis, too, and she is pregnant again...."*
>
> *His colleagues affirmed, "Abortion, of course!*
>
> *Then Dr. Lejeune said, "The outcome of that last pregnancy was a baby named Ludwig van Beethoven...."*

Besides, the ban on artificial termination of pregnancy is a part of the full version of the Hippocratic Oath taken by every newly qualified doctor of medicine: "...I will not give to a woman an abortive remedy." The version adapted by our Health Care Ministry omits that part. It is also desirable to make a ban on abortion a part of the Russian Fundamental Law, should the public deem such a measure justifiable.

If our liberals scream about "reactionary policy" again, maybe they should look up to their former American master, George Bush Junior, who introduced tough measures restricting pregnancy terminations. Arguably that was the only reasonable and useful deed that he had done during his term. In Russia, the issue of "life protection" is still decidedly marginal, and as to the understanding of its moral aspects, it is largely limited to followers of religion. The task of representatives of traditional religions of Russia is to progress from raising awareness of the issue in secular media and educational institutions onto a proactive public information campaign.

The nature generally allows for about 5% of all babies to be born with genetic abnormalities. Sadly, in the olden days many babies with disabilities were not making it beyond infancy or early childhood; the strong and healthy survived.

The "mass abortion healthcare" reversed this situation to the effect that the majority of healthy fetuses are aborted, whereas the weak and disabled survive due to the advance medical care. As a result of such health care, the Russian genetic fund started to deteriorate dramatically in the 1960s.

Obstetricians note an increase in pathology cases among women of childbearing age. Normal natural births account for 30% of all reproductive outcomes. More than half of all babies are born with some health deviations. Medical commissions note that about a third of young people of conscription age are not fit for army service.

What is probably worse is that the nation is not only shrinking in numbers but is degenerating "in quality", as more and more children are physically or mentally handicapped.

In pursuit of the additional state finance initiated by President Putin in 2006, regular schools are keen to accommodate as many pupils as possible so as to improve their statistics, mostly by keeping children with learning disabilities who would otherwise benefit from attending schools that cater for their special needs.

It does not take much imagination to know how years of studying beside a child with learning disabilities might affect a capable child.

The problem of neglected children goes hand in hand with the demographic crunch. Official statistics claim that there are 700,000 neglected or homeless children in Russia; unofficial studies suggest that the correct figure is close to 4 million, i.e. every ninth child. The majority of them are social orphans — children who were denounced or abandoned by their living parents. These children are an easy prey for criminals and abusers. Over a million of underage children were arrested for various crimes; 11,000 were convicted and are kept in juvenile prisons.

The other side of depopulation is the excessive mortality rate. Every year 2,300,000 people die in Russia.

The country also is ahead of the world in suicide rates — 40 people out of every 100,000 take their own lives, which is thrice as much as the average global rate.

Male life expectancy has fallen rapidly and is now below 59 years of age, which is lower than, for instance, in Egypt or Bolivia. To compare, male life expectancy is 77.3 in Japan, 77 in Sweden, 75 in the United Kingdom, 74.5 in France, 74.4 in Germany and 74 in the USA. Here one has to bear in mind that life expectancy started to grow in the USSR in the 1960s due to improved medical care and has been consistent with rates in leading European countries. People at that time could envisage the prospects for themselves and for their country. They had confidence in their future — something that was ridiculed at great length by journalists and TV jesters during Perestroika.

In fact, even all these figures do not reveal a lot. The full extent of the tragedy is not even the fact that our elderly do not live long lives, but that a great proportion of the population do not make it to the old age at all; many able-bodied men die literally of heartbreaks inflicted by the lack of personal prospects and hopes. It is no secret for medical practitioners that high mortality rate among the middle-aged and the elderly is largely caused by depression and despair. The reformists created a monstrous gap in the levels of income across the population. Whole generations were driven out to the margins of the modern life with a message that they were mere losers who had failed to find their way around in the era of total wealth-building.

Mortality is also very high among the young, which is linked to some other factors such as drug abuse and chronic illnesses inflicted by use of drugs.

Astute customs officials and Militia repeat in unison: it is necessary to impose strict control over the immigration influx that supplies heroin from Tajikistan to the Russian territory. As if to rub it in, our "liberals" respond with introducing a visa free regime for Tajikistan....

Astonishingly, this measure was explained something along the lines of Russians needing to be able to travel to Tajikistan on internal passports only. But is this what we really need? Exactly what is the proportion of Russians who require easy access to Tajikistan?

Heroin must be classified as a weapon of mass destruction in the genocide of younger generations of Russians, whereas production, delivery and distribution of heroin must be viewed as a full-scale assault on our country. According to the data from the United Nations Office on Drugs and Crime (UNODC), our special services confiscate about four out of approximately 70–75 tons of illegal heroin from Afghanistan that is smuggled through into the territory of the Russian Federation, i.e. less than 6%. The same UNODC statistics paint an equally grim picture of the situation on other routes. Countries of

Central Asia confiscate only about 5% of total heroin traffic volume, and Europe and Turkey — 9%.

In 2003 I happened to discuss the issue of Afghan heroin trade with the US Deputy Secretary of State Richard Armitage. In reply to my question why the US troops were not exterminating heroin plantators that had been steadily expanding during the years of the US occupation, the top American politician said, "But this heroin does not reach the United States!"

I think that his answer was very logical.

Recently the German press reported a scandal that rocked the top echelons of NATO. The unwilling perpetrator of the scandal was John Craddock, US Army General and former NATO Supreme Allied Commander for Europe[1].

It turned out that Craddock had ordered the execution of drug traffickers as they were deemed to be involved in terrorist activities. In the same letter Craddock ordered to bomb drug rehab facilities in Afghanistan.

Many NATO Generals categorically objected and did not wish to follow these orders. The "liberals" affirmed that the drug traffickers were not terrorists but criminals who should be tried, not executed. Apparently, the fact that the proceeds from drug sales were used to finance Taliban was of no major concern to them. I am certain that with such an attitude NATO would never win the war in Afghanistan.

The correct attitude to the problem of the current demographic crunch does not withstand hypocrisy. The same applies to the ethnic aspect of the problem. Research shows that the losses mainly affected the peoples of the Russian flatland. All ethnic groups that inhabit the flatland have shrunk by 10–40% in total, with the exception of Kalmyks and Bashkirs. All minority groups in Siberia increased in number by 20–40%. As for the large-numbered ethnic groups of the Caucasus, they have increased significantly; they almost doubled in numbers. Ossetians, who are the only Christian nation of the Caucasus, and Lezgins, are the only exception to this overall trend; both of these ethnic groups grew smaller.

It may be concluded from this data that the process of depopulation today is integral to the ethnic groups who are either part of, or close to, the Russian nation. Interestingly, the same process has affected Tatars

---

[1] On 1 July 2009 General Craddock has been replaced by US Navy Admiral James Stavridis.

whose reproduction trend copies that of Russians and not of the Islamic nations of Russia.

The birth rate is in decline across all areas of Russia with the exception of Chechnya. In all other regions and Republics of the Federation the birth rate is on the steep downfall. In some ethnic groups, such as Russians themselves, Karelians and Mordvins, this process already gained full speed. In others, it is a delayed threat that may only be lifted by a shift in the governmental policy. The first blow struck Russia like it happened so often in her history. The disastrous trend may be broken under one condition: if Russians and other indigenous nations begin a new life span and gain the will for revival and augmentation of the nation. As always, all other indigenous nations would support this trend if Russians would be the ones to pioneer it. The only alternative would be to invite immigrants of alien cultures, and that would undermine the right of our nation to exist.

We must encourage reproduction within the country instead of trying to improve the demographics by bringing into the country echelons of the Chinese, the Vietnamese, and the Afghanis. The sound demographic measures must take into account a real picture of birth and mortality rates in each Russian region separately. Such measures must be implemented to the full in those regions that are acknowledged to be "disadvantaged".

The governmental support must be selective and moderate in the demographically satisfactory regions, where the birth rate is stable and the indigenous population is growing; only the native population there should be entitled to the governmental support. If a region would demonstrate the stable natural growth of the population as a result of governmental demographic policies within at least four years, then that region should be re-classified as a demographically satisfactory one.

Another valid point of view exists: urgent measures of governmental demographic support must be directed not to the regions with plummeting birthrate, but to certain ethnic groups that experience this crisis. By them we mean Russians, Karelians, Komi, Udmurts, Mari, Chuvashi, and Tatars, as well as Lezgins and Ossetians in the Caucasus. At the first glance, such a policy might trigger an adverse reaction in general public, which is very sensitive to any ideas that are perceived to contain elements of racial discrimination. The public opinion can be and must be prepared for the acceptance of these ideas. The ethnic groups mentioned above are in the same demographic position today as is the group of indigenous small-numbered peoples of the North[1], which have been receiving the state support for a very long time. The issue is not just to maintain ethnical, cultural and folkloric identity, but also to save the ethnic groups that constitute the historical core of Russia. Governmental demographic policy can be differentiated both by geographical regions and ethnic groups.

The demographically stable Republics of the North Caucasus are in need of a different kind of support. High level of corruption, the spread of religious extremism, total disintegration of economic infrastructure and high unemployment as a result of it, are characteristic to those Republics. The governmental support in these regions must be designated to tackle those issues, and that would compensate for the fact that the demographic programme would not be applicable there.

The continuous child benefits must fluctuate in accordance with the level of income in families; however, a one-off grant upon the birth of a child must be the same for all. The total value of child benefits may vary from region to region (with consideration of extra provisions by local authorities), but in the demographically disadvantaged regions and categories this value must be no less than the equivalent of 20 minimum monthly wages. A progressive scale of payments with the birth of consecutive children in families must be established.

It is widely thought that Russian families have little or no motivation to give birth to the second or the third child. In reality, this is not the case. Every tenth family would like to bring up four or more children; one third of all families want to have three children; over half of all families — two children. A wish to have an only child or to remain childless is expressed in fewer than 4% of families. The problem is not that Russians have no desire to procreate, but that for some reason or other they cannot afford to. The major issue is the lack of housing; young families often have nowhere to live, and their only option is to share homes with their parents.

A special State Housing Finance Programme must be introduced in all demographically unstable regions (practically everywhere across Russia), which would be designed to provide credit finance to young families allowing them to buy their first homes. Such a programme may provide for 30%, 65%, and 100% credit write-offs upon birth of the

---

[1] Forty indigenous peoples live in Siberia, the Far East and North, such as Chukchi, Eskimos, Aleuts, etc.

second, third, and fourth child accordingly. Socially oriented businesses should be the Government's aides in this.

I do not agree with a view that married couples should be entitled to a financial grant solely on the basis of their decision to tie the knot. This is bound to give rise to a wave of fictitious marriages. Crooks would go through marriages and divorces repeatedly; the system would be abused, and the presidential programme of affordable housing, this good initiative of the Government, would be discredited and ridiculed. The state must encourage not the mere act of matrimony but the birth of children, when a married couple evolves into a large and content family.

As noted, the majority of young Russians think that a family should have two or three offspring. That is why the incentives for young married couples with children should be introduced in the regions with declining birth rate. A young family should be entitled to loans on preferential terms, including consumer loans, after their first baby is born. Upon the birth of their second child a couple should be receiving the whole social package which would include a free place in a nursery school; compensation of expenses for parents with children of school age; free use of public transport; free medicine for children; opportunity to buy children's clothes at discounted prices, concessions tickets, etc. Grandparents who devote much of their time to childcare are to be entitled to additional state pension benefits.

Over the last five years the number of people on nursery waiting lists has increased by four. A baby should be registered with a state nursery shortly after it is born. Russia needs about 2,000 extra pre-school nurseries. The cost of running the nurseries should be partially covered by the state, and partially by one-child families. Families with two children under the age of sixteen should be entitled to free places at a nursery. Some measures in support of foster family homes are needed as well.

I would like to stress separately that the job of a full-time parent must be viewed as being an equivalent of employment in public sector. If a woman chooses to look after her children on a full-time basis, she must receive a state salary equivalent to the national average wage. A mother who has brought up four or more children should be regarded as a citizen who has carried out her duty before society, and be entitled to the first category pension.

As to neglected and homeless children, I would accentuate the need for their adoption primarily by families in the Russian Federation as well as the need to set up a system of foster care that would replace the traditional orphanages. Families wishing to adopt an orphan should not have to pay to the state, as they would need the money for the child. The amount, that otherwise would have been spent on that child in an orphanage, must be made available to adoptive family, provided that they duly carry out their parental duties. Moreover, the Government needs to provide a legal ground that would enable the children who are adopted by a foreign family to maintain their Russian citizenship.

A full-scale designated campaign promoting family values; families of two parents and several children; mutual responsibility and marital fidelity should become an area of specific attention from the Government. We need a concise programme designed to establish a family cult, to sustain a socially attractive image of traditional family values, bring out motivation for child rearing, poeticize the state of expectancy and motherhood, and teach responsible fatherhood.

Propaganda and promotion of the perverse and degenerative forms of human behaviour, such as debauchery, prostitution, paedophilia and homosexuality should be the cause for criminal prosecution.

Instead of approving co-habitation, broken families, and other compromising forms of family relations as acceptable, it is necessary to form the adequate attitude to them. The foreign organisations which activities are aimed at the reduction of birth rate, breakup of family values, and promotion of an abortion as a method of contraception, should be named, shamed and banned from working in Russia. Those alcoholics who systematically undermine public morals must be forced by law to undergo compulsory treatment and rehabilitation. If this requires tighter, concrete legal definition, then it needs to be made in the shortest terms.

The television, this most powerful channel of public communication, should convey healthy life style messages to viewers. This should be done in an engaging and creative way, with the focus not on the process but on tangible results. Moreover, radio and television should come to terms with a ban on direct and indirect alcohol advertising.

Much harsher measures against the heroin aggression must be adopted. I can anticipate angry rejection of my idea by my partners in Brussels, but I will outline it nevertheless: in cases of heroin trade a moratorium on death penalty should be forgone. Death penalty must be applied to persons who are guilty beyond doubt of either production, or trade and distribution of heroin. In such cases, an execution should take place in five years after a sentence is passed, in order to prevent legal abuse. The law enforcement structures must be reliably controlled by the Parliament.

We have to acknowledge that the Russian southern border is an "open house". There all our border control points are nothing other than field gates. We must establish a proper border with Kazakhstan that would be impenetrable to criminals and illegal immigrants; incidentally, this border stretches for one fifth of the length of the equator. Our southern neighbours must be forewarned about the possibility of imposition of a visa regime for all countries of the Caucasus and the Central Asia, the area of drug smuggling routes into Russia, if these countries would not be willing or capable of putting an end to smuggling.

On the way to demographic recovery such a disgraceful social phenomenon as prostitution must be eradicated. The Russian Militia like to moan about how hard it is to uncover and close down the brothel chains, or to identify ringleaders and suppliers of "human commodity." This is a cynical brazen lie. Leaf through any yellowish newspaper and you will see plenty of contact numbers for various "VIP saunas" and "elite massage parlours" where in the clouds of hot steam priestesses of Love will generously share with you a bouquet of sexually transmitted diseases.

Prostitution that is killing the body and soul of the nation is currently "uncatchable" precisely because some Militia circles have appropriated control over this criminal business, taking it from actual criminals. The struggle must be commenced with the detection of werewolves inside Militia, those who have turned debauchery and epidemics into a source of private income.

I am convinced that the persistent practical implementation of these measures, along with democratic monitoring and without "excesses", will bring us closer to our main objective which I express as "our kin will not wear thin".

THE STONE GUEST[1]

Russia was never a country of immigrants, unlike, for instance, the United States of America. The vast majority of the population has always been indigenous. Throughout her history Russia absorbed various nationalities and ethnic groups together with the lands that they inhabited. The expanding Russia had been involving ethnic minorities and their habitats into the wholesome cultural and social circulation; we shared one fate and bread.

In this historical process the Russian nation acted as a consolidating and protecting force; Russia provided the nations of Eurasia with an access to universal knowledge and world cultures; Russia also gave these nations the freedom to develop their own cultures, native written languages, and, in some cases, own forms of governance. New human influx had been always growing at a relatively slow rate even in the periods of the most intense expansions of the national territory.

Unlike us, the United States thoroughly regulates the scale of immigration into their country. They endeavour to keep immigration within reasonable proportions over the recent years; the average annual population growth rate in the USA is 1%, only one-fifth of which accounts for immigration.

The situation in our country is quite the opposite. Immigration reconquista — something similar to the "great migration of people" — is taking place in defiance of our national traditions. According to the official statistics only, in the last decade Russia took the second place after the United States in the list of countries that are actively letting immigrants in.

So what happened? Why our country has suddenly become a popular destination for immigrants? There are two explanations for this.

The prime reason is the collapse of the USSR that, in turn, triggered the collapse of the system that divides labour between the Republics. Millions of people lost their jobs and found themselves on the edge

---

[1] *The Stone Guest* (1830) is Alexander Pushkin's powerful poetic drama based on the Spanish legend of Don Juan.)

of poverty. In the early 1990s a large proportion of highly qualified specialists, mainly of Russian descent, were forced to abandon their places of settlement in the Republics and fled to Russia under the wolf-whistling and jeering of local chauvinistic yobs; caravans of refugees and forced migrants staggered along. It was the first wave of repatriation.

Actually, I disagree with the customary interpretation of the word "repatriation". By definition, repatriation is the process of returning to a home country, but it would not be correct to assume that the home of Russians is limited to geographical borders of the Russian Federation. The Crimea, Donbas, Malorossiya, Kievan Russia, White Russia, the contemporary North and North-East of Kazakhstan, modern Latvia and Estonia, Transniestria — all these lands are cradles of the Russian nation and as such constitute parts of the Russian indigenous territory. Russians, as well as other indigenous nations, are in their rightful territory there.

The pathological greed and the criminalisation of our "business elite" are also at the root of the current massive immigration influx. That business elite is prepared to succumb to any criminal activity in order to squeeze maximum profits out of private industries, markets, and trade.

"The heavy step of a commander" of the immigration has muffled a self-preservation instinct in our entrepreneurs. Of course, initially the influx of labour force from Ukraine, Moldova, Middle Asia, and the Caucasus provided an ample opportunity to exploit immigrants with no legal consequences. But a couple of years went by, and exploiters regretted their course of action, as the uncontrolled labour force began to dictate its own rules to the market.

Liberals often refer to the list of occupations that are allegedly not viewed as prestigious enough by indigenous Russians, implying that without immigrant labour it would be impossible to get enough street cleaners, dustmen, plumbers, bus drivers and construction workers. It takes one glance at the current market situation to realise that such claims are a blatant lie. Unemployment has been high in Russia, particularly the hidden unemployment, and particularly in the period of financial and economic crisis. If employers were prepared to pay good wages for physical labour, then hiring Russian citizens would not be a problem. Their logic is simple: why overpay Russian citizens when there are so many foreigners around who would be happy to do the same work for peanuts?

Statistically, the rate of illegal immigrants to legal ones is 9 to 1. For example, in 2009 the Federal Migration Service officially registered 1.8 million immigrants, out of which only 270,000 were in registered employment. What about the rest; what are their occupations? And are all immigrants registered officially? And how many more immigrants live in Russia illegally?

Experts estimate that currently there are about 20 million illegal immigrants in this country, in other words, one fifth of all economically active population. At the same time, unemployment rate among Russian citizens remains very high. Almost 6.6 million (7.7% of the economically active population) are unemployed, and this number continues to rise as a result of recession. The sheer volume of immigrants is putting a pressure on social services. The state is obliged to meet newcomers' social demands; it has to provide them with adequate health care, schooling for children, and improved housing. If the number of newcomers exceeds the capacity of the state to accommodate them, then the house would become too crowded for its hosts.

The illegal immigration causes far greater damage to the country and the population. Unlike the people who are here legitimately, illegal immigrants pay their taxes not into the budget but into the pockets of corrupt officials and ethnic mob bosses, whereas Russian taxpayers have to cover the overheads of the illegal immigrants' stay.

Immigration does not solve the problem of workforce and skills shortage. There are practically none highly skilled workers among the uninvited guests. At the same time, the crime rate among Gastarbeiters has increased threefold in the last decade and continues to rise every year. Eight out of every ten street robberies and muggings are committed by "illegals". There is a threat that immigration would become a factor of social destabilisation.

Cases of money extortion from immigrants by the corrupt officials and Militia officers are commonplace in Russia. Illegal immigrants themselves also contribute to the process of corrupting the law enforcement system, as, in many instances, banknotes are the only convincing document that they are able to produce.

Repatriates encounter artificial barriers set up by officials in obtaining citizenship, in registrations at residential and temporary addresses, gaining employment and accessing social services such as health and childcare. At the same time, there are many thriving commercial firms that in exchange for relatively small sums readily "assist" just about anyone in obtaining paperwork required by the monitoring bodies. For example, one such firm offers certificates of the HIV test for about 100 Roubles (approximately 2.2 Euros) that one can get without taking the test; clients part with this sum and receive a certificate confirming that they are not infected.

As estimated by experts of the Russian Interior Ministry, the annual turnover of the fake documentation produced for the black market labour is at least 140 million USD in Moscow alone.

It is not completely out of the ordinary for the so-called employers to lock away passports of their immigrant construction workers, thus rendering them to a state of slavery or quasi-slavery; even though, sadly, in the aftermath of the two Chechen wars people in Russia are probably no longer shocked by the modern slavery.

Other, graver problems exist, too. Non-residents take out of the country and transfer overseas about 6 billion USD in cash every year. The Central Bank noted some cases when the citizens of some "brotherly countries" were withdrawing from bank accounts and, most probably, taking out of the country the sums of 20, 30, and 50 millions of USD in cash!

It is hardly a secret that illegal migration into the Russian Federation is the most important, if not the only one, source of refilling financial balances in some of the former Soviet Republics. We are aware of it, but we still tolerate the inappropriate behaviour that some of those countries display towards Russia, even though the physical presence of their huge ethnic diasporas in Russia provides us with a powerful instrument of influence on those countries' foreign policies.

The term "migration" (*migratio* — Latin) is only correct when it is applied to movements of birds and wild animals. When referred to humans, the word "migration" may have several meanings. Returning migrants, i.e. people returning to their native land, is one of them; when bearers of foreign spirit and customs arrive into a country, it is not migration but something else altogether. Just because the two categories are a part of the similar process, it is not acceptable to define them by one and same term "immigrants".

Finally, transit migration also takes place when people come to Russia regarding it as a transit base for a further move into Europe. Unfortunately, migrants in pursuit of such a transit are helped by dozens of thousands of firms including some travel agencies; such companies and their names and logos often provide a cover for organised criminal activities.

The exploitation of illegal immigrants by dishonest businesses with silent consent of regional authorities creates a favourable climate for street crime and other criminal activities. This is very alarming. The riots and arsons of the Autumn 2005 in Paris are a vivid example of what might happen.

Living and working in Belgium, I learned that the uncontrolled expansion of illegal immigration is a growing concern for all European nations. The Flemish and the Walloons are becoming alarmed by illegal immigrants and foreign criminals who are overtaking their city, aren't they? What exactly is happening in today's Europe that fears the immigration flood?

In January 2008, in Brussels, when I assumed the office of Permanent Representative of the Russian Federation to NATO, the first thing I had to look into was a sharp increase in the number of street assaults on Russian women who were either members of our diplomatic mission, or our diplomats' wives. In the period from January to April 2008, seven female Russian citizens, residing in Belgium, became victims of street robbery. As the police never replied to any of the diplomatic note that we had sent, I insisted on a meeting with the Minister of Internal Affairs of Belgium.

The Minister did not bat an eyelid when, by way of an explanation, he informed me that the growing street crime rate in Belgium was an objective factor and that "foreign diplomats should bear their share of sufferings on a par with Belgian nationals." This sounded quite extraordinary to me. I can imagine a fuss that would arise should seven Belgian diplomats' wives happen to be randomly assaulted and mugged on the streets of Moscow. A single case of a foreign diplomat becoming a crime victim would be an emergency event in Russia.

I always have and continue to hold an opinion that when it comes to protecting interests and honour of our countrymen, we have to shred the false delicacy that was pointed out by Dostoevsky as one of our negative features:

> *In Europe they look upon us derisively, while the best and indisputably clever Russians are regarded in Europe with haughty condescension. Even emigration from Russia — i.e. political emigration with complete renunciation of Russia — has not spared them this haughty condescension. The Europeans simply did not want to acknowledge us as one of their own, despite any sacrifices we made and despite the circumstances: Grattez le Russe, they would say, et vouz verrez le Tartare*[1]. *And so it remains to the present. We've become one of their proverbs. And the more we tried to please them by despising our own nationality, the more they despised us. We wagged our tails before them, we made servile confessions of our 'European' views and convictions, while they haughtily ignored us and usually added, with a polite smile, as if wanting to be rid of us as quickly*

---

[1] "Scratch a Russian, and you will find a Tatar."

as possible that we simply 'misunderstood' things in Europe. They were amazed that we, being such Tatars ('le tartare') had been entirely unable to become Russians; and we never could make them comprehend that we wanted to be, not Russians but cosmopolitans. It is true that lately they have managed to understand something. They have understood that we want something, something that for them is fearful and dangerous; they have understood that there are many of us — eighty million — that we are aware of and understand all the European ideas and they are not aware of our Russian ideas; and even if they did become aware of them, they would not understand them; they know that we speak all their languages, while they speak only their own. And many another things they have begun to realise and suspect. The result is that they have plainly labeled us enemies and future destroyers of European civilisation. You see how they have interpreted our passionate goal of becoming cosmopolitans!

After the Moscow Duma elections I visited France. In a series of meetings in the Government, the Senate, and the National Assembly I had an interesting discussion with a certain MP from a right-wing political party. There was a poster on the wall in his office featuring a copy of the famous *Freedom at the Barricades* painting by Delacroix with the tag line *"France: Love it or leave it!"*[1] I had a good laugh imagining how the "liberal community" at home would react to a similar slogan relating to Russia. In France, this politically correct country, people openly discuss immigration and national relations issues and debate the political and legal aspects of immigration and national identity; such debates are narrowed down to the need to respect and support immigrants' authentic national feelings, combined with the requirement to smoothly integrate them into French civil society.

By the way, in 2010 major Western politicians admitted the overall collapse of the so-called "multiculturalism", based on the false understanding of tolerance towards the imported by immigrants manners and behavior. Here and there right-wing EU politicians began calling against alien presence and went even further, attacking the religion of the majority of these aliens — Islam. The response followed rather quickly — Islamists cursed the West, and to counter-balance the right wing their ultra-leftist counterparts began emerging in European politics. The process completely undermined traditional and existing since the post-war years party system where the left and right wings have so far been interchangeable and didn't differ integrally. As

---

[1] "France, ou tu l'aime ou tu la quitte!"

a matter of fact, Europe itself is now at risk of disintegration due to the false premise of tolerance towards an alien cultural influx that may be seen as an aggression of sorts against customs and traditions of the host culture.

The Russian Federation should be an open country; however, the Government must adopt a clear, concise and consistent policy in relation to foreign workforce; such policy must reflect interests of indigenous citizens, first and foremost. Today, immigrant labour does not stimulate tangible economic growth but merely feeds irresponsible attitude of some employees; it breaches Employment and Labour regulations; it contributes to unemployment among Russian citizens, due to very low wages paid to immigrants, and often directly and aids indisputably criminal activities within certain businesses or industry sectors.

Entire business empires were built on the exploitation of disenfranchised immigrants' cheap labour, primarily in retail, construction and service industries. These business empires have been taking advantage of the lack of antidumping norms in the Russian law, which would have set a minimum wage rate adequate to the needs of citizens of Russia. So at the moment, they use gaps in the law that allow them to pay much smaller wages, not to pay taxes or insurance on behalf of illegal workers, and be negligent about health and safety regulations.

The construction mafia treats illegal workers worse than cattle. There were cases when workers on "grey" sites were not being paid upon completion of jobs. Workers who protested and demanded payment were menaced and some of them were murdered!

The supply of illegal immigration into Russia exceeds the demand for labour, which reduces the demand for the indigenous workforce down to zero. 40% of graduates from vocational training colleges and schools are unable to find work that would match their skills. At the same time, trade collectives of surviving factories and industrial plants consist of "reserve" pensioners.

The situation with emigration from Russia is also not to the country's benefit. 3.4 million emigrated since 1992, mostly skilled specialists and young scientists who went to join the economically active population in their destination countries. The so-called reform of the Russian science resulted in near-total disintegration of it. The emigration of scientists; the predominance of old-aged staff in the surviving scientific laboratories; the decline of science schools; the loss of research and technologies — it is all happening along with influx of the unqualified and uneducated mass of immigrant labour. People of no particular profession come to Russia to live, whilst top class scientists and professionals leave the country.

Of course, immigrants *per se* do not represent a threat to contemporary Russia. It is highly dangerous to count on the immigration as a means to resolve the demographic and economic problems; this would amount to the rejection of the indigenous population, which would be a direct threat to the survival of the Russian nation.

Immigration policy should be designed for the benefit of the nation. We must aspire to preserve the traditional spirit and the way of life that are inherent to our country and our civilisation, which means that Russia must encourage only the kind of immigration that would not undermine our values, our culture and customs. Immigration policy must be directed at the stabilisation of the ethnic composition of Russia and her specific geographical regions. Such policy must ensure that all citizens, regardless of their ethnicity, have equal civil rights; it would also help to preserve the authenticity of each indigenous nation and of Russia as a whole. We must throw away the fig leaf of political correctness and declare openly which immigrants we would like to welcome into the country and which we would not.

A welcome immigrant is a young person who is keen to work honestly in Russia, who either has a good command of the Russian language or is willing to learn it, and who shares the values of the Russian civilisation. In short, a welcome immigrant is a person whose cultural adaptation would not be overly lengthy or costly.

Belonging to Russia's indigenous ethnic groups must facilitate the process of obtaining Russian citizenship. The Russian, or other indigenous ethnic ancestry, must be an additional facilitating factor.

A good command of the Russian language must be a crucial condition not just of obtaining citizenship, but of a prolonged stay and work in Russia, in particular in the areas where intense communication is involved, such as the retail industry, education, service industry, mass media and public sector. Widely available language courses and a compulsory language test for immigrants would be useful in the expansion and promotion of the Russian language and culture and, ultimately, of the Russian influence abroad.

Russian Federal Law should impose quotas for admitting immigrants from particular countries and establish principles on which such quotas would be based. Immigration barriers must be minimal for the people who would easily adapt to life in Russia and who would be able to become an organic part thereof (this refers primarily to our compatriots abroad, i.e. citizens of Belarus, Ukraine and Kazakhstan).

An initiative to establish the so-called Slavic Trade Union is worthy of serious consideration. By this we mean a formation of a national professional trade union of workers from Ukraine, Belarus and Kazakhstan. The purpose of the Union would be the protection of workers' rights, assistance in legitimate job search in Russia, ensuring that jobs are undertaken under employment contracts that clearly define terms and conditions, salary, principles of taxation, holiday entitlement, etc. If we wish to sort out our immigration policy, attract young professionals and skilled workers to work in Russia legally, and educate immigrants in the spirit of respect for our country thus jeopardising economic foundations of the ethnic mob, we must find our own ways to remedy the existing situation which at present is a threat to our national interests.

The current situation in Russia is so critical that only a technological growth spurt can save her from declining any further, otherwise her physical disintegration is unavoidable. The following conclusion is obvious: Russia should become a Mecca for creative individuals and inventors from all around the globe, who would be capable of bringing in the technologies of the future. Russia should encourage scientists and inventors, primarily the ones who work on breakthrough technologies, to arrive into the country; it must be a matter of priority in the immigration policy. One might argue that this constitutes a policy of bespoke immigration, but, as they say, good things come in small packages.

The headhunting must be conducted with the help of the Russian diplomatic missions abroad; non-governmental organisations specially designed for the purpose must be set up to make enquiries within the "new economy" sector, in high technology industries and corporations, and in research and technology parks. The "import of brains" via the immigration strategy is not merely desirable but plainly necessary. We have to literally lure valuable human resources into Russia.

The definition and screening of "unwelcome immigrants" is one of the sore issues of putting the immigration policy to order. The influx of large groups of people of the same ethnic origin, who form enclosed separatists enclaves in the territory of Russia, is particularly risky. Such enclaves in the near-border regions are yet more dangerous as they will certainly lead to the further estrangement of these areas.

At the first sight, it seems that immigrants without Russian roots represent a cheap labour option. In reality, however, their capacity to quickly build ethnic-based criminal structures is very costly to the state. Indigenous population either gets under the pressure of ethnical crime, or is pushed out of the lucrative and profitable business sectors. This, in turn, escalates social tension and leads to ethnic rivalry. Clearly, this kind of immigration is hostile to us.

In the absence of an elementary order in the governmental immigration policy, ethnic mafias act as an intruding aggressor. By managing shadow clans of diasporas, the mob occupies entire sectors of economy and overtake the most attractive lines of businesses; the mafias' inside agents penetrate the Militia and corrupt regional authorities. The system of clans evolves indefinitely, and, as such, it is incapable of a reasonable self-limitation. One example: it takes one representative of a "diaspora" to achieve a position of some significance in a structure today, and tomorrow his numerous close-knit relatives and homeboys occupy all available positions in the same structure.

When market traders of the same nationality settle near their selling spot, it gradually results in a formation of a ghetto. Residents previously living in such a neighbourhood realise that the reputation and social environment of their area is now damaged, and set out to leave their long-inhabited homes.

An outbreak of segregation occurs as a result; the Russians tend to frequent one restaurants and shops, the Asians prefer others, and the Caucasians yet others. Such a "separate diet" only serves to deepen the mutual distrust and weaken the traditional community, which divides against itself into clans and Diasporas and steeps into ethnic dissension as a consequence.

Under the existing conditions of globalisation, criminal immigrants, who penetrate the businesses with quick capital turnover and opportunities for tax evasion, are using Russia as a gigantic money-laundering outlet. Fake trade contracts, unprofitable barter deals, over- or under pricing, bond speculation, unrestricted inflow or outflow or cash — all of the above allows for the illicit movements of funds and serves to legalise criminal profits.

As a general rule, the professional crime syndicates in Russia are ethnic-based. Even the most decent individuals among the illegal immigrants tend to stick with their fellow countrymen upon arrival into our country; thus, the enclosed national communities are formed. This environment is conducive to ethnic-based organised crime. "National" criminals seduce their compatriots into people trafficking, prostitution, drug smuggling and drug trade, apart from tax and business crimes. Clearly, the expansion of such diasporas cannot possibly have a positive impact on the national demographic situation. The Ministry of Internal Affairs claims that there were about 2,000 ethnic-based organised criminal groups actively functioning in the territory of the Russian Federation in 2004, out of which 516 were based in Moscow. Covered by the support of the city authorities, they ran the traffic of illegal migration on an international scale and managed the proceeds from it.

In this connection, it is interesting to refer to an interview by Saakashvili quoted by Information Agency *Rosbalt* on 31 March 2009. The interview was astounding in the extent of its openness:

"Ninety percent of the organised crime leaders in Russia come from our country. Our major export item into Russia is not the wine but the "thieves-in-law," criminals, and the like."

The unfortunate Georgian führer, not without a grain of boast, reminiscences furthermore: "A mere few years ago, when the thieves were arriving to Tbilisi from Moscow, they were escorted all the way from the airport; top officials of our Interior Ministry accompanied them into the best hotels and they partied together in the most famous restaurants".

Indeed, it is something to be proud of!

Whilst it is not entirely clear what was the reason for such sincerity on Saakashvili's part, in his interview he merely confirmed our theory that ethnic mafias' capitals are a solid surplus to the budgets of such countries as Georgia, that export national organised criminal structures into Russia.

In order to resist the illegal and unwelcome immigration, we need to enter into agreements on either visa-free, or simplified, entry into Russia only with those countries that would be prepared to sign re-admission agreements with us and assume legal and financial responsibility for repatriation of illegal immigrants, citizens of these countries. Generally, a basic order must be introduced into the system of a visa-free entry into Russia. Visa-free regime on the Southern direction must be foregone altogether; or, at the minimum, people from there should be able to enter Russia on a single type of document, such as their national passport for international travel. After foreigners cross the Russian border they should pay a fee for a personal immigration card containing biometric data and other information that would allow law enforcements authorities to exercise due control over labour immigration.

At the moment, it is possible to enter Russia on eighteen (!) different types of ID; they range from an old internal Soviet passport to a staff pass of the kind "Passport of Sailor of Tajikistan," despite the fact that insofar we were not made aware of the existence of a sea in that mountainous Asian Republic. It is hardly surprising that the relevant Russian authorities are not able to determine the authenticity of some such documents. Moreover, one could legally enter Russia merely on a birth certificate of a Soviet type, which is a folded sheet of paper with no official stamps or a photograph. Imagine a startled expression on the face of your average Militia sergeant who stops a suspicious person on the street to check their ID: he questions when and how a "stone guest" has come to Russia and asks for a registration proof, and the answer he gets is something along the lines of "I arrived yesterday on my birth certificate which was not stamped at passport control as stamping birth certificates is unheard of".

It is beyond my understanding what idiot and for which payment could have possibly agreed to introduce visa-free travel into Russia on the high-risk directions favoured by illegal immigrants the most, especially when they are able to travel not on passports but on birth certificates. As to the old Soviet passports, no Russian authority including our distinguished Special Forces can explain who got hold of the 23 million blank Soviet passports that were left beyond the Russian borders after the USSR ceased to exist. When I was heading the State Duma Committee on International Affairs, I repeatedly demanded a complete report on the fate of the blank passports from the federative authorities and insisted that the passports be destroyed.

A concise governmental immigration policy should be set against the current spontaneous "unwelcome immigration." Such a policy should comprehensively take into consideration the interests of national businesses and economy. Work immigrants, especially the ones from the culturally alien countries and regions, should be invited into the country exclusively to meet the particular requirements of an employer in Russia and become the responsibility of that employer. If this would be the case, foreign workers will have a right to enter Russia only on a genuine invitation from an employer for a specific period of time, which would be limited by that employer's requirements and the purpose of stay.

An employer must assume responsibility for the settlement of such immigrants in Russia and make sure that the medical, administrative and other conditions of their stay are observed. If a proportion of foreign workers in an organisation exceed 15% of the total number of staff, a special additional tax must be imposed. Personal criminal liability and sanctions for use of illegal workforce must be imposed; such sanctions may stretch to withdrawal of licenses and winding up businesses.

At the same time, highly skilled foreign workers should be offered favourable terms and working conditions, social guarantees and, should they wish, a fast track to Russian citizenship. Of course, the Government has to make a special effort in order to return our scientists and specialists who emigrated during Perestroika. A distinction between "welcome" and "unwelcome" repatriates is inappropriate; all of them are Russian citizens by right.

Quotas must be introduced in respect of foreigners who are looking for work in Russia, just like it is done in civilised countries worldwide. Diffusive settlement, which would prevent formation of ethnic ghettos, must be an essential rule in this type of immigration. For example, immigrants from China would settle evenly in between the settlements of migrants from other countries (such as the Koreans and the Vietnamese), which would prevent the formation of compact settlements with their autonomous infrastructures, communication systems, illegal financial structures, own laws and norms of existence. Carelessness in this matter might cost us a half of Siberia.

The sooner we impose a legal order in our immigration system, the better. We need to begin not by deporting individual illegal immigrants, but by ruthlessly suppressing ethnic mafia and eradicating corruption, which are thriving on the invasion of the "Stone Guests."

NOTES FROM THE DEAD HOUSE[1]

The processes that are developing in the Russian internal migration are no less dramatic. The most serious threat to national security and well-being lies in the disproportion between the European part of Russia with its 3/4 of the total population and economic potential, and Siberia and the Far East, which are inhabited by a mere 1/4 of the total population and amount to 3/4 of the country's energy and mineral resources.

The level of population density in Siberia is seven times lower than that of the European part of Russia. Moreover, seven million people in the Far East seem negligible when compared with hundreds of millions Chinese that inhabit the neighbouring territories. Imagine, if the population density in Russia were the same as in Japan, the Netherlands or Belgium, then the number of our citizens would be over six billion — same as the population of the entire planet!

Siberia and the Far East are the future of Russia in the new century. Russian monarchs, as well as Communists who replaced them, had never underestimated the utmost importance of developing the Russian Asia. Population of the Far East had increased threefold from 1926 to 1959 partially due to the internal migration, whereas population of the Russian Soviet Socialist Republic had grown by less than a third in the same time period. The migration inflow into the Far East in the 1960s and the 1980s contributed to the population increase by another two thirds.

However, in the 1990s due to the downfall of domestic production of commodities the migration process has reversed. Today a continuous outflow of population from the twenty-six administrative regions of the Far East and Siberia into the European parts of the country was registered. The number of people who live in the Far East today fell by about 20% compared with twenty years ago. Thus our richest land is turning into "the dead house".

The "deadening" of these territories adds to the problem of intense immigration flow from the neighbouring countries, primarily from

---

[1] *Notes from the Dead House* (1862), or *The House of the Dead*, is a novel in which Fyodor Dostoevsky describes life and characters of the convicts in a Siberian prison.

China. Our "liberals" should not indifferently brush aside the problem of "the Chinese expansion." As it is, population density on the Russian side of the border is one person per one square kilometre, whereas it is 125 per one square kilometre on the Chinese side!

While we are idly assessing the risk of divestiture of the Eastern Siberian territories, this process is already underway. It just takes a mere 1% of the population of the People's Republic of China to settle in the Russian Far East, and we can bid farewell to our strategic resources of oil, gas and water and mineral resources, and ultimately to the territory as such.

As yet, a state of conflict with Russia is not in the best interests of China. I can explain why. China buys modern weaponry from us; the military budget of China is on the increase by 10% annually. Beijing is developing the more backward western provinces of China with the aid of the Russian energy resources. China needs Russia not because we are a friend, a comrade, or a brother, but because we are the "reliable back" for the Chinese — the strategic backbone to draw resources from. China requires these resources in order to sustain her imperial ambitions in the South-East Asia. One of the Government leaders of this ambitious great country personally as much as spelt it out for me, and I think he was being sincere.

Two million people have moved to the European part of Russia from the other areas of the country over the last twelve years. The power of this human Gulf Stream has rearranged the proportionate distribution of population density in the Asian and the European parts. The internal migration pattern is the following: the main volume of migrants goes to the European Russia via the "Krasnoyarsk buffer"; the work migrants from Irkutsk partially settle in Krasnoyarsk; in turn, the migrants from Primorie and Khabarovsk fill vacant jobs in Irkutsk. Finally, Primorie and Khabarovsk absorb human resources from Chita[1] and the Northern areas. Thus, the migrating resources are stretched to the limit, as the donor regions do not have sources to draw extra people from. The regions of Yakutia, Magadan, Chukotka, Sakhalin, and Kamchatka are deserted more and more with each passing year.

It has to be taken into account that not only China but Japan, too, is closely watching the process of the human dry-out in Siberia and the Far East; the Japanese are waiting for the right time to commence political conquest and economic development of the South Kuril Islands; Japan

---

[1] *Chita* — a city 900 km east of Irkutsk. It is the administrative centre of the Zabaikalsky region of Russia.

has already begun to put her audacious territorial claims in legal forms. Whom shall we blame when our precious territories are lost due to our own bungling?

The weird and unhealthy migration patterns are also observed within the European part of Russia. Firstly, a Russian village is diminishing and turning into a "dead house", too. When I used to go hunting in the sticks of Russia together with my friends, we saw so many of these abandoned dead houses. Have you ever seen wild animals — foxes and bears — inhabiting deserted and dilapidated huts and chapels? Well, I have, and let me tell you, it is a grim sight.

The demographic potential of a Russian village is exhausted since the 1970s; a village no longer has anyone to send to a city. Now foreign work immigrants take a place of the "city peasants" of the past. Neither the foreigners nor the internal migrants from the East want jobs in the depth of the country. Primarily Moscow and the Moscow region are attractive to both of these categories; other megapolises follow closely, particularly in the South of the European Russia.

In the circumstances of the lack of conditions for simple reproduction of the nation the national genetic fund is being burnt in the cauldrons of megapolises.

This nightmare scenario — the swelling of cities and the agony of villages combined with the overpowering migration and the gradual capitulation of the North and the East of Russia — must be wrapped up and rejected as a malevolent one.

I envisage our future strategy in "a turn to the East", i.e. in the new colonisation of the Far East and in building an industrial carcass across the country. A significant amount of energy must be concentrated in "the backbone and the stiffening ribs" — in Urals and West Siberia. The Far East must become the new national gravity centre to counterbalance Moscow.

The centre of global activity is confidently shifting toward North-Eastern Asia; the Far East borders with Mongolia, China, North Korea, as well as with Japan and American Alaska by sea. This creates gigantic economic prospects and opportunities for us.

A turn to the East as an imperative of the governmental policy is necessitated by the Russia's demographical objectives of Russia and by rapidly advancing external challenges. Moreover, the meaning of our turn to the East would be the purposeful development and settlement of the Eastern lands; the new colonisation of Siberia and the Far East and the break-through into the global market of the densely populated and rapidly progressing Asia.

The highest stakes must be put on the young generations of Russians. Young people re-settling in the East and their participation in strategic projects must be encouraged with provision of well-paid jobs and housing on preferential terms; with sound social packages when an offspring comes along; by other viable material incentives. Voluntary resettlement of young people must be supported by the generosity of the state and by the stable growth of prosperity.

The future of Russia is in the East, on the shores of the Pacific Ocean. The sooner we realise this, the closer we will come to the national revival of Russia.

TARAS BULBA[1]

The process of national aggregation is the cornerstone of the patriotic project of national preservation, development, and growth. We have to reverse the process of erosion of the Russian ethnical core, which has been going on throughout the 20th century. The modern colonisation of Russia by groups of non-Russian ethnicity is largely of the archaic, trading character. The state must act in the interests of own development.

The return of Russians to the Motherland is a condition and a pledge of success in implementing the priority plan of economic development; importantly, it is also a crucial factor in the spiritual growth of villages, small towns and communities inside Central Russia, as well as in the revival of the Russian Far East. The Russian returning migrants represented a sufficiently high proportion of the overall immigration influx, particularly in the first half of the 1990s. In the recent years, however, the percentage has diminished significantly. Those who wished or were forced to return to Russia have already done so.

We have to realise that it is the duty of the Russian state to accommodate all compatriots who express the wish to come here to stay; this includes the unemployable and the people of old age. Proper care for the elderly is a distinctive characteristic of a cultured and a civilised nation.

The project of national preservation presupposes the understanding of the fact that the nation consists not only of citizens of the Russian Federation as such. The Russian nation comprises those who love Russia and relate to her culture, history and people; therefore, the concept of the nation encompasses our compatriots who, often unwillingly, found themselves beyond national borders, primarily in the aftermath

---

[1] *Taras Bulba* is a historical religious novel by Nikolai Gogol. Taras Bulba is an old Ukrainian Cossack who fights together with his two sons against the Poles who rule Ukraine west of the River Dniester. When one of the sons falls in love with the Polish princess and goes over to the other side, Taras Bulba allows his execution. The novel has been cited as the seminal work establishing the concept of the "Russian Soul".

of the collapse of the USSR. Being an integral part of the nation, these compatriots are fully entitled to move to Russia, following her much shrunk borders.

The descendants of emigrants who were driven out of Russia by the Communist Revolution and Civil War or who found themselves abroad in the turbulent wartime years are our compatriots, too, provided they have preserved the sense of belonging to Russia. We have to recognise that their rights in the territory of our country have a priority over the rights of foreigners.

I would like to stress once again that it is necessary to review and alter radically the existing attitude to the issue of granting Russian citizenship. It is great that the President restores Russian citizenship for the distinguished descendants of emigrants. However, this very action is evidence that the awards of citizenship are exclusive and may be subject to unaccountable personal tastes.

Under the current historical and demographic circumstances there could be no possible justification for the artificial constraints in the process of obtaining citizenship for individuals who have natural entitlement to it. Every ethnic Russian, or a member of an indigenous ethnic group of Russia, or anyone born to a Russian parent must have a lawful right to obtain a Russian passport upon the first application, i.e. automatically. I wonder how anybody could possibly debate this.

Germany, Japan and France, that had lost the majority of her colonies, returned practically all of their abroad compatriots following the active relevant policies in the post-war years, whereas Russia returned only 12%. We intend to give a right of return to the mother country to Russians and to members of other indigenous ethnic groups abroad.

The geography of "the Russian House" is not confined to national borders of the Russian Federation. The voluntary reunion of Russia, Ukraine and Belarus — the cause for which fought Taras Bulba and millions of his followers — is a key issue in the progress of our civilisation.

Today we must help the repatriates who have already resettled in Russia some time ago. Hundreds of thousands of the Russian compatriots lead a wretched existence; they live in huts in unsanitary conditions; they stand in exhausting queues for Russian citizenship, being sent away by officials with demands to come back with more paperwork. Before we accommodate newcomers in their dozens of thousands, we must pay closer attention to those who already live by our side and are persistently ignored by officials.

National preservation also means a reunion of nations who used to share one life and one fate. In order to gather Russian lands together it is necessary to have a centre of gravity; indigenous Russia must arise from the ashes of internal calamities and lead by example.

The former Soviet Republics (an expression that is much disliked by my colleagues in NATO, oh well) must be transformed from a hostility belt into a Russia-friendly environment; their nations must be encouraged to see the need to protect themselves from foreign dependency and demographic downfall that is happening at the similarly speedy rate there as it does in Russia. We must create conditions for voluntary reunion of the country within the natural geographic borders.

This is a much more serious task than the alleged re-establishment of the "Russian sphere of influence" that is sending the West into a panic. No, ladies and gentlemen, we do not intend to "influence spheres"; what we want is to aggregate the Motherland. A new political and cultural nation will be built in the process of this national aggregation. Only then our nation will be able to maintain its sovereignty and survive in the ruthless geopolitical race.

MY TENDER
AND AFFECTIONATE BEAST[1]

The autumn of 1996 saw Alexander Lebed sacked from his post of Secretary of the Security Council. The official reason for his dismissal was fancily worded as "...forming of unlawful armed units". The Kremlin had cynically used the charismatic General for the purpose of securing Yeltsin's power and afterwards threw him aside like some processed material, which was exactly what Lebed appeared to be in their eyes.

Ivan Rybkin, "a very flexible politician" and at one time Speaker of the State Duma, was appointed to fill the vacant position. By the time of the 1995 elections, the spineless Rybkin managed to lose the last remains of his authority and grew totally dependent on Berezovsky; Rybkin had no choice but to make the latter the Deputy Secretary of the Security Council despite all the speculations in the media on Berezovsky's dual citizenship, one of them being Israeli! Ivan Rybkin was elected into the State Duma from the Anna district of the Voronezh region; the district accounts for nearly half of the agricultural land and a quarter of population of the largest blacksoil Voronezh region of Russia (the town of Voronezh itself was not a part of the constituency). After Rybkin left the State Duma to join the Presidential Administration, by-elections were announced in the district. I resolved to test myself there.

My family is linked to the Voronezh region through my greatgrandfather, Boris Nikolaevich Mitkevic-Zholtok. As I previously explained, he had been one of the first Russian military pilots to fight in World War I. Despite his aristocratic descent, Mitkevic-Zholtok did not emigrate in the aftermath of the Revolution. The young Soviet country

---

[1] This title refers to a 1978 Soviet film. The film is an adaptation of Anton Chekhov's story *The Shooting Party*, also known as *The Hunting Incident*. It is a story about a country girl and three men who are fascinated by her. The soundtrack, the waltz, is very popular and lives a life of its own.

was in need of military specialists, and so my great-grandfather was invited to serve in the Red Army. In the 1930s he was a commander of an Aviation Regiment located in the city of Tambov and was directly involved in establishing first aviation schools in the Soviet Union. One such school was opened in the city of Borisoglebsk — an old provincial merchant city where cultural traditions that are long lost in metropolises are still preserved sacredly.

Voronezh region was an arena of severe battles between the Soviet and the German armies during World War II. Hardly anything remained of the city of Voronezh, which was split between the enemies by the river in the course of fighting. However, Borisoglebsk, the second most significant town of the area, was left intact. Not a single German bomb fell upon the city.

I tried to understand how such a miracle could happen and thought up a quite astonishing version. In the 1930s the German air cadets used to train in the aviation school that was founded by my great-grandfather, among other people. Naturally, the cadets used to go out in town in their free time where they could meet local girls; romances flourished. The romantic relationships proved to be so strong that even during the cruel war that followed the German Luftwaffe pilots were protective of the town where their girls lived. Indeed, love can overcome war.

Citizens of Borisoglebsk welcomed, and provided permanent settlement for, about 15,000 refugees from Tajikistan, Uzbekistan and Chechnya in the 1990s. The largest community of migrants was formed there. Their representatives frequently came to Moscow to resolve various issues and often stayed in the KRO executive offices. These people were the key influence on my decision to run in the by-elections.

We had just one month to conduct the election campaign. I traveled thousands of kilometres of country roads, holding hundreds of meetings; I received thousands of pre-election mandates from ordinary people. During my extensive travels across the region, the true scale of poverty, in which Russian people live, was revealed to me. There was no access to basic commodities, such as gas and heating; proper bathroom facilities were hard to find. Even communal baths, this essential feature of the Russian rural life, were almost all shut down in the course of Perestroika. Local village clubs suffered from neglect, and schools were dilapidated. The vast majority of the collective farms and agricultural communes had gone bankrupt and could no longer afford to pay wages to their members. On top of all that, pensions were paid out irregularly.

The refugees who settled in the Russian provinces having miraculously survived the Caucasian wars and ethnic cleansing had to exist in unbearable conditions. Many of the refugees carried on living where they had been initially housed — inside giant metal bunkers on the outskirts of Borisoglebsk. In winter, it felt like the freezing Antarctica, in summer, like the baking hot Sahara Desert. This is not to say that the Government had not been sending inspectors to the area, but those inspections did not change a thing.

One would be forgiven for thinking that someone was deliberately using the desperate circumstances of the refugees in Borisoglebsk to demonstrate to the Russian compatriots beyond the national border, who in their naivety looked forward to compassion and assistance, that back home nobody cared about them. At any rate, I cannot offer a better explanation of such a devil-may-care attitude that local administration displayed towards the Russian refugees.

Nevertheless, people in the Voronezh region did not become bitter and wrapped up in themselves even in living conditions that were far from civilised. If a place, where the national culture is still preserved and maintained, exists at all, then the Russian provinces are such places. Russian peasants are deserving of utter respect. Villagers are tough, smart and witty. They would not accept just anyone immediately and would watch you closely before opening an embrace.

There was a curious episode during my election campaign. I went to visit a rather large poultry farm. The farm's director was a beautiful tall Russian woman, bossy, as she kept ordering her colleagues around.

She sat down with me at the table, poured me some tea with honey, and said, "Feeble are our men lately! Put one underneath, and he would suffocate. Put him on top, and he'd be seasick. Put him on the side — he'd be crying for a mummy's breast! Ugh! I can see right away — you are a good man. Don't make any promises, we'll vote for you anyway!"

More accustomed to a rather different, the Moscow University manner of speaking, I could not help laughing at her words. Of course, what she really expressed was the desperate need of the ordinary people of Voronezh for a protector of their interests in Moscow; someone who would be strong, robust and independent of local clans. And their choice fell on me.

In March 1997, after the exhausting campaign, I won over my main rival, a candidate from the Communist party, and was elected Deputy of the State Duma where I joined the Committee of Nationalities.

My first legislative initiative was a draft of the proposal entitled

"On Development of the National Culture of the Russian People". That legislation act, if ratified by the Federal Assembly, would have defined Russians for the first time as "the nation that is key in the state development; is segregated and autochthonous throughout the whole territory of the Russian Federation". My proposal outlined the task of overcoming the existing segregation of the Russian nation as being one of the Governmental objectives. I suggested that the Government should prepare annual reports on the demographic situation in the country, the social self-perception of the nation, and the course of implementation of the programme of the Russian reunion. The reports were supposed to be presented to both Chambers of the Parliament at the end of every year.

It seemed that there could be no reasonable objections to that.

The draft law met an objective requirement of the national development at that stage; executive power institutions were supposed to assume a legal obligation to secure the well-being of the host nation, which was conditional to that of other nations in Russia. That was it. As it turned out, not everyone shared my view.

My legislative initiative stirred emotions at the top of the pro-governmental party "Our Home is Russia" as well as in the Yeltsin Administration. Typical procrastination under the various excuses followed, such as: the draft lacked the resume of the Government; a feasibility study had to be attached; the draft had to be distributed across all administrative regions for the review, and so on. One has to give credit to the parliamentary majority of Yeltsin's time — they had imagination and astuteness when they needed to wrap up a potentially risky draft law.

Passing time in the Duma pushing a pen was a hopeless waste; when this became all too clear, I started to look for a more worthy field in which I could apply myself to the benefit of KRO and in the interests of my constituents. That is how I came to occupy myself with the liberation of hostages — Russian soldiers, civilians, and construction workers who were abandoned in Chechnya by Russian authorities after federal troops were withdrawn from there. To begin with, I submitted a request to the Army Commandant of Voronezh to provide me with the official records of the number of conscripts from Voronezh who had gone missing in the rebellious Republic. The records showed that there were eighteen of them. The Russian Defense Ministry had no knowledge that would have thrown light on the location or a state of health of these soldiers. However, with the help of the Commission on War Prisoners Tracing we managed to establish the circumstances of death of three of the conscripts.

Strangely enough, the two abovementioned structures belonged to the same institution of executive power, but they were never exchanging information on the subject; each structure was taking its own steps to trace missing soldiers and officers. Moreover, the Government consistently refused to subsidise a much-needed technical update of the Rostov Genetic Research Laboratory where the remains of perished servicemen had usually been sent for identification. Bodies, and fragments of bodies, of hundreds of servicemen killed in Chechnya were kept in mobile refrigerators and stayed unidentified for years.

Agents of both the Defense Ministry and the Commission on War Prisoners Tracing carried on their searches in Chechnya independently, often putting their own lives at risk; a lot of the effort could have been saved, if DNA tests were duly carried out and processed. In short, it was "business as usual". I was pleasantly surprised when the State Duma passed my amendment to the 1998 budget, which had a provision to allocate some of the funds to the development of the Rostov Genetic Research Laboratory. The amendment helped to remedy an absurd and embarrassing situation.

Great help in releasing hostages who had been kept in captivity in Chechnya came from Nadir Khachilaev, State Duma Deputy elected in the constituency of Dagestan. This young, tough and charismatic man from the Caucasus was the Chairman of the Union of Muslims of Russia and the leader of the national movement of the ethnic group of Laks. He had some influential friends in Chechnya. After Raduyev's armed gang launched a terrorist attack on the town of Kizlyar, Khachilaev started to express his hatred for Chechen warlords openly and, as far as I know, had brought revenge on a few, whilst still maintaining his contacts in the separatists' circles. The Khachilaev clan was in conflict with the Dagestani establishment and soon went into opposition. On the demand of the official Makhachkala, the State Duma stripped Nadir off his parliamentary immunity accusing him of "organising mass unrest". When that happened, Nadir abandoned his home and, together with a group of supporters, took refuge in Chechnya across the border from Dagestan.

Nadir was demanding justice and fair treatment for himself and his family. He insisted that he remained State Duma Deputy and a true patriot. Driven by the desire to prove his cause, he kept "bombarding" the Kremlin with enquiries on the facts of corruption in the Dagestani government and in Makhachkala Mayor's office. In his free time Nadir searched for, and arranged releases of Russian hostages in Chechnya, often paying up a ransom for them. Such was this Robin Hood of Dagestan.

Every time I received a relevant message from Khachilaev's associates, I flew over to Makhachkala, traveled to Khasavyurt and from there headed for Chechnya via the Novolak region. Usually we never had to wait long at an agreed meeting point; Nadir and his people tended to appear suddenly beside our "khaki vehicle" and delivered to us yet another soldier, who had been exchanged from Chechen bandits and was barely able to move. We used to drive a liberated hostage in our car following the same route back to Makhachkala, where we used to stop for the night in the massive family home of the Khachilaevs. There a released lad could wash, have some light liquid food which would not make him collapse after a long period of starvation, change into some clean underwear and go to bed. They seldom managed to get any sleep. The released soldiers, having survived the ordeal of captivity, humiliation and beatings, all as one asked for some smoking material and spent all night just sitting at the front steps of the house, smoking and staring at the stars that were shining in the dark sky of the Dagestani night. In the morning we were taken to the airport where Khachilaev "had his people", who made sure that my precious cargo and I boarded a plane bypassing passport control and customs. As a deputy of the State Duma I was entitled to a free flight with no allocated seat, and, of course, hostages never had any proof of ID on them.

Fearing that the whole operation might fail, we usually gave the released hostage a chance to call home right before boarding. The times were uncertain; the warlords' agents infiltrated the Government and the law enforcement institutions of Dagestan, and no precautionary measures seemed excessive to us. The plane was usually full. Throughout each flight a ticketless hostage was locked in the front toilet right beside the pilot's cabin, and I sat opposite the toilet on a suitcase. Strangely enough other passengers hardly seemed to suspect anything and were using the toilet in the back of the plane. Nobody had ever voiced frustration by the inconvenience caused by a locked front toilet; or maybe people figured out what was going on.

Weeping relatives would collect a former hostage on our arrival to Vnukovo International Airport in Moscow. We carefully avoided any leak of information, particularly to media, as that would have inevitably disclosed the route and the mechanism of the hostage release operations. Publicity would have put an end to any future "field trips" and therefore to the very lives of the captured soldiers.

Sometimes other people went to Chechnya instead of me. Once Nadir told me that Minister of Internal Affairs Vladimir Rushailo had approached him with a similar request, and so on behalf of the Minister the Deputy on the run looked for certain people sunk in the black hole. I am certain that this was truly the case. The tough man seldom joked and never lied.

My most vivid memory of the hostages is of 72-year old Vitaly Kozmenko, a construction worker, one among the many sent to Chechnya to carry out the "reconstruction works". Vitaly was kidnapped and held hostage for fourteen months in the damp basement of a family house. He survived the ordeal due to his amazing willpower and wits. He persuaded his captors to supply him with some wooden boards; he slept, did some physical exercise, and generally lived on those boards in the basement for over a year. To save himself from losing his sanity and to be able to feed his mind, Vitaly begged the Chechens to drop down to the basement all the reading material that they could find in the house; there were mainly some prison memoirs (maybe, the monster family had a special affection for prisons) and poems by Yandarbiyev, my old "chum" whom I met in the residency in Starye Atagi.

A few journalists witnessed the release of Vitaly Kozmenko. Khachilaev was in need of public approval and so he asked me to invite the press along on that occasion. All the way from Khasavyurt to Makhachkala, the old man, incredulous of his miraculous escape, was reciting poems by the Ichkerian president; he had learnt those poems by heart under the light of the gas burner in the pit during his endless agonising imprisonment. Vitaly Kozmenko was not cursing his tormentors, but kept recalling how the whole family used to gather around the table to have their meals right above the door to the basement where the old man had been kept. All members of that family, young and old alike, were aware of the elderly hostage wasting away right there, in the basement of their house, and, apparently, considered it to be a trivial matter. As if in a hurry, the man could not stop sharing with me further details of his ordeal, and I was wondering to myself, how did he sustain the will to live; from where did he get this remarkable ability to preserve human dignity in such inhumane conditions? The strength of his spirit kept his body going, and we know that the resilience of the Russian spirit and character has no limits.

Our last attempt to send home a large group of fighter pilots that were released from Chechen captivity ended in disaster.

The people from Nadir's team called me again in May, 1999 and asked me to fly over to the Caucasus urgently. Nadir knew that on that particular occasion a large group of the so-called visitors was supposed to meet him for the purpose of picking up the released pilots, but he still asked me to come along to assist in making sure that the handover of hostages went smoothly.

Nadir Khachilaev was in despair. His petitions were being ignored by Moscow. It was unsafe for him and his team to stay in Chechnya for as long as they had done already. Nadir was eager to return from exile; he was hoping that he deserved to do so by merit of personally rescuing dozens of Russian soldiers and officers. But they did not think so in the Kremlin, and wanted the unpredictable, harsh man in Chechnya, and only there. Various officials used Nadir in rescuing hostages from Chechnya with fanfare, thus trying to publicly redeem their own crime of allowing the warlords to gain the upper hand in Grozny. Khachilaev's name was certainly never mentioned in official reports, and all the credit went to some officials.

Khachilaev was at a loss. In defiance of any common sense, he decided to arrange the handover of the captured pilots to a Russian Parliamentary delegation headed by "the Soviet nightingale" Joseph Kobzon, singer and "distinguished entrepreneur" who had a wide circle of the so-called business associates among Chechens as well as in Moscow high society. Nadir chose to forgo the customary secrecy of our operations and exposed the next one to TV networks. As Nadir explained to me later, he was motivated by a desire "to let them know at last that I am a parliamentarian who carries out his duty to voters and to the country, and not a traitor".

Of course, that was the climax of insanity. Khachilaev had an explosive spirit but a reasonable mind, and such an idea could only have occurred to him in the circumstances of isolation from the outer world. Unfortunately, I knew nothing about the proposed scenario of the events, otherwise I would have done my best to convince Nadir not to turn the undercover operation into a live performance. When I found out, I was at the Chkalovsky military airport base on the outskirts of Moscow, and it was too late for me to refuse to go to Chechnya.

The Commander-in-Chief of the Russian Air Force afforded his private plane for us to go and bring the released pilots back. I found out that it was not just Joseph Kobzon, but that the whole parliamentary delegation was flying to Chechnya for the purpose. Among others, the delegation included Valery Kurochkin and Telman Gdlyan, as well as the Deputy Commander-in-Chief of Air Force whom I do not wish to name for ethical reasons. A bunch of the writing and filming reporters accompanied the delegation.

The whole set-up would have been more appropriate on a private holiday flight to the Canary Islands then on a rescue mission to Chechnya. In the Makhachkala airport we were met by what seemed to be the entire Dagestani government, who gathered there not as much to honour the delegation but to greet Kobzon (who incidentally at the last minute cancelled his trip under an excuse of being unwell). Even though Kobzon was absent, "the dear guests" were invited to meet leader of the Dagestan Republic Magomedali Magomedovich Magomedov. The authorities were clearly stalling for time and trying to sabotage our trip to a Chechen village of Zantag where Nadir and the hostages were due to meet us.

In the atmosphere of confusion I took an opportunity to get away from the VIP escort. Together with Alexey Zhuravlev, my assistant from Voronezh, we took another, more modest car and drove off, leaving Makhachkala behind. I instructed the Laks driver to shake off the surveillance and to head for Chechnya by the route that I knew like the palm of my hand. We passed OMON check point by Novolak village and entered Chechnya.

I instantly identified a house where Nadir was waiting for us. There was a machine gun nest made up of sacks of sand in about ten metres away from the house, and it would have been hard to miss. An old Lada with toned windows was parked nearby. The driver seat door flung open and my old pal Vladimir Kozlov emerged out of the car. Kozlov was a gutsy young General who at the time headed the Main Office for Combating Organised Crime in Ministry of Internal Affairs of the Russian Federation. He arrived to the village earlier than me, probably by a day or two, and stayed there, eagerly anticipating the handover of hostages. As I was telling him about "the wedding procession" that was to follow shortly, I could see from his expression that he smelled trouble. The pompous convoy of black BMWs and white Mercedes' inescapably attracted death, like a magnet. It was a prey that the field fighters could not resist, and that was exactly what happened.

Nadir had been inside the house waiting for his contact to show up, when, all of a sudden, a procession appeared from over the mountains. Minibuses filled with TV reporters with their equipment closely followed the cars carrying the parliamentarians in search of an adventure. "Circus is coming to town," came to my mind. At that point Deputy Commander-in-Chief of the Air Force, in plain clothes, came into the house. He was already slightly drunk, which was a sign that the meeting in Makhachkala had been a success.

"So, where are my pilots?" rubbing his hands, the heroic Deputy Commander addressed Khachilaev.

"They will be here soon. We have to wait." Khachilaev replied.

I sat down by the window and watched the road that ran in the middle of Zantag. Presently three military trucks appeared from the direction of the village. The trucks suddenly stopped, and armed militants ("Gorrillas," was Nadir's derogatory remark) started to jump off the trucks, one after another. To my estimation, there were about 150 heavily armed young fighters, all of them camouflaged and with masks on their faces. In split second, they semi-circled the front of the house and laid down onto the ground, following a command. Next moment they jumped up simultaneously, ran forward for about ten metres, and were on the ground again. Proceeding this way, 'gorrillas' cut off all possible escape routes for us.

We all ran out of the house. General Kozlov had a hand grenade on him; he got into his car and observed the events from there. The Deputy Air Force Commander locked himself in the outdoors toilet at the far side of the back garden. He sat there very quietly, possibly having immersed into the character, so quietly that later we nearly forgot about him and almost left him behind after everything was over.

I was a bit slow and so found myself in the centre of the semi-circle at the gunpoint of about 150 weapons. I had my service pistol in the inside pocket of my leather coat. Wanting to reach for the weapon, I stopped myself, thinking that I better not make any jerky movements in front of the militants. Besides, what use was my "fly-flap" against a squadron of professionals?

A group of scared and sobered reporters kept close together, like sheep in a flock, about fifteen metres away from where I was standing. The cameramen were brave — they were trying to film everything as best as they could under the circumstances. Maybe a professional habit of watching the world through a camera lens eventually suppresses the feelings of fear and the understanding that the recorded events are real. The warlords jumped up again, ran for another few metres, and fell onto the ground, as if they were acting for the benefit of the cameras. The circle narrowed. Now a distance of about fifty metres separated them from us.

In the meantime, Nadir was calmly observing the militants through his binoculars. He claimed to have recognised the leader's face, a large robust individual who was issuing orders to the 'gorrillas' in a harsh voice. "These people are not Chechens," Khachilaev whispered and, lifting his arm, started to walk in the direction of the field commander. Later we discovered that our attackers were Avars — the Wahhabi from Dagestan who had been trained by Basayev and Arab militants. The people who had informed the Avars of our scheduled arrival knew all the details of the forthcoming operation. Apparently, someone in Moscow leaked that information. I wonder if that was the reason why very well informed Soviet Nightingale Joseph Kobzon suddenly cancelled the trip to Chechnya. The warlords were hoping to hit the jackpot — to take valuable hostages and get hold of the expensive cars and equipment.

Khachilaev seemed to be cool and collected, but it was obvious even from the distance that he was engaged in a tense dialogue. By all accounts, the rescue of the pilots had already failed, so Nadir's next step was to prevent the taking of more hostages. He had to move the people who arrived to collect the pilots away from danger.

I don't know what made me join in the conversation between Nadir and the field commander. I came up to them, greeted the warlord as if I had met him before, and asked if he wanted to hear the latest Moscow anecdote. He was interested. The anecdote was about how God once allowed a righteous man to visit Hell so that he could see for himself the torments of sinners. However, the sinners had thrown a lavish party for the man, and he very much enjoyed his short trip to Hell. So the man asked God to be sent to Hell forever. When God did just that, the righteous man bitterly regretted his wish; devils were frying him up, saying: "Now you know that you shouldn't mix tourism with immigration!"

The warlord liked the joke. He roared with laughter and then looked me in the eye and asked:

"So what do you mean by that?"

"Well, these people came here as tourists. They don't know that it is hell here, and you are the chief devil!" I said with a smile and indicated the group of the Duma deputies and reporters.

"All right, give us the money and get lost," and he waved at his warlords who promptly got up from the ground, split into three groups and headed towards their trucks. The tension began to fade.

"Just look at us. Who in their right mind would come to Chechnya with a load of cash?" My heart was beating fast but I tried my best to demonstrate indifference. Only conspicuous self-confidence could possibly impress armed bandits in situations like these.

I left Nadir one to one with his compatriot and went to talk with

Telman Gdlyan, State Duma Deputy, one of the few who managed to remain calm in that dramatic moment. Telman made sure that everyone got into the vehicles, and we slowly drove off heading back towards the Dagestani capital. 'Gorillas', too, boarded their vehicles.

When our convoy had finally left the ill-fated village far behind and out of sight, we stopped. The reporters got out of the cars and started gulping vodka that had appeared from God knows where. They drank in silence; the bottles were passed around. Then all returned to their seats, without saying a word, and the cars were on the way to Makhachkala again. None of the "tourists" mentioned the hostages. Thankfully, they were finally rescued a month later, that time with no grand processions and no fuss.

I returned home thoroughly convinced that the second Chechen war was inevitable in the not too distant future. I saw with my own eyes the young Wahhabi warlords from Dagestan trained by Arab and Chechen terrorists. My prognosis was that these warlords will act as a "fifth column" of the separatists and will be prepared to launch a full-scale war against Russia in the whole territory of the North Caucasus, from the Black Sea to the Caspian Sea. My premonition was absolutely justified. The war in Dagestan broke out three months after God helped us to escape from the imminent captivity.

An unusual visitor brought back memories of the events in the village of Zantag two years later. He was wearing civilian clothes again, and I did not recognise him at first. He turned out to be the same Deputy Air Force Commander who was with us in Chechnya. I hoped never to see him again, or at least not to have to deal with him. Of course, I did not forget how he was hiding in the outdoors toilet from the warlords.

But the General was comfortably sitting in the chair in my office, presenting me with some paperwork. He had prepared a draft of my recommendation, addressed to President Putin with a request to assign the honorary title "Hero of the Russian Federation" for "the outstanding courage displayed on a critical mission" to the bastard. With no hesitation, the General explained the reason for his visit and his request: "My sons are growing up and they are in need of a role model". I had to shove the beggar out of the door.

Every time when I recall the dramatic events that took place in Zantag in May 1999 I feel guilty because, hurriedly evacuating the people from the village, I never said farewell to Nadir Khachilaev. Dozens of Russian hostages, including one conscript on my "Voronezh List", were rescued thanks to Nadir. I do not know the whole truth about what Khachilaev had done and why the Dagestani Government had turned against him so badly. Shortly after the events of May 1999 Nadir was arrested and later acquitted. In 2003 he fell victim of a hit man. Who had commissioned his death, remains a mystery to investigators and myself. All I do know is that Nadir Khachilaev returned many Russian boy soldiers back to their mothers alive; those soldiers, disregarded by politicians and abandoned by the Army Commandment, survived against all odds and came back home. And for that I will forever remember my "Tender and Affectionate Beast" with fondness and gratitude.

THE GAMBLER[1]

The year 1999 was abundant with dramatic events. Prime Minister Yevgeny Primakov was dismissed, and a short-lived reign of Sergey Stepashin followed; shameful broadcast on state television of a sex video showing a man who looked a copy of Prosecutor General Yury Skuratov in the company of two prostitutes and the subsequent scandalous dismissal of the top prosecutor; fierce battles took place between the clans of Yeltsin and Luzhkov for places in the State Duma; Boris Berezovsky formed the pro-Kremlin political movement Unity; a series of apartment buildings explosions in Moscow organised by Chechen bandits; Wahhabi intervention in Dagestan; and, last but not least, Vladimir Putin entered the large-scale political arena and, referring to Wahhabi, promised to "sink them in a loo". The pre-term resignation of President Yeltsin was the final accord of 1999. "Tsar Boris", who had brought Russia so many troubles, handed the key over to Vladimir Putin and left the Kremlin for good. Everyone breathed a sigh of relief.

Young and energetic, Vladimir Putin got down to business straight away. Closely following the decisive presidential measures on re-establishing order in the North Caucasus, I was saying to my colleagues, "This guy is going to render KRO jobless". Frankly, I took a liking to "Putin the Hawk".

Having come first in the toughest elections of December 1999, where the governor of the Voronezh region and his network of Communist campaigners were in an open confrontation with me, I began to serve my second term as State Duma Deputy. I successfully defended my PhD thesis on the subject of philosophy of war in the Lomonosov Moscow State University a few months before the campaign (I had earned the Master's Degree back in 1996, a few weeks before our first successful

---

[1] An amazing short novel by Fyodor Dostoevsky about a young Russian tutor who is in employment in a noble but impoverished Russian family in Germany. The novel reflects the writer's own addiction to roulette. Dostoevsky completed the novel under strict deadline to pay off his gambling debts.

election campaign). The topic of my thesis was relevant to modern times: *"Russian National Security on the eve of the 21st Century."*

In January 2000 the newly composed State Duma elected me the Chairman of the Parliamentary Committee on International Affairs. The job presented unique opportunities for implementation of my academic findings and ideas in the practice of parliamentary diplomacy. Busy at work or on work-related trips for weeks on end, I still found time to compile and issue the Glossary *War and Peace in Terms and Definitions* in cooperation with several prominent military scientists. My father helped me tremendously in this huge work. Of course, we had scarce resources to promote the Glossary. I personally purchased 5,000 copies from the publishers and donated them to the Defense Ministry and the Education Ministry to be distributed in libraries of military schools and academies throughout the country, as well as in military departments across civilian universities.

I have to say, my candidacy for the position of "the chief parliamentary diplomat" was not to everyone's liking. Some time later, patriarch of the Russian politics Yevgeny Primakov himself told me about the hysteria my appointment had caused in "liberal circles" and among Luzhkov's aides. Mr. Primakov was even delegated to speak to the new President about securing my dismissal. Later, "the Wise Primus", as he was affectionately nicknamed by my colleagues, acknowledged that I was doing a good job as head of the Committee on International Affairs and apologised to me in the presence of President Putin.

Relations between Russia and the European institutions were under the sharply increasing strain in February 2000, which was caused by the opposing views on the methods of our military campaign in Chechnya. The Council of Europe and its Parliamentary Assembly (PACE) took up the role of conflict instigators. In response, the State Duma and the Federal Assembly appointed new members to make up the Russian delegation to PACE, and I was elected to chair the delegation for the duration of my term as State Duma Deputy (prior to that the position's turnover had been high).

The Russian permanent delegation participated in the Council of Europe Parliamentary Assembly plenary sessions since 1996, when our country became the 39th member of this international organisation. There are twenty-four State Duma Deputies and twelve Federal Assembly Deputies in the delegation.

In April 2000 we faced a scandalous discussion on "the grave human rights violation in the Chechen Republic". Russian Foreign Minister Igor Ivanov suggested that we missed the session in Strasbourg altogether.

"Man, let's just skip the trip! Let's delay sending the registration form, and we will not be accredited in time. Let them have a chat in our absence and calm down at that," insisted the head of the Russian Foreign Affairs establishment. I disagreed, saying that it would be better to cede the Council of Europe altogether than to wail and tail away. "If we are confident in the correctness of our position, why must we avoid a discussion with the European parliamentarians?" Disappointed, "the dove of peace" Minister Ivanov reported to President that "Rogozin is frenzied" and instructed his Ministry to take the wait-and-see approach.

Indeed, the April session of PACE did not hold in store any joys for us. The Westerners were buzzing in anticipation of an opportunity to rub it in and to clear score with Russia for her position on Kosovo, however timid, but, nevertheless, different from that of Europe. Objectively, the excesses of the Russian military operations in Chechnya provided ample grounds for criticism. Moreover, our delegation had the "fifth column" within — the opposition group made up of "the liberals" of the State Duma; "the conscience of the nation" and "professional dove of peace" Sergey Adamovich Kovalev was among them.

Mr. Kovalev was always on a look out for a chance to do dirt on Russia and personally on me, and "old pal" of his.

We knew the scenario of the forthcoming public humiliation of Russia in Strasbourg: if our delegation does miss the session, it would be ridiculed and deprived of voting rights; if it attends the session, it would be denied voting rights all the same and forced to sit in a "naughty corner". I was not happy with either of these options. I arrived to Strasbourg, the Alsace capital city, fully intent on publicly defending our right to resist separatism and terrorism. I was not going to bow and scrape in front of the political pygmies of PACE, neither did I wish to appear rude. What we thought of ourselves was more important than what they were going to think of us. Strasbourg was a perfect test of political courage for my parliamentary colleagues.

I began to prep our delegation ahead of time: "It is crucial for us not to be intimidated. The main thing is to not be afraid of our own opinion or responsibility. Remember, we can only win if we play as a team!" Nobody had any objections, apart from the three renegades who had ignored the delegation meeting held prior to the assembly. It was a threesome of "plucked doves" — two Yablochniks (members of "Yabloko" coalition)[1], who were of the opinion that "we must be

---

[1] Yabloko (Russian for "Apple") — the Russian United Democratic Party Yabloko, a social liberal party originally established as a public organisation by Gregory

friends with the West even when they are wrong", and, of course, our omnipresent "bird of peace" Sergey Adamovich Kovalev.

Finally, the Black Thursday — the day when the Chechen dossier was scheduled to be on the agenda — arrived. The Assembly Hall of PACE was full. Visitors' boxes were occupied by the Strasbourg onlookers and by the dregs of "Ichkeria" that had comfortably settled in Europe under the semblance of unfortunate refugees. Everything was ready for the public whacking of Russia, and so the show began.

The microphone was passed from one passionate orator to another. Every speaking "dove" was describing events in Chechnya, as if they had personally returned from there. Every next speaker seemed to try to outdo the previous one at the art of telling stories of "the atrocities of those Russian military". In contrast, none of the speaking Lilliputians referred to the warlords as bandits or terrorists, preferring to use such expressions as "partisans", "freedom fighters", "rebels," and "autonomists". The term "warlords" was the harshest form of reference to Chechen fighters, but even that term was voiced just a couple of times during the three and a half hours of the session's duration. The triumph of double standards and hatred towards Russia was clearly manifested in that audience.

The detailed account of "the Russian Army crimes" was supported by verbal "documentary evidence", supposedly thrown in for good measure by Movladi Udugov and his aide "professor". As if drawing physical pleasure out of it, the members of PACE were savouring with gusto the gruesome details of Moscow's cruelty.

I don't think that someone who ever witnessed the horrors of any civil war and seen bloodshed of civil population in real life would feel that it appropriate to share their impressions in public with such enthusiasm. Notwithstanding our delegation's vociferous protests, the participants of the show continued to stick to their scenario. Our amendments to the final document were unanimously rejected, and each new allegation against Russia was accepted with the same unanimity.

The European populace was entranced by the list of Russian atrocities presented by a succession of PACE speakers. The sounds of a woman's sobbing were coming out of a visitor's box. Two speakers had the floor, one after another: Lord Judd of the United Kingdom and a social democrat Rudolf Bindig of Germany. Bindig's father was one of those "blond beasts" that had intervened upon the Russian land under Hitler's

---

Yavlinsky in the early 1990s.

command and met their death there. Maybe, the son of the "tourist" wanted to clear score with Russia, too.

Having worked up the audience to a suitable state, the pair of "doves" put forward a resolution that demanded to initiate the procedure for the suspension of Russia from her right to vote during the whole period of the assembly. However, the most diligent russophobes did not stop at that: they suggested suspending us, Russians, not just from voting, but also from speaking from the PACE tribune.

If this resolution were adopted, our delegation would have been left with a limited choice of either sitting nicely, like fluffy toy rabbits, on the "penalty bench" at plenary sessions of the Assembly, or never coming to Strasbourg at all.

Interestingly, none of the European parliamentarians went to the length of putting forward a proposal to exclude Russia from membership in the Council of Europe. They could afford to be spiteful against us, but still wished to continue living at our expense. When Minister Kozyrev agreed upon the matter of Russia's accession to the Council of Europe, this European waiting room, with President Yeltsin in the middle of the 1990s, he also persuaded the President to undertake the financial obligations of the main sponsor of the Council. From then on, 20 million Euros were sent from Russia to Strasbourg every year, which accounted for 13% of the Council of Europe's gross budget. This amount even exceeded the official contribution of the Russian Federation to the United Nations! In return for this inexplicable generosity, Russia received the right to send to Strasbourg the representation of 36 members of the Russian Parliament four times a year, again at own expense, who went there only to be scolded by the Western democracies on a regular basis, much like some inveterate underachieving schoolboys for their overdue homework.

After the exposure to what had essentially been an irredeemably anti-Russian activity of PACE, I made five (!) attempts to convince President Putin, whenever I met him, to cut down the monetary contributions to PACE. Each time he expressed an agreement with that and endorsed my paperwork by his signature, ordering fulfillment, but things still are where they had been — at the beginning. I wonder whether our officials will ever learn to treat an endorsement by the country leader with due respect, and whether they will finally leave the slanderers of Strasbourg without their crème brulee for dessert.

Coming back to the events of the PACE session in April 2000, at last, the heated discussion was over and the voting by a show of hand began. Not that the arguments put forward by our delegation had completely failed to achieve a positive effect, as some of the European representations, namely the Italian and, partially, the French and the Spanish, did not support the suggested sanctions against us. Our buddies from the former socialist camp, though, showed their rotten nature in full glare.

In the end, the resolution on suspension of the Russian delegation from its right to vote at PACE plenary sessions was adopted. Everything else, such as access to the canteens and restrooms, and even an odd squeak from a tribune, was graciously allowed.

As the Chairman of the Russian delegation, I was called out to speak. I knocked on my mic and, with due attention, looked at the audience.

A few hundred self-contented European parliamentarians, who had just ridiculed Russia and the truth behind her, were looking at me triumphantly.

You have just been picking on my tragic country that had to face the aggression from chauvinists and separatists. We came here specifically to tell you about Chechnya and the North Caucasus and introduce the people who rendered the armed resistance and defended their homes from the bandits and the rapists. We wanted to find ways to resolve these difficult problems together with you, but instead you preferred to impersonate teachers that scold the unreasonable Russians.

You are not teachers. You are pupils, just like we are. If you were proper teachers, we would be sitting here today writing down your recipes for solutions to the problems of Ulster, Corsica, and the Basque terrorism in Spain. If you had managed to find a wise and bloodless way to put a stop to wars in Kosovo, Serbian Krajina and Bosnia, we would be applauding you now.

Unfortunately, we have not seen you succeeding in those areas. Who gave you the right to lecture us, when you are the feckless masters in your own European house?

As to the adopted resolution on suspension of our delegation's right to vote… Ladies and Gentlemen, I did ask you to be polite! We called for a dialogue of equals and urged you not to humiliate us, because we are the colleagues of yours. You, however, did the opposite.

As for your freshly adopted resolution to rid our delegation of the right to vote, you can stuff it… in your briefcases.

In front of the surprised audience, the Russian parliamentarians got up from their seats and walked out of the Assembly, quitting in the midst of the plenary session. Some remarks were exchanged behind our backs, but on the whole, the leadership and the members of the Assembly did not expect such a turn of events. They all were in shock. They had seen the obedient Russians much too often in recent years; they got used to Russia's "politeness and servility for Europe", as Fyodor Dostoevsky expressed it; they witnessed the spineless humility of the feeble Russian liberals and their lackey's readiness to lick the boots of any foreigner who would assume an air of importance. For the first time in ten years, the Europeans suddenly saw the Russia that demanded respectful attitude, and they were taken aback.

Outside the door, the Russian reporters came up to us. They seemed to realise that they had witnessed a historic moment. As I joked grimly, that was "the awakening of the Russian national pride". This pride was dormant for so long under the vigilant watch of our liberal supervisors, that it was nearly obliterated. And all over sudden, there it was again.

All the members of the Russian delegation were very excited. These guys gained self-belief; they felt strong and confident. Three of the delegates were not there — the same threesome that I have mentioned already. An hour later, when the European parliamentarians had gone to their restaurants and hotels where they could discuss *une demarche russe* privately, I went back to the Assembly Hall to pick up my mobile that I had forgotten by the microphone. Thanks to my forgetfulness, I became an unwitting witness of the remarkable *mise en scene*. The "conscience of the nation" Kovalev was sitting in the empty hall, his back turned on the Hall entrance. Two local journalists were interviewing him.

As far as I could tell, the French journalists had already finished extracting a regular portion of poison from the human rights campaigner; they were transcribing some Russian swear words with which Kovalev was describing President Putin and me. "Spell it, write it down!" Kovalev prompted, "Rogozin is a bas-tard. Got it? Good. Spell it — Putin — scum-bag."

At that point I felt slightly embarrassed on behalf of Kovalev. The spiteful and shallow old man looked sad and desperate. I did not interfere, collected my phone and left.

Next morning, I took the flight back to Moscow where I had to report on the status of the Strategic Arms Reduction Treaty (START-2) ratification by the State Duma in front of the Security Council board. That one-sided Treaty was highly dangerous for Russia: according to the START-2 our country was obliged to destroy all ground-based strategic nuclear ballistic missile warheads. The United States was rather afraid of this masterpiece of the Soviet military science. They nicknamed these missiles "Satan" due to their reliability, counterattack survivability, and power of destruction. It would take just one missile to erase the entire East Coast of the United States.

Americans used their connections in the Russian Government and succeeded in getting President Yeltsin to sign the Treaty that was unfavourable for Russia. The Treaty could not come into effect until ratified by the Parliament. The United States, along with all NATO member countries, urged Russia to stop procrastinating and put the draft ratification on the agenda of a parliamentary plenary session as soon as possible. The Kremlin did not have enough resolve not to make the Treaty a subject of a parliamentary discussion at all, as that would have been perceived as an open demarche of Putin in the very first month of his presidency, and would have inevitably created a deep rift in the Russian-American relations. Nobody in the Russian Government wanted that to happen.

A rather clever solution was found. In order to reinstate the safeguard of the Russian military security, the decision was made to include in the draft ratification the amendment, which meant the following: Russia would comply with the START-2 if the USA would not withdraw from the Anti-Ballistic Missile Treaty of 1972 (ABM Defense), and if NATO would not expand further. We knew that the Unites States would not consider agreeing to either of these conditions. "We have to protect our land from nuclear threat coming from Iran and North Korea," such was the explanation behind the intention to disturb the strategic balance with Russia. Donald Rumsfeld, for instance, had assured as early as in 1998 that by 2003 Teheran will produce missiles capable of reaching the territory of the USA. Surely, we did not believe a word of it; likewise, our opponents did not consider our concerns. As for NATO expansion, we had been aware of the plans for a while. The Kremlin run by President Yeltsin no longer had either the will or the skill to counteract those processes. Members of the Security Council approved the idea contained in my report — to make the ratification of the START-2 Treaty conditional to preservation of the ABM Defense, along with abandonment of its further expansion by the NATO Council.

When the meeting of the Security Council was over, everyone was coming up to Vladimir Putin, who chaired the meeting, to say good bye. I approached him, too, and delivered the report on the latest PACE session in Strasbourg. The President read through the report and said, "Maybe we should not have gone there after all". I knew then that he had already spoken to the Foreign Minister. "I think we were right to go there. We put up a fight because we were confident in our cause," I replied.

"You are probably right," Putin shrugged, and that was the end of the conversation.

The State Duma adopted the decision on the PACE issue, outlined in my proposal. Firstly, we were not going to step a foot there until the rights of the Russian representation were reinstated in full. Only the Chair of the delegation was given the authority to discuss with PACE leaders the terms and conditions of unblocking the cooperation. Secondly, the Duma did not refuse to continue the ongoing cooperation with the Council of Europe on issues of mutual interest, such as seeking common ground in the human rights protection. In order to achieve that, I proposed to set up a Joint Working Group of the Duma and PACE on Chechnya. The Group was supposed to visit the Chechen Republic regularly and to lift anxieties of our European colleagues. Strasbourg bit at the bait.

As a result, being the head of the State Duma Committee on International Affairs I had to spend a lot of my time in the Chechen Republic, accompanying various international delegations and the rapporteurs on that sore spot in the Russian external relations.

I have to say, our parliamentary delegation in PACE was very strong and representative. It included the leaders of all Duma factions as well as some prominent members of the Council of Federations[1]. Of course, the most fascinating representative of Russia was the State Duma showman Vladimir Zhirinovsky. Strasbourg was taking Mr. Zhirinovsky in all seriousness; the Europeans were terrified of him, and even did not allow him to join any of the five political groups within the Assembly. One day, I had an idea to use the demonic image of Zhirinovsky in order to gain advantage in a matter of crucial importance for Russia.

The issue was that a group of PACE deputies in the height of battling against Russia demanded from the Committee of Ministers of the Council of Europe to set up a special international tribunal. The Russian civil and military officials, allegedly (the allegations were made by know-it-all deputies) implicated in war crimes in the course of anti-terrorist campaign in the Chechen Republic, were supposed to be summoned before the tribunal. Naturally, I had to do my best to nip this extremist and dangerous anti-Russian idea in the bud. Supportive votes among deputies of PACE clearly were expected to be in short supply, and so I made up my mind to play a game.

In the course of debates the president of the Assembly first calls

---

[1] *The Federations Council* — the upper body of the Federal Assembly of the Russian Federation; the upper Chamber of the Russian Parliament.

a deputy to support an amendment proposed by him or her, and then addresses the Assembly, asking if anyone wishes to speak against it. Upon this, the president declares the amendment in question to be either accepted or rejected.

I was acutely aware of the fact that a number of deputies of the anti-Russian inclination would speak against my amendment with great pleasure. They would make the Assembly maintain the initial version of the draft resolution that contained the macabre plan for setting up the international war crimes tribunal. What if I asked Mr. Zhirinovsky to object to my amendment? Zhirinovsky to them is like a red rag to a bull. We needed to engineer a situation when all those who wish to "punish" Russia would be forced to associate with "the Great and Terrible" Vladimir in order to achieve that.

I approached Zhirinovsky, who was looking bored, in the Assembly hall and gave him a low-down on my desperate plan. He called me a gambler but was pleased to oblige. The President of the Parliamentary Assembly of the Council of Europe, Austrian socialist Peter Schieder, announced that the debates on amendments to final resolution on conflict in Chechnya were open. When my turn to speak had come, I used the time slot to bring the sound arguments against the unacceptable and ultimatum-like proposal of setting up a supranational legislative body specifically for the purpose of examining the implicated crimes in the Chechen Republic. The Assembly members were hardly paying attention. From their lack of reaction it was obvious that they had already made up their minds and were only listening to my speech because such was the protocol decorum. Schieder said his usual dry "thank you", and, looking around the audience, asked if anybody wished to object to the amendment.

"Me, me! I am against it! Give me floor!" suddenly Zhirinovsky shouted from his seat, muffling up other volunteers. That made even the experienced "been there, done that" Schieder gape with astonishment. Naturally, he found the intrigue amusing. Nobody had the heart to refuse Zhirinovsky an opportunity to speak out against Russia and against the Chair of the Russian representation in PACE. I don't think that anybody suspected a catch.

"I call Mr. Zhirinovsky to speak against the amendment!" the President rapped out. And so the show began. Zhirinovsky grabbed the microphone and literally screamed into it:

"I am against it! I am categorically against the amendment supported by Rogozin! I think it's a good idea to set up a tribunal on Chechnya! I am ready to explain why we do need this tribunal! We need it to incarcerate your entire Assembly, all of you rascals and scoundrels; all of you will sit before the tribunal there! Bindigs-shpindigs, lords-mylords[1], all of you, until you drop dead! Therefore, I am against the Rogozin's amendment!"

Upon hearing this passionate and, indeed, offensive speech by Zhirinovsky the President called the audience to order, debarred Zhirinovsky from rights of presentation for the rest of the day, and finally put the amendment to the vote. The Parliamentary Assembly, terrified by the leader of the Liberal Democratic Party of Russia, unanimously approved my amendment, thus negating all the efforts of our opponents.

---

[1] Zhirinovsky was referring to Rudolf Bindig, a left-wing deputy from Germany, and to Lord Frank Judd, a Labour Member of the House of Lords of the United Kingdom.

A HERO OF OUR TIME[1]

My visits to Chechnya with the important foreign delegations became a sort of routine over time. On such visits we often had to communicate with the warlords who had switched over to Moscow's side. The most distinguishable of all was Akhmad Kadyrov, the man on whom the Kremlin had put the highest stake in regulating the post-war Chechnya. At a glance, the newly appointed leader of the Chechen Republic, and former Chief Mufti, came across as a man of an unrestrained temper, but that was a misleading impression. Mr. Kadyrov-senior turned out to be a real "hero of our times". Due to his psychological insight he had a very clear understanding of what Moscow expected from him, and he did in all fairness his job of persuading warlords to lay down their arms.

It was he who started to lure Chechen "partisans" down from mountains, lobbied for their amnesty, and offered them placements in the so-called law-enforcement structures under his personal guarantee; in short, he effectively legalised the majority of the armed gangs under his wing. In the State Duma just a few deputies, apart from me, stood up against what we saw as a policy of connivance to bandits. The majority, though, not only voted in favour of the highly dubious Decree on Amnesty to members of the armed gangs, but also turned a blind eye on the fact that yesterday's extorters and killers were given a legitimate opportunity to carry personal weapons and serve in the Militia and in Kadyrov's guards. Still, Vladimir Putin trusted Akhmad Kadyrov; the President valued own "political investments" in the new Chechen Government. President Putin was brushing aside warnings and criticism, voiced by the Defense and the Security officials, and directed at the former Chief Mufti. General Victor Kazantsev, Presidential Plenipotentiary Envoy to the South Federal district, had also issued warnings against Kadyrov, and this antagonism cost Kazantsev his position.

Kadyrov-senior used to treat me in an informal and friendly way:

---

[1] *A Hero of our Time* is a novel by Mikhail Lermontov written in 1839. It is famous for its Byronic hero, or anti-hero, Pechorin and the beautiful descriptions of the Caucasus.

he often invited me to have lunch with him, offered to use his car and personal bodyguards for the trips around the Republic, and usually was receptive to my requests with regard to cooperation with international observers.

In March 2001, on one of the many Lord Judd's excursions to Chechnya, the helicopter that carried the important guest very nearly crashed. We were about to land in Znamenskaya Cossack village when our helicopter got caught in an air funnel produced by the plane that had landed shortly before. The helicopter hanged in the air at about 70 metres over ground. The Spetsnaz fighters, who were with us, fell down on the steel floor without letting go of their machine guns. The faces of the deputies froze with fear. They were looking at me, as if I was supposed to know what was going to happen next.

My first thought was that we had been hit. I took out my duty pistol, unlocked the bolt, and waited. I put my sports bag behind my back with my free left hand. I thought for some reason that the soft fabric — my jeans and my warm jumper — would help to soften the blow, should we hit the ground. Strange ideas come to mind in mortal danger!

I caught a glimpse of the scene below. People on the ground looked like ants. They were running in all directions away from the spot on which the helicopter was about to drop. Suddenly, the machine stopped turning around, and banked sharply towards the flat field at a distance from the village.

We landed. I was still suspecting that we had been shot at, and was not in a rush to leave the helicopter. Finally, I pulled the handle of the emergency exit and jumped outside on the dry grass.

The ground was smouldering in about forty-fifty metres away from us. The black smoke from the underground oil burning up went up in the air.

Like Rambo, I kneeled down, held my pistol tight and looked around. There was nobody out there.

In a second, the helicopter doors opened and two of the officers jumped out. They went past me, without paying attention, to look at the rotor at the back; they smoked and looked around the deserted field, too.

I realised that, with my pistol in hand, I looked stupid in a Hollywood kind of way. Laughing at myself, I went to see what was happening in the passenger section. The people there were recovering from the shock.

One of the parliamentarians felt ill, maybe due to his cardiac problems. I literally poured some cognac into him, and in a minute his face regained colour. An FSB minibus appeared from nowhere and took us to the Cossack village where we were greeted by the local authorities.

Kadyrov was promptly informed about the incident and called me straight away.

I communicated with Chechens a lot, and once I tried to put some of my personal observations in writing, hoping that they would be helpful in composing a psychological portrait of the Chechen people. With no understanding of specifics of the Vainakh psychological type and mentality, our politicians and military should never have attempted to tamper with Chechnya in the first place.

Any national army worldwide must not only be trained to shoot well, fight skilfully and take settlements by storm, but also be able to retain the once-established control of an area by building a non-hostile rapport with local population. Moreover, in some instances an insight into mysteries of a national soul may allow to overtake territories without striking a blow; as a result of the correct approach to the national issue, a backfire just might be substituted by flowers, and nice ladies would welcome soldiers with traditional bread and salt.

When thinking about it, I could not grasp why the Kremlin plunged yesterday's schoolchildren into the thick of Chechnya; they had no combat survival skills and a very limited understanding of where exactly they were put and what kind of people they had to deal with. Then I decided to have a go at a brief analysis of Chechen national character and came up with the following:

Until we learn to understand Chechen people we will never succeed in establishing peace in the Chechen Republic. The mentality and value system of Chechens are significantly different from that of Russians. Like all mountain peoples, Chechens get quickly excited about an idea and then cool down just as quickly. At the same time, educated Chechens possess clarity of vision to spot potential gain. Their behaviour is always motivated by pursuit of these gains.

The showy vehemence of Chechens may bring them sympathy from a Russian who would typically take it as a display of amiability, truthfulness and altruism. However, one must remember that behind all such manifestations there is almost always a practical goal that a Chechen is set to achieve.

Where a Russian would find an ambiguity, for a Chechen there is none. He might act friendly towards someone whom he had nearly murdered five minutes ago. He might hate a person with whom he was on the warmest terms until recently. This great difference between our two value systems means that something that you regard as a treachery, may be seen by Chechens as a mere cunning, luck, or the proficiency in dealing with outsiders.

Ordinary Chechens see Russians primarily as conquerers who tread upon "the land of forefathers". This is a consequence of the implantation of the false historical concept of Russia as a "prison of nations" and of the myth on "the 200-year Russian warfare" combined with the rapid post-war expansion of the Chechen flatland population. When speaking to Chechen people, you should defer to their misguided opinion on Russians and disprove them in a calm and reasonable way.

You must remember that Russia represents a link between Chechnya and the global civilisation. This demands that Russians must at all times be conscious of their mission in the territory of Chechnya. You have to realise that such things as sloppy language, swearing, signs of disrespect towards women and the elderly, and ostentatious rudeness give Chechens an impression that the greatness of the Russian culture is a fake. And if this is the case, a step from contempt to enmity will be a short one.

Drinking in public and drunken debauchery repel the religious Chechens. The dry law must be imposed in all military quarters in the territory of Chechnya. Rowdy drunken servicemen in the Muslim environment irritate religious people; this in turn contributes to the formation of a disrespectful perception of the Federal Army. Soldiers and officers who have been partaking must not be allowed on duty, particularly, they must not take part in special operations.

A Chechen, as well as any other person whom you may encounter, must be treated with respect. You never know whether a Chechen may be a friend or a foe; therefore, it is best to assume that he might be helpful if you manage to gain his sympathy. The simplest way to achieve this is to be considerate. Even a slightly exaggerated admiration for a home of a Chechen, his possessions, or his professional skills would not go amiss.

We must not forget that due to the history of deportation into the Russian-speaking Kazakhstan, Chechens have a better command of the Russian language than other peoples of the Caucasus; their good Russian pronunciation can always serve as a cause for a genuine compliment.

A perceived air of superiority of a Russian over a Chechen is bound to be met by either a criticism of the Russians' behaviour in general, or an open demonstration of a Chechen's superiority. You would react in almost the same way if you were in his place — if you were being condescended to.

You will earn respect of Chechens if they can see that you are familiar with the local customs, and if you display your knowledge of Islam, which should be not inferior to theirs, at the least. Ordinary Chechens, although not deeply religious, have high regard for those who practise religion; they are not averse to pointing out that they live according to the Law of Allah. Manifestation of live faith in a Russian instead of talks about religious tolerance or debates on the verity of one religion as opposed to another — this is what will earn you respect from a Chechen.

Russian Orthodox rituals serve to prove to Chechens that we are not conquerors but a cultured nation and the bearers of one of the world's mainstream religions.

Chechens have to be reminded of the "pre-war" times when they used to live without hatred alongside Russians. The memory of that might trigger a desire for returning to the state of peace amongst the mature generations and would give hope for overcoming today's fear and instability to the young.

The sore spot for any Chechen is an issue of deportation during the Stalin's era. Chechens would be offended by a suggestion that the deportation had been anything other than genocide. At the same time, you should remind Chechens that they had not settled in their land exclusively, and that Russians, too, suffered horrendously from Stalin's repressions.

Hospitality of Chechens is of a rather different sort than that of Russians. They customarily show hospitality to near strangers, and a guest of theirs might be ever so impressed by the kindness of his hosts. However, such hospitality does not imply a beginning of a special friendship or any ties or duties on a host's part. It is very important for a Chechen to feel his magnitude. Because of that, they enjoy receiving symbolic awards and occupying administrative positions, which also gives them an opportunity to help their numerous friends and relatives.

In order to strengthen your ties with a Chechen, you have to lavish him with signs of attention. It is advisable to invite him to your home rather than to continue visiting his.

It is important to realise that once a Chechen holds an administrative position he becomes a potential target for a warlords' attack; it takes plenty of courage for him to accept and maintain such a position (unless, of course, he had entered into a deal with criminals beforehand).

High respect for the elderly, particularly for patriarchs and for secular and spiritual authorities alike, is still preserved in the everyday Chechen life. The Chechen parents enjoy dutiful affection of their extended families.

Please take into consideration the specifics of the Chechen men's attitude to women. Whilst Chechen men appear to treat women in their families in a strict manner, they are very protective of them and will not tolerate from others any rudeness or disrespect towards their women. Making passes at Chechen women, dubious jokes, attempts to introduce "free love" — in the eyes of a Chechen all this contributes to the "image of an enemy" who impinges his most sacred, i.e. his family.

Chechen warlords often use women in public scandals or in armed provocations of all sorts.

The federal government and the military find themselves cornered: either there will be no order imposed at all, or it would be necessary to "insult" Chechen women or even apply force against them in the presence of Chechen men. In situations like these, you have to identify the man to hold negotiations with. We know from recent experience that confusion of federal military during a "psychological attack" on Chechen females inevitably results in victims on the side of the federal authorities. Whenever possible, you should avoid even engaging in conversations with Chechen women. We must succumb to the Chechen way of negotiating with males and dismissing females from "men's business".

The practice of taking hostages is an ancient Chechen custom, the one that even the Soviet power failed to eradicate. Hostages are typically treated with extreme harshness. That is why it is not advisable to conduct oneself irresponsibly or in a colonial mode while on a mission in Chechnya. It is of the utmost importance that you take precautions so as to avoid becoming a hostage and feeling on your own skin the full extent of hostility that Chechens have built up against Russians.

Your colleagues must be aware of your whereabouts and the expected timings of your returns at all times. It is advisable to move around either well armed, or together with reliable guards and in groups of at least five. You must also be on alert if approached by a group of locals, even when there are onlookers nearby, including persons familiar to you.

However, if a disaster strikes, and you fall into the hands of bandits, you must prepare yourself for a release by all possible means. Escaping from captivity used to be extremely risky in the period of the warlords' total control over the territory of Chechnya;

however, today an escape could be your only option and deliverance from imminent death. One has to prepare for escape by lulling the vigilance of bandits in every possible way. Only take action when absolutely certain.

Do not protest in any way. It is best to hide all your protests behind a virtual wall of silence. Do as you are told, but only what you are able to do in your condition, and without undue eagerness. Never look your tormentors in the eyes. When prompted, answer their questions but give brief answers. Do not engage in discussions or offer revelations. Any pleas for mercy, attempts to flatter or please would only cause the opposite effect. Similarly, a hostage who threatens his captors with revenge or assumes an air of superiority may spark a cruel reaction.

It is important not to disclose the residential addresses of your family and friends or relatives, as they might become a target for ransom demands and threats. If forced, you should name an outdated or an altogether non-existent address. The crucial thing is to play for time and prepare for an escape.

A Chechen wishes to come across very persuasive in his conversations with others; with this purpose in mind he often exaggerates his merits and success stories. In doing so, he sometimes grows to believe that his estimations reflect reality. One must be aware of this trait and take it with good grace, and without irony that might seem offensive to a Chechen. There are many dreamers among Russians, too.

A conflict or an argument that has been resolved verbally is not deemed to be exhausted by a Chechen. Even if the duelists shook hands and agreed that one of them, the Chechen, lost the fight, this does not mean that he would not launch into a battle again five seconds later. Therefore, it is not advisable to give one person a chance to prove his physical superiority. Use of military force and actions of law enforcement must be concise, predictable and correct, but with no leniency, as this would be viewed as a sign of weakness, and Chechens would be tempted to test your resilience again.

Quarrels between Chechens may be quite dangerous, as they have no restraining boundaries. An ordinary argument could potentially evolve into a full-blown conflict and an ongoing antagonism between family clans. This is why Chechens, unlike Russians, readily appeal to a third party to resolve their internal arguments. To become such a party, it is enough to hold any official status and to be prepared to act as an amicable compounder, motivated not by own interests (which would be spotted by Chechens at once, and their trust in you would vanish) but by fairness. Participation in resolution of Chechen internal conflicts is one of the most effective ways to affirm the need for Russians in them.

The tragic events of the last decade reinstated such mountaineer customs as "blood revenge" in Chechnya. The inevitability of revenge to an offender or to his family members is an expression of the self-preservation instinct in the conditions of rampant crime. The lack of similar traditions among the non-Chechen population largely created a sense of impunity, with which warlords or gangsters committed their crimes against the defenseless Russian civilians. Your conduct in Chechnya must be based on the moral and political principle of inevitability of a punishment for a crime that has been committed.

In their molding and feeding the feelings of hatred for Russia and her people, Chechen bandit leaders are prepared to come up with dirty frame-ups; often they do not stop at sacrificing their own people's lives at that. It has been known for Chechen militants (including those of Slavic descent and Slavic looks) to wear federal uniform by orders of their "field commanders" and to slaughter Chechen civilians in front of their fellow villagers. External ill-wishers of Russia refer extensively to the facts of such crimes in their criticism of the federal Government's actions in the North Caucasus; these facts are used in order to create the criminal and barbarous image of the Russian military.

The explanatory work among the population in Chechnya requires greater attention on our part; this work should be done with the help of local activists and the Chechen intelligentsia. Communication with Islamic religious leaders and Orthodox priests is of utmost significance. People must see that the law applies indiscriminately to local criminal elements and to representatives of the federal power, if they are guilty of criminal conduct.

Chechnya today feeds on rumours, gossip, and myths. The Chechen society is in need of true and objective information. Chechens have a high regard for the concept of fairness and equality; if they see that the actions of the federals are tough but just, they would be favourably impressed.

By nature Chechens are rather credulous; they might follow a positive or a negative example with equal enthusiasm. We need to earn more credentials in our treatment of the local population. It is important to bear in mind that Chechens respect strength and value justice and fairness. However, cases of ungrounded arrests or unjustified use of force may break the fragile trust between the locals and the military, which has taken so much effort to achieve.

Another thing to remember is that the familial, local, patrimonial, and clannish bonds have always been very powerful in Chechnya. Elements of the mutual cover-up culture are still well alive there; because of this, chances are that any information coming from locals might be inaccurate and, therefore, it has to be verified carefully. Unfortunately, it is not uncommon among the Chechen federal agents to knowingly give false information, wishing to get even with a hostile clan; any information from them must be handled with extreme caution.

Prior to conducting a special operation in a settlement, it is very important to detect a circle of authority figures on which the federal forces can rely for support in establishing relations of trust with the population. The same circle may be responsible for the formation of a self-governing local body and for the law and order maintenance in an aul or village. In the agitation campaign, it is necessary to stress the need to resist Wahhabi, Arab mercenaries and terrorists who are entrenched in the territory of the Chechen Republic.

These groups are considered to be the major enemies of the people, and such a view is now beginning to dominate in the Chechen circles.

Russian servicemen must treat with care the cultural sites and artefacts in places of military dispositions, and in the course of military operations; they must never allow desecration of mosques and of places of worship, destruction of burial places of Ustaz Sheikhs or Islamic tower complexes, mausoleums, and cemeteries. In the aspect of gaining trust of the population, it is extremely important to protect the natural environment, areas of natural beauty, and cultural monuments.

You must remember at all times that law is on your side, and that law is the power of the Russian presence in Chechnya. You are a living embodiment of the law. Any unlawfulness, any acts of anarchy (even those that do not cause tangible damage) would be discussed among Chechens, prone to exaggerating matters and fabricating details. Any action that implies infringement of interests of the Chechen population must be sustained by an administrative decision and backed by relevant documentation. A Chechen needs to see that he is dealing with the law and not with somebody's private will.

Remember, chances are that if you antagonise a Chechen by your inappropriate conduct, he would turn into a bandit, and a series of killings and atrocities will follow. Innocent people will suffer, and your own life will be at risk too. The task of all representatives of federal power, including officers and soldiers on anti-terrorist missions in the territory of Chechnya, is to learn how to win friends there, even if these friends would not be entirely loyal. Otherwise, we will not be able to achieve our main objective, which is to establish peace and to reinforce national integrity of the Russian state.

I wrote this memo, based primarily on my personal impressions, in February 2002. It was submitted to heads of the Defense and the law enforcement structures. Unfortunately, very few of the recipients showed interest in the material or seriously thought of putting it to use in their fieldwork.

The President agreed to study the memo. He asked me which additional references I had used in preparing the document. "I used the poets Alexander Pushkin and Mikhail Lermontov as well as Leo Tolstoy. All three of them wrote about the Abrek traditions and the customs of mountaineers. Russian classical literature is full of extensive descriptions of the Chechen history, as well as the history of other nations of the Caucasus and their customs. We simply have to re-read the classics, and that would stop us from falling into the same trap over and over again," I answered.

There are no reasons to believe that my sketch on the mentality of Chechens served as a reference in the military personnel anti-terrorist indoctrination programmes, or that it helped to save a single Russian or a Chechen life, at the least. I doubt that the top military officials, overloaded with personal preoccupations, found the time to acquaint themselves with my memo. A possibility of its practical implementation is even more remote.

Just as I submitted the memo to the President, I made a request to be sent to Chechnya in the capacity of his envoy with the objective of securing the constitutional order there. I was certain that I would be capable of accomplishing the task of coordinating activities of the law enforcement bloc there; I was also keen to establish the due control over expenditures out of the budgetary funds allocated for reconstruction of Chechnya and to ensure that the spendings were legitimate. "We need you in the Duma", the President pointedly cut me off, and the question was never again raised at our subsequent meetings. Pity, though. The murder of Akhmad Kadyrov, the terrorist attacks on Nazran, Nalchik and Beslan, terrorist attacks in the Moscow Metro and in the Domodedovo Airport, almost daily bomb explosions in Dagestan — all of this is a confirmation that the Russian policy in the Caucasus is not as effective as it could be. There is no guarantee that horrendous acts of terrorism will not happen again tomorrow, and this means that Russians continue to live on the Caucasian volcano.

WAR AND PEACE[1]

The work in the Committee on International Affairs of the State Duma presented me with unique opportunities to implement my academic knowledge in practice and apply the practical experience accumulated in the Congress of Russian Communities.

I was fortunate enough to be invited by His Grace Kirill[2] to take part in the complicated negotiations on restitution of the church property in the territory of the Estonian Republic on behalf of the Estonian Orthodox Church of the Moscow Patriarchate. Until the intermediation of the State Duma Committee, the self-proclaimed "Swedish Synod" was the official proprietor of all Orthodox churches in Estonia; this right of ownership was granted to the Synod by Estonian authorities "in gratitude" to Russia for their newly received independence. I had to go to Istanbul twice to meet with incompliant and uncompromising Ecumenical Patriarch Bartholomew of Constantinople. There I came very close to arranging an eponymous night, frustrated by the Patriarch's aching jealousy of the Moscow Patriarchate and his destructive stance on the Estonian issue.

The Union of large-sized industries of Estonia played a massive part in the resolution of that conflict, which was far from being a purely clerical one. The Union persuaded the political leadership of Estonia to mellow their attitude. The entrepreneurs and industrialists had a vested interest in unblocking bilateral contacts with the huge eastward market, and so they managed to break the resistance of Estonian "hotheads" in the bastions of power.

As soon as the news of the long-awaited successful outcome of the dispute on ownership had reached Moscow, Patriarch Alexiy of Moscow and All Russia went to Estonia to personally support the Orthodox

---

[1] The fine novel *War and Peace* by Leo Tolstoy does not need a special introduction. It is regarded to be one of the greatest works of fiction. The epic novel describes the events leading to Napoleon's invasion of Russia and the impact of the war as seen through the eyes of five Russian aristocratic families.

[2] At the time Patriarch of the Russian Orthodox Church Kirill headed the External Relations Department in Moscow Patriarchate.

congregation there, as well as to visit his parents' graves there at long last. His Holiness was recovering from a grave illness at the time, and I hope that the good news brought by us helped him to heal.

The events of 11 September 2001 were some of the most memorable during my work in the Committee on International Affairs. I had to comment on the American tragedy live from a studio on the top floors of the Rossiya Hotel. I was moving in between the studios, in a rush, trying to change headphones in time to be able to comment on the breaking news, now on Channel 1, and then on NTV, and observed the overwhelming panic everywhere. Mostly I feared a hysterical reaction from Washington — in total commotion or due to a software error the suicide terror attack could have been mistaken for an aggression from somewhere else, and an attack in retort could have followed.

I discussed with the US Congressmen a threat of the Islamic fundamentalism on a number of occasions, both during official inter-parliamentary negotiations and in private conversations. The discussions were fruitless. Overconfidence and complacency of our US colleagues went beyond acceptable levels. However, after the 9–11 the Congressmen turned sorrowful overnight and, at last, began to pay some attention to our advice and admonitions. Still, judging by some of the comments on the tragedy, the attitudes of some Congressmen remained as hopeless as ever.

I recall a meeting with a tall and handsome Congressman from Arkansas who shook my hand in the characteristically casual American manner and asked me where I had come from. I replied that I came from the largest country in the world. "From Poland?" he probed, and I felt instantly bored.

Nevertheless, I have never belonged to the category of my compatriots who habitually make fun of Americans, because I think that it is unfair. True, the USA is a self-oriented country, and its citizens sincerely believe that America is the centre of the world. After all, they do have solid grounds for such a belief.

Whilst thieves pocketed assets of the former superpower in our country, and our Army hurriedly evacuated from Eastern Europe and the former Soviet Republics, the US politicians endeavoured to increase the military power, which was becoming a weighty argument and a trump card at trade negotiations tables. What is so laughable about that? Why mock and snigger?

True, an average American with his cultural and geographical knowledge or, to be precise, with the lack thereof, may produce an everlasting impression on an average Russian. At the same time, the small-numbered, but educated, cultured, and patriotically-minded elite, the power of which is restricted by the balanced political system and independent courts, governs the American society. Americans are not afraid to work hard; they have flexible employment market; they possess a healthy adventurous spirit without which it would be impossible to develop an advanced, proactive, assertive and successful business. And, of course, in the United States it is not embarrassing to be a patriot.

After all, until recently, "patriot" was a dirty word in our country thanks to the efforts of the liberal propaganda. Every so often my opponents in various debates on air and on television, wishing to come across as liberals and intellectuals who are free from national prejudices, throw in a famous quote: "Patriotism is the last refuge of a scoundrel". Perhaps they do not comprehend that the quoted writer Samuel Johnson was a zealous patriot of Britain and that the true meaning of his words was a comparison of the true patriotism with the ostensible.

The North American politicos choose not to see, or not to remember, the courage and consistency with which Russia had supported the USA independence from the claims of the British; how Emperor Alexander II of Russia helped the United States to establish control and sovereignty over Hawaii; how Russian Monarchs gave the Russian America[1] over to Washington for a symbolic price, practically as a gift; how the brightest Russian minds campaigned for racial equality in the USA over one hundred years ago, clearing the future triumphant pathway for President Obama. Sadly, the USA had not always repaid my country in kind and often did not show gratitude and grace.

One does not have to love Americans, but one can and must learn by their example. For instance, we need to learn from them how to jump to rescue of own compatriots in trouble. It is well known that the US Government would be prepared to send an aircraft carrier for just a few of their citizens, should their lives become endangered abroad. Does Russia have the legal tools to protect her countrymen abroad, as the USA do? The horrendous killings of our diplomats, taken hostages in Iraq in 2006, prompted both chambers of the Parliament to endow the President with authority to use force outside national borders if Russian citizens were in need of rescuing; in fact, such a right of Russia has already been recognised in the international law.

I think it was the summer of 2002, when I received a phone call from the Chief Prosecutor's Office with the message that one Mr. Khramov on

---

[1] "Russian America" used to be a name for Alaska discovered by Russian navigators in the 17th century. Alaska was a part of the Russian Empire until 1867.

behalf of some trans-radicals (must have been some radicals entranced by their own radicalism) filed a complaint, accusing me personally of "aggressive war propaganda". It was a demand for criminal proceedings against me.

In February 2002, when the US "commandos" grounded in Georgia, the relations between Russia and the USA sharply deteriorated. It seemed that the Americans were trying to block Russia's right to use force in order to eradicate the camps of Chechen raiders in the Pankissi Gorge in Georgia.

I urged to "quit mumbling" and to apply the concept of preventive strike in order to eliminate a threat of a terror attack against Russia. The "trans-radicals" regarded that to be a call for a war and filed a complaint in the Prosecutor's Office.

The prosecutor advised me to use my MP immunity and avoid engaging into an argument with Mr. Khramov due to negligibility of the group that the latter represented. However, I thought it was necessary to compile an extensive reply to the Prosecutor's Office. I intended my reply to serve as a legal base for sanctions that involve use of armed force in protecting lives and safety of Russian citizens. This is the text of the letter:

I confirm that in an interview to Russian information agencies (13 May 2002 — Interfax) following a barbarous terrorist act in Kaspiysk (the explosion of a military housing complex) I expressed an opinion that the Russian Special Forces should launch an anti-terrorist operation in the Pankissi Gorge in Georgia. (...)

As concerns the legitimacy of such an operation, it is necessary to analyse restrictions on use of armed force in a war on terror and in protecting compatriots outside national border, which are imposed in the Constitution of the Russian Federation and in the international law. Can a blatant violation of Russian citizens' human rights (in our case of the Russian servicemen and the Chechen refugees who are held hostages and terrorised in the Pankissi Gorge) be regarded as an act of hostility against the Russian state? And if the answer is yes, then can it be a valid cause for use of armed force in defense of Russian citizens?

I believe that there is legal framework for saying "yes" in answer to both of these questions.

First of all, in modern history there were precedents when governmental policies of using force in defense of citizens were regarded a form of self-defense. In addition, in these cases the governments in question actively employed the Army or the Special Forces for the purpose of protecting citizens of a foreign country, if they were clearly subjected to genocide. It suffices to recall, for instance, the allied forces of Russia, Great Britain, and France intervention in Turkey in 1827–1830 in order to save Orthodox Greeks from mass slaughter. Another precedent was the military actions that Russia undertook against the Ottoman Empire in 1877–1878 to protect the Orthodox Slavs of Bulgaria, Bosnia and Herzegovina from slaughter.

Secondly, the Constitution of the Russian Federation does not prohibit use of state power for the purpose of protecting citizens in peril; on the contrary, the Constitution confirms (Article 2): "The recognition, observance and protection of rights and freedoms of a man and a citizen shall be the duty of the state." It follows that a damage caused to one citizen is paramount to a damage caused to the state, the main function of the state being protection of its citizens in general. As to a geographical location where force may be used, the Constitution does put any limitations on that. Moreover, according to Article 5 of the Citizenship Act, the state has a duty to protect and defend its citizens within the Russian Federation and beyond; Russian authorities have an obligation to protect rights and freedoms of the people of Russia and to take necessary measures if such rights and freedoms are violated.

These statutory provisions are fully compliant with the international law. This is confirmed, for instance, by the words of a member of the International Law Commission Professor Sir Derek Bowett: "There are sufficient grounds to affirm that defense of citizens in the territory of the country or abroad essentially constitutes self-defense of a state."

Thirdly, one can easily detect a number of precedents of use of force for the purpose of protecting compatriots beyond national borders in the contemporary policies of the USA, the United Kingdom, France and Israel. The widely known precedents that spring to mind are the following:

1965 — joint Belgian-US operation in Zaire, when Belgian paratroopers with the US and the UK technical and logistical support conducted a military operation in defense of 2,000 foreign citizens in Zaire;

1976 — Israeli "commandos" in Uganda rescued hostages taken by Palestinian terrorists;

1983 — the USA armed intervention in Grenada on the grounds of protecting thousands of the USA citizens whose lives were at risk as a result of a coup-d'etat in that sea-locked state;

1989 — the USA brought troops to Panama. The need to protect the

American citizens in Panama had been one of the main declared reasons;

1991 — 4,000 French and Belgian paratroopers landed in Zaire for the purpose of evacuating their compatriots and foreign citizens.

Another vivid example is the USA "Operation Enduring Freedom" (OEF), a part of the war on terror, and an operation of the International Security Assistance Force (ISAF) in Afghanistan, launched by NATO in 2001 under the mandate of the UN Security Council.

Not all of the above operations were unquestionable from a moral standpoint. However, the subject of our discussion is the international legal framework for military operations, and not their details and particulars.

I quote Nikolai Krylov, Doctor of Law, a prominent Russian expert on the international law:

> *"Opponents of the concept of use of force in defending its citizens abroad often refer to various forms of potential abuse of this concept. They claim on this basis that any use of force may have dire consequences; therefore, it is too dangerous to permit a government to have a right to employ military force. Indeed, history of international relations is abundant with examples of abusive actions that were committed under the banner of the citizens' defense and resulted in tyranny. Suffice to remember Hitler's intervention in Czechoslovakia under the pretext of protecting Sudeten Germans, among other things. Self-defense under the international law may be used as a legal cover-up of a military assault on other states. However, self-defense in criminal law may be also unjustified in some cases; and freedom of speech, this rock of democracy, may often lead to clashes or to irresponsible statements. Would it be reasonable to restrain freedom of speech together with liberty of the press and to forbid people to protect their homes and families on that basis? The question is: would Hitler have stopped in his aggression, if the aforementioned pretence of protecting rights of the German minority was not available to him? Certainly not, he just would have invented a different excuse. The real issue is how to draw a thick line between lawful and unlawful use of force."*

Analysis of all precedents of use of force in the international war on terror and in defense of compatriots allows us to develop criteria to determine the legitimacy of use of force in the framework of international law:

- Occurrence of an imminent and real threat of terrorist aggression, or imminent and real danger to human lives, or a systematic gross violation of human rights;
- Absence of alternative peaceful means of resolving a conflict, which necessitates a recourse to extreme measures of self-defense;
- Humanitarian purpose of an armed operation, i.e. when a liquidation an international terrorism cell or a rescue of compatriots abroad is the exclusive, or at least the prime, motive behind the military action;
- Proportionality, i.e. a set time frame and restricted means of rescue. A decision to use force may be undertaken only by government for the purpose of neutralising terrorism and defending people; these actions must not spread beyond immediate defense.

In our case of the necessity to "clean-up" the Pankissi Gorge, it is clear that the anti-terrorist actions would be more effective if they were undertaken by a joint Russo-Georgian effort. This is the point that I am trying to convey to the official Tbilisi.

It stands to reason that governments worldwide should adopt national security policies of a preventive and prophylactic direction. Such policies would prevent a threat to the security of a state as a whole and of its individual citizens. A government must not put itself in a political deadlock, where a direct use of force would be the only option to resolve a given critical situation.

The above recommendations were written back in 2002. I would like to stress, at the risk of repeating myself: both chambers of the Russian Parliament finally ratified the principles of armed self-defense and use of force in rescuing compatriots abroad after the long four years passed since our diplomats had been killed in Iraq. These principles have become a part of the Russian legislation.

Foreign policy of a powerful state must manifest itself not merely by the existence of highly trained and educated diplomats, who are fluent in foreign languages and able to wear a dress coat and kid gloves with ease and grace. Underneath a kid glove there must be an iron fist of a state that sticks up for its own.

THE BRONZE HORSEMAN[1]

When venesecting the Soviet Union, Mikhail Gorbachev and Boris Yeltsin "forgot" not only about the Crimea, Sevastopol and the fate of 25 million compatriots abroad. They also overlooked the city and region of Kaliningrad with its near 1 million of population.

The contemporary Kaliningrad region used to be a part of East Prussia until it merged into the USSR in 1945. The city of Kaliningrad, once known as Koenigsberg, had been a German strategic fortress city. Adolf Hitler affirmed to his generals: "Berlin may fall but Koenigsberg will hold" — so confident the führer was of the fortress city defensive capacity.

Hitler was wrong. Koenigsberg fell ahead of Berlin, on 10 April 1945. 150,000 Red Army soldiers and officers laid down their lives in the battle, three weeks prior to total and unconditional surrender of Germany. That land has still not dried from Russian blood. That is why it is beyond comprehension that in 1991, when three Baltic Republics were declared independent, nobody bothered to agree with them on the terms of a visa free passage for Russian citizens between the Kaliningrad exclave and the mainland. Our people put their lives on the sacrificial altar of the WWII; did our nation not earn the right to move freely across our national territory?

Even during the Cold War the Soviet Union, out of humanitarian considerations, agreed with the Western democracies' proposal to set up a visa free corridor for West Berlin residents residents who travel to the Federal Republic of Germany through the territory of the Democratic Republic of Germany.

However, during the admission procedure of the Baltic States to the European Union, "thankful Europe" repaid us with a demand to

---

[1] 'The Bronze Horseman' is a reference to Tsar Peter the Great statue by Falcone in Saint Petersburg. The statue is one of the symbols of this great Russian city. There is a narrative poem of the same name about the statue, written by Alexander Pushkin in 1833, which is widely considered to be one of the greatest works of literature.

introduce transit visas for Russian citizens traveling through Lithuania, even though transit trains did not stop in Lithuanian territory.

The State Duma Committee on International Affairs established the following facts: approximately 1 million crossings of the border that divided the Kaliningrad district from Lithuania and Poland were registered in 2002; on average fourteen times more than on other state borders of the Russian Federation. We singled out several categories of Russian travelers who crossed the Lithuanian border and whose rights were going to be affected by the EU visa regime.

Kaliningrad's "Suitcase traders", who cross the border almost daily, are the largest category. Usually there are the people who live in the Kaliningrad district and go to Lithuania and Poland to purchase retail goods or, vice versa, to export locally produced commodities. Such people could have simply obtained a Schengen or a Lithuanian visa. We did not detect any signs of human right's violation in their case. Any country, whether it is Russia, Lithuania or Mongolia, is entitled to impose or to lift entry clearance regulations at its discretion. The fact that a visa regime would incur additional costs to our citizens, which would ultimately add to retail price of goods and would be borne by end customers, is another matter; opposing to that would have been far too complicated.

The second category comprises Russian citizens, residents of Kaliningrad and "metropolis" alike, who travel to other EU countries via Lithuania. They have been traveling on Schengen visas for years, and so the introduction of a visa regime by Lithuania would not have significantly altered their situation.

However, there is a third category — citizens of the Russian Federation who travel between the Kaliningrad exclave and the mainland with no intention of stopping in Lithuania on any business. This category was going to be largely affected by the introduction of a visa regime. Moreover, an intention to introduce a visa regime gave rise to a political issue of Russian sovereignty over the Kaliningrad district, as our citizens now needed a foreign state's permission to travel to other regions of their own country!

We estimated the number of people whose civil rights would be violated. We determined that 600,000 — 650,000 passenger tickets on the train route Kaliningrad — Moscow — Kaliningrad were sold annually, about a half of which, 300,000, were two-way tickets.

We also calculated that the score of transit trips by passenger cars and other vehicles was approximately 200,000 a year. Thus, we were talking about approximately 400,000 — 500,000 transit passengers who crossed the Lithuanian border both ways every year (excluding those travelers for whom Lithuania was the point of final destination and those who traveled to other EU member states).

If this transit visa regime were imposed, Lithuanian consulates would have been receiving at least 1,200 applications daily for a minimum of two transit visas. The Lithuanian consulates in Russia could not possibly process such a high volume of applications.

Not underestimating the power of public opinion, the Lithuanian authorities via their agents in the circles of the Kaliningrad separatists (they exist, too) spread disinformation. Rumors were going around that their country was prepared to grant free multiple Lithuanian and even Schengen visas to residents of Kaliningrad district, but Moscow objected to that. That was a sheer lie: we were never approached with a proposal to this effect; nobody intended to let Russian citizens, residents of Kaliningrad district or not, out of the visa trap. We only ever discussed the visa regime that Vilnius and Brussels intended to introduce from as early as 1 January 2003.

The Member States in the Schengen Agreement routinely discriminate against Russian nationals in issuing Schengen visas. Good-looking women (this effectively means all women in Russia), owners of medium-sized businesses, and even individuals with minor police records, such as of minor car accidents, are aptly put onto the so-called "stop-lists" — the black lists of persons who are refused entry into Europe. Applying the same draconian visa policy to the Kaliningrad transit passengers would have meant a grave humiliation for Russia and would have led to the isolation of the exclave territory.

Trying to fool us, Western diplomats promised to partially offset passengers' expenses by covering a share of a ferry or an air ticket that exceeded the cost of a bus travel card. At that, they ignored the fact that due to health, or other, reasons, a significant proportion of travelers only ever used overland transport. Moreover, air connections between Kaliningrad and the mainland Russia are limited, and such an approach would have inevitably led to discrimination of the large-numbered provincial population.

For example, there was a direct train that bypassed Moscow and went between the town of Safonovo in the Smolensk district and Kaliningrad. Under the proposed transit visa regime, a resident of Safonovo had to travel to Moscow first (it takes seven hours by train), where he or she had to submit a visa application in the Lithuanian consulate, queue there for a few days, and then come back to Safonovo, also by train. Only then he or she could have boarded a direct train to Kaliningrad. Thus, taking into account the cost of traveling to and from Moscow, accommodation, expenses, and the consular fee, the cost of a trip to Kaliningrad increased two- or threefold. This would have been an insurmountable expense for pensioners, and a breach of their human rights. There are at least 50,000–60,000 people in provinces who habitually travel to Kaliningrad every year. That figure implied the human rights' violation on a large scale.

Diplomatic negotiations between Russia and Europe on the Kaliningrad issue finally came to a halt by late spring 2002. I noticed that President Putin was thoroughly annoyed with the way things were moving. He sensed an upcoming public humiliation of his country and was not sure how it could be avoided. "I could say without exaggerating that the future of the Russia-EU relations depends on how the question of passenger and cargo transit between the Kaliningrad district and Russia is resolved", Russian President declared at the time. He noted that the proposals of the Russian side "were not met with understanding" and that "after the Cold War funeral has taken place, a comeback of the old times attitudes is not understandable". Only six months remained until the imposition of Lithuanian visas for transit passengers; the Kremlin and Ministry of Foreign Affairs did not foresee any levers of pressure on Brussels, now thinking of the best way to explain another international defeat to the Russian people. This time the defeat would have affected the right of approximately 1 million people to travel freely within their own country; as if it was not enough that Eastern Europe, which was opened to us until very recently, now sent our citizens to stand in exhausting queues for visas. Now Russian people were supposed to apply and pay for visas in order to travel to their own homes.

Russia needed to find a different strategy to negotiate a way out. Like "the Bronze Horseman" — Tsar Peter the Great — we needed "to cut a window through to Europe."[1] Members of the Duma Committee on International Affairs surrounded themselves with heaps of documents and literature and set out to study the Schengen Law with the objective of finding internal discrepancies and snags to support our position.

We applied our experience of parliamentary intrigues acquired

---

[1] A quote from a poem by Alexander Pushkin *The Bronze Horseman*. 'A window to Europe' is a reference to Saint Petersburg, the city build by Tsar Peter I (Peter the Great).

during the work in PACE instead of resorting to the usual head-on ingenuous approach, which was so characteristic of our officials. One of us suggested trying to use the Euro bureaucrat's own favourite weapon — human rights protection — against them in order to divert the chamber diplomatic negotiations into a broad, public human rights discussion.

The strategy of negotiations with the European Union on the Kaliningrad transit issue was aimed at achieving two objectives.

Firstly, we suggested that the issue of Kaliningrad transit could be resolved in the perspective of the total lift of the visa regime between Russia and the EU member states. In this connection, we submitted to the President the draft of his letter to the European Union state leaders; his message was a starting platform for our "storm" of Brussels and Vilnius.

In the meantime, we pointed out the gaps in the Schengen Law for a legal resolution of the conflicting issue. For instance, Clause 5.2 provided for a right of the Schengen member states to make exceptions or to lift visa regime in relation of certain categories of citizens for reasons of "humanitarian considerations", "national interests" or in connection with other international obligations. Clause 141, which we read through and through, gave the EU member states an open opportunity to advocate changes in the Schengen visa regulations, if "fundamental changes of circumstances" occurred. The appearance of a part of territory of the Russian Federation in the Schengen zone met this definition accurately.

The creators of the Schengen Agreement could not possibly foresee back in 1985, or even in 1990, that the USSR would collapse and the European Union would rapidly expand; these processes, indeed, constituted "a fundamental change of circumstances".

Secondly, aside from a purely tactical approach, we started to develop plans to revitalise the near-border collaboration and to set up a special economic zone in Kaliningrad. The grave social and economic lag of the region, ever more evident in comparison with neighbouring Lithuania and Poland, induced a dangerous tendency towards separatism, especially among the young. Ideas to form a "Baltic Republic" with its further joining the European Union were spreading among the citizens of Kaliningrad. In the midst of the tedious talks with the EU, such moods were a knife in the Russian negotiators' backs. Moreover, rampant crime, prostitution, HIV epidemics, drugs trade, and the general ongoing deterioration of the socioeconomic and environmental situation in the Kaliningrad district presented the additional arguments in favour of consolidating the European position on entry clearance and transit visa regime for Kaliningrad residents.

Having identified weaknesses in the EU legal position on the issue, I was keen to assist the President in breaking the negotiations logjam; it was imperative to take negotiations to a level of a broad, public human rights advocacy.

I picked up the receiver of the Government internal communication and dialed the "Reception One", the number for the President. Operator connected me to Mr. Putin. He listened to what I had to say and told me to come and see him in the Kremlin straight away. Fifteen minutes later, I was in front of the President, outlining our detailed plan of Kaliningrad transit issue resolution.

"I want to assign to you the mission of my special envoy at the negotiations, otherwise the talks might crumble. In the Foreign Ministry they ran out of ideas on how to maintain visa free transit and avoid a crisis in our relations with Brussels at the same time. Your plan might work. We accept what you have just detailed. Now let's agree your assignment with Igor Sergeyevich Ivanov". The President pressed a button on the communication panel. Foreign Minister happened to be at his desk.

Mr. Putin informed him about his plan of appointing me as his special envoy. Mr. Ivanov balked at the idea. Probably he did not want to admit that his Ministry had all but failed the negotiations; or maybe he just thought that I had a cunning plan of overtaking his chair. (I wonder why our officials think first of their chairs, and then of their duties?) "Igor Sergeyevich objects categorically," the President informed me when the phone call was over. "I shall await the decision," I replied, said good bye and left the presidential office.

On the next day, 12 July 2002, the Russian Federation Ambassadors Meeting was scheduled to take place in the Assembly hall of the Ministry of Foreign Affairs on Smolenskaya Square. Everybody was waiting for the President to arrive. As usual, Mr. Putin was held up. The ambassadors were aware of that, and nobody took their seats in the Assembly hall at the appointed hour. The foyer and the smoking area were crowded.

I came up to the Foreign Minister and his Deputies and greeted them. Tensely glancing at their watches, they waited for the ministerial reception to indicate that the President got into his limousine and was on the way from his dacha to Moscow. Just as he saw me approaching, Ivanov straightened up and said loudly for all the Deputy Ministers to hear: "I don't know what you've been whispering to the President yesterday, but you will become his envoy in Kaliningrad over my dead body. I would be prepared to quit. Be my guest, take my chair, and then command, but while I am still the Minister, my Ministry will deal with the problem of Kaliningrad transit!"

I replied: "You haven't resolved it so far, have you? Perhaps you should not mention your dead body with such ease."

It was an awkward and, frankly, an unattractive scene. The last thing I wanted was to compete with the Ministry of Foreign Affairs over an issue of such a great importance. Our opponents would have used the smallest crack in the Russian position to their advantage, and the whole country would have lost, as a result. That is why I was determined to smooth our internal differences as quickly as possible and to join efforts in implementing the new strategy.

The morning after the Ambassadors Meeting I went downtown to run some domestic errands. I automatically switched on the radio in the car and heard a host reading out the Decree on appointing Dmitry Rogozin as the Russian Federation President's Special Envoy to Kaliningrad on issues following the EU expansion.

"A complicated but accurate title," went through my mind.

I gathered our experts together in order to discuss the plan of action. These were not easy circumstances. We knew how we intended to conduct the negotiations; the President signed the Decree. We had that much in credit, but what did we have in debit? I did not have rights or powers to coordinate work of the Government institutions involved in the Kaliningrad transit issue. I did not have a chance to familiarise myself with practical experience of the Ministry of Foreign Affairs in their negotiations with the European Commission. No instructions to cooperate with me were issued to the Russian Embassies in Lithuania and Belgium or to diplomatic missions within the European institutions. No state funding was allocated for travel expenses; we did not have an office or even a minimal number of additional staff, required for the effective work on such a serious issue. We did not have any of the above, and the Presidential Decree in itself arranged for nothing. In other words, we landed on the Moon with a mission of the kind "Go there, I do not know where, get that — I do not know what"[1]. However, there was

---

[1] A reference to a Russian folk tale, where a hero receives unclear and unspecific instructions but still manages to outwit his rivals.

now the scapegoat in case the whole thing would fail. The most amusing in this situation was the fact that I had "imposed myself" voluntarily.

I recalled an anecdote and shared it with my colleagues who were beginning to look a little desperate. The anecdote was about the difference between the Italian and the Russian manner of land troops assaults of the past. It went like this: when a Russian officer gets out of a trench to lead the attack he shouts, calling for his soldiers: "Brothers! For Mother Russia! Charge! Hurrah!" The soldiers follow their commander in a brave and tough attack. In the Italian Army things were not the same: a courageous officer shouts from a parapet: "Avanti! Avanti!" (Charge!) Soldiers remain in a trench and applaud with admiration, exclaiming: "Bravo! Bravo!"

"Just like us", I pointed out to my colleagues, "We are already on a parapet calling for an attack, and all they do is applaud to us from a trench."

We thought it over and decided to barge for a room to manoeuvre by means of the intellectual pressure. Having cancelled the August family vacations that most of us had planned, we got down to business.

I immersed deep into the theory of the Kaliningrad transit issue; however, I realised that in reality things might happen quite differently. To start with, I made a phone call to Oleg Groznetsky, a correspondent of the Russian TV Channel 1 in Kaliningrad. This brave and talented journalist had been in the midst of all global trouble spots. He had great powers of observation. Oleg and I had discussed a problem of Kaliningrad transit a number of times during my visits to the amber land of Russia, prior to my official appointment. His knowledge of the issue was much deeper than that of any diplomat, as he himself made work-related journeys from Kaliningrad to Moscow and back several times per month and tried all available means of transport.

Oleg colourfully described to me the sufferings of our compatriots, who had to face the problem of the region's isolation on a daily basis, and offered me his assistance. He suggested that we crossed both borders — Belarus/Lithuania and Lithuania/Russia — in his Lada 10 Series so that I obtained an informal understanding of the process and could see the sore spots of the transit. I gratefully agreed.

A couple of days later, Oleg with his cameraman met me in Minsk Airport. We got into Oleg's car and headed towards Lithuania without delay. Having gone quickly through formalities at the half-deserted border control point in Belarus, we entered Lithuania and drove in the direction of Vilnius at high speed.

We were received with extreme caution in the capital of the Lithuanian Republic. They knew me rather well there; they had been also familiar with the fighting spirit of the Congress of Russian Communities, represented in the Lithuanian Seim by the Union of the Russians of Lithuania. Nevertheless, our meeting was conducted "in the constructive manner" and "with substantial filling", as our diplomats would have put it. In the few hours spent in Lithuania, I managed to meet with President Valdas Adamkus along with his special representative; with Chairman of the Seim Committee on Foreign Affairs Gediminas Kirkilas; with late Algirdas Brazauskas, then Prime Minister, and with other leading figures of Lithuanian Seim, Ministry of Foreign Affairs and the Internal Ministry of the Lithuanian Republic.

I delivered to Mr. Adamkus the message from Mr. Putin; the Lithuanian side in turn reassured me that "they will resolve the Kaliningrad problem in a way that would be of maximum benefit for both our neighbouring countries". True, Lithuanians are actively involved in the Russian Baltic; they participate in numerous joint ventures over there and do not wish to fall out with us due to stubbornness of European bureaucrats.

Our business in Lithuania finished, and we drove towards the Russian border. It only took a few hours on the motorway. I noticed in the rear mirror that a car with people in civilian attire was in our trail. I did not think that such care and consideration for us was necessary, as driving across Lithuania was safe and comfortable. We whizzed to Sovietsk[1] with no problems or complications.

A black Mercedes belonging to the Russian Consul General waited for us at a spot in about 20 kilometres to the Russian border. We stopped to greet him. I refused to leave the steering wheel of the Lada, thanked the diplomat, and asked him to follow us.

My simple trick worked. A proper procession, headed by the governor of the Kaliningrad region, the federal inspector, and the Commander-in-Chief of the Baltic Fleet expected us on the Russian side of the border. Thank God, they did not bring a brass band along. They assumed that I would be arriving in the Mercedes. As our Lada was blocking the way on the bridge for the fancy vehicle, the border control officer came up, running, to us. He hurriedly stamped our passports and ordered to get

---

[1] *Sovietsk* — A town formerly known as East Prussian town of Tilsit.

out quickly "because there is a big fish behind you". Barely restraining laughter, we nodded our understanding at him.

I accelerated and drove around the group that was there to greet us. People were stomping from foot to foot in anticipation of "the big fish" arrival. The cameraman got ready to film, Groznetsky connected the microphone; we got out of the car and approached the governor from the other side. I tapped him on the shoulder and said: "Could you give me directions to the library, please?"

That was our happy first meeting with head of the Amber land Vladimir Yegorov.

In the three months left to the Russia-EU Summit, I visited Kaliningrad dozens of times. I held numerous meetings with the regional authorities, with the Commandment of the Baltic Fleet, with the leaders of the business community, and with local media. I observed the queues by the Lithuanian Consulate, where many Kaliningrad residents, anxious about their region being cut-off in the near future, waited for the promised transit visas, night and day.

The Envoy Bureau was established in the former capital of East Prussia; Andrey Saveliev moved to Kaliningrad for six months to run it. The Bureau prepared for the Government unique materials and proposals on developing the regional infrastructure, setting up Special Economic Zone of the tax-exempt type for the EU citizens; it suggested measures aimed at easing tension at the border and customs controls and tackling crime and separatism.

The Envoy's team ensured that the negotiations with Lithuania and the European Commission reached a different level of quality.

The media in the West started to touch upon the subject of legitimacy of Russia's claims in the issue of Kaliningrad transit; a relevant discussion took place in PACE and in the European Parliament; hearings on the subjects were held in the German Foreign Policy Society in Berlin.

The main negotiator of the European Union Commission, the British Euro Commissioner for External Affairs Chris Patten, was the toughest person to deal with. Mr. Patten demonstrated in every way the lack of consideration for the Russian position on the issue; one of his arguments was, as he put it, that trains crossed Lithuania on the way from Moscow to Kaliningrad at such a slow speed that anyone could "easily jump off of a train and momentarily vanish in the vast space of the European Union." I was deeply frustrated by such an approach, which seemed to be not entirely competent. Finally, I offered a bet to Mr. Patten: the two of us board a train to Kaliningrad and then jump off together at an agreed time. I said that if we both survived the experiment I would be ready to admit publicly that my opponents were right, and would accept their terms of transit. After this initiative of mine Chris Patten no longer resorted to light argumentation.

The leaders of the largest European countries, as well as some renowned public figures of Europe with whom I had discussed the issue beforehand, put a particularly strong pressure on the European Commission to review their position. President of Lithuania Mr. Adamkus, President of Poland Mr. Kwasniewski; Italian Prime Minister Mr. Berlusconi, Spanish Prime Minister Mr. Aznar and the late Lithuanian Prime Minister Mr. Brazauskas; heads of Foreign Ministries of France (Mr. Dominique de Villepin), Italy (Mr. Gianfranco Fini), Greece (Mr. Andreas Papandreu); State Secretaries of the Foreign Affairs establishments of Austria, Germany, Finland and Denmark; the European Union commissioners Romano Prodi, Chris Patten, Gunter Verheugen, Loyola De Palacio, Javier Solana; the veterans of European politics Martti Ahtisaari and Hans-Dietrich Genscher — this is an incomplete list of persons whom we cooperated with on a daily basis in resolving the issue of utter importance for Russia and Europe.

The visit to Italy for a meeting with Italian Prime Minister, "Hawk" Silvio Berlusconi, was the most memorable of all. I was treated as a guest of honour in Rome. They even rolled out the red carpet in front of Palazzo Chigi. Brave cuirassiers (or dragoons, frankly, I was not able to tell) were standing along the two sides of the carpet. They were waving their swords in salutation. Overall, I felt like a guest from Planet Earth during an official visit to the Pisces.

Things were running smoothly until the moment we got into the lift. We only had to go up one level and could have easily used the staircase, but the grandeur of the welcoming reception required us to use the lift. A funniest incident happened there. A sign inside the lift informed that its capacity was up to 10 people, or 500 kg; apparently, the lift was designed to carry slim Italians, who, as I realise now, were meant to weigh no more than 50 kg each. We only noticed the sign that said "10 people". We are Russians and, therefore, on average we weigh about twice as much as Italians do. The lift did not know that. It went dead the moment its doors closed. We were stuck inside for about seven minutes, surprised, silent, and motionless, intensely listening for a sound of life in the lifting mechanism and feeling uneasy about the exclamations in Italian behind the lift doors. Then I heard loud swearing in Italian: "You idiots, get these people out right now! My friend Vladimir[1] sent his Envoy here, and you buried him inside this ugly lift!"

I knew at once that it was Mr. Berlusconi in person, condemning his aides for slowness in rescuing the prisoners of the ancient Roman lift. The machine jerked a few times and finally delivered us up to the first floor where we happily embraced the long-awaited freedom.

Berlusconi hugged me, enquired if I were not suffocated in the company of my heavy friends in need, and took me to his office. As we were walking together, I asked him about the results of the latest Milano game. A mention of his beloved football club pleased Berlusconi even more, and he immediately assured me of his assistance in resolving the Kaliningrad transit issue. He kept his word, and, for this, I will always be grateful to the incredibly charismatic friend of Russia.

Two weeks prior to the Russia-EU summit, on 23 October 2003, I flew over to Copenhagen for the final meeting with the Danish negotiators. Those turned out to be the most stubborn of all.

In accordance with the informal allocation of responsibilities within the European Union, Denmark was a curator of the Republic of Lithuania. Vilnius reported to Copenhagen all the details of transit agreements with Moscow and complained about "the Russian envoy twisting an arm".

Denmark used her position as Chair of the European Union at the time and took the most uncompromising stance on the Kaliningrad transit issue. The six months period of the Danish chairing of the EU happened to fall into the second half of 2002, which was the time of the most tedious discussions. Copenhagen was interfering in all the particulars of our talks with Lithuania and the EU and put obstacles wherever it was possible.

Moreover, the Danes themselves gave grounds to doubt their intention to hold an open negotiation with Russia. In October they allowed the emissary of Chechen underground, officially known as the World Chechen Congress, to hold one of their regular gatherings in Copenhagen. On a number of occasions I warned my Scandinavian negotiation partners that we deemed such antagonistic actions against Russia to be unacceptable. They reaction was to be taken aback with astonishment at "how was it possible to ban a forum of Chechen dissidents in a democratic environment".

The evening of 23 October clarified everything.

At the precise time when our difficult talks with Danish diplomats rounded up, the Barayev gang took hundreds of hostages — peaceful

---

[1] I assume Silvio Berlusconi was referring to Vladimir Putin — *Author's comment.*

civilians, Muscovites, and visitors to Moscow who were on a night out in theatre to see the *Nord-Ost* musical. In the morning of 24 October I boarded the earliest plane to Moscow and went to Dubrovka, to the operative headquarters of hostage release, right from the airport.

There I went down to work with dozens of foreign diplomats, who had been aimlessly wandering the headquarters' hallways before my arrival, trying in vain to obtain any relevant information. Together we managed to establish telephone communication with the foreign hostages and received some information from them, which, I hope, was of use to Special Forces. Together with Sergey Yastrzemski, an aide to President, we took over a group of children hostages from Doctor Leonid Roshal; the Doctor had been begging the terrorists, and the children were released a few hours prior to the rescue operation. At the Kremlin's request, I went live on "Rossiya" TV channel at 4am on 26 October and commented on the Special Forces assault on the theatre and on the entire hostage release operation.

Neither on 24 October, nor on 25, nor 26 we received a reply to our request to cancel the Ichkerian gathering in Copenhagen, despite the telephone messages that I left for the Danish right from the operative headquarters. We understood everything clearly. In the aftermath of the tragedy on Dubrovka it was unthinkable to go to Denmark to take part in the Russian-EU Summit there, as if nothing happened. My insistent recommendation to President was to select an alternate place for the Summit. In the end, we agreed on holding it in Brussels.

President Putin showed himself a hard negotiator and refused to sign a Summit Joint Statement until it included all amendments that reflected our interests, notwithstanding lures by Danish Prime Minister Fogh Rasmussen[1], who was at the root of the change of the Summit's location, and by Chairman of the European Union Commission Romano Prodi. As a result, the negotiation partners agreed to our terms.

The Summit went into a recession. The main negotiators proceeded to a different room to conclude the final amendment to the Joint Statement. Putin stuck to the initial plan, and I was terribly grateful to him for that. Together with Deputy Foreign Minister Sergey Razov (he is now the Russian Ambassador to China) we remained face to face with Euro Commissioner Chris Patten, and finally "pressurised" the Brit. Time was running out, but we succeeded in bringing him to convince the European Commission to include the final amendment in the Joint Statement; the

---

[1] *Anders Fogh Rasmussen* is NATO Secretary General since 1 August 2009.

amendment fully complied with our demands on obstacle-free travel of Russian citizens to and from Kaliningrad.

Finally, as he was leaving the room, Mr. Patten, who in his time held a post of the British Governor in Hong Kong, said to me: "Mr. Rogozin, you are as bad as the Chinese. I thought it is only they who know how to push a cork back into an open bottle of champagne." Of course, this experienced, highly skilful negotiator was flattering me, but he was absolutely right in one instance: I actually did put up a fight for each and every comma of the final document. If reaching an agreement on Kaliningrad transit was a formality for Chris Patten, for me it was a fight for Russia's honour. I did not have a right to surrender my position, and that is why we won.

So what did we achieve in the end? The European Union made significant alterations in its law, specifically to accommodate the purposes of Russian citizens' travel to and from Kaliningrad, which was something that previously the European bureaucrats did not even wish to consider. In accordance with the new transit rules, effective from 1 July 2003, our citizens did not have to apply for visas in a Lithuanian or any other consulate. They can just buy a train ticket and go.

After a ticket is purchased, both Russian and Lithuanian sides check whether the passenger has a crime record in the Russian Federation or the European Union member states. The checking is equally important for Russia, as a criminal on the federal or international wanted list may board a transit train and escape the country. For example, there were a few cases when Chechens pulled a train to an emergency stop for illegal alightment on the Lithuanian part of a route. The new transit terms eliminated those risks.

At the point of border crossing passengers show their passports to the Lithuanian border patrol officers and receive a Facilitated Rail Travel Document for two visa free trips both ways. Before 1 January 2005, Russian citizens could travel on internal passports. On my insistent request, then head of the Government Mikhail Kasyanov issued an urgent decree that permitted to insert photographs of children traveling with parents into internal passports. That lifted a series of problems during school holidays and minimised the moral and financial burden on our citizens.

So that is all there is to the new procedure. Apart from that, we managed to include in the final Joint Statement our proposal on launching a high-speed non-stop train that would eliminate all remaining inconveniences for transit passengers.

The successful resolution of Kaliningrad transit issue demonstrated the ability of the Russian side to take a firm stand on protecting the interests of Russian citizens; it also helped to ease the tension in our relations with Europe.

The Joint Statement of the European Union and the Russian Federation on transit between the Kaliningrad region and the rest of the Russian Federation is a documented evidence to the fact that Russia and Europe are capable of resolving complicated issues together in the shortest terms possible; it proves that Russian and European politicians can achieve tangible results, and not just engage in diplomatic twitter about the importance of "strategic partnership" without properly understanding what such a partnership implies.

The Decree, signed by Vladimir Putin, officially expressed gratitude to me personally. The practical implementation of the agreement on Kaliningrad transit was delegated to the Ministry of Foreign Affairs and to the Presidential Administration. Unfortunately, the historic decisions of the Russia-EU Summit were carried out only partially. Somehow, everybody forgot about preparing a feasibility study for launching a high-speed nonstop train, as well as about the plans on developing infrastructure in North-Eastern Europe with involvement of the Kaliningrad region. The decision sank to the bottom of wine glasses that had been shared during endless and senseless diplomatic parties. Politicians and diplomats succumbed to the routine, until the push would come to shove.... And the push should come, I am certain.

MOTHERLAND[1]

In June 2003 Vladimir Putin had a meeting with President Kwasniewski in Kaliningrad. The leaders of the two neighbouring countries went out to sea on board of the Baltic Fleet military ship to observe joint military exercises. In Baltiysk (formerly the base of the German submarine Fleet Pillau) we observed the moor where cargo and passenger ferry between Kaliningrad and Saint Petersburg was to be launched. In the evening, after an intense day, the delegation went to the Central Bank residence on the Kurshskaya Sand Bar to stay overnight.

Being left on my own with the President, I took the opportunity to discuss the status of the Russian preparations for the launch of Kaliningrad transit on 1 July under the new terms agreed upon with the EU and Lithuania, as well as the deepening complications in the circumstances of Russian citizens in Turkmenistan. When we were about to finish going over these issues, Mr. Putin unexpectedly asked me how I intended to participate in the forthcoming elections.

I replied that I was very busy working for my constituency in the Voronezh region and intended to run for the Duma in the same constituency for the third consecutive term, but that at the same time I thought it would be necessary to form an electoral coalition. Representation of political forces in the State Duma as of 2002 was unbalanced and did not reflect interests or demands of society. The monopoly of United Russia was being pushed by the Union of Right Forces[2], by the Liberal Democratic Party[3] (party of Zhirinovsky), as well as by the Communist faction, whose members' average age was 64. Even

---

[1] *Motherland*, or *Mother Russia*, is a poetic appellation to our country. Mother Motherland is a symbol made during the Great Patriotic War immortalised in a famous poster. There are many monuments of this name in the former Soviet Union.

[2] *SPS* — The Union of Right Forces– a liberal political party founded in 2001. SPS is the heir of 'Democratic Choice for Russia' party, which was founded in 1994 and merged SPS along with other smaller parties of democratic orientation.

[3] *LDPR* — The Liberal-Democratic Party of Russia led by Vladimir Zhirinovsky since it was founded in 1991.

so, with their artificial proletarian directness, the left wing was merely playing at "being in opposition"; they exploited nostalgic and protesting moods of the senior generation and never thought of fighting for real power. The Duma was becoming impotent; the level of public trust to it was falling, which undermined proper governance of the state.

I was of the opinion that the country was in need of a real alternative, a source of fresh ideas that would meet public demand. Such a new force was to be orientated towards establishing democratic freedoms and social justice, and aimed at economic growth and protection of national interests (not to be confused with the interests of large corporations).

I was certain that under the circumstances, when the ruling elite consolidated under the banners of United Russia, the President needed such political force, too, in order to achieve a balanced system of restraints and have a healthy opposition. In the foreseeable future such a political force might be prepared to assume responsibility for the executive power in the country. I shared these ideas with Putin.

My previous personal experience of contacts with Mr. Putin led me to believe that we held similar views. I was almost certain that the President, as a personality placed above political parties, was interested in the emergence of a project that would be put together by young, but experienced, people in search of new forms of applying themselves in politics.

I told Mr. Putin that during the elections of 1995 I had closely worked in the Congress of Russian Communities with a young economist Sergey Glaziev; and that with him now we could form a new election bloc, which would not only be able to gain voters' support, but also do a good job representing their views and interests in the State Duma.

"I like Glaziev, and I have already discussed with him a possibility of launching a socio-democratic project. Sooner or later Communists will have to be replaced by a serious and modern-thinking left-wing party. And it would be good for the country, too," the President concluded the conversation.

Frankly, the prospect of creating a left-centrist party did not excite me much. I have always considered myself to be a traditionalist, a follower of good old values — family, religion and the national spirit. Because of that, I always treated with prejudice any ideas that belonged to the left from the centre. "Why don't we combine ideas of healthy conservatism with the struggle for social justice in this country that is ripped off by corrupt thieves and oligarchs?" I thought and decided for the time being not to attempt to unconvince Putin as to potential ideological and practical objectives of a new project that we had come up with.

On my return home I called Glaziev and briefed him on the conversation with the President. I did not sense enthusiasm on his part. Possibly, Sergey counted solely on his numerous personal talents and dreamed of creating some "broad national-patriotic coalition" under his leadership. Many organisations that might have been candidates for such a coalition existed only on paper or in Glaziev's imagination. It would have been useless and uninteresting to collect zero entities. I thought that to follow a path of misleading the voters and trying to convince them that we were "a broad coalition" would be a dishonest, as well as a doomed, strategy.

I suggested to Sergey that we pick two or three little-known political parties to formally put the coalition together; bring in several respected individuals who had shared our platform; produce an election manifesto consisting of the sound proposals previously voiced by these figures, and we can go ahead!

On a piece of paper we sketched a list of well-known and respected personalities whom we wanted to invite to appear on election list of a new bloc. As the list was filling up, we realised that we were putting together the "all stars team" of the Russian patriotic movement.

Inventing a name for the new bloc was quite hard. Glaziev deemed it necessary to carry out an analysis with participation of "prominent political scientists and experts." Frankly speaking, I was fed up with all those political scientists. They could never suggest anything specific or practical but were very good at assuming important poses at the meetings and using quasi-scientific words to cover up their "absence of presence". (By the way, I wonder, how many of these "centres of strategic studies and tactical prospects" and "institutes of tactical appraisal and strategic research" are there in this country?) If it were not for Glaziev, I would have kicked the useless and greedy creatures out of the election headquarters. In the end I decided to stop at some "intellectual teasing". I announced in front of the political scientists that I had finally made a decision on the name of the new bloc: "Fraternal United Coalition 'Key'".

"It's not bad," one of Glaziev's experts remarked. "I do not like it, it is rather tedious and inexpressive," someone else objected. "Maybe so, but I like the abbreviation," I said. You should have seen their faces, those quasi-scientists, when they realised the direction this humble enterprise was taking!

Later that night I told Glaziev that I insisted on the name "Rodina" (*Motherland*). As usual, I joked that the words of Lermontov "*I love the Motherland but with a love so strange!*" would be the epigraph to the bloc's name. Typically, Sergey did not get a joke and insisted that the tag "People's Patriotic Union" must be added to the name Rodina. We agreed that I would lead the election campaign and Sergey would become number 1 on Rodina electoral list.

On 13 September each Member Party approved the list of candidates for parliament members from Rodina (People's Patriotic Union) at their internal congresses. The following day the founding conference of the actual bloc took place in the Golden Ring Hotel in Moscow in the presence of the media.

Glaziev was the first to speak. As appropriate to the leader of the list, he made a presentation of our election bloc manifesto, which was written with participation of the best economists — members of the Academy of Sciences of the Russian Federation. Undoubtedly, it was an important and substantial document, however, the members of the bloc had already been familiar with it, and the journalists were not particularly interested and started to make their way to the exit too soon. I decided that my presentation should be made in contrast with Glaziev's rather dry report. I realised that we had very little time left for the campaign, as we were starting from zero rating and had very little public awareness and recognition. Such circumstances required some healthy epatage on our side. In my speech I stressed that our task was to prevent the restoration of state power circa 1990s with its liberal thieving privatisation, economic downfall and Russian national interests' sell-off. I finished my speech with the children's rhyme from the Russian blockbuster *Brother-2*:

> "I have learnt I've got a huge family.
> Grass, woods,
> Every corn head in the field,
> The Sun, Blue sky —
> That's all my kin.
> That's my Motherland.
> I love everybody in the world."

Of course, everyone in the audience had seen that popular film a few times at least and remembered an episode where the main hero recited this rhyme and then reloaded the gun and shot at the gang of American criminals. Getting the hint, the whole audience applauded; the journalists came to the conclusion that, at any rate, thanks to Rodina the forthcoming elections were not going to be boring. This proved to be the case. Rodina literally took the election campaign by storm.

Our campaign started with a TV commercial that showed Glaziev and me peacefully conversing over beer. "Oh, Dima, I don't like those oligarchs!" Glaziev exclaimed from the screen. "Serega, if you don't like it — don't eat it!" my reply followed. To be honest, Glaziev was a lousy actor. We had to go through twenty-four takes before the commercial was cut. Each time I took a sip of fresh beer from a large glass. By the end of the shooting I felt rather tipsy and jolly.

After the meeting in our headquarters, the day after the TV commercial was released, a rather odd girl, a university friend of Glaziev whom he for some reason put on the election list, angrily scolded me: "How did you dare to arrange for such a thing to be broadcast! The Society of Teetotalers is indignant!"

"Tell the Teetotalers that the beer was non-alcoholic. Is that right, Sergey Yuryevich?" I winked at Glaziev. Everyone looked at him. Glaziev's face betrayed traces of the exhausting filming of the day before.

"The Beer footage" intrigued viewers and attracted attention to our election campaign; from then on the campaign was led in an assertive and strict tone. We could not afford to procrastinate or mobilise support of the masses. We did not have enough people to distribute news lists and other agitation material in the regions. That is why I concentrated key efforts and resources on televised debates. There were some excellent polemists, some bright and distinguished individuals on the Rodina lists, and it would have been a shame to waste the team's talents, so we aimed at a direct dialogue with our electorate.

It was useless to try challenging the parliamentary majority. Their representatives were ignoring pre-election debates on state television channels, as well as in the *Freedom of Speech* NTV programme presented by Savik Shuster on NTV.

Communists appealed exclusively to their core electoral base and did not aim to broaden it, and so they also chose not to appear on *Freedom of Speech*.

Regular faces in televised debates aside from Rodina were people from Yabloko, the People's Party that had since discontinued senselessly and prematurely, LDPR, and SPS.

In the course of the live debates I practically had a duel with representatives of the Union of Right Forces who had singled out Rodina and me personally as their private enemies. I paid back in kind. Here is an extract from one such debate that probably attracted attention of the whole audience:

> **Host:** Please, Boris Nemtsov[1]. Boris Yephimovich, I address you with the same question about the President's statement. Yes, there are journalists and foreign politicians who are used and who are paid out of large capitals; but on the other hand the President said that there would be no reviews of policy, no change of political track. Does this unite or divide you?
>
> **Boris Nemtsov:** You know, I did not like the President's statement very much. The thing is, by making such a statement he is dividing civil society apart. Judge for yourself: Khodorkovsky was incarcerated before his trial; let me draw your attention to this fact. He has not been proved guilty so far. Have they increased pensions or stipends since? There are students in the audience; maybe they received an increase in stipends? Capital was taken out of the country, large contracts were terminated, investments were reduced, jobs were lost, and inflow into the budget has shrunk. The result? Poor country, more poverty, no economic growth. We totally agreed with the President when he said that we needed to double our gross domestic product. What he is doing now is in direct contradiction with that statement.
>
> The second thing: I have looked and our lawyers have looked into the crimes that Khodorkovsky is accused of.
>
> Ten million people can be put into prison for such crimes. These are the crimes, for instance, of business activity without registering a legal entity. Instead of incarcerating people like Khodorkovsky, you need to tax them. And so our proposal is the following.
>
> Yes, truly they have mega income. Yes, we can and we must increase the rent on natural resources, but not the way that Rodina proposes — absolutely mad figures — but by 120–150 billions of roubles. At the same time, it is necessary to reduce taxes in all other, non-natural resources sectors of economy in order to develop industries, agriculture, small and medium-sized businesses, scientific technologies. This is the essence of our proposal. We proposed to the Kremlin to do this back in August. We submitted our proposals to them. The result — he was imprisoned, the money left the country, the economic growth

---

[1] *Boris Nemtsov* — a co-founder of the union of Right Forces. Boris Nemtsov was Deputy Prime Minister in 1997–1998. He is an avid critic of Vladimir Putin.

was suspended, and the prestige of Russia is going downhill. That's all there is to it.

Host: Dmitry Rogozin, your word.

Dmitry Rogozin: Boris Yephimovich, what do you think, is Chubais going to prison? (the audience laughs and burst with applause)

Boris Nemtsov: You know, this question makes me think of Nikolai Ivanovivh Yezhov[1]. If Dmitry lived in Yezhov's times, he would have worked in the same style. I have to tell you, we (*SPS*) are one team; we have been together for thirteen years. Nobody has managed to divide our team, nobody, and neither will Rogozin. We are stuck together, we will continue stick together, and we will win these elections....

But these words of the faded cowboy Nemtsov were spoken in vain. After my brief question the audience was not listening to him any longer. They unconditionally supported Rodina in the uncompromising struggle with oligarchs and with "devil's advocates". That was the major problem of our liberals: in their routine criticism of Putin and pathetic campaigning for Khodorkovsky they could not understand why people did not trust them anymore. And the reason people did not trust them, was precisely because such "reformers" as Chubais and Nemtsov were chiefly responsible for the excesses (what a mild expression!) of Yeltsin's times. The anti-Putin rhetoric, coming out of the mouths of Nemtsov & Co., sounded like a cynical lie, which merely served to achieve the effect of affirming the President's authority.

At times the debates on Savik Shuster talk show were so astute that the audience hardly paid attention to Mr. Zhirinovsky, who had already existed in the state of an ongoing hysteria, trying to redirect all the attention towards him, as always. The LDPR leader could not forgive Andrey Saveliev who had awarded a slap to Zhirinovsky for publicly offending the memory of General Shpak's son, killed in Chechnya[2].

Opinion palls were supposed to be monitored in the course of the televised debates. At the end of the very first round of the debates

---

[1] *Nikolai Yezhov* (1895–1940) was a senior figure in the NKVD (People's Committee of Internal affairs), the Soviet Secret Police under Stalin.

[2] *General George Shpak* was the Russian Air Force Commander in 1996–2003. His only son Oleg, Lieutenant Shpak was killed on a mission in Chechnya in 1995.

we received 40% of total votes. That was our first achievement. The impressionable Savik Shuster remarked: "Gentlemen, we are witnessing the birth of the new political force."

After the further two rounds, when it became clear that Glaziev was getting the majority of votes, the practice of interactive voting stopped. I had my ideas why but still wanted to check with Savik. He looked down and said: "The software broke down...." That meant that our growing popularity alarmed the competition.

Boris Berezovsky made his mark by issuing a couple of nasty remarks in the heat of the elections. As he could not dig any dirt to throw at us, he, like a skunk, decided to use internal resources and publicly alleged that I had asked him for money. I conveyed a responding message to the "London outcast", saying that I thought that planting a "Birch tree" (a nickname of Berezovsky)[1] was a major life goal of a real man, not, of course, underestimating such missions as to raise a child and to build a house.[2]

The same week I received an email with a threat from another outcast — leader of the Chechen bandit underground, "the hero" of Budyonnovsk maternity ward Shamil Basayev. We had announced a reward to be paid out of our election fund for information on his whereabouts. We did that publicly signing all necessary legal guarantees. Basayev took our actions seriously and distributed on his network of separatist information agencies the following curious piece of writing (original Basayev's spelling and style is preserved):

> *To the election mob Rodina.*
>
> *Recently in the media of Rusnya[3] the election mob Rodina held a cheap campaign offering 500,000 USD for my head. In this connection I address one of the leaders of Rodina mob Rogozin — "Why you bastard offer so little? Or you ran out of dosh? Where is the 150 million that you together with Lebedev and then deputy Finance Minister Vavilov stole from Moscow district, devaluing their stock through National Reserve Bank and Inkombank? Where are 480 million from so called Indian contract that the three of you — plus Potanin — laundered through Seychelles*

---

[1] The surname *"Berezovsky"* originates from the word "bereza" meaning a birch tree is in Russian.

[2] A Russian proverb says that the three most important things a man has to do in his life is to build a house, plant a tree and raise a child.

[3] *Rusnya* — a derogatory name for Russia often used in the Chechen underground circles.

and Comoros islands and invested some of it through Swiss banks into Svyazinvest?"

If you spent all that money you could borrow from Zhirinovsky at least, to whom Saddam paid 5 million American dollars in cash for one sitting on the toilet.

My advice, goner, don't be mean and don't tremble over the dosh like Gobseck.

With no respect whatsoever,

Abdallah Shamil Abu-Idris

It was not clear what money the major Chechen bandit was referring to in his letter. Now, after he had accidentally tripped his own mine in 2006 and became "a goner" himself, it is unlikely that I will ever find out. Probably he confused me with my namesake — a former Deputy Head of Security under Boris Yeltsin, "the Kremlin Medium" General George Rogozin, or with someone else altogether. But the very fact that Basayev worried about his skin was self-evident — even international terrorists, warmed up by the fire in the cold mountains of the Caucasus, were thinking of Rodina!

Going back to the subject of SPS, in 2003 the team of privatisation forefathers aspired to the state power again.

A threat of restoration of the liberal thieving ideology was present and manifested itself vividly in Russia. In fact, what the liberals represented did not even deserve to be defined as an ideology. Its apologists, the young and pushy mediocrities of the 1980s, all those chiefs of social sciences laboratories and fresh Doctors of Philosophy, who sharpened their wit in the perfectly safe criticism of political economy of socialism and the Communism studies, simply were on demand by Yeltsin's regime in the 1990s.

Naturally, they inherited all the inhibitions of Soviet intellectuals, based on the mixture of hatred for the USSR and the mania to always start a new project with demolition (as per the well-known hymn *Internacionale*). These odd people in power despised all things domestic and especially all things Russian; they were prepared to conduct social experiments over their people.

As soon as they found themselves at the steering wheel, they put aside their proclaimed manifesto of economic effectiveness, democracy and the importance of public opinion, and then the hell broke loose.

Chances to almost instantaneously build up capitals, equal only to royals and captains of transnational corporations, were intoxicating; such opportunities suppressed their instinct of self-preservation and the ability to think straight. It is hardly surprising that many of that generation did not live to witness the "bright future" in which we exist now.

Soon I had a chance to prove correctness of my estimations to the liberal spiritual guru Anatoly Chubais. The dynamic growth in the number of our supporters and the fatal weakening of SPS position became all too apparent at the final stage of the election campaign.

Chubais made a desperate attempt to remedy the situation and invited me for a one-to-one debate in a popular TV talk show *To the Barrier!*

Only three days remained until the Election Day.

The Ostankino TV studio was filled with security staff of the Russian Joint Stock Company "Single energy system of Russia" (JSC "EES Russia"), which was then chaired by Anatoly Chubais. Chubais must have done many things in his life to necessitate such a high level of protection and security. A solid group of his supporters settled on tribunes. Some of his supporters were constantly making faces at me; one unbalanced lady of the literary last name Tolstaya showed me her tongue. Probably, these were the sophisticated psychological methods used by our liberal intellectuals to destabilise opponents.

Chubais made up a scary story to name and shame Rodina throughout the country, labeling Glaziev and me as "socio-nationalists". To follow his logic, judging by my views on issues of national security, foreign policy and crime resistance, I was a nationalist; and Glaziev was a socialist as he promoted social justice as the founding base of economic growth. As a result of a simple mathematical compilation of two words, Chubais deduced that we were indeed "socio-nationalists" and called for "all progressive mankind to unite against the brown menace".

I got the impression that Mr. Chubais was accustomed to performing solo. He was blowing his affirmations into the listeners' ears and never tolerated a disagreement or as much as a hint of polemics. Several Old Testament Communists in the audience were the only opponents acknowledged by him; he repeated to them, not missing a single opportunity: "I hammered the last nail into the coffin of Communism."

During one of Chubais' TV appearances, two glamorous hosts asked the man to name his favourite piece from Russian classical literature. I was startled when Anatoly Borisovich thought long and hard, and failed to name a single title; he blamed his inability to answer the question on the Soviet school that had allegedly undone his affinity for literature. However, this should not be too surprising, given Chubais's public image and his practices of managing the state's assets. Astounding is how people like him ever came to power.

All sorts of people surface in uncertain times. 150 years ago Fyodor Dostoevsky wrote about the imminent advance of demons on Russia:

> *What constituted the turbulence of our time and what transition it was we were passing through...*
>
> *Yet the most worthless fellows suddenly gained predominant influence, began loudly criticising everything sacred, though till then they had not dared to open their mouths... guffawing foreigners, poets of advanced tendencies from the capital, poets who made up with peasant coats and tarred boots for the lack of tendencies or talents, majors and colonels who ridiculed the senselessness of the service, and who would have been ready for an extra rouble to unbuckle their swords, and take jobs as railway clerks; generals who had abandoned their duties to become lawyers; advanced mediators, advancing merchants, innumerable divinity students, women who were the embodiment of the woman question—all these suddenly gained complete sway among us....*

The demons, by the way, reciprocated the great writer with the equally intensive hatred. Below is Chubais' message to Dostoevsky, taken from an interview to *The Financial Times*:

> *You know, I've re-read Dostoevsky over the past three months. And I feel nothing but almost physical hatred for the man. He is certainly a genius, but his idea of Russians as special, holy people, his cult of suffering and the false choices he proposes make me want to tear him to pieces.*

Back at *To the Barrier!* the host signaled the start of the show and Chubais and I began the duel. "The notorious crook Ostap Bender[1] knew thirty three methods of voluntary extortion of money out of population. How many methods do you know, Mr. Chubais?" was my first strike. The debates (if they could be called that) went on for about three hours. Emotions were running high; a fight nearly broke out among supporters on tribunes. I was dead tired by the end of it. Emotionally overloaded,

---

[1] *Ostap Bender* — a fictional con man and antihero from the novel "The Twelve Chairs" (1928) by Soviet writers Ilya Ilf and Yevgeny Petrov. "The Twelve Chairs" and its sequel "The Golden Calf" are a source of popular quotes in Russia.

I felt the stress of the past weeks building up. Just a day before, I returned home from a field trip running high fever.

The programme was aired the following night and attracted a multi-million audience. I was leading the polls until the final commercial break, whereupon the counter of my votes stopped, and a number of phone calls for Chubais suddenly sky-rocketed.

In the end, I lost the public vote by a small margin. The television screens showed the name of the company that supplied technical software for counting votes: MTU-Intel. Only a fool wouldn't guess that JSC "EES Russia" was the main shareholder in that company.

All his tricks played a bad joke on Chubais. The Elections Day, three days after the duel, showed that the Rodina bloc gained three times as many voters as SPS did; Rodina entered the State Duma, having achieved the sensational 9% in the elections.

My personal score in a single mandate constituency was a country record — 79.3%. Voronezh region, by then already so dear to me, did not let us down, too — 20% of electorate there voted for Rodina; the share of Rodina supporters exceeded 50% in single cities of the Voronezh region.

FATHERS AND SONS[1]

In the end of August 2004, when the State Duma stopped fighting over the "monetisation law"[2], I went to South Ossetia in the company of Yury Saveliev, Nikolai Pavlov, and Mikhail Markelov, deputies of our faction. Relations between Russia and Georgia were getting increasingly conflict-ridden. The Chechen underground terrorists were still hiding in the Pankissi Gorge. The warlords acted blatantly, training new recruits in their paramilitary camps.

In that same year Mikheil Saakashvili came to power in Tbilisi. A former "anti-corruption" activist and a first-class demagogue, he literally crushed down flabby Shevardnadze's Administration. However, the new President depended on the Georgian thieves as much as the Grey Fox did during his presidency. New Georgian authorities were not overly preoccupied with economic revival of the Republic or with establishing good neighbourly relations with Russia. Official Tbilisi followed the logic of keeping people in implicit obedience and regarded the chauvinistic appeals for a "victorious war" against Abkhazia and South Ossetia to be the most effective tool of mobilising the starving masses. Cynical Saakashvili understood that very well. With a solid backup in Washington, he marked the beginning of his term with threats addressed to Tskhinvali and Sukhumi.

As a result of Georgian leadership's aggressive conduct, an extremely tense situation developed around Tskhinvali. The capital

---

[1] *Fathers and Sons* (1862) is the best-known work by Ivan Turgenev. The literary translation of the title is "Fathers and Children" which does sound epiphanic in English. The main character Bazarov is a nihilist and rejects the old order despite having affectionate, yet distant, relations with his parents. The novel is about a growing divide between generations.

[2] *Monetisation law* — in 2005 Russia transformed most of the in-kind benefits into monetary compensation. Rodina faction in the State Duma voted against the measures, and after the law had been adopted some of the deputies went on a hunger strike. The monetisation largely affected pensioners and caused a wave of protests and discontent throughout the country.

city, just as the whole of South Ossetia, is cut off from North Ossetia by the Caucasus Mountain ridge and Georgian villages. It is not easy to get to Tskhinvali. First you have to take the mountain road that is at risk of an avalanche, till you reach the Roki Tunnel at the height of 3,000 metres. Then, after passing the border control, you have to make it through 3,660 metres of the obscure "road of life", perforated in the Sokh Mountain. Next, you have to drive across four Georgian villages where the locals cast sharp glances at strangers and throw Russian flags and Putin's crumpled portraits under the wheels of passing cars. Finally, you can slow down at the South Ossetian checkpoint before you enter Tskhinvali. The journey takes almost half a day, but in bad weather conditions, or if an armed confrontation occurs, one can get stuck in the mountains for days.

We were lucky. We reached Tskhinvali without problems. In the capital of this brave Republic we were warmly welcomed by South Ossetian President Eduard Kokoity, by the Parliament's Speaker, and by our party's local activists. Practically all the residents of the Republic were Russian citizens, so we had not had difficulties in setting up a party cell in Tskhinvali.

After the brief protocol meetings and interviews to the Republican television, the guests, journalists and accompanying officials left the office of the President. I remained tête-à-tête with Mr. Kokoity. In a military-like manner the President briefed me on the situation around the Republic. Armed provocations became common practice. The city was regularly subjected to shelling. Citizens of the Republic were taken hostages on a regular basis and released only following the harsh response measures from Tskhinvali. Several dozens of the South Ossetian citizens were kept in prisons in Georgia and deprived of the right to see their relatives.

The Georgian leadership pretended that they had nothing to do with all that business, as if the hostage-taking and the shootings were the deeds of an unspecified "third force." At that, Saakashvili's people were pointing at Chechens. No one believed those tales, of course. Everybody understood that the units of the Georgian regular army operating in the conflict zone were behind the violations. Those units had been trained by US instructors and tasked with spreading fear and pushing Ossetians out and into Russia.

Meanwhile, a crowd waited for us in the Tskhinvali theatre. It looked like the whole town gathered together to see and hear the deputies of the popular Russian patriotic party.

The spacious hall, the corridor, the boxes, and the balconies of the theatre, as well as the entire square in front of the theatre and the streets adjacent to it, were filled. "See, they greet you with such a warm welcome!" the President of the Republic, who sat by my side in the presidium, winked at me delightedly.

"They are not here to greet me, they are greeting Russia!" I replied.

Indeed, South Ossetians greeted us with enthusiasm that inspired all of us, and we all shared their elated mood. Every word pronounced into the microphone was caught on by the audience and spread all over the town. The people of South Ossetia dreamt of breaking away from Georgia, but only together with their indigenous land, where the remains of their ancestors were buried. The people of South Ossetia sought Moscow's protection, they turned to Russia, and they trusted her. I introduced my colleagues — Yury Saveliev, Mikhail Markelov, and Nikolai Pavlov — and Ossetians gave them a standing ovation. Some people cried the tears of joy.

I ended my speech with the promise to do everything in our power to facilitate the reunification of the Ossetian people. The audience burst with delight. At that moment I felt a truly happy man. Thousands of people thought alike; they were dreaming of Russia; they had faith in the greatness of the Motherland and were ready to defend her with weapons in their hands. Perhaps, you can only love Russia that much when you are far away from her, like those dear people, who welcomed me in their homes so warmly. In moments like these, a political leader feels needed; it is a test whether the ideas that he represents are related to people's aspirations. That was, indeed, a moment of truth in politics, a minute when a politician feels one with the people.

The meeting lasted longer than we expected; we also spent some time saying good byes outside. At last we got into cars for the return journey.

Head of the Supreme Council of North Ossetia Mr. Taymuraz Mamsurov spent a few hours in a Vladikavkaz hotel, waiting for us. He asked us to come back early, so that on 1 September we could visit one of the local schools to celebrate the Day of Knowledge[1] with children and parents before flying up to Moscow from Beslan Airport. We were supposed to visit school #1 — Mamsurov's children attended it. We were

---

[1] *Day of Knowledge* is celebrated every year in Russia on 1 September, the start of the school year.

going to discuss the results of our journey to Tskhinvali on the way to the school and then to the airport. That had been our arrangement.

However, our journey back to Vladikavkaz was, indeed, held up. South Ossetian leader Mr. Eduard Kokoity warned us that his patrol guards had obtained intelligence about a planned ambush near the Roki Tunnel, orchestrated by Georgia; Mr. Kokoity insisted on taking a different route. We went down a picturesque, albeit worn-down, bypass road. There was only one advantage to that road — it was entirely under control of the South Ossetian Armed Forces.

At last our convoy stopped right at the entry into the Roki Tunnel where we could feel perfectly safe. The Ossetian patrol towers were clearly visible on top of the hills despite the dusk. In a few seconds car bonnets were transformed into improvised dinner tables. The traditional Ossetian "three pies", greens and fresh vegetables — everything came in very handy. We shared a drink before parting, hugged our new friends, got back into the cars and drove into a dark, long tunnel.

We arrived in Vladikavkaz late at night, past 2am. To my dire surprise, I saw Teymuraz Mamsurov who had been waiting for us in the hotel lobby. "Our hospitality law does not permit me to leave you on your own", he said in a voice that did not tolerate protests. We talked for another hour and in the end decided to skip the next day's school; we needed to sleep after the exhausting journey. Teymuraz showed compassion and agreed with that. He said that in this case he would not accompany us to Beslan Airport but would remain in Vladikavkaz and go to the Republican University in the morning to congratulate students on the Day of Knowledge.

In the morning we drove off in the company of a Republican Press Office staff member and a Militia car. The journey took less than half an hour. The local journalists had already set their microphones in the press area and waited for us in the Airport Deputy Hall. I positioned myself in front of the mics and began the briefing, when suddenly my assistant came by my side, leaned towards me and whispered worryingly that some strangers had just locked down a school in Beslan, seven minutes drive from the airport.

At that point none of us could comprehend the true scale of this tragedy; nevertheless we immediately decided to postpone our return to Moscow. At the time we did not know that Beslan Airport was going to be closed shortly, all flights would be cancelled and all passengers taken off the plane that was about to fly to Moscow.

At full speed we drove to Beslan, where we nearly got under machine-gun fire, bullets were shooting just fifty metres away from us. The driver pulled up the car, and we quickly got out. Right at that moment an APC carrying Ossetian OMON fighters in helmets and full body armour stopped in front of me. Soldiers jumped off the tank, clicking the shatters of their sub-machine guns, and spread to form an immediate blockade.

A man was standing by the entrance to the militia station that adjoined the school. He was extremely anxious. Judging by his soaked with sweat shirt, I gathered he had been one of the few lucky ones to miraculously escape from the school building, seized by warlords.

The man described the first moments of the lock-down and told me that the approximate number of hostages was 800. According to him, there were at least thirty terrorists inside the building.

I forwarded the man for further questioning as an eyewitness to a Militia major who had just come up. Then I switched on my mobile phone and dialed the special commutator[1] number. Briefly explaining to the lady who took the call who and where I was and what had just happened, I asked her to put me through to the Government urgently. I also asked her to urgently arrange for a vehicle equipped with special mobile government communication line so that we could set up headquarters of hostage release; we needed to establish a direct line with the Kremlin, FSB, and the Chief of Staff of the Armed Forces.

We realised from the first minute of our arrival to Beslan that a large-scale catastrophe was unfolding. Obviously, under the circumstances the principal decisions on the course of the operation had to be taken not in Vladikavkaz, and not even at the level of the Plenipotentiary Representative of the President to Ossetia, but only in Moscow, personally by the Head of State.

I noticed Alexander Dzasokhov, the President of North Ossetia, among the military. Taymuraz Mamsurov was standing beside him. He looked awful. Mamsurov's children — son and daughter — were among the hostages inside the school to which he invited us earlier for the celebration.

We went into the backyard of an office building. Breathless Dzasokhov's aides finally brought the city map and the plan of the school building. About ten minutes later, a note with the terrorists' initial demands was thrown out of a school window and delivered to us. The note read as follows:

8–928–738-33-374. We demand that President of the Republic Dzasokhov, Ingush President Zyazikov and children's doctor Rashailo

---

[1] *Special commutator* — governmental communication switchboard.

negotiate with us. If one of us is killed, we will shoot down fifty people. If one of us is injured, we will kill twenty people. If five of us are killed, we will blow up the building. If electricity or communications are blocked for one minute, we will shoot down ten people.

As it turned out later, that phone number was wrong. As for the "children's doctor Rashailo", the headquarters assumed that the terrorists meant Leonid Roshal, chairman of the Relief Fund for Children in Catastrophes and Wars.

Terrorists were acting competently. Unlike some of our excessively chatty Federal Security officials, who complacently blurt out inside secrets and details of counter-terrorist activities on television, the bandits had learned a lot from the "Nord-Ost" experience; they had foreseen a possibility that Special Services might use soporific gases and other special means. On our part, we couldn't even find intelligent negotiators or renowned intermediaries who would be able to negotiate the release of at least some of the hostages. Those who were involved, including Doctor Roshal, with all my respect for their professionalism and courage, turned out to be too loquacious.

In the aftermath of the terrorist attack on Dubrovka in Moscow, TV channels reported in detail how the children's doctor passed the most valuable information to the Federal Security Service after the terrorists had given him access to the hostages; Leonid Roshal described the characteristics of the terrorists' explosion devices in full detail and indicated where the female suicide-bombers were positioned inside the theatre. After this "promotional act", when the Doctor was granted a well-deserved official award, could he have been of use in rescuing the Beslan children? Of course he could not. Terrorists considered Leonid Roshal an FSB informer.

One might think that the militants called the Doctor to come inside the school on purpose, so that they could execute him in revenge for the deaths of their accomplices. Knowing a bit about their behaviour, I will never believe that this was the case, just as I did not believe it then. My version is that this note was dictated by a terrorist to one of the women-hostages, who got killed afterwards. This poor victim was heavily affected by the situation and not only made a mistake when writing down the telephone number, but also added "children's doctor" (that had not been dictated to her) after the surname "Rashailo".

In reality, the terrorists demanded to speak to Vladimir Rushailo, Secretary of the Security Council of Russia and former Interior Minister. I shared my version of the interpretation of the note with heads of the operative headquarters right away. But no one gave these considerations a proper thought; the request to urgently bring in the famous doctor to Beslan was passed on to Moscow. The note was carelessly left on a desk in our headquarters; I had to prompt one of the senior officers to put it away. I saw plenty of examples of such negligence and confusion during the hostage-release operation.

The team finally decided on the headquarters' location, opting for the district council building nearby. A group of chief officers set to walk there and was nearly hit by a shell fire. In order to protect the Republican chiefs from terrorist shooters, one of the military came up with a plan to block gaps between buildings by OMON APCs. That was not the wisest of decisions, either. According to this suggestion, the Speaker of the North Ossetian Parliament, the Russian MPs, and a group of the Militia and Army generals were supposed to hop in between the houses like rabbits, moving through the shelling zone in the sight of the whole troubled town that now resembled a hive. The Special Forces were meant to simultaneously shield that horrific sight with fire, armour, and own bodies. Angry remarks and swearing between the political and military figures of North Ossetia followed, and the decision was made to get to headquarters by cars via a by-pass road.

We were there in five minutes. Dzasokhov, Mamsurov, and my colleagues occupied two small rooms on the second floor where the special governmental communication office was equipped quite soon. The military officers and the FSB Combat Units staff took all other available rooms. They set up the military headquarters on the ground floor. Even Dzasokhov had no access there. Senior officers of the Special Forces took the first floor and the adjacent wing of the second floor.

A little later, Plenipotentiary Representative of the Russian President in the South Federal District Vladimir Yakovlev, Deputy Prosecutor General in the South Federal District Sergey Fridinsky, and the FSB Deputy Director Vladimir Pronichev arrived in Beslan. Everybody was there with the exception of the President of Ingushetia Murat Zyazikov. I had his mobile number and tried calling him just to check if the number was correct; unexpectedly I got through to him at once.

"Who is this?" asked Murat cautiously.

"Murat, hello, it's me, Rogozin! Glad to have reached you. Do you know what is going on here? In Beslan, I mean. Where are you? Everyone is looking for you. Dzasokhov and the Muscovites are here…" I was shouting.

"I am far away," said Zyazikov and cut off.

I told Dzasokhov and Fridinsky about the phone call. They exchanged a look but said nothing. No one mentioned Zyazikov any more.

Everybody was desperate for some new information. Eduard Kokoity with whom I had parted at the entrance to the Roki Tunnel came from Tskhinvali. He alone seemed to keep cool. Kokoity and Dzasokhov were on tense terms — they exchanged chilly greetings and barely spoke to each other at all.

Doctor Leonid Roshal's arrival in Beslan was met with agitation.

Generals were following him everywhere, as if he was our "master key" from the treasure chest, seized by the bandits. A separate room and a telephone line for communicating with militants in the school were immediately allocated to the Doctor.

Doctor Roshal shut the door behind him and started to dial the number. He did not get an answer. As I had mentioned already, there was a mistake in the number in that note.

A couple of hours later the FSB operating officers finally established the connection with terrorists. They put through "Rashailo, the children's doctor" to one of the terrorist leaders, but the conversation was not a success; they did not expect the Doctor in the school and, despite his insistent offers, denied him access to the children.

Roshal was dispirited. His mood immediately spread around. Only one of the generals, who kept stopping Dzasokhov from walking into the school building alone, repeated theatrically, "It's not that bad! We've seen worse."

The operational headquarters never came up with a specific plan of how to rescue the hostages. But there were no cowards either among those who stayed in Beslan back then — each and everyone was ready to volunteer being a hostage in exchange for the children. After consulting with my party colleagues, I offered that we, State Duma Deputies, go there in exchange for the children hostages. Dzasokhov thanked me and said that our help could indeed be essential; however, the Security agents and Government in Moscow flatly refused such an action. Nevertheless, I once again assured the North Ossetian President that we were ready to be exchanged for the children. Considering my status of head of a Duma faction, I thought that the terrorists would agree to release at least a hundred kids in exchange for myself.

It is easy to write about it now. How do I convey the feeling of utter responsibility mixed with an understandable fear of imminent death that we experienced then? I did not have the slightest doubt that if the exchange took place, I would not have been able to get out of that school alive. This repulsive and clinging fear, which I had never felt before, not even on the front lines in Transniestria and Bosnia, made me listen carefully to the sounds of every movement behind the door. I waited for them to come and call for me. I waited for it and wanted it to happen.

I was imagining how those frightened innocent little creatures suffered so much with no food, no drink, and no hope. I hated those who in their fanaticism were prepared to kill our most vulnerable: defenseless children who could not possibly put up a fight.

My entire being was desperate to help them, but I did not want to be slaughtered, like a lamb, by their tormentors. It is one thing to go down fighting with a weapon in hand and taking a couple of bearded bastards with me, but to surrender to terrorists and to accept death with complacency is quite another.

I had plenty of time to think it over and took an immediate and irreversible decision to be ready to go inside that school but… continuous waiting-around during the first day and the sleepless night and up to the climax on 3 September were wearing me out.

If someone says to you that in times like these a person is not afraid to die, do not believe it. All sane people fear for their own lives, but sometimes circumstances do not leave us a choice. If you are a public political figure, if you value your name and reputation, you will walk into that damn school, no matter how powerful is your fear's grip.

Time was running out. On 1 September we decided that two of our deputies, Nikolai Pavlov and Yury Saveliev, should go to Moscow and try to persuade the Duma leadership to hold an extraordinary parliamentary assembly.

Mikhail Markelov, a journalist who had worked almost in every hot zone of the former USSR, and I stayed in Beslan. North Ossetian leader Alexander Dzasokhov, an experienced diplomat and just an intelligent man, also supported our idea to hold an extraordinary session of both chambers of the Russian Parliament, thinking that this would trigger the mechanisms of foreign and international pressure on the terrorists; the latter had some foreign hirelings in their midst, according to the operative data of the FSB.

Meanwhile, now and then some strange and inadequate suggestions came from Moscow. These ideas brought about even more disarray. For example, I was asked to receive a delegation of Chechen women, who, following the initiative of Vice Prime Minister of Chechnya Ramzan

Kadyrov[1], intended to stage a rally in Beslan in support of the hostages. I strongly objected to that idea. I smelled a provocation. Infuriated Ossetians of Beslan would have come pouncing at the unbidden guests.

Then, Speaker of the State Duma Boris Gryzlov called, saying that we should be expecting a bunch of United Russia MPs. I could not stand it any longer, so I called Dmitry Medvedev who was head of the Presidential Administration at the time, and asked him to put a stop to all this "tourism". The city longed for some real help from the headquarters and Moscow and did not need more of the official visits. Medvedev promised to intervene, and awkward initiatives finally stopped.

At night the city was buzzing. It seemed that nobody slept at all. Armed with hunting rifles or even sub-machine guns, the severe men on the streets of Beslan looked warily at every stranger.

At about 2am Eduard Kokoity and I went outside the headquarters to get some fresh air. People on the street immediately knew who we were and asked us to talk to the hostages' relatives. Turning back to check if we were catching up, people hurried us into the yard of the local Palace of Culture. A live human procession literally carried us inside. We sat down in silence. Those who could not find a chair remained standing in the corridors.

Only yesterday, a similar Ossetian crowd in Tskhinvali gave me a standing ovation for every word that I said. Today, I stood at the stage level in the front aisle, a microphone in my hand and heavy thoughts in my head.

The Beslan Ossetians, whose sons and daughters, wives and husbands, sisters and brothers were lying on the school gym floor covered in blood, with no food or water, and with a faint hope for survival, were watching me closely, expecting to hear news of any kind. I looked back at the President of South Ossetia and, very quietly, requested him to open the meeting.

Kokoity started to speak in his native language. We heard some exclamations and sobbing in the audience. But the majority was listening to their fellow countryman with great attention. Eduard switched to Russian language and introduced me. "We know who he is! Let him speak!" someone cried out from the back rows.

I climbed up the stage and said the following:

"My dear citizens of Beslan! It happened so that the trouble that descended upon your city caught me in the course of a visit to your Republic. I stayed here to try and help as much as I can to save your

---

[1] Ramzan Kadyrov is now President of Chechnya.

children. I can promise you one thing for sure: my friends, who are now in Beslan, and I are prepared to be exchanged for your relatives and the loved ones. If the bandits agree, we will proceed with this exchange immediately.

Another thing. The best counter-terrorism experts are already here in your city. They are highly professional. Let's all of us pray for success of their task.

I have nothing more to say to you for the moment. God be with us."

I went off the stage and headed for the exit. Nobody tried to stop me or asked awkward questions. People were waiting for a miracle, believed in the fortunate destinies of hostages, and were afraid to betray a premonition of disaster.

As we were walking away, someone shouted behind our backs: "Tell Dzasokhov to speak to people! Let us look him in the eyes! If you go for an assault, you are all going to die!"

The voices were silenced by the sounds of gunfire coming from the school and grenade explosions 200 metres away from us. With heavy hearts, Eduard and I returned to the operational headquarters. The gloomy anticipation of an outcome lingered all through the night.

It is important to note that the lack of any information whatsoever and the reluctance of the Republican leadership to talk to people infuriated residents of Beslan. People suspected that the National Security agents were planning to storm the school. No one believed the promises that the storm would be a Hollywood-style bloodless exercise.

Director of the North Ossetian Republican FSB branch, General Valery Andreyev, appointed the Head of the operative headquarters, was the one to talk to the mass media the most, somewhat assuming a role of a lightning conductor. It was clear that it was not he, but his immediate bosses, somewhere in the vicinity, were the ultimate decision-makers in planning the operation.

Beslan citizens were utterly indignant that the information about the number of hostages was made public. I have no clue as to how and who came up with 365. Most probably, this was not an intentional deceit but simply the incomplete data compiled on the basis of the information provided by the hostages' relatives. Some of the relatives saw the operative headquarters' phone number on the news and managed to get through. However, that number could not possibly reflect the real number of the people in captivity inside the school.

First of all, entire families might have fallen into the terrorists' clutches, and there could be plainly no one left in the family who would be able to call the headquarters. Secondly, many Beslan citizens were outdoors all the time, did not watch the news, and were unaware of the headquarters hotline. Thirdly, many citizens thought that they should better not give any extra information to the Muscovites, fearing that this might only harm their beloved ones in trouble.

Whatever the reason behind it, the incomplete data about the number of hostages caused resentment in the city. Beslan citizens were convinced that the headquarters disseminated an intentional lie in an attempt to disguise the fact that an armed storm of the building was being planned, so that the eventual death toll could be grossly underestimated.

Beslan residents were quite disheartened by the news broadcast on federal channels that featured the agenda of the Government meeting held on 2 September 2004 — the ministers were discussing agricultural issues.

"They will be showing us "The Swan Lake"[1] soon. Your Putin is hiding the truth about Beslan!" that is how people voiced their outrage over the phone calls to the operational headquarters. It was hard to explain to them that Moscow was thinking of nothing else but how to help the children hostages. President Putin was trying to find a solution. He was, truly, extremely worried about the hostages. I know that for sure.

The terrorists' operatives in the city (and I am sure there were quite a few of them) were agile enough to snatch this wave of disarray. They inflamed the crowd, promoting the idea that the only way to save the children would be to form "a human ring" that would impede any forced action of the Federal Special Forces. A risky possibility of a "second front", formed by armed and infuriated Beslan citizens, became real by the mid afternoon.

It turned out that there were simply no such leaders in the operational headquarters who would be capable of relating to the people, calming them down and encouraging them to cooperate with the counter-terrorist forces. Republican and federal authorities demonstrated their inability to take a complex situation under control; they were unable to

---

[1] This is an allusion to the funerals of Communist Party General Secretaries as well as to the events of August 1991 when ballet "The Swan Lake" was continuously broadcast instead of scheduled TV programmes and news bulletins.

assume responsibility. Instead of theatrically kneeling down in front of children's graves at funerals after the tragedy, they had a chance to avert the situation. Way before, when hundreds of little Russian citizens from the hands of rapists and bandits was still a possibility.

The Ossetian leadership awaited an instruction from Moscow, and Moscow waited to see how the situation developed. My attempts to establish at least a minimal interaction between different influence groups in the operative headquarters stumbled over a polite refusal each time.

In the afternoon of 2 September a significant development took place, which consolidated our hope to save the children. Terrorists agreed to allow Ruslan Aushev, the respected former President of Ingushetia and retired Army General, to enter the school building. Having received final recommendations from the headquarters, Aushev strode confidently in the direction of the school. He reappeared shortly with a baby in his arms. A few more hostages with infants in their arms followed him out.

The headquarters rejoiced. This success was inspirational. The leadership was disturbed, however, by one circumstance — Aushev returned from the school with a new note that contained demands from Shamil Basayev (himself not present in Beslan). The headquarters considered the demands to be unrealistic. The note read:

> *From Allah's Slave*
> *Shamil Basayev*
> *To President of the Russian Federation*
> *Vladimir Putin*
>
> *Vladimir Putin, it was not you who started this war. But you can put an end to it if you have the courage and determination of De Gaulle.*
>
> *We offer a reasonable state of peace based on mutually beneficial principle of "independence in exchange for security".*
>
> *If federal troops are withdrawn from Chechnya, and the independence of the Chechen Republic of Ichkeria is acknowledged, we will take upon the following obligations:*
>
> - *We will not form any political, military or economic unions against Russia with anyone;*
>
> - *We will not deploy foreign military bases in our territory, not even temporarily;*

- *We will not support or finance groups and organisations that pursue armed methods of the struggle against the Russian Federation;*
- *We will remain in the common currency zone (rouble);*
- *We will adhere to the Commonwealth of Independent States (CIS)*

Moreover, we can sign the CST[1], but we would prefer the status of neutrality.

We can also guarantee that all Russian Muslims will give up armed resistance to the Russian Federation for at least 10–15 years under the condition of observing the freedom of faith (which is, by the way, guaranteed by the Russian Constitution).

We have nothing to do with the explosion of apartment buildings in Moscow and Volgodonsk, but we can assume responsibility for this, too, in an acceptable form.

Chechen people are leading a national struggle for liberty and independence and for our self-preservation, and not with an objective to destroying or humiliate Russia. When we are free, we will be interested in having a strong neighbour. We offer you peace, and the choice is yours.

Allahu Akbar
Signature
30.08.04

The note was immediately sent to Moscow for examination and for a decision. One of the opinions in the headquarters was to conceal the very existence of the note and the demands that it contained. That was a yet another stupidity. It was the Ingush leader in oblivion who had delivered the note from the school building. He had read it and he could confirm its contents, if necessary. What would be the point of hiding it then?

On the second sleepless night I went to see my friend Mikhail Markelov, an MP. Being an experienced journalist who had been around all war zones, he made friendly contacts among the Ossetian militia officers and settled in the Republican Interior Ministry headquarters. All this time Mikhail and I were exchanging text messages, shared the latest information between us, encouraged each other and prepared ourselves for the possibility of being exchanged for the children-hostages.

---

[1] CST — apparently, Basayev meant the Collective Security Treaty.

Both of us anticipated the approaching climax. Sociable, and at an ease with people, Mikhail established trustworthy relations with representatives of the Ossetian paramilitary and with local Cossacks, who were giving him the precious updates on the situation in Beslan, particularly in the vicinity of the school. We soon parted, and I returned to the operational headquarters.

Mikhail sent me a new text message in a couple of hours: "We need to meet up ASAP." It was 7am. The day 3 of our waiting-around for outcome had begun.

Five minutes later Markelov came into the operative headquarters, literally flying up the stairs. He said at one breath that he, together with some Cossacks, had managed to crawl up to the school building at the distance of just a few metres, and remained totally unnoticed. He heard the militants speaking in hushed voices; he saw how a few terrorists came out to check ignition of the cars parked outside. Our scouts managed to retreat undetected in the same manner.

The obtained information had to be transmitted urgently to the Federal Security agents. If a Duma deputy could get so close to the school entrance, then, surely, the Special Forces would be able to easily re-enact such a feat.

On the second floor of the headquarters we found Chief Military Prosecutor Sergey Fridinsky and the senior "Alfa"[1] officer. Mikhail repeated his story; he spread the field map and pointed out the concealed approaches to the school building. The FSB officer thanked us and rushed off to see his chiefs.

In the headquarters, the tension mounted with every passing hour. Dzasokhov was pacing up and down the room; he felt frustrated and helpless.

Suddenly Taymuraz Mamsurov had an incoming call on his mobile. His children were ringing from inside the school. The Ossetian Speaker did not even have a second to find out if they were okay, when one of the terrorists snatched the mobile from the kids. He warned against storming the building, saying that, otherwise, Mamsurov's children would be the first to die; he demanded that relatives of the hostages must prevent the Federal Security Forces from an armed operation. My suspicion that the terrorists planned to use the "human ring" of the hostages' relatives as a shield was confirmed.

Someone reported upstairs that a militia sniper had noticed some movement inside the school building; the sniper had an impression that

---

[1] *"Alfa Group"* — Spetsnaz Unit — the Russian counter-terrorist unit established in 1974.

the terrorists were installing TV equipment and a satellite to broadcast from the building that they had seized. "Now that's the last thing we need!" someone cried out in the corridor.

At last, North Ossetian President Dzasokhov decided to convene a small meeting in one of the offices on the second floor. He had just returned from a meeting with Beslan citizens during which he swore to them that he would not allow a storm of the building. Everyone was agitated to the limit. The morning of 4 September was the deadline of the ultimatum imposed by the terrorists. Time was sweepingly running out. Food and water deprivation was taking its toll on the condition of the children-hostages. Moscow was digesting Basayev's letter; they were thinking something up but did not come up with a decision. The Federal Security Service was silent too.

I turned the television on. The time was 1pm sharp. A breaking news issue of *Vesti* (News) reported from the Republic of Ingushetia. The TV showed a video recording of an interview with a militant's wife; her husband had been identified by the FSB as a member of the armed gang that had taken hostages in the school. The woman was speaking in Vainakh language; the running script below gave the Russian translation. I was flabbergasted. The woman was plainly making it known that she and her four children were taken hostages:

"I did not get here by my free will, you understand me... You must do what you can. Make sure that the children are unharmed. I don't know what to do. You will just understand me, I guess. [...] May Allah be with you. Let Allah turn everything to the best, as you desire. No one did anything bad to me and no one will. Nothing will go wrong, Allah is mighty".

Then she switched to Russian and murmured something about the need to set the children-hostages free.

I looked at Yakovlev and Dzasokhov who were standing beside me. Both of them were in wide-eyed astonishment. Such a development resembled a provocation. I wondered if any of professional propagandists had monitored this instigating madness before it was released on air. "One should lose their balls for such work!" I said to the stupefied group who were watching the news with me. Just then we heard gunfire and explosions coming from around the school. "Now, this is how they reacted!" Dzasokhov cried out. Others kept gloomy silence.

At 1:03pm there was a terrible explosion.

We flew downstairs and rushed into the FSB headquarters. Apart from General Pronichev and some other officers in civilian clothes, Ruslan Aushev and Ingush businessman Mikhail Gutseriyev were there.

Mikhail was on his mobile, trying to reach the terrorists' leader. As he was dialing the number, another powerful explosion followed.

At last, the connection was established: "Hello, hello! What did explode there? No! No, the school is not being stormed! What? Cease fire? Ok, we are ceasing!"

Gutseriyev was trying to outshout the roaring sounds of combat and desultory fire, but the connection broke off again.

"He thinks that we are storming and he said that everyone is going to die now!" he repeated terrorists' last words' leader to the Generals who had been listening to the exchange with the terrorist. Then, not trying to hide his despair, Gutseriyev moaned and plumped into the sofa.

Ruslan Aushev covered his face with his hands. Dzasokhov howled. Everyone rushed to the inner yard of the building. The mushroom-like light-grey smoke rising above the school building was visible from the yard.

I texted my wife: "Explosion in the school. Battle."

The combat was in full swing. Special Forces officers were running and buckling their flak jackets and spherical helmets on the move. "To the school, to the school!" the officers were shouting to one another. I regretted that I had left my pistol back in Moscow.

The patrol guards abandoned the headquarters without a cover. One of the FSB officers ran up to me and urged me to "leave fast; the two 'shahid'[1] women and a group of militants broke free from the school and may attempt to seize the headquarters or the city hospital". That was unlikely, even considering the chaotic planning of the school rescue operation. "But then, Mikhail managed to crawl up close to the school and was not noticed either by bandits, or by Security Forces!" I thought. "Anything can happen!"

Headquarters' representatives kept together like a flock of sheep on the landing between the ground and the first floors. No one knew where to run or hide from a possible terrorist counter-attack. Plenipotentiary Representative of the Russian President, Vladimir Yakovlev, went as far as suggesting to shoot off the lock on the lattice frame door that led to the basement, and to hide there. That would have been too panicky.

I left the scared group and climbed the stairs up to the second floor, where the governmental switchboard had been installed. Quickly running past the window that was exposed to fire, I got into the headquarters room. Amidst the roar of the battle helicopters

---

[1] 'Shahid' — here refers to suicide bombers.

whirling in the sky and the sounds of explosions and machine-gun fire, I heard the special communication telephone bursting to be answered.

It was the Armed Forces Chief of Staff General Yury Baluyevsky ringing. He asked me to find any of the FSB chief officers to coordinate actions of the GRU[1] Spetsnaz. I asked General Baluyevsky to hold the line and looked out into the corridor. There I saw the officer whom I needed, Commander of the FSB operative group in the North Caucasus; I grabbed him by the arm and shoved him into the special communication room. The colonel reported to Baluyevsky on the first casualties among Spetsnaz officers and the reconnaissance conducted by helicopters in the nearby woods, where the "second group of militants" was allegedly hiding, as well as on other key details of the battle.

"Colonel!" I addressed the officer. He covered the receiver with the palm of his hand and stared at me.

"There is an opinion", I pointed a finger to the ceiling, "that we must capture one of the terrorists alive". I looked into his eyes. The Colonel nodded and continued with his phone conversation.

I left the room and ran outside, to the school. Ambulances were filling the street. Civilians were hiding from stray bullets around the corner of our building. Grenades were blowing up in the vicinity of the school. The battle did not abate. The hostage situation collapsed into a bloodbath.

We were very close to the school when the children who had miraculously survived the explosion came running out of the inflamed building. From under fire, men carried children in their arms and passed them over to paramedics and territorial guards.

I must say that all of my comrades displayed outstanding courage during the battle.

At about 4:30pm I was urgently called to the headquarters. President Alexander Dzasokhov, in bitter grief, took me by the hand and told me: "I am asking you to fly to Moscow urgently. The plane is waiting for you in the airport. It is all over here. Thank you for everything. What we have to do now is to prevent a new war between Ossetians and Ingushi. My people want to take revenge on Vainakhs. Go to Moscow and try to persuade the leadership to block our administrative border with Ingushetia immediately. You will manage to do that."

Dzasokhov hugged me, we said good bye to each other, and I left

---

[1] *GRU* — Main Intelligence Directorate; the foreign military intelligence Directorate of the General Staff of the Russian Armed Forces.

the headquarters. I stopped for a second at the exit. Spetsnaz soldiers were dragging a captured terrorist, pushing him with their rifle butts down into the basement. Into the very basement door that some people from the headquarters wanted to shoot open with a gun only a couple of hours before.

The terrorist — he would be identified later as Nur-Pashi Kulayev — was screaming vehemently, asking for mercy, kissing officers' boots. A nasty scene....

It is beyond my knowledge what really led to the explosions in Beslan School #1. I think that the findings of the official parliamentary commission are incomplete and do not reveal the whole truth behind the horrific tragedy that broke out during those hot September days in the North Ossetian town. Politicians and experts will debate for long about the true culprits behind the tragedy. Meanwhile, Beslan continues to live by the memory of 335 innocently killed children and adults — terror victims, just like those in the ill-famed Stavropol city of Budyonnovsk — "The Sacred Cross" that lives on.

IDIOT[1]

In the beginning of 2006, after Rodina had been taken off the ballots in the elections to the Moscow City Duma (in my book *Enemy of the People* I wrote about this unappealing story that involved Mayor Luzhkov), I found myself in a situation where I had to resign from all significant positions both in the party and in the parliamentary faction. I felt that I had no right to put at risk my political creation — the party into which I invested all my passions and energies and on which I placed my hopes for positive changes in the country. But the decision to leave the party could not be have been made by me single-handedly. I would never have left the captains' wheel, if the team required me to stay. I wanted to test my comrades' cohesion and loyalty because I needed to know whether they were ready to compromise their personal comforts in the name of the cause.

I made the decision to call the Extraordinary Party Congress and raise my blunt question there: will the party activists be prepared to maintain their leader, or will they agree to accept my resignation in exchange for promises by the outside enemies to quit blackmail, persecutions and threats to take the party off the election?

The Extraordinary Congress took place on 25 March 2006. I submitted my resignation and named the successor — Alexander Babakov, the Co-Chairman of the Rodina faction in the State Duma.

Hiding their eyes, all my comrades raised their hands up in favour of my resignation. Then, all of a sudden, as if prompted by a signal, they all got up on their feet and gave me a standing ovation. I bowed before the congress and left quickly, not stopping for the journalists that were crowded in the hall. I took my car and drove home. That very night Babakov told me that Yury Skokov, who as the press secretary presided over the congress for the rest of the day, had addressed the "guests of the congress" in the audience with the

---

[1] *Idiot* is a fine novel by Fyodor Dostoevsky in which he portrayed Prince Myshkin, "a positively beautiful individual" who represents Christian values. He wishes to sacrifice himself for others and is ridiculed by society.

following words: "We fulfilled our promise. Now we expect that the Presidential Administration fulfills theirs." Later I heard that even my most tough and consistent opponents were disgusted by such an open betrayal. Skokov and his circle simply traded me for the promises that the obstacles and the pressure on Rodina before the elections would be stopped, as if participation in elections could be the only reason for existence to a political organisation.

Unfortunately, after Rodina renounced its leader, it lasted as a political party only until the fall of 2006. Soon it merged with the political project "Russian Party of Life", which was unsuccessfully promoted by Chairman of the Council of Federations of the Federal Assembly Sergey Mironov. The joint party was named "A Just Russia"[1], and it went on to thread on thin ice of the Russian political life. Soon, Mironov and his circle took care of remaining Rodina adepts of whom the most faithful and stubborn returned to KRO.

Rodina, that lived a brief but full and bright life, turned into a dormant party. Hopefully, not for long. Surely, not.

I am not going to describe in detail, dear reader, what a bird feels when being shot in the air. As if all sound and light suddenly goes out....

Somehow, the phone stopped ringing. Acquaintances crossed to the other side of the street whenever they saw me as if I was infectious. The only exception was a phone call from Foreign Minister Sergey Lavrov who wished me a happy birthday and said the words of much-needed support....

One of my old friends called me an impractical idiot, but I felt more like a complete idiot. The main thing was that I could not understand where I had gone wrong. I managed to organise a vivacious election campaign that resulted in the unexpected success of the new political force. It was under my leadership that the Rodina Political Party evolved from a parliamentary faction (and not vice versa!) and united hundreds of thousands of activists in one short year of its existence; Rodina confidently took the second place in elections, stepping on toes of the Russian bureaucrats. And then, all of a sudden, a total defeat. The first political test on stability of our ranks, the first test of our activists' resilience, and everything cracked. The majority of Rodina regional leaders, as well as the people who surrounded me within the party core, easily broke down under the pressure, applied by our political opponents, and turned away from their leader. I only had myself to blame for that.

---

[1] Also translated as "Fair Russia".

The idea to write the book *Enemy of the People* did not come to me out of the blue. I wanted to analyse my thoughts and emotions and count back in time in order to understand where I made a crucial mistake. In August 2006 I sent the script to editors. The first edition was out by the time of the Moscow International Book Fair, held in the Pavilions of the famous Exhibition of Achievements of the National Economy — this masterpiece of Soviet architecture. To my joy, plenty of the Book Fair visitors were keen to get a copy of *Enemy of the People*, freshly printed and still smelling of ink.

As was to be expected, unbidden guests were there, too — young thrashers from a certain scandalous youth movement. Their specialty was to sabotage events organised by politicians of a different platform. A provocation was attempted, but my team had looked out for something of the sort and chucked out the youths under the approving remarks from the Book Fair visitors.

By the way, these "pogromers", recruited mostly from a football factory, followed us everywhere. They tried and failed to sabotage all the presentations of my book; they launched fights and even attempted arson in the largest bookstores of Moscow and Saint Petersburg; they distributed demeaning articles, caricatures, and similar rubbish. In the course of another vagary, my supporters obtained a curious trophy: a digital camera that belonged to one of the guys. We looked at the pictures and nearly lost the gift of speech! The pictures showed these lads in some office, apparently bored to the bone by having nothing to do; on the photos they appeared trying to outdo one another in... pulling condoms over their heads.

It is a shame that mature mentors dragged young people into dubious actions and provocations. I am sure that the vast majority of them acted against me with little enthusiasm — maybe some of them needed to earn a bit of money, and for others all these activities were the mistakes of their young age. Some people are easily led astray. I do not bear a grudge against those guys.

It has to be said that the repulsive actions of my political opponents only served to stir up public interest towards my book. Ultimately, the book took on a life of its own; it was re-edited several times and became a political bestseller in Russia.

Despite the popularity of *Enemy of the People*, I decided not to pursue a writing career. The time for that had not come yet. Together with the group of co-thinkers we started to reanimate the Congress of Russian Communities, which had been led to a miserable condition by its former leader Sergey Glaziev[1]. The congress was held; the manifesto and the chart were adopted. KRO public receptions were established all over the country. Andrey Saveliev played the first violin; he undertook the executive management of the Congress of Russian Communities. On my part, I was deeply immersed in the public court case of the two servicemen, Sergey Arakcheev and Yevgeny Khudyakov. Despite the two previous verdicts, the magistrates were preset to find the two officers guilty for the war crimes in the territory of Chechnya, which they had not committed. I was spending a lot of my time in Rostov-on-Don, where the hearings took place, and I also covered a sizeable part of legal and travel expenses of the defendants and their witnesses.

It was there, in Rostov-on-Don, where a phone call from Moscow reached me. They called me on behalf of Putin. The President was offering me a job. In Brussels. In NATO Headquarters. To represent Russia in the military bloc by which, as a joke, naughty children are taunted.

Even though I had been in Russia's domestic politics for years, I always maintained an interest towards international politics. Besides, I read up on international relations during my college years, and my academic interests were related to NATO and the European security issues. So my chance presented itself.

The job of Permanent Representative of the Russian Federation to NATO has given me a unique opportunity to put my ideas of peace consolidation in Eurasia to practice. Moreover, the position did not precipitate either a change in my personal views, or a review of my principles. Being in opposition is not a natural state for a true, professional patriot. However, the reverse also applies: if true patriots are in opposition, it is a sign that something is wrong within the country.

I accepted the President's offer. In order to explain to my supporters and comrades the motives behind that decision I issued the following statement:

Dear friends!

Today the President of the Russian Federation signed a Decree appointing me the Permanent Representative to the North Atlantic Treaty Organisation (NATO). I regard this decision of the state leader to be an offer of an interesting and responsible job that is of a high importance to my country.

---

[1] *Sergey Glaziev* was KRO Chairman from 2000 to 2006 — *Author's comment.*

I assume that the Decree arrived unexpectedly for many of you. Our relations with the party in power have not been trouble-free lately. However, the fact that our political views and professional qualities are on demand meets my desire to serve my country and to contribute to the prosperity of the Motherland.

I call to my comrades, colleagues, and supporters: do not be afraid to integrate into the structures of power, primarily into its executive branches, where you can make an impact on the evolution of power from within. In this crucial time, when our Motherland is in transition and when it is being determined whether our country can eventually regain the status of a great power, the patriots must not stay aside.

I have to say, when the first rumors of my possible appointment appeared in the press, before the official announcement, many thought that it was a hoax. When the Decree was published, my political ill-wishers stirred like snakes in a pit; they bade farewell to me long time ago! It could not even occur to them that President Putin might have other ideas. Anyhow, at that moment rumors and speculations were the least thing on my mind. The most exciting job was ahead of me, and the subsequent events in Brussels and in the Caucasus confirmed my expectations.

The day before leaving for Brussels, President Putin invited me for a short talk:

"Let bygones be bygones. Do you copy?"

"Understood. Agreed."

"Well then, Godspeed. Don't disappoint me there."

Nothing else needed to be said.

THE DUEL[1]

When I moved to Brussels, the thing I had to adapt to the most was not the capriciously changing Belgian weather (like they say here, if you are not happy about the weather, wait for fifteen minutes) but the entirely different cultural environment. I have to say that people of the European Union member states do not regard us Russians to be proper Europeans. To them, we are rather like astronauts that resemble humans but wear weird spacesuits. This impression was reinforced even more when I took to reading Western newspapers regularly; I was forever coming across samples of artificial contraposition of Europe against Russia, as if they were two separate historical and cultural civilisations with manifestly ill-matched values. Such an approach sustains mutual suspiciousness and speculations that each pole of the European continent follows "a special path." This vision, at best, is a profound and ignorant delusion multiplied by historical amnesia and blindness.

Russia is, and always will be, a European nation in the literal meaning of the word; at the same time, Russia always represented the Eastern, sun-facing vector of Europe's political and cultural development. Ever since the European civilisation split into the Roman and the Byzantine empires, there was a certain rivalry between the Europe's West and East. Today, this rivalry manifests itself in Russia's relations with the European Union and NATO; however, this confrontation of opposites serves to prove their dialectic unity. The EU and Russia are the two ends of the thread that binds the entire European continent together.

The identity of the West, that faces the globalisation process, is challenged by the colossal cultural and spiritual pressure from the South. Over time, the West with its guilt complex of the colonial past lost all of its competitive advantages. The nations that were conquered in the past are now conquering Europe, changing dramatically not

---

[1] *The Duel* is Anton Chekhov's lengthiest story in which he describes the confrontation between the scientist consumed with Nietzschean concept of superman and the indolent and disappointed young man. The duel between the two that nearly ended fatally transforms both men for the best.

just her exterior, but also her inner life. The conquests provoked a retaliatory conquest. Self-assured as ever, contemporary Europe can no longer assimilate and digest the powerful inflow of alien cultures. By having misinterpreted the wise principle of tolerance, the West, in fact, abandoned the struggle to preserve values inherent to European civilisation. Instead of inviting newcomers to share in the invaluable European cultural heritage, instead of instilling the indigenous European values in those who chose to anchor here, the West's elites concealed their problems in ghettos. One day it dawned that it were the elites that had been in ghettos all along.

Sadly, the cowardly denial of the harsh realities of globalisation will inevitably lead to the gradual demise of Europe and her culture. The South's heady current is already wearing away the ancient stones of Europe.

In convulsions, the Western elites sought to substitute the ongoing process of globalisation with salvation plans for the European world, such as NATO's expansion to the East; the Eastern Partnership — these essentially Trozkyist projects undermine Europe even greater than taking no action would have done.

The European leaders resemble a folk hero who smears one spoonful of porridge over a plate and convinces himself that his plate is full. This wishful thinking is dangerous. The wider NATO's and the EU's areas of responsibility are, the weaker they become, as such expansion is sustained by nil potential growth. Nevertheless, Europe takes it upon herself to settle the problems of others; she interferes into disputes and arguments of the neighbours. This is thinning out the Europe's spirit of identity.

Whether Brussels, Paris, and Berlin like it, or not, the reality remains: Russia is becoming the centre of the European tradition. Russia is patiently moving in the eastern direction, imparting European culture to more of the new lands. José Manuel Barroso and Javier Solana, who visited the grand city of Khabarovsk in the Russian Far East, could see for themselves how dramatically outdated the Charles de Gaulle's slogan of "Europe from the Atlantic to the Urals" is. The Russians have opened the Urals for Europe and expanded the European space to the shores of Alaska and the Kuril Islands.

Whatever wailing there is about the modern Russia's developmental problems, these problems are nothing compared to the imminent threat to the very existence of European civilisation, in the Western understanding of it. The recent procurement of Eastern European countries for the West has not had a positive impact on the current trend. Europe is not growing in a genuine cultural and spiritual sense; on the contrary, it is shrinking like La Peau de Chagrin.

I discussed these issues with many of my colleagues in Brussels. I noted their disappointment and annoyance, barely concealed, at the peculiar fact that Eastern European countries had brought into the Western world the unsavory spirit of parochialism upon their escaping from the socialist camp. We, Russia and the West, have played tug of war with these unfortunate countries for too long, and so their tug of the European culture wore out.

The paradox of the modern world is that Europe's Western half is shriveling whilst her Eastern half is expanding. Russia now acts as Europe's spiritual guardian, just like Byzantium that prolonged the "cause of Rome" for the millennium after Rome collapsed under the onslaught of Barbarians. There is nothing surprising about it. A fear of the new Russia, inflamed by Russophobes, is not justified. Russia is a natural, and the most reliable, ally of the Western cultural elites. The sooner the West grasps this, the higher the chances are that we all will be able to refer to our common European destiny not just in the past tense.

The above fully applies to the relations between NATO and Russia. These relations do not exist in a vacuum and do not evolve per se; on the contrary, it is in them where Russia's relations with the West are reflected like in a mirror.

NATO's export to the East did not reinforce but, on the contrary, weakened the security in the West. Following geopolitical gluttony, NATO is suffering from poor digestion. Stretched like a rubber, the body of the Alliance is not fit to sustain own military presence in the high priority areas such as Afghanistan; sending an extra tank or a squadron there to fight Taliban is a big deal. All serious ideas or initiatives sink in endless discussions, and this is hardly surprising, as the number of staff in the EU institutions and the NATO Headquarters in Brussels already exceeds the number of soldiers in the Belgian Armed Forces! The number of staff in the EU bodies has swollen to 41,000, and that of NATO — to 4,000. For the sake of comparison, there are only about 39,000 servicemen in the Belgian Army.

Every action is supposed to have a meaning and an objective. What are the meaning and the objective of NATO's expansion? "Democracy enforcement", human rights protection, etc. — all this is demagogy. The Council of Europe and other humanitarian organisations were designed to serve such purposes. NATO is a military alliance, and not a Philatelic Society; therefore, its main mission should result in the increased level of security. But has NATO expansion to the East established greater security? Judging by the permanent crisis in Ukraine and the breakup of Georgia, no, it has not. Then why does NATO expand further? Is it to diminish the bloc's military potential, overstretching its area of responsibility to include scandalous countries? Or maybe NATO wishes to become a pledge and a subject of manipulations by its new members, who resolve their inner petty problems and settle territorial disputes at the expense of Europe and the USA, and whose only contribution to NATO are their ancient phobias and squabbles?

NATO's energy went into a whistle. The Alliance has turned into the Paper Lion and is living by memories of the past victories, both real and imaginary. The "Hawks" of NATO like to claim the credit for the victory in the Cold War. Personally, I find these contentious tales of my opponents in Brussels to be ridiculous. Do they not realise that the USSR and the whole Communist empire collapsed for whatever reason, but not due to NATO; that, by its mere existence and weapons-clacking, the Alliance served to prolong the agony of Bolshevist dinosaurs? However, I have already elaborated on that in the beginning of this book, so I go back to the subject of NATO.

When the USSR and the Eastern bloc disappeared, NATO was "at a bit of a loss". "Whom are we going to be friends against?" its leaders contemplated. The ethnic war in the Balkans instigated by the West, as well as the rapid acceleration of radical Islam, provided a hint for the answer to this question, and, there you go — international terrorism, organised crime, religious extremism, illegal drug trade and piracy were proclaimed to be the new enemies of NATO. This raises a further question: in this case, why NATO does not wish to undergo a makeover, transferring itself into a worldwide security provider, a kind of a super Special Service that would gather and exchange intelligence, launch special joint anti-terrorist and other operations in order to resist the above mentioned threats efficiently? Clearly, ballistic missiles and systems of air defense are of little use in a war against terror.

Sometimes they say of NATO: when a rhino has poor eyesight, it is not his problem; it is the problem of those unnoticed by the beast. So can this military alliance, frozen in a condition that is suitable for military resistance to an opponent of a similar scale, be an effective instrument in the struggle against new challenges and threats? Personally, I doubt that it can.

NATO members often justify the reasons for preserving the alliance in its conventional military form by the existence of "rogue states" that are potentially capable of terrorising the West with WMD. Well, let us see these weapons. Maybe something has been found at Saddam Hussein's, at last? We all remember how members of President Bush Jr. Administration assured the UN Security Council that there were weapons of mass destruction in Iraq.

In the end, the United States and its allies assaulted Iraq. It was an action that had not been sanctioned by the UN Security Council; they occupied and destroyed that country, they caused deaths of masses of people including their own servicemen, and for what? Even if we do accept that there are countries in this world whose people are not keen on the West, America, Christians, Jews, white people etc., etc., would it be a valid cause for a war? So what, if some people do not like other people? Maybe the Germans are very fond of the Poles? Or maybe the French suddenly have grown to love the English, and the English have become overly fond of the Irish? No, in general, different nations in this world are not particularly fond of one another, but this should not be a reason for a war.

In any event, the "offending states" such as Iraq, North Korea, and the rest of them are times weaker than NATO's military machine.

So what is the point of possessing such a great power? Arguably, it is NATO's military power combined with its tactics of "weapon-rattling" and ultimatums, made on behalf of "global community", that is the main reason why some countries go into active defense and urgently acquire "heavy bats" for themselves.

The war in Iraq manifested: if Saddam really had possessed weapons of mass destruction, Washington would have never sent its troops there. After Iraq was defeated, the governments of some countries arrived to an important conclusion: if you do have weapons of mass destruction, no one would dare to start a war against you, but if you do not have them, you might expect a military intervention. Is this not the case?

Today, the Alliance is trying to lull the Kremlin with assurances that Russia would not be affected by NATO's imminent transformation. "Moscow does not believe tears," especially not crocodile's tears. This is what former Foreign Minister of France Roland Duma thinks about the true worth of NATO's promises:

> *The Alliance's course on moving closer to the Russian borders is a very dangerous thing, indeed. I remember, when the Cold War was at its last gasps in the late 1980s — early 1990s, at the time of Germany's reunification, the Western countries undertook the liability that NATO would not expand in the direction of the country that was the USSR*

then. What happened to those promises? They were forgotten, as if never made. Very recently, the USA insisted on having elements of the anti-missile defense in Poland and the Czech Republic, trying to impose on them the role of a shield against the outcast countries, all the while knowing that Russia would see it as a threat to her security, and not unreasonably.

I can only comment that, unfortunately, the West's politicians only ever share with us evidence and opinions of this nature upon reaching their retirement.

Cooperation, establishment of trust, and joint analysis of common threats between Russia and NATO are the key to mutual success of the united European security project.

Of course, the above does not imply that Russia should join NATO.

Remarks by the US Administration officials that "we cannot exclude a possibility of Russia's integration into NATO, if Russia meets the due criteria, or if the Alliance reaches consensus on the matter" are regarded by the Kremlin to be awkward and insubstantial. Gentlemen, do you genuinely think that we dream of joining your "pique waistcoats club", where, incidentally, we would have to be "marinated" in the waiting area first?

Russia has her own independent means and methods to ensure her national security. We intend not to give up an ounce of our sovereignty. We are not going to forfeit the rights and guarantees of safeguarding our independence to an uncle from overseas. Different political and economic approaches notwithstanding, we, Russia and the West, must learn to protect both our European houses. This will be best achieved by the concerted actions along both perimeters of Europe.

Some people prefer to reside in secure gated developments. Living in such a community does not presuppose that one must become close personal friends with neighbours, or do business with them, or, for instance, encourage one's son to marry a neighbour's daughter. However, in the conditions of crime escalation in a modern city, residents of a gated development start out with setting a system that would ensure safety and security for all. Residents join resources for the purpose, for example, together as a community they erect a fence, install a barrier, or hire security guards.

In a similar way, European civilisation today does not have a sufficiently effective system to protect itself from "the challenges and threats of today", as diplomats like to put it. Maybe we, Russia and NATO, should build a safe and mutually guarded "residential development" together. I would stress once more, the intention is not to hurdle Russia and the West into one communal flat or a shared European house. Russia does not need to join NATO, and NATO does not need to join Russia. Neither of us needs to squeeze and live on top of each other. But why can't we take the shared common perimeter of security under our protection and establish the wholesome European security system?

In order to pursue this sound, transparent idea, Russia is prepared to work with patience and consistency at strengthening the relations with the North Atlantic Alliance; to evolve these relations into strategic cooperation in the cause of Europe's survival. This cooperation must be based on principles of equality, integrity, safety, and mutual trust.

It is only through the understanding of Europe's political processes in their historical context that we can forge the truly secure future for all nations from the Atlantic to Khabarovsk, this European city built by Russians near the Chinese border.

But what is authentic Europe in the eyes of a European? What does it represent? What does the Western world expect from Russia, and what can it reasonably expect? Conversely, what does Russia expect from the West, and what can she expect? Is it possible to translate the romantic sentiments for "Europe from Vancouver to Vladivostok" into the pragmatic principles of international accords?

The logic of the previous era commanded that the West erected bastions around the USSR. The state of opposition to the Eastern bloc was accompanied with the launches of ideological viruses into the territories of the Soviet Union and its "brothers". The Soviet propaganda stroke back and broke through the defense lines by imposing "the socialist projects" on other continents. Some "cannibalistic" regime in Africa only had to declare itself "a country of the socialist choice", and Soviet ships with skilled specialists and economic aid on board sailed there immediately. This was happening during the period when in Russia there was the shortage of the most basic commodities. The Soviet internationalism turned out to be hard labour for Russia's people in the name of the outdated and morally redundant expansion of Marxism.

In fear of a head-on armed conflict, for a long while the West and the Eastern bloc made each other's blood boil by arranging no-nonsense local conflicts in the third countries every now and again. Moreover, in the spirit of confrontation, ideological engineers of the two opposing sides were creating live cyborgs in the Cold War laboratories. Whilst

NATO and the US military camps trained the future Afghan Taliban fighters, preparing them for a war against the Soviet Union, the Soviet military instructors were busy teaching the methods of partisan war to the left radicals of Palestine, South America and Africa. A few years went by, and the Palestinian terrorists, trained in the USSR, appeared among the gangs of Chechen bandits, whereas the nurslings of the West turned against their teachers and plundged them into the war of terror. It all became too clear on 11 September 2001 — the cyborgs rebelled against their creators.

By inertia of the confrontational mentality, the West encircles Russia and exports "colour revolutions" designed to clear the pathway for the new Atlantist crusade to the barbarian East. Instead of uniting Europe, the West erects new bastions and lays bypassing pipelines of the Nabucco sort, an unashamedly and provocatively anti-Russian project. Matters like these seed distaste for the West in Russians and motivate Russia to look for allies beyond the European borders.

Possibly, our European and North American partners do not have an insight into the inner life of Russia and do not understand the specifics of the Russian soul. I am ready to explain: Russians cannot bear being condescended to. This is so, due to the five centuries long total lack of Russia's foreign fiscal dependence; it is a unique phenomenon in history — no other country in the world can boast anything like it.

The confrontational attitude and the ongoing crusade against Russia do not help to resolve a single problem intrinsic to the West. Excessive immigration influx, illegal drugs mafia, environmental problems and moral disintegration; the projects that are designed to undermine Russia's strength have no relevance to any of the above issues.

So, what do such projects achieve? Are they aimed at Russia's weakening, down to her complete decline? Will it be a part of a desirable future for Europe? Is it not clear that such a scenario would be Europe's nightmare? Would life next to an entire continent immersed in the humanitarian catastrophe add to anyone's safety and comfort?

If politicians of the West really do envisage their future without Russia, then the most energetic efforts to overturn such a vision should be reasonably expected on the Russian part. This would mean that my NATO partners would be getting nothing but false smiles and endless imitation of cooperation around negotiations table.

The future of Russia-free Europe is not enviable. The future of Russia-free Europe is terrifying. A Europe of such kind will no longer be able to enjoy stability, wealth or the values of its civilisation. In order to prevent that, the West must view Russia as an integral part of Europe, and Russia must recognise the advantages of the alliance with European countries.

What can constitute a basis of the European integrity with Russia's full participation?

Strange as it might seem, in the course of "real politics", an extremely important aspect of the problem, namely our value orientations, are almost inevitably removed from the agenda. The European integrity and unity were founded not on political doctrines but on Christianity that knits together the fabric of European civilisation. Fyodor Dostoevsky wrote about Europe that lost its sense of own history:

> *To the Russian, Europe is as precious as Russia; every stone in her is cherished and dear. Europe is as much our fatherland as Russia...Oh, those old stones of foreign lands, those wonders of God's ancient world, those fragments of holy marvels are dear to the Russian, and are even dearer to us than to the inhabitants of those lands themselves! They now have other thoughts and other feelings, and they have ceased to treasure the old stones.*

Just to think that European bureaucrats, fearing allegations of intolerance, rejected every mention of Europe's Christian roots in the European Constitution draft!

The roots of modern humanitarian values, business and economic practices go back to the postulates of Christianity (the Protestant ethic and the spirit of capitalism according to Max Weber). These essential Christian values remain unchanged today. The sociocultural environment is still formed by Christianity, even in the societies where the Christian faith has almost vanished. The public ideal of Europe cannot be perceived without referring to the faith of the fathers. Thus, it is possible to achieve Europe's unity, and Russia's isolation would be imprudent to the extreme.

Ensuring European security presupposes protection of spiritual and ethical heritage, historical traditions and social norms, as well as preservation of cultural assets that belong to all. Traditional national and all-European ways of life must become an object of protection. To a certain extent, this way of life belongs in the past already. Good old England, La belle France, Holy German union, Holy Russia.... These affectionate names are not in contradiction with one another. All of them are imbedded in the great cultural and historical heritage of the European Christianity. This past that we shared will give us hope for the shared future.

A FEAST IN THE TIME OF PLAGUE[1]

NATO will never be at war with Russia. This conviction of mine was ultimately reinforced during my work in Brussels as Ambassador to this military and political giant. Of course, there is an "if" — NATO will never be at war with Russia, if Russia remains a strong and independent power. The Western world values its comfortable and trouble-free life too highly, and it is unlikely that it is ever going to risk it. Russia presents a problem for the West as it is; Russia is a continuous source of fear and annoyance, and nobody in Europe wishes to face additional problems in connection with her.

In Switzerland, recently, I watched a remarkable local TV feature that portrayed the hard life in the Alpine Republic during World War II. An old lady was movingly sharing with the viewers the tales of her bitter fate: in the wartime local shops had only thirteen sorts of cheese on sale instead of the usual thirty-nine. Poor thing, didn't she suffer!

Here, in the heart of the Old Europe there are medieval towns that look a lot like displays of dollhouses. Course of time and destructive wars of the 20th century did not affect them. Why is that? This is because certain European nations always surrendered to aggressors, even before a war was actually declared. To this day, people in those ancient domains

---

[1] A prophetic manifestation of Russian character from Alexander Pushkin drama *A Feast in the Time of Plague*:

> There is an ecstasy in battle,
> And at the edge of darkest chasm,
> And in the enraged ocean
> Amidst furious waves and turbulent night,
> And in the Arabian sandstorm,
> And in a breathing of the Plague
>
> All, all, that is frightening with destruction,
> To the mortal's heart covertly holds,
> The inexplicable pleasures —
> The immortality's promise, perhaps!
> And happy is the one who amidst the turmoil –
> Can find and feel them.

A Feast in the Time of Plague, Alexander Pushkin, *Little Tragedies* 1830. Translation by M.Korsakova-Kreyn.

live peaceably and without a care in the world. They eye random Russian tourists with caution.

What can I say...? These are the ways of the modern European bourgeoisie. The United States, too, never had to fight a foreign aggressor off the American land. Americans never knew what it was like, for example, to deal with a hunger siege of San Francisco or with tanks on the banks of the Potomac River; their notion of the reality of war is blurred. Russians, on the contrary, fought for every inch of their land, for every village. Whatever anyone may say, no other nation in the world values its national independence and dignity as much as we do. Our problem is that we win on a battlefield and hopelessly lose on political arena, and let go of our military gains.

Still, at a risk of repeating myself, in the modern day and age a war between European countries (this includes Russia) is not possible. A series of circumstances eliminate all chances of an internal European war. I am pleased to point them out:

> Today no major ideological or political contradictions exist between European countries.
>
> European citizens have no desire to fight and they forgot how to, anyway.

It is impossible to imagine a war in the modern European environment in principle. The whole continent is packed with the infrastructure and facilities of superior technology, such as dams, nuclear power plants, chemical plants, etc. A strike on the infrastructure would cause catastrophic damage paramount to the destructive power of a nuclear bomb. A conventional military war in Europe would inevitably regress into the bilateral use of strategic nuclear weapons, which would bring life on Earth to its end.

As the 20th century passed, the nature of modern warfare had changed forever. Now a war is never declared. If a war does occur, it is not due to a conflict between two or more separate states but within one state. Outside parties usually take sides and interfere, but that is another matter. Again, this also happens without a prior announcement.

The latest European wars were linked to the collapse of the USSR and Yugoslavia. In the case of the USSR, other countries or guerrilla armies got involved behind the scenes (I described this in detail in the chapters dedicated to two Chechen wars). In the second instance, NATO committed a savage act of aggression against the disintegrating Yugoslav Federation.

Whilst Russia found inner resources to extinguish fire and suppress the rebellious armed gangs, in the Balkans the fire is still glowing, maintained by internal fights and not by international disputes.

No matter how much NATO forces bombed anything they could set their eyes upon and beyond, they still did not manage to put a stop to what went down in former Yugoslavia.

So what is a modern aggressor? Primarily, it is an underground radical organisation formed on the grounds of ethnic, religious or political extremism and hatred. Such an organisation may be acting on a local and/or transnational scale. At times it attempts to assume some of the functions of a government and forces the opponents to negotiate on equal terms, as was the case when General Lebed signed the Khasavyurt Accords with Maskhadov. The latter posed as a "representative of the Government of the Ichkerian Republic". Typically, the ill-wishing outsiders are keen to abuse such an "interesting situation" and encourage a legitimate government to enter into hopeless negotiations with rebels. By the way, such a conduct represents one of the legal indirect methods of hostile actions against a sovereign state.

The objective of an "unclassical war" is to undermine and compromise statehood as such. Invasions, usurpations of territory, establishment and maintenance of control over population — all this belongs in the past. No terrorists or rebels want to look after civilians in an occupied land; in modern warfare, civilians are nothing more than hostages.

A typical sequence of actions by the new type of aggressor is the following: his priority is to satisfy the private interests of ethnic or criminal groups; then the regional political map is redrawn, at which stage a legal base for statehood is finally established (the attempt to establish "Independent Ichkeria" in the territory of Chechnya was the most advance project of the kind so far). Thus, the object of military aggression and violence is not a state per se, but an ethnic group, represented in that state (like ethnic Russians in the Caucasus or Serbs in Kosovo).

The material resources required to conduct an "unclassical war" are gained out of proceeds from human trafficking, slavery, weapon and drug trade. Naturally, international humanitarian law does not apply in such cases. "Unclassical war" is always characterised by uttermost cruelty and the indiscriminate use of means and methods. In the course of such a war civilian population is pulled into participation therein, and the distinction between militants and civilians gradually becomes blurred, as a consequence.

Full retreat, human, territorial and material losses are no longer the testimony of the defeat in an "unclassical war"; disintegration of the national unity is. Predacious interests, that serve to escalate a conflict, manifest themselves in the most egregious ways — state budget funds are embezzled, new channels of illegal arms trade are established, enclaves out of control of law enforcement bodies are set up, and so on.

All this is usually set against the background of provocative diplomatic and political debate on "irrepressible differences" between the two concepts of nation-building — the concept of sovereignty and territorial unity vs. the concept of a nation's right to self-determination. Juggling with these two principles is the most vivid example of the double standards policy; it is a favourite game of cynical manipulators who are interested in instigating warfare in a country which they can then destabilise or bring to ruins. Influential Western circles, interested in destroying Serbia (that was the initial experiment) and followed by Russia, turned the notion of a nation's right to self-determination into the slogan of recognition of minorities' rights' priority over rights of the indigenous population. This slogan is harmful to a wholesome nation and serves to justify armed separatism. Just how shortsighted are these people! Can they not see that the genie of separatism, let out of the bottle in Southern Europe and Russia, will not stop but will move on to Central and Western Europe and take it to pieces as he goes.

I am certain that in the debate on relative merits of a nation's right to self-determination and right of a state for its territorial integrity, the latter has higher priority. However, there can be one exception to this general rule: an ethnic or a religious minority may be entitled to exercise their right to self-determination fully (up to secession from a state and gaining an independent status) only if such a minority is subject to a danger of physical extermination. But this perfectly harmonious combination of the two principles of international law became a target of intrigues, too, over the last two decades.

For no apparent reason, in the end of the 20th century the United States positioned itself as the hyper power that aspired to have the monopoly over global regulation of self-determination processes and review of sovereignty rights. Washington endeavors to re-adjust the global political map by either atomising large countries, or else by diluting their sovereignty in imperious international organisations, of which NATO is a classic example.

Thus, one power, which means one cultural and historical type, undertakes active attempts to impose its way of life on the rest of the world. Incidentally, this way of life is far from being ideal, to put it mildly. These attempts cannot fail to be met with a spirit of resistance, equally powerful. Of course, the United States is enjoying their power. They are intoxicated by their own global financial and political strength but the circumstances are bound to change soon. The plague of new threats will push Washington in the direction of cooperating with other states, and then it will have to take these states' national interests into account comprehensively.

THE INSPECTOR[1]

It is well known that while the fools fight, the wise men talk. Pan-European security may only be safeguarded by the joint ability of European states and nations to restrain, block and eliminate both internal and external threats to their sovereignty, territorial unity, cultural, social and economic structure, their nation-building base and their existence as one civilisation. I would say to those who question Russia's capability to play in the orchestra of European states: this is nonsense.

Russian population equals in number to the combined population of France and Germany. Denmark also has a large territory, if you count Greenland in, but this fact does not bother their colleagues in NATO or the European Union in the least. Even the newly elected NATO Secretary General is a Danish national. Russia is the largest country in Europe, not an elephant that might stamp out the sprouts of European life, which is a concern that Brussels officials so often express in their conversations with me.

Objectively, Russia today cannot have any expansionist plans. We have a headache of a different sort, which is how to maintain such a vast and rich country with the population that is very small in proportion to the territory. Considering that new generations of Russians might go down the demographic whirlpool, this problem will only exacerbate in future. Considering also the rapid population growth in the neighbouring Asian countries, we must seriously think about how to increase the level of effectiveness of the existing national security systems.

Try guessing whom these words belong to:

> *If one nation or other succeeds in conquering very large territories, this does not oblige other nations to acknowledge this fact as final, and set in stone. All it proves is the fact that the conqueror was strong enough at*

---

[1] Nikolai Gogol's 1836 masterpiece of dramatic satire *The Inspector* tells the story of a young civil servant who is stranded in a small town, where he is mistaken for an influential government inspector.

> *the time of the conquest and other nations were weak enough to let that happen. The conquerors' entitlement to these territories is based solely on military strength. If today our nation is squeezed into an unbearably small territory and, therefore, faces a future full of hardships, it does not mean that we have to accept our fate. We have a lawful right to rebel against it. It would be silly to think that some divine force has ruled forever that some countries may enjoy vast territories, whilst we must obey to the unfair order of the territorial division. Besides, the lands that we inhabit now were not bestowed on us from the skies. Our ancestors gained them in severe struggle. Likewise, in the future we will conquer new territories in a hard struggle, with weapons in our hands.*

Do you give up? I will tell you, the above is a quote from a speech by Adolf Hitler. Don't some Western politicians and some of our Southern neighbours think along the same lines today?

The history of the interaction between Russian civilisation and European political structures is not confined to the 20th century with its iron curtain and the Berlin wall. Apart from that, there is a history of the Russian participation in coalitions of the European and the North Atlantic powers, and what a history! I am referring to the Vienna Congress of 1814–1815, to the Entente of World War I and, of course, to the Anti-Hitler Coalition of 1942–1945, the success of which was secured by the unparalleled heroism and bravery of the Soviet people, 27 million of whom lost their lives in that war.

European nations are indebted to my country for that victory; it would be inappropriate for them to assume superior poses and condescend to Russia, inviting her to join European orchestra.

I think that a potential new confrontation should be replaced by a new philosophy of European security — a new code of conduct for countries that stretch from Vancouver to Vladivostok. Such a code must take a legally binding form, the need for which has already been indicated by President Dmitry Medvedev.

Future generations, who are going to be wiser than we are, will later decide on the fate of foregone military alliances. Before it happens, however, the existing military blocs have to be reformed in such a way that all cannons on the European continent are positioned to face in the outward direction. Clauses of existing collective security treaties must reflect the need to resist outside threats. We have to extract all the poisonous teeth out of the European war risk, thus rendering such a war impossible in principle. NATO should abandon its excessive egocentrism and acknowledge that the security of all countries within the Euro-Atlantic region must be indivisible, and not just that of NATO member countries.

Ideally, national laws of all European and North American countries should impose a moratorium on military planning against one another. Same laws should also forbid use of force, as well as threatening with use of force, in resolving any international disputes that may arise within our civilisation. Personal or collective safety cannot be achieved at the expense of that of a neighbour or partner. It is important to realise that freedom and security of one nation ends at the doorstep of another as other nations are equally entitled to their own freedom and security.

NATO should officially announce that Clause 5 of the Washington Treaty (on collective defense) does not apply in relation to Russia. NATO must treat and decrypt the notion of collective security as the preparedness to restrain and resist threats from beyond the North Atlantic area. All partners of NATO, including Russia, must know: in extreme circumstances they may count on the Alliance's assistance; likewise, the Alliance must expect similar support in return. Two-dimensional guarantees of security between NATO and the Russian Federation at the initial stage, followed by the practical cooperation in ensuring European and international security and the creation of coalition of Trans-European security would represent the optimal measures of cementing the mutual trust. The coalition would comprise the USA, European Union, and Russia.

Such form of Trans-European security coalition would resemble a Russian doll Matryoshka. Each European nation would be protected by several layers of defense, such as national defense and security system; existing alliances, such as NATO; new Pan-European alliance between the EU, NATO, and the Russian Federation.

Zbigniew Brzezinski, a famous American "Hawk", a political scientist, suggested in his notorious *New York Times* article of 19 August 2009:

> "*A good first step might be an agreement on security cooperation between NATO and the Kremlin-created Collective Security Treaty Organisation, which consists of Armenia, Belarus, Kazakhstan, Kyrgyzstan, Russia, Tajikistan and Uzbekistan.*"

The irredeemable hawk of American democracy elaborated furthermore: "*In return for this concession — which Moscow has long sought — such an arrangement should be made conditional on provisions that* confirm the right of current nonmembers to seek membership of their own choice in either NATO or the CSTO."

How peculiar they are, these American hawks. If Zbigniew thinks that we are prepared to renounce our principal position against NATO expansion onto Ukraine, Georgia, and other post-Soviet states in exchange for the formal acknowledgement of the CSTO, then all his years of Soviet and Russian studies taught him nothing.

Some Western politicians and experts go much further than Brzezinski. They come up with a seemingly harmless "dual citizenship" formula for states that are keen to keep an existing, and to acquire a parallel, membership in a more than one military and political alliance, such as NATO and Collective Security Treaty Organisation, at the same time. This idea of dual membership implies the non-antagonistic nature of the alliances and underlines their regional and influential differentiation.

Moreover, from their point of view, such a formula would ease tension in cases when a choice of an alliance takes political dimension in view of conflicts of the bygone era.

I immediately saw two 'buts' in this seemingly harmless and reasonable proposal.

First of all, for this to be implemented in practice, the NATO Chart must undergo substantial corrections, as up until recently only European countries could become NATO members (however, there has already been an exception of Turkey). Secondly, would it not result in a situation where NATO would include the majority of Middle East countries that insofar are politically weak and dependent on the West? As to NATO member countries, I cannot imagine them joining the CSTO in a rush. Believe me, democratic as it is, NATO is run with steel discipline, and no European state would exert its free and independent will to such a great length without an approving nod from Washington.

Nevertheless, I am optimistic about the possibility of Europe's and Russia's integration into a single security system from Vancouver to Vladivostok. The path to such reintegration lies through an equal and consistent planned rapprochement of NATO and the CSTO. A coalition of two military and political organisations, headed by the USA and Russia accordingly, will be the basis of peace and prosperity on the European continent, and possibly worldwide.

This is my personal view and my intellectual contribution, if you please. These ideas stand a chance of becoming a reality if NATO finds the inner courage to give up the fruitless attempts to be a global police force and a global competitor of the United Nations. Just because the

United Nations Organisation suffers from excessive red-tapism, it does not mean that it may be dismissed or ridiculed.

Overall, I think that the entire Euro-Atlantic security system would benefit from a visit of a good inspector. Old rules and outdated amoral codes of conduct of military blocs must be subjected to a ruthless scrutiny. However, the revision must be carried out in an evolutionary way. The existing norms of the international law were gained with plenty of sweat and blood, and this blood cannot be injected back into arteries of our mothers and fathers....

UPON THE HILLS OF GEORGIA...[1]

In the morning of 8 August 2008 I got up earlier than usual. Tuscany's bright sun and chirping birds outside woke me up. Together with my wife and children we were spending holidays in a small rented villa in Italy. I went out on the patio to lay table for breakfast. We had just arrived a couple of days before and still hadn't unpacked properly.

My mobile went off somewhere in the vicinity. Stepping over a yet unpacked suitcase, I grabbed the phone quickly so that the loud signal wouldn't wake up the children who were still asleep in the house. On the other end of the line someone was shouting: "Why do you not reply? We are all being killed here! Have you betrayed us, tell me!" I recognised the voice. It belonged to an Ossetian friend of mine whom I had first met in the Beslan crisis headquarters. I tried to calm him down and to understand what all the fuss was about. He slowed down a bit and went on to tell me about the tragedy that descended during the night. Saakashvili just started a war against South Ossetia. Georgian air force and artillery struck the sleeping town of Tskhinvali at midnight.

I gave my friend the special communication number in Moscow (I have learnt it by heart while in Beslan) and told him to whom he should give the detailed account of the events. At that, I understood, of course,

---

[1] This is a title of a beautiful poem by Alexander Pushkin:

Dark falls upon the hills of Georgia,
I hear Aragva's roar.
I'm sad and light, my grief — transparent,
My sorrow is suffused with you,
With you, with you alone...My melancholy
Remains untouched and undisturbed,
And once again my heart ignites and loves
Because it can't do otherwise.

Alexander Pushkin, *Upon the Hills of Georgia...*, 1829

that the Russian Government and military most definitely were already aware of the full-scale intervention of the Georgian Army into South Ossetia that happened on that night. The Georgian forces could not have possibly entered Ossetia bypassing the Russian peacekeeping troops; therefore, the positions of our military must have been crashed by the time of the phone call.

If so, casualties among the Russians were inevitable — unlike the peacekeeping Western troops in Srebrenitsa, our lads would not have left their positions without putting up a fight. I turned the TV on hoping for some coverage of the events. There was everything on the few Italian channels but the news on the war that had just broken out. I went online via my mobile. The first news that I saw confirmed that my Ossetian friend was telling the truth — it was the war!

I woke up my wife and asked her to help me pack as quickly as possible. Then I reached my assistant in Brussels and asked him to book me a seat on the nearest flight to the Belgian capital from any airport in Italy within my reach. We were lucky to get a seat on a plane that was taking off in a couple of hours, so it looked like I was going to be in Brussels on time. My wife offered to take me to the airport. We quickly got into the car and set off on an almost empty, sunny motorway.

On the way I called every person on whom the success of my mission in NATO Headquarters depended. I realised that the objective of the Georgian government was to internationalise the armed conflict and persuade the Allied NATO Armed Forces to take Georgian side. My duty was quite the opposite — to restrain NATO from making rushed decisions and stop the Georgian adventurers from provoking a third world war. Of course, great many things were far beyond my authority, but I set my task precisely in those terms.

I needed all my people to be at work. It was the month of August, and many of my staff were away on holidays, but I prompted everyone to come back to Brussels. We submitted urgent enquiries for operative information to Moscow. I still maintained my old reliable sources of information in Vladikavkaz and Tskhinvali. A dramatic picture emerged out of my phone conversations with Moscow and Vladikavkaz. Just as I suspected, the Georgian Armed Forces assaulted Ossetia in a deceitful way, without a prior warning. Russian peacekeepers were targeted at patrol points and in observation spots. As to the how many civilians were killed during the night bombing and the early morning tank battles, we could only guess.

Just when the plane was ready to take off I took another phone call. Interfax Information Agency parliamentary reporter Lyudmila Shcherbina, whom I knew well from my days in the State Duma, was asking me to comment on the situation in the South Caucasus. I felt that the circumstances called for independent and responsible initiatives, and so decided to comment at length without waiting for guidelines from "the centre":

Today, Saakashvili committed the last one of his many mistakes. The assault on the Russian peacekeeping contingent on duty is paramount to an armed attack on the Russian Federation. This is an aggression, and we will respond to it with harsh military actions. The bombing of the peaceful city in the middle of the night was a barbarous action, undertaken with an aim to murder as many innocent people as possible, particularly women, children, and elderly. It is an act of ethnic cleansing and should be classified as a war crime. Russia's duty is to put an end to the slaughter and to punish the aggressors using armed force against them.

When I landed in Brussels an hour or so later, my comment was already quoted by Russian and international newsmakers. I did not realise at that point that I had stepped on the warpath myself — a path of informational and propaganda campaign that was just as mean and cruel as the combat in South Ossetia.

As we were leaving the Brussels Airport, I received a phone call from John Craddock, NATO Supreme Allied Commander for Europe. He knew that I was back to Brussels.

"Howdy, Ambassador! Where're you?"

"Already in Brussels. How about you?"

"Sunbathing at the beach."

"Keep sunbathing, General…"

I needed to stall and take the initiative out of my interlocutors' hands, so I suggested holding the briefing in the Belgian town of Mons, during which I was going to inform the NATO SHAPE[1] on the situation in the conflict zone and answer the questions.

The US General agreed to that. Having verified the volume of information with Chief of Staff of the Russian Armed Forces General

---

[1] *SHAPE* — Supreme Headquarters Allied Powers Europe, the central command of NATO military forces, located north of the Belgian town of Mons.

Nikolai Makarov, the next morning I received Chief of Staff SHAPE General Karl-Heinz Lather in my office. A group of senior officers from Mons came along.

The conversation was as professional as it was difficult. The message that I got across to the NATO generals was that our peacekeepers were killed and there was an unspecified large number of casualties among the civil population. Russia had no alternative but to draw Armed Forces into South Ossetia. The operation would be limited in time and locality. Russia's objective was to achieve peace with Georgia, the country that started an international armed conflict. We did not intend to occupy the Georgian territory or to change the political regime. However, I said that we will eliminate any object of military infrastructure if it is deployed against us, or against civilians in South Ossetia. I also confirmed that Commander-in-Chief of the Russian Armed Forces President Dmitry Medvedev ordered to avoid striking civil objects in Georgia as much as possible under the circumstances and to stay within the responsibility zone of our peacekeeping troops. We will return all our troops to their bases upon completion of the operation on reinstating peace in Georgia. We expected from NATO one thing only: not to interfere in the conflict.

The German General listened to me attentively; he never interrupted me and clarified just a few details. I read suffering or, maybe, compassion on his face. Then General Lather thanked me for the frankness and the disposition for a dialogue.

I was physically aching for the entire five days of the war in the South Caucasus. I knew wars from before, from my experience under fire of artillery and snipers. But never previously did I witness this rise in patriotic spirit in all my comrades in Moscow and our mission in Brussels, this despise for the war instigators, and such a strong sense of personal responsibility for establishing the state of peace.

On 12 August Major General Victor Zinoviev, Head of the Russian Military Liaison Office to SHAPE wanted to speak to me as a matter of urgency. He informed me about a recent visit of a US colonel to our office in Mons. The colonel said that the Alliance had arrived at the decision to send paratroopers to Georgia. Of course, I could not take seriously an idle talk of an American officer, especially when I knew that this was not the usual way that NATO did things. NATO military commandment had to get an official sanction of the NATO Council prior to the use of force. The Council was comprised of my colleagues, Permanent Representatives of various countries to NATO. If such a decision had indeed been made,

I would have been one of the first people to know about it. Nevertheless, I passed the information supplied by General Zinoviev to the Centre and contacted NATO leadership.

General Lather replied without delay. I briefed him on what I had heard and asked for an explanation. From Gen Lather's tone, I gathered that he was rather embarrassed. He asked me the name of the American prankster again, assured me of NATO's neutrality in the South Caucasus, and said that the incident would definitely be investigated. I thanked the General. Still, the incident was an unpleasant surprise. It revealed that there were some officers in NATO SHAPE who quite enjoyed tickling nerves. I hope that they answered for their words.

Hours into the war in South Ossetia, the Russian mission to NATO turned into headquarters and the around-the-clock live press-centre. I spent the first half of every day taking part in various televised debates, televised bridges, and in interviews to the Western press.

I also worked on articles and comments to be published in leading US and European newspapers, explaining the truth behind the events of that war. I spent the afternoons in NATO Headquarters advising my colleagues the Ambassadors and NATO International Staff leaders.

All of them, somewhat reluctantly, cut short their annual leaves and returned to Brussels.

The US delegation blocked an extraordinary session of the Russia-NATO Council that I had initiated. By doing so, NATO deprived itself of a significant political role in the conflict and passed it over to the European Union and to the French President personally. Nicolas Sarkozy presided in the EU at the time. My colleagues in NATO found themselves in an informational vacuum and lost track of the rapid developments in the South Caucasus; they asked me for the daily updates on the situation in the war zone and actions of the Russian Armed Forces.

The whole affair was over in five days. The intimidated Georgian Army, trained and provided for by NATO member countries, deserted the battlefield, much to the shame of its instructors.

Astonished, the Ambassadors to NATO were asking me: "Dmitry, please tell us how did Russia manage to bring troops and defeat Saakashvili in such a short momentum?" I just shrugged. These people have been living side by side to us for centuries; they try to pick on us, and yet when we answer back, they are genuinely surprised.

The "5 days war", as it is known in the West, ruined Saakashvili's plans to include Georgia into NATO and turn the country into a splinter on Russia's body in the South Caucasus.

But Saakashvili, along with his Washington paymasters, refused to be defeated. The military campaign against Russia and the two young Caucasian Republics, Abkhazia and South Ossetia, was a proper aggression. Tons of lies were showered on ordinary people in the West. In the West, the only counter-force to this madness were my staff and reporters from *Russia Today*. The propaganda machine was levered mainly by two diplomatic missions — the Russian mission to NATO, and the Russian mission to the United Nations. The Russian Ambassador to the UN Valery Churkin and others has proved that underneath their diplomatic attire they had hearts of Russia's true patriots and citizens.

On 19 August 2008, Foreign Ministers of the 26 member countries came to Brussels to participate in the NATO Council meeting. NATO Secretary General, the Dutch national Jaap de Hoop Scheffer spoke before journalists after the Assembly. He accused Russia of a disproportionate use of force against sovereign Georgia. At that moment NATO's attitude reminded me of a matron of dubious behaviour, past her prime and mentoring a youngster.

I could not believe what I was hearing: the accusation came from the one and same NATO that had "proportionally" bombed Serbia in the spring of 1999 and killed 2,000 civilians! Truly, NATO's cynicism outdid the worst cynics of this world.

The Foreign Ministers Council declared that relations with Russia may not carry on as "business as usual". That was a serious political mistake. The Alliance went over the limits in the South Caucasian drama and compromised its reputation.

All NATO propaganda work in presenting the Alliance to the Russian public as "nice and sweet" went up in smoke. In the critical moment for Russia, NATO took side of women's and children's murderer who had ordered the killing of our peacekeepers. Even the most sceptical NATO critics could not imagine such hypocrisy.

My press conference in NATO was scheduled for the same day. NATO leadership never used to mind it when Ambassadors of partner countries wanted to talk to the press inside the NATO HQ.

A few hours before the press conference, our mission received a reply from Secretary General Jaap de Hoop Scheffer informing us that "there were no vacant press-halls in the NATO Headquarters at the moment". It was a bad move by NATO PR officers, who, undoubtedly, had advised the Secretary General on the matter.

By restraining the Russian Ambassador from speaking to the

accredited press, NATO put itself in a bad light. Of course, I could hold the press conference anywhere, with a megaphone in my hands, on an armoured tank, wherever! I did learn a great deal while in the Russian State Duma.

I instructed the Russian mission administrator to take down temporary partitions in my office and put as many chairs there as he could find.

News about the cancellation of the scheduled press conference had reached foreign journalists, and naturally they stormed into my office in pursuit of sensational announcements. The press briefing took place, and I can only thank NATO bureaucrats for that. By their unprofessional actions, they inadvertently helped to create the perfect environment for my every word about the war in South Ossetia and NATO conduct to be subsequently printed in millions of copies of leading newspapers in the West; and my comments were not entirely flattering.

Following the derogatory press statement issued by the NATO Council, which accused Russia of all mortal sins and announced the policy of 'no business as usual', the Kremlin had no alternative but to acknowledge independence of the two young Caucasian Republics. Russia saw no other possible guarantees of stability on her southern borders, as we could not be sure that the Georgian leadership would not attempt an armed intervention again. Besides, the acknowledgement of independence was made in response to the insinuation that "Russia intended to annex South Ossetia and Abkhazia".

President Medvedev personally informed me about this decision on 25 August in Sochi, where he required me to come for a political consultation.

At that time, Americans who had "missed the last train" suddenly decided to demonstrate their military might and stationed a group of battle ships in the Black Sea.

Small-numbered Georgian criminal elements that had settled in Europe's capital cities, where they felt quite at home, arranged provocative street meetings in front of Russian Embassies. Georgian intelligence service and diplomatic missions abroad directly supervised these street rallies; in this respect, I made an official statement at one of the EAPC meetings at ambassadorial level. In order to prevent another aggression by the Georgian Army, the Kremlin, by invitation of authorities in Tskhinvali and Sukhumi, made a decision to position Russian troops in these cities.

A new war was cut at its root. Refugees were returning to South Ossetia. Relatives were trying to identify the places where their loved ones had been killed and buried in the course of the aggression. Destroyed Tskhinvali was being cleaned up; reconstruction works started. As for Brussels, it went back to its favourite pastime — having a bone to pick with the "Russian bear" that, to everyone's surprise, woke up from its sleep and tweaked the aggressor's ears. Oh well, gentlemen, don't you awaken the Russian bear!

A MISFORTUNE OF BEING TOO CLEVER[1]

As it often happens, when trying to rectify other people's mistakes of others, one puts oneself at a risk of being ridiculed and brandished by those who made these mistakes in the first place. That's life. One example of this is the criticism of Barack Obama's corrections to the plans of strategic missile defense.

I would like to remind the reader that, a few years ago, the Republicans in the White House planned to place interceptor missiles in Poland and accompanying radar in the Czech Republic, under the pretext of defense against possible missile attacks of the "rogue states," such as Iran. Their plan aggravated military experts for a number of reasons.

Firstly, the confidential information exchanged between experts confirmed that in real terms in the next twenty years Iranian President Mahmoud Ahmadinejad would not manage to develop a missile technology that would be capable of hitting the European NATO member countries, let alone the territory of the United States. Moreover, Iran did not even have such plans on the agenda, as its main military interest was to develop small- and medium-range weapons capable of striking the Middle East, primarily Israel. This meant that interception facilities in Eastern European countries were not needed and would have been rusting and collecting dust there.

Secondly, Russians knew that the US anti-missile systems in Poland and the Czech Republic were not designed to counter-attack Iran; naturally, this prompted a question: what these American weapons in such proximity to the Russian borders were really aimed at? Washington offered awkward explanations, and our observers were denied access to the military objects in question. The Kremlin leadership frowned at that.

---

[1] Half of the lines of this 1823 Alexander Griboyedov comedy that is also translated as *Woe from Wit* had become proverbs. This fierce satire of the Russian 19th century officialdom was banned at the time and is still relevant to our day and age.

Russia faced the need to come up with a military and technical solution that was duly found soon.

In the autumn of 2008 Dmitry Medvedev announced his intention to deploy the short-range SS-26 ("Iskander") missiles in the Kaliningrad region. That statement caused anxiety among the Poles and the Czechs, who realised that Russia was through with joking, and their countries were pulled into a big political game, their territories exposed as potential military targets. Washington's plans awakened the public opinion and triggered mass protests in both of these Eastern European countries.

The late President of Poland Lech Kaczynski, cleverly using the anxieties of the Polish nation, put up the price for accommodating the US missiles.

Warsaw demanded from the Pentagon the full modernisation of the Polish ballistic missile defense in "compensation for moral damages." Poland's financial claims amounted to the astronomic figure of 20 billion USD.

President Kaczynski initiated the sort of bargaining that upset Moscow furthermore. Russians knew very well that Iran did not possess a single air missile plane that would be capable of flying to Poland, not even one way; however, Russia, Poland's neighbour, had the Air Force. Thus, the Kremlin received another confirmation of President Bush Jr.'s manic desire to build a defense shield in Poland and the Czech Republic, and its anti-Russian, and not anti-Iranian, vector. Moscow regarded Iranian missile programme nothing else but a "smoke screen".

From Russia's standpoint, the prime objective of the US missile defense programme was to neutralise the Russian divisions of heavy ballistic intercontinental missiles located in Russia's European part.

And finally, when reaching agreement with Warsaw and Prague, George Bush Jr. Administration either did not bother, or deemed it unnecessary to keep their allies in NATO informed. Perhaps, somebody in the White House condescendingly assumed that the allies had no choice but to eventually join the notorious "Atlantic solidarity". President Bush was wrong in his estimation again: Western Europeans took all these separatist agreements for a slap in the face and resolved to prove that they, too, had their pride and personal opinions.

A suitable occasion presented itself soon. The question of granting Membership Action Plan to Ukraine and Georgia, which is the first step towards the membership, was on the agenda of the NATO Bucharest Summit in April 2008. Berlin, Paris and London vetoed the decision to accept Ukraine and Georgia. As a result, Kiev and Tbilisi never received the coveted invitation to the "Atlantic gentlemen's club".

The plan of building ballistic missile defense system in Poland and the Czech Republic very nearly accelerated a new arms race; it increased tensions in the relations with Moscow, weakened historic links between the US and European allies, undermined authority of the pro-US politicians in Warsaw and Prague, and killed off all chances of Ukraine's and Georgia's accession to NATO for the next fifty years. The only winners in that situation were Iranian President Ahmadinejad and the radicals in his entourage. It is they who should be ever so grateful to George Bush and his darling Condoleezza Rice for the US missile defense system taking a wrong turn.

As for the Nobel Peace Prize laureate Barack Obama, he merely rectified the mistake of his predecessor. He acted exclusively in American interests and was not overly considerate towards his allies.

Stated purpose of American activity on the missile defense program is phased to be implemented during next 10–15 years; it's a multi-tiered global missile defense system with many elements of different types of home base (land, air, sea and space) designed to protect against ballistic missiles of all types the U.S., its allies, and significant in size zones of military activity.

Barack Obama came to power at a time when the United States plunged into a crisis most severe since the very Great Depression of the 1930's. This financial crisis has affected the economic, social, political and military fronts. Pursued by George W. Bush's neo-liberal economic policies and a new arms race presented a heavy legacy for President Obama. In the circumstances, his administration was forced to carry out the "New Deal", just as Franklin Roosevelt once saved American capitalism from the reign of uncontrollable market forces. The main focus was on increasing state intervention in the economy. In addition, Obama's economic strategy counted on the new technology market, which should ensure America's leadership in the global economy of the 21st century, and intended to review the structure of government spending.

All this led to a revision by the new occupant of the White House of the U.S. approach to missile defense. In his message, Obama set the following policy priorities in the field of missile defense:

- The United States will protect its territory from the threat of possible limited impact of intercontinental ballistic missiles;
- The United States will protect its forces from regional missile threats, also protecting its allies and partners, providing them with opportunities for self-defense;

- Before deploying new means of defense, they should be tested to assess their effectiveness in conditions close to real combat situations;
- Development of new military remedies must be secured in the long term;
- U.S. missile defense must be flexible enough to adapt to changing threats;
- The USA will look for opportunities to enhance international cooperation in missile defense.

Let us assume that Mr. Obama heartily wishes to improve relations with Russia. Suppose he is a kind person and a wise politician. I honestly want to believe that this is the case. In any event, he will leave his post in one or two terms. Who can be sure that his successor, whoever he or she may be, would not attempt to aim the strategic missile defense system against Russia?

That is why we should not indulge too much. The decision to correct the missile defense system removes one splinter in the Russian-American relations and opens a way to a new agreement to cut strategic nuclear arsenals. True. On the other hand, we can never be too confident that a mobile defense system placed, for instance, on ships in the Mediterranean Sea, would not bring us new problems in the future. Nor does the Pentagon intend to forfeit the overland component of its defense system in Eastern Europe.

A battleship equipped with interceptor missiles and far-range reconnaissance systems can be like Figaro, here today, gone tomorrow. If necessary, cruisers Aegis will lift the anchors in the Mediterranean and approach the Russian coastal line. If that happens, instead of missiles in Poland there will be the same missiles on US battleships sailing in Polish of Norwegian territorial waters. In what way would that be a better option, and why must we suddenly trust the Americans after the long years of deceit?

If the new US Administration is genuinely open to the strategic rapprochement, its actions must be concise. This necessitates drawing a "road map" of the missile defense system.

At the first stage, Russia's, the US, and Europe's experts must work together on the appraisal of missile threats. At the second stage, together still, we must devise a set of political, diplomatic, and economic levers of pressure on those who breach the existing regime of non-distribution.

Only at the final stage of such cooperation, should it become apparent that things are not working out as intended, it would make sense to build a collective system of military and technological efforts on creating the missiles defense shield with participation of the USA, the Russian Federation, and NATO.

We must engage the West into the common cause and closely knit our mutual interests together. Only then we all could relax a little bit. The alternative — escalation of military capacity and further self-isolation of Russia — is too grim to contemplate. Should this scenario become reality, we will no longer be able to avoid difficult choices.

EPILOGUE

It is a common perception that the respective national interests determine relations between different countries; it may seem that international relations have no room for morals, compassion, decency, charity, and other categories inherent to relations between individuals. One might think that foreign and international policies serve a pragmatic purpose, and only that. This is true to a certain extent; however, it is equally true that international relations are based not only on immediate national interests but also on national passions and, in some instances, on the passions and phobias of national elites.

A monarch, a president, a member of a government, or their aide — are they robots that mechanically promote national interests that were formulated someplace by someone else? Of course, they are not. Do you remember how Russian-German relations have improved due to the friendly links between President Vladimir Putin and Chancellor Gerhard Schroeder; or how much Italy led by Silvio Berlusconi and France led by Jacques Chirac did to unblock the Russia-Europe political affairs? One should never underestimate the importance of personal contacts between national leaders. These contacts discipline the character of the links between national elites, which, in turn, influences public opinion. For example, a suspicious, I would say, even negative, attitude towards NATO dominates among the Russian general public. In contrast, the European Union is viewed as a "sweetie". I think, though, that the devil you know well is better than the devil you hardly know.

Politics is made by individuals and depend on their talents or the lack thereof. If the state powers at all times conducted their international policies in accordance with their predominant national interests, Russia would have never got involved in World War I that shook her entire statehood. The Soviet Union would never have fed "the socialist camp", encouraging hypocrites, free-loaders, and small-scale traitors with damage to itself.

Recently my wife and I spent a weekend in Prague. During my years in college, it was compulsory for us to study a language of a socialist country. I chose to learn the Czech language because I loved Prague. Its cosy streets always filled me with a sense of harmony. However, on that last occasion I was shocked and offended by what I saw.

There was this legendary tank T-34 on one of the central Prague's squares, the very same tank that had been the first of many to roll into the city in order to help the dying Prague Uprising in 1945 and liberate the city from the German occupation.

In May 1945, after the total and unconditional defeat of the Nazi Germany had been announced and the Soviet red flag was raised atop the Reichstag, the Russian boys — the crew of the T-34 — did not want to die. Nobody wanted to die, especially when the war is over. However, even though the war in Europe officially ended, certain Nazi troops in Prague did not surrender. They continued to assault the Czechs, who suddenly realised the value of their freedom.

The entire crew of that first tank was killed. Grateful Prague citizens put the tank on the pedestal after the city had been liberated. Years went by, and so it came to the "democratic times". Fastidious Czechs thoroughly wiped their feet over the memory of those perished Russian boys who had sacrificed their young lives so that Europe today could enjoy its trouble-free life. First the tank was painted pink, then it was taken off the pedestal all together, its turret was taken off and tossed into the flowerbed, and the rest was disposed of as scrap metal. Now, Czech youngsters use the burrs of the tank turret to open the glass bottles of their famous beer. If you do not believe it, go to Prague and see for yourself.

Now, after that, what do I have to think of the leadership of that country? What would be my opinion on its national elite, the moral and ethical state of the Czech civil society? Obviously, I have drawn my conclusions. It is also obvious that these conclusions would influence my attitude towards that country and its people. Given a chance, the negative impression that I got while in Prague would influence the Russia's policy towards the Czech Republic, if I ever work in this direction. Having said that, I mean the above to be just an example, for the argument's sake.

Today, when I write the last pages of *The Hawks of Peace*, I am full of ideas and stamina. I am forty-seven years old. Over the last twenty-five years, same as millions of my compatriots, I have lived through grand tectonic events of Russian and global post-modern history.

Unlike many others, I had a good fortune to be a part of the events I witnessed. I saw war; I saw heroes and traitors; I saw "doves of peace", profiting from the war and receiving awards and titles, and I saw "hawks" who struggled to establish peace for their nations.

I wish for my nation to learn at last to enjoy fruits of own victories.

We are a great nation and we never surrender in wars. But why do we regress to our national vices and shamelessly waste away our lives in the times of peace?

Explaining our faults with "scheming by enemies" would be the simplest option. Of course, Russia's enemies exist, but this does not mean that we must be politically isolated forever.

As a Russian saying goes, we are not a dollar to be liked universally.

Other nations are not overly fond of one another, either. Grassroots xenophobia, ethnic clashes, instinctive rejection and suspiciousness towards strangers are present to some extent everywhere, including NATO and the European Union. It is not compulsory to love one another, but we are obliged to learn to live in peace and respect each other's choices. The main principle that I follow in my diplomacy is this: turn an enemy into a neutral, a neutral into a partner, a partner into an ally, and an ally into a friend.

I am positive that Russia will regain power and authority. Our people are gifted and our land is mega-rich; we are energetic and able to stand up for ourselves. However, a lot depends on the state power in Russia. Until some of the influential members of the elite continue to view the power as a means of personal enrichment, we would not be able to achieve a lot. The time has come for them to think of Mother Russia.

My dear hawks of peace! Let us be on guard so that the Russian Troika[1] does not stray from its path!

---

[1] *Troika* is a Russian word meaning three of a kind; here is means a traditional Russian carriage drawn by three horses harnessed side by side.

Dear Reader,

Thank you for purchasing this book.

We at Glagoslav Publications are glad to welcome you, and hope that you find our books to be a source of knowledge and inspiration.

We want to show the beauty and depth of the Slavic region to everyone looking to expand their horizon and learn something new about different cultures, different people, and we believe that with this book we have managed to do just that.

Now that you've got to know us, we want to get to know you. We value communication with our readers and want to hear from you! We offer several options:

- ❖ Join our Book Club on Goodreads, Library Thing and Shelfari, and receive special offers and information about our giveaways;
- ❖ Share your opinion about our books on Amazon, Barnes & Noble, Waterstones and other bookstores;
- ❖ Join us on Facebook and Twitter for updates on our publications and news about our authors;
- ❖ Visit our site www.glagoslav.com to check out our Catalogue and subscribe to our Newsletter.

Glagoslav Publications is getting ready to release a new collection and planning some interesting surprises — stay with us to find out!

Glagoslav Publications

Office 36, 88-90 Hatton Garden

EC1N 8PN London, UK

Tel: + 44 (0) 20 32 86 99 82

Email: contact@glagoslav.com

Glagoslav Publications Catalogue

- *The Time of Women* by Elena Chizhova
- *Sin* by Zakhar Prilepin
- *Hardly Ever Otherwise* by Maria Matios
- *The Lost Button* by Irene Rozdobudko
- *Khatyn* by Ales Adamovich
- *Christened with Crosses* by Eduard Kochergin
- *The Vital Needs of the Dead* by Igor Sakhnovsky
- *METRO 2033* (Dutch Edition) by Dmitry Glukhovsky
- *A Poet and Bin Laden* by Hamid Ismailov
- *Asystole* by Oleg Pavlov
- *Kobzar* by Taras Shevchenko
- *White Shanghai* by Elvira Baryakina
- *The First Oligarch* by Michel Terestchenko
- *The Stone Bridge* by Alexander Terekhov
- *King Stakh's Wild Hunt* by Uladzimir Karatkevich
- *Depeche Mode* by Serhii Zhadan
- *Saraband Sarah's Band* by Larysa Denysenko
- *Herstories*, An Anthology of New Ukrainian Women Prose Writers
- *Watching The Russians* (Dutch Edition) by Maria Konyukova
- *The Hawks of Peace* by Dmitry Rogozin
- *Seven Stories* (Dutch Edition) by Leonid Andreev

More coming soon...

www.ingramcontent.com/pod-product-compliance
Lightning Source LLC
Chambersburg PA
CBHW020900080526
44589CB00011B/379